6m

Analysis without measurement

Analysis without measurement

DONALD W. KATZNER
University of Massachusetts at Amherst

CAMBRIDGE UNIVERSITY PRESS

Cambridge
London   New York   New Rochelle
Melbourne   Sydney

Published by the Press Syndicate of the University of Cambridge
The Pitt Building, Trumpington Street, Cambridge CB2 1RP
32 East 57th Street, New York, NY 10022, USA
296 Beaconsfield Parade, Middle Park, Melbourne 3206, Australia

First published 1983

Printed in the United States of America

Library of Congress Cataloging in Publication Data
Katzner, Donald W., 1938–

Analysis without measurement.

Includes bibliographies and index.

1. Economics – Methodology.   2. Economics –
Mathematical models.   3. Social sciences –
Methodology.   4. Social sciences – Mathematical
models.   I. Title.
HB131.K37   330′.0724   82–4469
ISBN 0 521 24847 7   AACR2

for
J. B.

Contents

Preface

The origins of this volume emerged from an interdisciplinary course in which I participated while at the University of Pennsylvania during the 1969–70 academic year. Four instructors representing their different fields of study were present: an anthropologist, a political scientist, a sociologist, and myself, from economics. Our forty students were among the brightest freshmen and sophomores the university had to offer. The first term we split the class into four sections, and each instructor exposed ten students to a quick but sophisticated introductory survey of his area. For the second term the class was reunited and a single problem was chosen to be considered by the group as a whole. It was hoped the students would develop an appreciation for social science in general rather than the feeling that our four subjects were distinct and unrelated spheres of knowledge.

The problem selected for the second term was to gain some insight into what it means for a society to modernize. Our attention focused on four books, one from each field: W. H. Goodenough, *Cooperation in Change* (anthropology), D. E. Apter, *The Politics of Modernization* (political science), E. E. Hagen, *On the Theory of Social Change* (sociology), and A. O. Hirschman, *The Strategy of Economic Development* (economics). Frequently we met with our first-term sections to discuss these books from the point of view of our own disciplines; at other times we met as a single group to educate each other and to obtain an overall perspective. Each student summarized his thoughts in a term paper at the end.

The first version of what turns out to be Chapter 10 here represents my initial attempt to put together and to make sense of as much of the material from our joint study of modernization as I could. As an organizational device, I was led to define variables that seemed incapable of measurement and to employ mathematical techniques that were lifted, by analogy, from the standard procedures I used as an economist to model the quantifiable world. When several colleagues unexpectedly began to show interest in what I had done, it became necessary to go back and see if my reasoning by analogy could be justified. With that out of the way, I turned to further applications, the question of empirical verification, and miscellaneous odds and ends. The result is now recorded for all to see.

Actually, the thrust of the book is mostly theoretical in nature. Part I develops a conceptual framework employing accepted mathematical tools. Part II puts them to work but on an abstract level. The purpose of these latter chapters is not so much to present certain propositions concerning subject matter to those working in the areas from which they are taken, as it is to provide theoretical illustrations of the ways in which a new technique can be applied in various fields. And, although Part III is devoted to empirical testing, only one detailed statistical analysis of a concrete problem is presented. On the other hand, I realize that the usefulness of any theory lies in its practical empirical applications. Theoretical work is justified, in the long run, only if it provides answers to real questions where no answers existed previously. I firmly believe that the methodology developed here will be an important aid in the resolution of such unsolved problems and hope that the potential for this shows through, especially in Chapters 11 and 14.

The argument in the text – both the rigorous development of Parts I and III as well as the less exacting presentation of Part II – is meant to be relatively self-contained. (There are exceptions, notably the coverage of factor and regression analysis in Chapters 2 and 13.) Parts I and III (excluding Chapters 7, 14, and 15) require some degree of mathematical sophistication; it is impossible to justify the rules for conducting analysis in any other way. Nevertheless, the theorem–proof style of exposition is used sparingly and only where convenient. The material in these chapters will be new to some, but at the same time, it is only a very minor extension of standard results. Included for the sake of completeness, as well as to provide an interconnected body of propositions that focus explicitly on mathematical analysis in the absence of measurement, much of it can be skipped without introducing serious obstacles in the way of understanding the main ideas. The applications of Part II and Chapter 14 relax rigor, although formality necessarily remains. Simpler applications are presented first. Considerable repetition from these and other chapters is introduced so that each chapter of Part II and Chapter 14 could easily stand as an independent paper. (In fact, Chapters 11 and 14 are almost exact reproductions of previously published works.) I have done this to make the main points as accessible as possible to the less mathematically inclined reader. Hopefully anyone, regardless of background, could, by reading Sections 1.1, 1.2, and the particular application of Part II and Chapter 14 in which he might be interested, obtain a pretty good idea of what analysis without measurement is all about.

The intellectual debts acquired while completing this book are heavy indeed. I have shamelessly imposed myself upon many people in many fields and, what is worse, not always followed their advice. I apologize as well as thank them for their generous help. Space permits acknowledgment of only a few by name. I owe considerable gratitude to Janos Aczél, John Conlisk, Richard Emmerson, Wolfgang Eichhorn, Jan F. Narveson, Larry R. G. Martin, Daniel Orr, Ivor F. Pearce, Richard S. Rudner, Hans Schneeweiss, Douglas Vickers, and my brother Louis, all of whom willingly submitted themselves to my intrusions. Special thanks are due Mihajlo D. Mesarovic not only for making his own (then) unpublished manuscript available for Chapter 6 and for his efforts to explain it to me, but particularly for his general interest and warm support.

I am also grateful to Gordon & Breach and to M. E. Sharpe for permission to lift substantial parts of Chapters 3 to 5 from, respectively, my "On the Analysis of Systems Containing Non-Quantifiable Elements" [*Kybernetes* 2 (1973), pp. 147–55; © Gordon & Breach Science Publishers, Ltd., London, 1973] and "On Not Quantifying the Nonquantifiable" [*Journal of Post Keynesian Economics* 1, No. 2 (Winter 1978-9), pp. 113–28; © M. E. Sharpe Inc., White Plains, N. Y., 1979], and to Academic Press and Sage Publications for permission to reprint Chapters 11 and 14, respectively. Finally, I acknowledge with pleasure the patience and understanding of my wife, Ruth, and children, Todd, Brett, and Tara, during my long hours of isolation over the past several years.

The first step is to measure whatever can be easily measured. This is okay as far as it goes. The second step is to disregard that which can't be measured or give it an arbitrary quantitative value. This is artificial and misleading. The third step is to presume that what can't be measured easily really isn't very important. This is blindness. The fourth step is to say that what can't be easily measured really doesn't exist. This is suicide.

Daniel Yankelovich as quoted by Adam Smith (pseudonym for G. J. W. Goodman), *Supermoney* (New York: Random House, 1972), p. 286.

CHAPTER 1

Introduction

1.1   Purpose

Although the modern trend of analysis in areas such as the social sciences is to favor those problems and techniques that can be expressed and explored through the use of numerical representation, it is still readily apparent that many of the important issues of our day involve phenomena exceedingly difficult, if not impossible, to measure. Examples abound. Human behavior would seem to involve a complex of interrelated, nonquantifiable elements. Economic (e.g., labor–management) and diplomatic–political bargaining illustrate the point. At times the significance of numerical information pales in comparison to the many hard-to-scale political, social, and psychological pressures under which negotiators operate. And the outcome is likely to depend further on the personalities involved. In another context, nonquantifiability turns up in many "resistances" to economic development (e.g., cultural patterns) that have been discovered in so-called underdeveloped countries. Kuznets [33] has also suggested that there are institutional and structural changes (urbanization, etc.) accompanying growth that are equally tough to gauge. It follows that purely quantitative analyses of economic development are of limited usefulness because important inputs and outputs of the growth process cannot, at present, be calibrated. Recent concern and interest in the "quality of life" also runs into a similar barrier. Attempts to measure it (see, e.g., Liu [34] and Ontell [38]) have not yet and may never be able to capture its essence fully. Hence the concept itself cannot be defined and understood solely in numerical terms.

   At the same time, nonquantifiability has implicitly, if not explicitly, been handled in surprisingly sophisticated ways. For a political scientist to say "different types of political systems produce different career patterns" (Apter [1, p. 163]) or an anthropologist to write "the established modes of action and belief, to which we refer as a people's customs, are something they have made out of experience..." (Goodenough [19, p. 63]) is tantamount, in either case, to asserting the existence of a relation[1] between two nonscalable entities. (The meaning of the term

---

[1] The idea of determining and using relations between things goes back at least to Hume. See his discussion of causation [25, pp. 375–7].

1

"nonquantifiable" is discussed in Section 2.2.) Paraphrasing Parsons on social behavior, Homans [23, p. 958] is more direct, "variables characterizing the behavior of each man are functions of variables characterizing the behavior of the other." Witness further the debate between Gerschenkron and Hirschman [15] over the nonquantifiable relation between ideology and economic systems. Also, Galbraith [16] must have a structure of these kinds of relations in mind when he tries to introduce the "power" of large corporations into the principles of established economic theory.

Relatively complete analyses based on the use of nonquantifiable "variables" are also commonplace. Weber [50], for example, argued the existence of a connection between what he called the Protestant Ethic and the spirit of capitalism. The former consists of certain beliefs contained in the original dogmas of Calvinism, Methodism, Quakerism, and several of the Baptist sects. The latter is also an ethic for the conduct of life, but in which the ideal is that of an honest, hardworking man who is completely devoted to the accumulation of wealth and material possessions. Weber's link is developed by exposing the rationalization for the pursuit of wealth contained in the foregoing religious doctrines. It is checked empirically by noting that "business leaders and owners of capital, as well as the higher grades of skilled labor, and even more the higher technically and commercially trained personnel of modern enterprises, are overwhelmingly Protestant" (Weber [50, p. 35]). This effect occurs in several Western countries that have proportionately more Protestants so engaged than their relative share of population within each country would suggest. In terms of the concepts of Section 12.4, Weber would say that the Protestant Ethic and the spirit of capitalism are positively associated characteristics of certain populations of the Western world.

Later, Weber [51] further isolated this relation and placed it in global perspective. "Modern" capitalism, after all, arose in the presence of the Protestant Ethic and certain other material factors (which many believed, at the time, were the sole reasons for its emergence). But it did not appear with the material factors when the Protestant Ethic was absent. In particular, capitalism turned up only in parts of Western Europe, whereas in Asia, where the major religions were Buddhism, Hinduism, and Confucianism, and in the Middle East, with Judaism and Islam, it remained dormant. Therefore the Protestant Ethic, rather than the material factors, is intimately related to the development of capitalism, as well as to the spirit behind it.

Although subsequent explorations (e.g., Sorokin [47]) have permitted numerical calibration of several of its features, these measurements have not been able to grasp the relation's conceptual substance entirely. As originally proposed by Weber, it remains a statement that connects two nonquantifiable notions.

Similarly, Durkheim [13] has considered a relation among knowledge, freedom, religion, and (egoistic) suicide. Durkheim's thesis is that a loss of cohesion in man's religious society not only leaves him with greater freedom of action, but also places the responsibility of justifying his actions (formerly derived from religious society) squarely on his own shoulders. Thus man is led to the pursuit of knowledge to guide him in his use of freedom. But when the knowledge so obtained is insufficient to compensate for the religious loss, suicide often results. Durkheim empirically examined this hypothesis by comparing religious cohesion and suicide rates among various religious groups.

More recently, to explain the process of social change, Hagen [22] has developed a theory of evolution of "innovative personalities." Although described more fully in Chapter 10, it is worth noting here. Hagen's argument begins when, for one reason or another (e.g., a change in the holders of political power), some group in society feels that society in general and those whose esteem it values in particular no longer respect its aims and purposes. This withdrawal of respect makes it impossible for the group members to achieve satisfaction in life. Because they are still bound by the customs and traditions of their time, they repress their rage, retreat from society, and relieve their pent up frustrations on their children. As a result, the latter grow up feeling these pressures more acutely. Repression and rage thus become greater from generation to generation. Eventually innovative personalities emerge, who are willing to break with tradition in order to regain the respect withheld from their fathers. They endeavor to become powerful enough to force acceptance and respect by others.

Hagen attempts to check his evolutionary sequence against the histories of various societies. He is, perhaps, most successful with Japan. Since about A.D. 400 the historical experience of Japan has consisted of long cycles that fluctuate between feudal localism and national integration. The social system absorbing these oscillations could not at times have satisfied many people. As one might expect, lords who felt wronged were sanctioned to use force or influence. But the lesser elite, caught in a world that overwhelmingly accepted the proper place of the individual in the natural order of things, and hence scrupulously honored the obligations due to those higher up, could do little to correct the lack of respect for their values and status. And so retreatism and the resulting emergence of innovative personalities appear throughout the history of Japan.

The most oppressive of all periods of national unity was the Tokugawa era (1600–1867). Attempting to perpetuate their power and to avoid the errors of earlier rulers, the Tokugawa enacted measures that, in addition to their intended purpose, left the merchant, samurai, and wealthy peasant classes with an acute feeling of loss of status and respect. The descendants of these classes went on to play a major role in the subsequent modernization of Japan. Hagen endeavors to establish a statistical association between these characteristics (i.e., being a descendant of one of the declassed groups and being an innovator) in the early twentieth century, but his data are insufficient for the results to be conclusive.

Pareto [40] and Parsons [41], on the other hand, have investigated entire systems of simultaneously interacting nonquantifiable relations. Pareto explicitly identified the twelve relations arising among "residues," "interests," "derivations," and "social heterogeneity and circulation" by thinking of each element as "acting on" the remaining three (Pareto [40, Sect. 2206]). He also considered the "cycles of interdependence" among them that generate dynamic sequences of cause and effect (Pareto [40, Sect. 2207]). Parson's concern was with the collection of simultaneous relations that comprise his theory of social action. Although it is too complex to describe in detail here, its analytical structure is easily summarized:

The ultimate unit is always the unit act with the fundamental structure of the elements that make it up. Then there are inherent in the frame of reference a certain number of "elementary" relations between the various unit acts in any system. These are mainly derived from the fact that the existence of other units in the same system is necessarily a feature of the situation in terms of which any one unit is to be analyzed. Finally there are the emergent relations of units in systems. These are not logically inherent in the concept of a system as such, but they are empirically shown to exist in systems beyond certain degrees of complexity. (Parsons [41, p. 734])

As a final illustration, consider the attempt of Dalkey, Lewis, and Snyder [9] to study individual and aggregate rankings of eight career-living environments. These ranged from a supervisory program analyst position in Saigon to the directorship of a public administration training program at Dartmouth College. Each alternative was described verbally. Participants were asked to evaluate and order them according to the "strength" of such qualities as meaningfulness, security, newness, and so forth. Personal preferences were also requested. Dalkey, Lewis, and Snyder found considerable variability in environmental qualities and were able to suggest improvements to make the lower-rated alternatives more attractive. They also applied their technique to investigate rankings of various modes of travel (also described in prose) between two points.

These examples illustrate the directions in which researchers, lacking a means for measurement, have turned. Of course, whenever legitimate forms of calibration are available, any analysis naturally receives all the benefits and conveniences numbers bestow. But applying quantitative methods without valid measures is a fruitless exercise that has little relation to the real world. Even as a pedagogical device, how is van Riper's [43, p. 309] stuttering equation, which adds, multiplies, and divides things such as frustrations, anxieties, guilt, and morale, to be understood? No effort is made to quantify these variables in any way.[2] Sorokin [48] has used the term "quantophrenia" to describe what he sees as rampant misuse and abuse of mathematical and statistical procedures stemming from a mania for precise, quantitative research. The preceding examples suggest that it is also unnecessary: Analysis without measurement can be a feasible – even rewarding – pursuit. In fact, van Riper's point can be made (as he shows) without resort to meaningless mathematics.[3]

The quantophrenia observed by Sorokin (and others) seems to have emerged from the wholly justifiable introduction of numerically mathematical and statistical reasoning in social and psychological science. However, these tools must be used with care. There have been periodic debates in a variety of fields over the limitations of the quantitative method in clarifying reality (e.g., the Sociology literature on this point has been summarized by McKinney [35, pp. 85-7]). The thought that there are facets of experience that cannot be ensnared in the numerical net is not new. Keynes, for example, in discussing with Tinbergen some of the latter's earlier statistical work, took such a position. His doubts about analysis that excludes the "unmeasurable" are neatly summarized in his concluding remark:

No one could be more frank, more painstaking, more free from subjective bias or *parti pris* than Professor Tinbergen. There is no one, therefore, so far as human qualities go, whom it would be safer to trust with black magic. That there is anyone I would trust with it at the present stage or that this brand of statistical alchemy is ripe to become a branch of science, I am not yet persuaded. But New-

---

[2] Parsons's equations [41, pp. 77-82] that schematically outline system types in the theory of action do not suffer from this sort of ambiguity, provided that the "+" symbol is interpreted as a general form of composition. This, apparently, was Parson's intended meaning.

[3] It is interesting that, in another context, after presenting a totally inadequate and arbitrary technique for cardinally measuring product qualities (e.g. color), and after admitting its shortcomings, Kuenne felt compelled to add the following disclaimer: "Those readers who are horrified by this procedure may be assured at this point that it is a nonintegral part of the analysis, used at only one point in the study, and is easily removed without damage to the results" [31, p. 233].

ton, Boyle and Locke all played with alchemy. So let him continue. (Keynes [29, p. 156]; see also Keynes [28])

Even with the recent surge of mathematical usage in the social and psychological sciences, Keynes's point has not been completely eclipsed. In economics, for example, it remains a major theme of the modern Austrian approach (see, e.g., Dolan [11, pp. 6, 7]), and Georgescu-Roegen [18] (himself a sophisticated, non-Austrian mathematical economist) in arguing not long ago both for the use of concepts whose definitions are fuzzy enough to overlap their opposites and for reasoning that is something less than mathematically precise, also has reaffirmed its presence.

However, most studies involving nonquantifiable variables (including those previously cited) have been handicapped by serious methodological difficulties.[4] Unlike situations in which variables are capable of interval (cardinal) or ratio measurement, there are few hard and fast rules guiding the construction, manipulation, and empirical verification of theoretical models. All arithmetic operations on the variables are prohibited and familiar procedures for, say, solving systems of simultaneous equations or systems of difference and differential equations no longer apply. As a result, issues such as the internal or logical consistency of these constructs have been all but ignored. In models involving several relations between variables, for example, no one has ever asked if it is logically possible to conceive of all relations simultaneously; for it can easily happen that assuming some subset of the relations to hold precludes the satisfaction of others. Thus it is not yet known if the foregoing models of Pareto and Parsons are internally consistent. Nor are the kinds of tests that could be applied to answer such a question very clear.[5]

But the matter of internal consistency cuts still deeper than this. Implicitly or explicitly, many simultaneous relations models seek to assert that the concomitant interaction of their component relations excludes all but a single phenomenon. The resolution of the relations, in other words, explains or determines a real thing. Thus Pareto is interested in determining what he calls "social equilibrium"; Parsons, in determining social actions. In any event, without resolution, little is explained by the model. Lacking uniqueness of resolutions, explanation may not be complete (although narrowing outcomes to a restricted set of

---

[4] A notable exception is Arrow's [2] impossibility theorem for social welfare functions. This result is based entirely on set-theoretic ideas and applies regardless of whether the objects of choice in social decisions can be measured.

[5] In this regard, Pareto actually bemoans the fact that he is unable to make use of the rules for analyzing scalable phenomena in the nonquantifiable context. See Pareto [40, Sections 1732 and 2091].

possibilities, no reason is given why a particular one, in actuality, occurs). Now internal consistency in such a context, that is, the property of simultaneous interaction free of contradiction, means that once parameters are specified, the relations "resolve themselves" into at least one point. Determinacy, then, cannot occur in the absence of internal consistency, for it requires that resolution be both possible and unique. From a dynamic point of view, determinacy can be taken to mean the existence of an explanation for a uniquely observed evolution or history moving through time in visible directions. Here, too, determinacy necessitates internal consistency. And how are these problems to be handled when dealing with variables for which measures are not yet available? Little is known. Again, the query does not even seem to have been raised. Whether Pareto and Parsons, in fact, have specified their models sufficiently to guarantee unique determination of, respectively, social equilibrium and social action, remains a mystery.

This book addresses itself to these questions. It is mostly about methodology and makes only a very modest attempt to produce results that are directly relevant to the real world. New techniques are explored and applied to define concepts and to develop formal structure. Because the latter is so important for the effective use of any analytical tool, and because it ensures that tacitly assumed conditions and circumstances are made both explicit and precise, it is a major focus of attention. Considerable effort is devoted to illustrating the creation of formal structure for analyzing certain issues. In these contexts, avenues for further study involving additions to, modifications, or the compounding of structures are implied. The application of the techniques to gain an understanding of entirely different phenomena at conceptual and practical levels is another possibility. In any event, statistical methods are introduced for empirical testing; but (with one exception) they, too, are not directed toward the solving of concrete problems.

It should be emphasized, however, that subsequent discussion is not intended merely to show how new variables can be added to scientific investigation by expanding the setting in which certain propositions are known to apply. A much deeper level of analytical penetration is achieved in demonstrating that such variables may be integrated operationally into the modeling process itself. Thus the potential for novel and meaningful relations between these variables and between these and already included variables arises. New policies and new effects of old policies could then be explored, and new predictions could possibly be made.

If there is any single theme unifying the following pages, it is that a lack of ability to measure is no barrier to the conduct of rigorous theo-

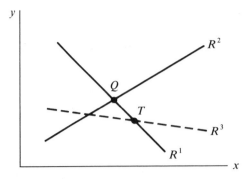

Figure 1-1

retical and empirical inquiry. Rules to carry out these investigations are suggested that permit the construction of internally consistent structures. All analyses of quantifiable phenomena are held up for comparison against such an ideal; the same should be true when measurement does not seem to be possible. For those already engaged in analyses without measurement, a methodological framework is thus provided. Hopefully it will aid in the prevention of logical errors and, by furnishing a core of general propositions that are applicable to diverse circumstances, will remove the necessity of repeating various arguments. On the other hand, for those who have previously limited themselves to variables that are capable of measurement (and relied on the standard methodological foundation already well developed for that situation), the possibility of greater flexibility and comprehensiveness is opened up. There is no doubt that studies based only on the quantifiable aspects of particular questions have not always led to satisfactory results; indeed, they are not always able to obtain solutions in the first place.

Because much has already been and will continue to be made of the notion of internal consistency, it is worth pausing for a moment to examine its meaning in greater depth. Perhaps the concept is most easily understood in terms of an analogy drawn from elementary algebra. Suppose x and y are two quantifiable variables. Let R^1 denote one relation between them and R^2 another. For example, R^1 and R^2 may be linear as pictured in Figure 1-1. In that diagram R^1 determines a line in the x-y plane, R^2 specifies a second, and both relations taken simultaneously identify the unique point of intersection Q. If there were a third relation R^3, then no point could simultaneously satisfy R^1, R^2, and R^3. Thus all three relations could not hold at the same time. The system is overdetermined. If there were only one relation, R^1, then the structure would be underdetermined: A unique point on the line R^1 could not be designated. Hence in order to have a determinate (linear) structure, that is, one that resolves itself into a unique point, one must require that the number of relations be exactly equal to the number of variables.

Of course, the fact that the number of relations equals the number of variables does not itself guarantee that the structure is determinate. Thus R^1 and R^2 could turn out to be two ways of writing the same thing, or they could describe two nonintersecting parallel lines. There are well-known mathematical conditions that, if met, ensure the existence of unique intersection points. The precise form these conditions take is immaterial here.

One more comment about this analogy: R^1 and R^2 depend on parameters (i.e., variables determined independently of all structural relations). Each time a parameter changes, a relation will "shift." For example, a change in parameters could cause R^2 to become R^3. In this case the intersection point would move from Q to T. Hence the intersection point depends on the values of the parameters as well as on the nature of R^1 and R^2. Specifying R^1 and R^2, then, determines a new relation that associates a point of intersection to each set of parameter values.

Matters relating to these kinds of issues are concerned with internal consistency. What structural circumstances allow the construction of general, simultaneous relation models that are amenable to analysis? When and in what ways can solutions exist and be unique? If it is desirable to examine the stability of sequences generated by some dynamic process over time, what are the structural requirements that provide a logical basis for doing so? There is already a vast literature devoted to such questions in the quantifiable case.

Part I below presents additional answers for more general situations when measurement may be absent. Arithmetic operations are replaced by function composition or substitution of variables and the ideas of "closeness" and convergence of variable values are given an abstract meaning that is independent of numerical distances. Conditions are derived under which a collection of relations can hold simultaneously, and a method of solution is provided so that the "unknowns" may be expressed as "functions" of "parameters." One required condition is that the number of unknowns be equal to the number of relations. Thus a possible first rule for the construction of internally consistent models of simultaneous relations is identical to the preceding standard for a system of quantifiable, simultaneous equations. That approach to model building, therefore, may be transferred directly to phenomena not, at present, capable of measurement. Alternative procedures when solutions do not exist are also considered. Similarly, restrictions are developed that enable "periodic" relations to be solved in the sense of determining stationary paths and the stability of other paths relative to them. The notion of stability naturally depends on the foregoing definition of convergence. Choice and maximization problems are also considered. Lastly, the connection between these structures and those associated with the general concept of "system" is explored in some detail.

The upshot of these results is that many of the fundamental techniques applied to analyze and understand the quantifiable world carry over when measurement is not available. For example, the framework in which a converging system is disturbed by parameter changes that subsequently send its time path moving toward a new (stable) equilibrium does not require calibration of any of the variables involved. Such analytical notions as equilibrium, change, stability, and the like are not limited to scalable reality. Nonquantifiable phenomena can thus be modeled in much the same way as their numerical counterparts. Reasonable conclusions, although perhaps not so powerful or as easy to state, can still be obtained through the use of familiar and just as meaningful theoretical processes. Of course, methods for testing the internal consistency of already existing models (such as those of Pareto and Parsons) are provided.

To illustrate the use of these techniques, Part II applies them in various theoretical contexts. Unfortunately, due to the immense complexity of both Pareto's and Parsons' models, the latter are not included among the applications considered here. Hence no direct test of their internal consistency is given. Simpler models, taken from the literature of various fields, are examined instead. Thus political structure is distinguished from political system by thinking of the former as a system of simultaneous relations and the latter as a solution that is dependent on parameter values. In the absence of solutions, political cycles may arise. Planner's concepts of society and the parametric controls they attempt to use are modeled in a more intricate way. And the notion of society in general is viewed in terms of a solution of a system of simultaneous relations that comprise personal, political, cultural, social, and economic structures. Change and the process of modernization are analyzed within this context through the use of periodic relations that describe appropriate dynamic transformations. As a final application, social interactions among individuals in the economic firm are explored, along with their implications for the firm's efficiency (Pareto optimality) and profitability.

Throughout Part II, arguments are presented rather formally. For example, interpreting a relation between coercion used by governments and the information they receive (Chapter 8) to assert that each possible (nonquantifiable) collection of information leads to a particular (nonquantifiable) kind of coercion, permits the dependency to be abbreviated in functional notation as

(1.1-1) $c = f(z)$

where c represents the variable coercion, z the variable information, and f is the symbolic name of the relation. Equation (1.1-1) means simply that f associates to each possible value for z a unique value for c. This mathematical shorthand is more than just a quick way of writing down several phrases or sentences. For once all symbols are properly defined, it is also the form in which the methodology of Part I is (necessarily) presented and justified. It, therefore, exposes the obvious link between Parts I and II: Concepts, propositions, and structure that are developed in the former are easily transplanted to the latter. In addition, it provides a simple means for checking internal consistency.

Part III investigates the possibility of empirical verification of hypotheses that are derived in a nonquantifiable setting. Various procedures are available, ranging from the statistical association techniques employed by Weber and Hagen in their previously cited works to a more general but weaker version of the standard methods of hypothesis testing. Also considered is the use of dummy variates and regression analysis in estimation and prediction. An application to an analysis of the "quality of life" is provided to illustrate the ways in which actual empirical verification may proceed.

1.2   A reader's guide

Intellectual curiosity is an immensely varied phenomenon. Different individuals have different backgrounds and proclivities, and consequently, approach scientific inquiry in different ways. What is interesting, even exciting, to one bores another to grief. Thus, on one hand, to convince as large an audience as possible that analysis without measurement is both a viable and potentially fruitful endeavor, one must speak to a broad range of concerns. On the other, it is highly likely that many readers will not want to emerse themselves into every topic that such an approach requires. In charting a course between this Scylla and Charybdis, the present volume attempts to cover as wide a variety of topics as feasible and, at the same time, to present them so as to permit readers to choose those they would like to pursue and to ignore (without impairing their understanding of the parts they read) the rest. The intent, then, of the next few paragraphs, is to guide readers through subsequent chapters. Detailed summaries of each chapter are provided first, followed by suggestions for various routes through them.

Chapter 2 and the remainder of Chapter 1 are given to different issues that are somewhat peripheral to analysis without measurement. Because it would be comforting to know that, in areas where nonquantifiability arises, the philosophical underpinnings of inquiry do not depend on measurement, the following section deals with philosophy. Without attempting to be exhaustive, only a few ideas and viewpoints are considered. Characterizations of such notions as "theory" and "prediction" are furnished; the meaning of "definition" and "argument" is discussed; and a distinction between physical and nonphysical science is drawn. The point is merely to suggest the independence of philosophical foundations from the question of whether the subject matter under investigation is capable of numerical measurement. (Several epistemological problems arising in relation to the analysis developed in Part I are deferred to Chapter 7.) Section 1.4 contains a sketch of systems concepts and their applications preliminary to subsequent material. Brief, highly simplified, and omitting particulars (the rigorous development promised earlier appears in Chapter 6), it is also based on the existing literature that, for the most part, tends either to preclude or to neglect the nonquantifiable.

Chapter 2 focuses on the meaning of various kinds of measurement and outlines conditions under which they are possible. It then becomes readily apparent what must be lacking when quantification seems unattainable. The most primitive form of scaling, namely, classification or the sorting into categories, is considered first and several classification schemes are discussed briefly. A formal presentation of nominal, ordinal, interval (or cardinal), and ratio calibration follows. Both the definition and the meaning in terms of an "underlying phenomenon" of these measures are examined. Several difficulties arising from the use of arbitrary, "non-natural" scales are also mentioned and special emphasis is placed on the pitfalls of employing ordinal data as if it were interval or ratio data in factor and regression analysis.

The chapters of Part I are intended to provide a methodological basis for analysis without measurement. Chapter 3 begins in much the same way as standard mathematical textbooks on set theory by building up through notions such as point, set, relation, and function. No form of quantifiability is assumed. The idea of a topology is then introduced to be able to talk about convergence, closeness, and continuity. The relationship between topologies and the existence of a metric (i.e., a function that provides a numerical measure of the "distance" between two points) is examined in Sections 3.2 and 3.3. Approaches to closeness and convergence, derived from topologies, turn out to be slightly more general than those resting on metrics. Thus it is possible to avoid all reliance on the latter when dealing with them. A specific example of a topology that can be employed sensibly to characterize closeness and convergence but which is not even pseudometrizable is given. The chapter concludes with some theorems on fixed sets and points that are introduced for later use.

Commonly, when interval or ratio measures of relevant variables are available, analysis often proceeds in terms of manipulation that is based on the algebraic operations of addition, subtraction, multiplication, and division. But in the absence of measurement, such techniques obviously must be discarded. The purpose of Chapter 4 is to develop formally a replacement, namely, function composition or substitution for variables. In other words, given two functional relations such that the image (or dependent) variable of one appears as an argument (or independent) variable of the other, the argument of the second function can be eliminated by substitution of the first. One natural algebraic structure in which such an operation may be framed is the semigroup of partial transformations. The existence of certain kinds of inverses of partial transformations turns out to be important for subsequent use and is also examined in this context.

Modelers of the quantifiable world frequently construct systems of simultaneous equations, systems of differential or difference equations, and systems of maximizing and/or choice behavior as an aid in understanding the phenomena they are investigating. Chapter 5 demonstrates that analogous models may be employed in a nonquantifiable setting, by showing that each system can be defined properly in the absence of measurement and that the fundamental questions pertaining to them can be resolved appropriately without numerical scales. Thus sufficient, nonquantitative conditions can be given to ensure that systems of simultaneous relations have solutions, that systems of periodic relations have stationary paths and reasonable stability or cyclical properties, and that certain maxima exist. The analysis of finite Markov chains is also considered. This chapter rests on the mathematical background that was developed in Chapters 3 and 4 and, in turn, provides a basis for the models exhibited as applications of analysis without measurement in Chapters 8 to 11 and 14.

Chapter 6 takes a broader view of systems analysis still, of course, in the absence of numerical calibration. A general definition of "system" is given and each of the specific systems considered in Chapter 5 is shown to arise as a special case. Several concepts of systemic causality are introduced along with the ideas of feedback and connecting systems.

Control (and optimal control) possibilities in systems are analyzed in some detail. The chapter concludes with a classification scheme for studying systems and their interrelationships derived from mathematical category theory.

At this point, the present development of a methodology for guiding theoretical analysis without measurement is more or less complete, except for several epistemological issues that remain unresolved. These pertain to the relation of nonquantitative analysis to reality, the meaning of "infinity," the representation of time and change, and the nature of the "space" over which variables are to range. Chapter 7 (the concluding chapter of Part I) argues the following: First, nonquantitative analysis occupies the same position in relation to reality when calibration is not available as standard quantitative analysis occupies in relation to reality when numerical yardsticks are present. Second, a lack of ability to measure does not mean that sets of infinitely many nonquantifiable elements are impossible to conceptualize. In fact, such visions are commonplace throughout the nonphysical sciences. Third, time and change arise in the absence of numerical scales (except, of course, that time itself is often identified with such a scale) in much the same way as they appear with them. Fourth, the question of what geometric proper-ties should be assigned to the universe of discourse (i.e., the space of variable values) of an analysis needs to be considered with care.

The aim of Part II is to provide a series of four examples that illus-trate how the methodology of Part I may be applied to specific theoret-ical problems. The first three are merely formalized reworkings of already existing literature; the fourth, however, is more original. Part II begins with an example of a simultaneous relations system in Chapter 8. The "political structure" of a society is thought of as a collection of simultaneous relations among such variables as ideology, coercion, and accountability. Society's "political system" is then taken to be charac-terized by the solution of its political structure. Resolving a political structure into political systems leaves the particular outcome (i.e., the latter) dependent on certain parameter values. The possibility of cycles of political systems also is discussed.

Chapter 9 provides an example of a periodic relations system that is taken from the area of land-use planning. Attention focuses on spaces used by individuals, activities performed by the individuals in them, kinds of communication between those performing the activities, com-munication channels used by the individuals, and the like. Values of these variables for each person in any time period are assumed to depend primarily on values of the same variables arising in the preceding period and on individual goals. The evolution of this system over time is examined and the logical constraints imposed on planning possibilities by the structure of the system are explored.

Both simultaneous and periodic relation techniques are combined in Chapter 10. The aim here – to build a setting in which the notion of "modernization" can be characterized and discussed – is met by providing (a) a very general, abstract, and admittedly simplified description of what constitutes "society," and (b) two (for comparative purposes) alternative visions of how society changes over time. The former is accomplished by thinking of the structure of society as a simultaneous relations system that is comprised of the persons making up the society, society's political structure (from Chapter 8), its "cultural structure," and its economic "investment structure." Society itself is defined as the solution of the social structure and is dependent on certain parameter values. To execute (b) these latter parameter values are assumed to vary over time according to periodic relations that reflect psychodynamic (personality) modification and industrial linkage in one case and learning by individuals and the same industrial linkage in the other. It is in this context that the concept of modernization is finally considered.

In addition to the construction of a fairly complex simultaneous relations system, Chapter 11 shows how formal analyses of such models may be pursued in the absence of measurement. The particular model in question has to do with (i) the work-related activities of individuals in the firm as affected by those individuals' incomes, the value orientations and premises and goals of others, the various kinds of information flowing around the firm, and the restrictions imposed on individuals by their supervisors, and (ii) the relation of all this to the firm's output and profit. Various theorems are established to elucidate the ways in which individuals' motivations, values, willingness to be influenced by superiors, preferences, and skills interact with the Pareto optimality and profitability of such a firm. The firm's provision of incentives to its employees and its receptiveness to new skills obtained by them also figure in these results. Chapter 11 is a reproduction of a previously published paper and is more technical than the other chapters of Part II. Proofs of the major propositions are relegated to an appendix to enhance readability.

Part III shifts direction and takes up the question of empirical verification. The statistical background is provided in Chapter 12. After a short, preliminary discussion of the meaning of empirical verification, the notions of probability, random variable, density, and distribution are introduced in the standard textbook manner. This is followed by a sampling of a few well-known statistical techniques that apply in the absence of measurement. The topics covered are limited to hypothesis testing, estimation, and nonparametric tests for dependence and association.

Apart from tests for the existence of relations between variables (i.e., statistical tests for dependence or association), there are the questions of obtaining information about relations themselves and of using them for prediction. These issues are taken up in Chapter 13. Now empirical observations of structural relations are usually thought of as observations of the structure's "reduced form." Hence the possibility of recovering structure from knowledge of the reduced form is considered first. Next, dummy variables (based on nominal measures) are introduced and their use in characterizing the reduced form (still in the absence of ratio, interval, or ordinal scales) is discussed. Then prediction from nonquantifiable data is examined, and some of the unique features of reduced forms having both quantifiable and nonquantifiable variables are explored.

An example of an empirical study employing nonscalable variables and a statistical test for dependence appears in Chapter 14. It focuses on the basis for occupational choice by examining the nature of individual preferences that are expressed in terms of abstract characteristics such as security, freedom, and pride. Both verbal and "quantitative" models of this preference structure are tested successfully, and a rough upper limit is set on the ability of individuals to specify their "quality-of-life technology." Although based on different kinds of information (each with its own independent usefulness), the two models yielded almost the same test results. The chapter is also reproduced from a paper published elsewhere.

Chapter 15 provides some concluding remarks about dealing with the nonquantifiable.

This completes the summary of what readers should expect to find on succeeding pages. Although (as previously described) the sequence of presentation moves from development of method to application, with theory construction preceding empirical investigation, readers will find that any chapter can be taken up in any order without seriously hampering their ability to understand it. Thus they may choose to skip from here immediately to one or more of the applications of Chapters 8 to 11 and 14. Then they might reasonably look over Chapter 5 upon which these applications most directly rest. Subsequent perusals might include Chapters 3 and 4 if readers are interested in mathematical background; Section 1.3 and Chapter 7 if they want to consider some philosophical matters; Chapters 12 and 13, to follow up on the foundations for empirical verification and prediction; Sections 1.4 and Chapter 6, to pursue general systems analysis; and Chapter 2, if a discussion of the measurement problem is desired. Of course, one could always read through *Analysis Without Measurement* as it is ordinally "measured" by its page numbers.

1.3   Philosophical setting

This section deals with what many philosophers consider to be scientific investigation: What it does, how it accomplishes what it does, and the rules and structures it uses in the process. Because there are often no clear-cut, generally accepted approaches to these issues, and because space will not permit inclusion of more than one or two of even the well-known possibilities, only a small, unbalanced sampling of views is presented. With one exception the discussion is primarily definitional, principally to illustrate that scientific inquiry – especially in the nonphysical sciences – is just as sound philosophically in dealing with nonquantifiable elements as it is when specializing only in those entities capable of measurement.

The end of scientific investigation is taken to be clarification, that is, the furthering of our understanding. Clarification proceeds by organizing information and developing arguments that link its various facets. Definition is an important aspect of the latter. In what follows, each of these elements are discussed in turn. Distinctions between the physical and the behavioral and social sciences are emphasized.

Before proceeding, note that the term "behavioral science" applies to those areas of inquiry whose primary concern is with various aspects of human behavior. It may, therefore, be interpreted, as it is here, to include a substantial part or all of psychology, urban and regional planning, the social sciences (anthropology, economics, political science and sociology), and so forth. The term "nonphysical science" will be used synonymously with behavioral science.

1.3.1   Organizational structure

Science in general is regarded as free and independent. There is no requirement to investigate certain kinds of problems, follow the rules of logic, or employ a particular methodology. One science may borrow elements such as concepts, techniques, or laws from another; but each develops its own standards of competence to which its practitioners adhere. According to Kuhn [32], most research within a mature science is inspired by, conducted, and evaluated in terms of some accepted paradigm. The paradigm is established through a revolutionary process involving competition among potential candidates. This process is not biased in favor of any particular one: In principle, any guiding base is free to emerge. Once established, the paradigm serves to further research within specific bounds. In time these bounds can become inadequate, and the paradigm may be replaced through another revolution.

One organizational structure of information for clarification in the behavioral sciences has been detailed by Kaplan [27]. With a few modifications, his view is now presented. It is developed by taking simplest notions first and building the more complex ones upon them.

Logic, as applied in the behavioral sciences, is a discipline that operates on human understanding in solving problems. It has to do with the truth-preserving derivation of statements from other statements without any reliance on empirical investigation. Logic is useful because it works and it produces solutions without a prior commitment on the part of the user as to what the solution might be like. Logic also deals with proof. In this context it is not concerned with how conclusions are obtained but only with whether they are justified. Logic is distinct from methodology. A specific procedure employed in a scientific inquiry is called a *technique.* The *methodology* of the inquiry is the collection of techniques (or methods) used. A *methodological study* is an investigation into the properties and limitations of a methodology. Logic may be applied in methodological studies to obtain or justify techniques, but it is not a technique itself.

Because behavioral science differs from other sciences in its subject matter, differences in techniques are required. The data relevant for behavioral science are human actions and not physical movements. Particular acts can be viewed from both the perspective of the actors themselves and the observer who is studying their action with reference to its broader implications. A vote in favor of a particular candidate, for example, can be seen by individuals in terms of their feelings toward all candidates, but it also has distinct consequences for society as a whole. The behavioral scientist must understand both. Physical movements, on the other hand, only have one aspect – that observed by the scientist. It is this duality that is, in part, responsible for the distinctive techniques in the behavioral sciences.

If science is to provide any insight into the real world, it must somehow contain or be linked to empirical elements. Information about the world is obtained solely through observation. Neither worldly knowledge nor meaning can exist independently of experience. A proposition is (empirically) *meaningful* only if it is capable of comparison with reality so that its empirical truth may be tested. The idea of concept is also related to experience. A *concept* is a mental construction that organizes the elements of reality. Concepts are the components of beliefs and propositions; they provide a vocabulary with which to talk about the world.

One of the purposes of scientific study is to discover laws. For Kaplan [27], *laws* are nonaccidental generalizations that result from successful inquiry. (Particular outcomes of inquiry are *facts*.) Now, although no two persons are identical, there can still be similarities between them. Thus laws in the behavioral sciences deal with the common elements among individuals. There are empirical laws obtained from direct observation and more abstract theoretical laws concerned with the explanation of appearances. *Hypotheses* are potential laws that have not yet been fully established. They may be formulated during the course of an investigation but become laws if verified by the outcome. *Assumptions* are generalizations set forth so as to test their consequences.

There are specific types of laws that are worth mentioning. A *distribution* is a law stating that certain characteristics appear in certain proportions in the field under consideration. When a distribution is discovered in a sample taken from a larger population and then attributed to the population itself, it is a *trend*. Statements of trends that lack statistical precision are *tendencies*. Asserting the occurrence of a tendency implies only that in the absence of other unspecified factors, a particular outcome is likely to occur. An excess of supply over demand tends to lower price although there are many circumstances exhibiting excess supply under which prices do not fall.

Formally, laws usually appear as follows: For all elements x in some field of discourse, if x has property p, then x also has property q. The field of discourse indicates which entities the law is about. The law that all ravens are black says something about ravens. But it also asserts a complex property of those things in the field that are not black: namely, they are not ravens. The *content* of a law consists of its field along with both antecedent and consequent properties.

Laws are often approximated rather than stated and used in a precise formulation. A statement can approximate a law as the number 3.14 approximates π; or it can approximate a law by asserting, say, "Normally such-and-such is true," without specifying the conditions under which this is so.

A *model* of something – call the thing A – is a system with enough structural properties in common with A to enable one to gain some insight into A by studying the model. As an example, the *postulational model* is a model that contains a set of postulates and axioms from which propositions or theorems are deduced. Empirical verification of the propositions indirectly "validates" the postulates; that is, it is necessary but not sufficient for their acceptance. The latter are required to be independent of each other and mutually consistent.

It is now possible to describe Kaplan's notion of "theory." A *theory* is a collection of laws, containing its own forms of argument, concepts, hypotheses, and even models. But it is still more. Its laws are interconnected so as to produce something in addition to the laws themselves: Each is explained and derives its purpose and force in terms of its relation to the others. The way in which the elements of a theory are tied together provides its distinctive character.

To appreciate what it means to experiment, one must first consider observation. A scientific *observation* is the outcome of a search under carefully controlled conditions whose outcome is something that is seen. An *experiment* is a process of obtaining observations under circumstances that are specially contrived for a particular purpose. It is a more complex procedure than observation, often requiring a series of interrelated observations to achieve its end. The experimenter, for example, may first design and construct his experimental situation. Next, he sets the controls and awaits an outcome. He then interprets, generalizes, and perhaps repeats after resetting the controls. Of course, many experiments in the behavioral sciences cannot employ such a technique. Neither the experimental situation nor the controls may be amenable to the experimenter's manipulations. Nevertheless, it is still possible to look through history for combinations of situations and controls that are desired by the experimenter. The outcomes of these events may then be treated as the results of an experiment – performed by nature – that provide the sought after empirical documentation. Thus events such as the dropping of the atomic bomb on Hiroshima and Nagasaki, the great stock market crash of 1929, and the 1960s ghetto riots in the United States can serve as experiments for the behavioral scientist.

In addition to understanding, laws and theories may provide a basis for prediction. *Prediction* is an assertion put forward that is derived from something already known. Predictions can be made without understanding (based, say, only on some empirical law), and it is possible to understand without being able to predict (e.g., when the values of certain parameters are unknown). However, successful prediction can only add to the credibility of any law or theory from which it comes.

It might seem from the preceding discussion that, except for minor differences, a social science is merely a transfer of the idea of a "science" from a physical to a social application. Mill [37] argued the same point: There is no logical difference between the principles required to explain physical and social phenomena. "Just as the irregularity of the tides [across]...the globe does not mean that there are no regular laws governing them, so in the case of human behavior" (Winch [52, p. 69]).[6] The fact that human beings are considerably more complex than tides reflects merely a difference of degree rather than of kind.

But Winch [52] contends, that this view is mistaken. His case is based on the notion (due to Wittgenstein) that in order to understand and communicate concepts, the researcher must have learned rules that tell him to identify repeatedly specific things with specific words. A horse is called a horse because a rule has been accepted asserting that a creature with certain characteristics shall be called a horse. Similarly, behavior can be meaningful only if it involves the application of a rule. To cast a vote is to follow a rule that identifies a particular action under particular circumstances with the behavior "voting." The learning and application of rules necessarily takes place in a social setting.

Now in any scientific investigation the objects of study must be observed, facts about them noted, and then, perhaps, theoretical constructions developed. But to be able to notice means that the researcher is able to identify certain characteristics; and to do this he must have some concept of what the characteristics are. The Winch argument suggests, however, that the latter is possible only with appropriate rules that identify communicable symbols with the characteristics, and these, in turn, will depend on what has been socially acceptable to others working in the area.

So far Winch's argument applies to all scientific inquiry. In the case of the physical sciences the phenomena under investigation are controlled by "nature"; rules are important only in so far as they preside over the investigation itself. Whereas the physical sciences require consideration of only one set of rules, in the behavioral sciences, the researcher's objects of study as well as his study of them are human activities and thus governed according to rules. And it is the former rules, not those governing behavioral science and the investigation, that must serve as the basis for identifying and communicating symbols. Whether or not two persons uttering dissimilar phrases are both praying depends on the rules they are following, not on those accepted by the researcher. Therefore the relationship between the observer and the observed is different for inquiry in the behavioral sciences. This, according to Winch, is more than a mere contrast in degree. The physical and nonphysical sciences differ in kind.[7]

---

[6] Here Winch is summarizing Mill's point of view, [37, pp. 552–5].

[7] The more radical aspects of Winch's argument are not considered here. They have been discussed, for example, by Rudner [46].

1.3.2   Argument

The most popular approach to argument has been presented, for example, by Carnap [8]. Because this view is so well known, its description here is very brief.

Carnap begins with inexact, "prescientific" concepts that can only be characterized and communicated through the use of informal explanations and examples. The first step of argument is to transform these prescientific concepts through a process of "explication" into exact, "scientific" concepts. These should be similar to their prescientific counterparts, useful and simple. Using scientific concepts, the next step is to construct an axiomatic system consisting of axioms and the propositions derived from them according to the rules of logic. The final step is to interpret the axiomatic system by providing at least one collection of entities that satisfy the axioms. The process of explication itself may be accomplished through the use of an axiomatic system and its interpretation as is done, for example, when explicating the natural numbers.

Without doubt, this type of formal argument appears often throughout the behavioral sciences. As Toulmin [49] points out, however, there are many circumstances in which the "current state of the art" or the nature of the problem under consideration may prohibit its use. Toulmin takes a more general, informal approach, turning on the use of modal qualifiers (such as "probable" and "impossible") and structural form.

Modal qualifiers can be understood in two ways. The *force* of such terms lies in the practical implications of their use. To say that something is impossible means that it has to be ruled out of consideration for certain reasons. The *criteria* for use of modal terms are the standards that permit one to decide when their employment is appropriate – in the preceding example the standards for accepting the reasons whereby the thing in question is ruled out. Different standards may apply for different usages of the same qualifier but its force never varies.

The structural form of argument consists of the following:

   i. A claim or conclusion to be established.
  ii. Data or facts on which the claim is based.
 iii. A general assertion or "warrant" that provides the authority to pass from the data to the claim.
  iv. A modal qualifier backed up by the conditions, when they exist, under which the warrant might not apply.
   v. The source from which the warrant's authority is derived.

For example, the claim that a particular man is a U.S. citizen may be based on the fact that he was born in the United States. The warrant could be an assertion that any person born in the United States is generally a U.S. citizen and its source of authority is the U.S. citizenship law. But the claim has to be qualified by a modal such as "most probably," for there are circumstances under which the man might not be a U.S. citizen. He may have left the United States and become a citizen of another country.

The standards for judging arguments are determined by the discipline within which they are set. Furthermore, it is clear that rational discussion depends on the possibility of establishing appropriate warrants. The source of authority of one warrant may, of course, be another. If challenged, an argument based on other warrants must be presented to uphold the first. Eventually some warrant must be accepted without "proof" in order for any argument to exist at all. The force of a warrant is universal but its source of authority depends on the particular context in which it appears.

An argument is analytic if checking the source of authority of its warrant involves, at the same time, checking the truth or falsity of its claim. The formal approach of Carnap is analytic and therefore a special case of Toulmin's more general scheme.

1.3.3 Definition

When the cat comes home, he can not tell you what he has seen. And this is not because he has no leisure, for the busy bees can tell each other that they have found honey; it is because he has no symbols. (Robinson [44, p. 28])

According to Robinson [44], the only purpose of a definition is "to report or establish the meaning of a symbol." This may be accomplished by either affirming that a particular word means a particular thing (which may also be described in words) or stating that it has the same meaning as another word. In the former case three elements may be identified: the word or symbol, the thing symbolized, and, as mentioned earlier, a rule asserting the word is to be taken as symbolizing the thing.

Definition is *lexical* if it involves only reporting on the meaning others (e.g., a dictionary) have attributed to words. It is *stipulative* when one's own meaning is chosen. The so-called "primitive" or "undefined" terms used in constructing mathematical systems all have lexical definitions. They are primitive only in the sense that their meaning cannot be drawn wholly from within the system and must rely, at least in part, on the general stock of common language that is available at large.[8] The remaining terms in such systems are often defined stipulatively.

---

[8] Criteria for the choice of primitives have been discussed by Goodman [20, Chap. III].

There are many methods for defining words. A synonym may be given. An analysis of the thing meant (i.e., a description of its distinctive features) can be provided. Or the object to be defined may be synthesized into a more general scheme. Whereas the analytic method displays the object as "a whole of parts," the synthetic approach exhibits it as "a part of a whole." Defining the wheel of an automobile in terms of its roundness and chemical makeup (e.g., rubber) is analytic; defining it by explaining how it translates energy from the car's engine into movement is synthetic. Still further, words may be defined by implication, by the use of examples both expressed in words or derived from the listener's past experience, or by explicitly announcing the rule that indicates how the word is to be used.

To illustrate, suppose a list of values (such as honesty and fairness) that human beings may or may not hold is agreed on as relevant for some purpose. For concreteness, suppose there are twenty entries on the list. Let S be the set containing all possible combinations of entries taken one at a time, two at a time, and so forth, up to twenty at a time (i.e., the list itself). Then S is defined analytically. On the other hand, the variable that may assume as "values" any of the elements of S is a variable, call it x, representing actual values present in particular human beings. In this case x is defined by articulating a rule.

For the moment, regard entries on the original list as primitives. Thus "honesty" could be defined lexically by appeal to Webster: "fairness and straightforwardness of conduct."[9] Such an approach, however, may not be precise enough to permit practical distinctions. Perhaps it is even necessary to consider degrees of honesty. Under these circumstances, it may be better to push the primitives one step back and define honesty (and the rest of the list) entirely within the system.

1.3.4   Conclusion

Nothing that has been said thus far relies in any way on a capability of measurement. Laws, theories, experiments, predictions, argument, and definition are all possible without it. Brodbeck put it this way:

Although quantification has considerable merit, it is neither a necessary nor a sufficient condition for science... [It] clearly is not sufficient... A science looks for laws to explain individual facts and for theories to explain the laws. If its concepts are not quantified, then its laws cannot be expressed in the form of [the standard type of] equations or other "mathematical" formulas. Yet they are laws all the same. They may be about biological properties of organisms, about individual behavior and personality, or about the links between, say, technological

9 *Webster's Third New International Dictionary* (Springfield, Mass., 1965), p. 1086.

innovation and institutional change. A discipline that formulates and tests such laws and theories is a science. Quantification is not a necessary condition. Concepts may be significant without being numbered. (Brodbeck [6, p. 547])

Thus it is quite legitimate for a scientist to work in terms of qualities as opposed to quantities. A *quality* is a descriptive property of something. A *quantity* is an amount of a quality. All quantities, then, are "measured" qualities, although it is not yet known how – if, indeed, it is even possible – to quantify all qualities.

Measurement, of course, is a means to an end. Its great advantage is that in its most restricted sense it permits standardizations (a variety of distinct objects can be made to conform to the same weight), fine distinctions (e.g., between the dimensions of various blocks), and, above all, application of the vast reservoir of mathematical techniques. It is not something that can be dismissed without cost.

1.4   The idea of a system

The idea of a system and the issues surrounding it are nothing new. In a sense they can be traced as far back as ancient Greece.[10] For Aristotle's conception of a whole as more than the sum of its parts suggests one of the distinguishing features of modern systems, namely, in addition to being made up of distinct parts, the parts themselves interact with each other in a variety of ways. Systems notions have appeared scattered throughout the history of ideas ever since. In the first century, Dionysius the Areopagite speculated about a hierarchic order among choirs of angels. Nicholas of Cusa, in the fifteenth century, perceived conflicts among parts within a whole leading to a higher form of unity. Leibniz's seventeenth-century hierarchy of monads resembles those of today. The nineteenth century produced Hegel's dialectic, the Marxian application of it, and Fechner's anticipation of modern ecosystems.

It was not until the 1930s, however, that the concept of system was separated from the particular processes it was used to describe. This abstraction gave birth to a new discipline: the theory of general systems. Although there were precursors and simultaneous discoveries, the person whose name is most closely associated with its initial development is Ludwig von Bertalanffy. Based on propositions from the theory of differential equations, Bertalanffy outlined an approach to the analysis of general systems and described several system properties. Subsequent development has been quite rapid.

This is not the place to pursue the evolution of Bertalanffy's abstrac-

[10] This paragraph and the next are based on von Bertalanffy [5, pp. 21–8].

tion. Instead, an attempt will be made to describe briefly some of the meanings it has today.

The notion of system seems to have appeared on at least three distinct levels: (i) as applied to practical problems, (ii) as used to reorganize approaches and redefine concepts in various disciplines, and (iii) as studied to gain a better understanding of its logical foundations and properties. Each of these is considered in turn.

Perhaps deriving inspiration from the highly publicized complex of systems used to land a man on the moon, the "systems approach" has recently become quite fashionable. It has been applied to business decision making, waste management, prevention and control of crime and delinquency, and so on.[11] It has been advocated as a means to study the prevention of war and population control [42]. The approach consists, essentially, of tackling a problem from an overall point of view and possibly dividing it into smaller problems that, when solved together, may provide the solution to the original. It's most notable successes have been in the field of engineering; its applications to social, political, and public affairs problems have left something to be desired.

The disappointing results with social (and other) questions are due, in part, to the assumption, on which the systems approach has been based, that a system consists of quantifiable, controllable elements, and relationships among them that are well defined and amenable to standard manipulations. Social systems, on the other hand, "are by their very nature so laden with intangible, human variables that concentration on their measurable aspects distorts the problem and confuses the issues" (Hoos [24, p. 25]). Thus, for example, to design a transportation system for improving community life, one must have some utopian society at which to aim and take into account various forms of travel, the use of leisure time, where people want to live, their tolerance of noise and other pollutions, and so on. The difficulties encountered in giving numerical meaning (i.e., interval scale representation) to most of these variables is enormous.

On a somewhat higher plane the impact of the system notion is felt in a wide variety of disciplines. Economists think of a capitalist economy as a system of economic units, each of which pursues its own self-interest. (Alternative approaches are suggested by Debreu [10] and Kornai [30].)

---

[11] In 1964 the state of California commissioned four aerospace concerns to apply their systems approach technique outside their own area of expertise. One was to study waste management, another was to develop programs for the prevention and control of crime and delinquency, the third was to design a statewide information system, and the fourth was to investigate basic transportation problems. For a critical discussion of the results see Hoos [24].

Psychiatrists have begun to view the human being as an "active personality system" instead of a robot (see Part I of Gray, Duhl, and Rizzo [21]). The brain has been analyzed as a mechanistic system that produces adaptive behavior [3]. Operations research, cybernetics, and information theory are three fields whose development is based largely on the study of systems. The systems viewpoint has further been applied in political science [14] and biology and history [4]. It has been suggested as the way to approach the sociocultural aspects of society [7] and has been used to model the simultaneous social, political, economic, and regional inter-relationships of society as a whole [26].

A definition of "system" appropriate to this usage of the term has been given by von Bertalanffy: A system is "a complex of interacting elements" (von Bertalanffy [4, p. 55]). There are "closed" systems – those existing in complete isolation from their environment – and "open" ones that take from and give back to their environment. Systems can be stable or unstable. They can grow, stagnate, reach for a goal, and so forth. In most cases the variables dealt with have been assumed capable of at least interval measurement. Even Isard [26] who explicitly postulates relations among nonquantifiable variables, treats them as if they were quantifiable presumably in the hope that some day scales will be found on which they can be measured.

At the uppermost level, mathematicians seem to have arrived at the notion of system through efforts to generalize specific systems such as systems of differential equations. Perhaps the simplest approach is to define a system as something that accepts inputs and produces outputs (Drenick [12, p. 6]).[12] It may be represented mathematically by an operator B on a domain D; that is,

$$y = B(x)$$

where x and y, respectively, denote inputs and outputs and x is in D. Diagramatically, it is often pictured as a so-called "black box" (Figure 1-2).

To place B in a dynamic setting, let T be an appropriate space of time. Time may be thought of as either continuous or discrete. As an example of the latter, suppose a particular one hundred-year period is to be studied. If observations are taken once a year, then T would consist of the points $\{1, 2, \ldots, 100\}$. In either case T is a subset of the real line. Now each x in D becomes an array of numbers whose components x_t are associated to points in T:

$$x = \{x_t : t \text{ is in } T\}$$

---

[12] The next three paragraphs are derived from this source.

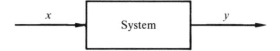

Figure 1-2

Thus x is one possible complete set of inputs over all time. A similar interpretation is given to the range of B.

The operator B may be written in a more explicit but still equivalent form as a function (or functional). When this is done each of the components y_t of y is specifically related to x:

$$y_t = b_t(x)$$

for all t in T and where each b_t is defined on D. A system is sometimes called *stationary* whenever the b_t are identical for all t.

One difficulty with the preceding definitions is that both B and the b_t need not be unique (solutions to differential and difference equations depend on initial conditions). Thus, for example, the functional representation may have to be written

$$y_t = b_t(x, p)$$

where p is a parameter that indexes the values of y_t for each x. A value for p is sometimes referred to as an *initial state* of the system.

Once a black box is specified the question arises of how to design a structure that yields the same relation between inputs and outputs as the given black box. Without such a model the box could not provide a greater understanding of reality than the assertion that inputs and outputs are related in a particular manner. To say that a machine accepts inputs and produces outputs does not reveal much about the way it operates. As an example, consider the case in which T contains a single element. Suppose (dropping the subscript t) the equations

$$y^1 = f(y^2, x^1)$$

$$y^2 = g(y^1, x^2)$$

where superscripts denote distinct inputs and outputs, may be solved as

$$(y^1, y^2) = b(x^1, x^2)$$

Of course b is the black box; f and g may be regarded as its structure. The question as posed here is directed toward obtaining an f and g given b. But there is no reason why, in a particular situation, it might not be possible to determine f and g first in order to derive b.

Another example when T is a single-element set is the system

$$y^* = h(x^*)$$

where x^* and y^* are, respectively, vectors of distinct inputs and distinct outputs, and h represents a vector of functions. Such systems have been studied both for their local [45] and global [17] invertability properties.

There are, of course, more sophisticated approaches. Systems have been defined by first identifying the traits of various system types and then providing specific definitions for each type [39] and by specifying mathematical structure as in the characterizations of various finite-state machines [53]. Also, they have been defined more generally as relations on abstract sets [36]. The last approach is the basis for the subject matter of Chapter 6.

References

1. Apter, D. E., *The Politics of Modernization* (Chicago: University of Chicago Press, 1965).
2. Arrow, K. J., *Social Choice and Individual Values,* 2nd ed. (New York: Wiley, 1963).
3. Ashby, W. R., *Design for a Brain,* 2nd ed. revised (New York: Wiley, 1960).
4. Bertalanffy, L. von, *General System Theory* (New York: Braziller, 1968).
5. Bertalanffy, L. von, "The History and Status of General Systems Theory," in G. J. Klir, ed., *Trends in General Systems Theory* (New York: Wiley, 1972), pp. 21–41.
6. Brodbeck, M., *Readings in the Philosophy of the Social Sciences* (New York: Macmillan, 1968).
7. Buckley, W., "Society as a Complex Adaptive System," in W. Buckley, ed., *Modern Systems Research for the Behavioral Scientist* (Chicago: Aldine, 1968), pp. 490–513.
8. Carnap, R., *Logical Foundations of Probability,* 2nd ed. (Chicago: University of Chicago Press, 1962), Ch. 1.
9. Dalkey, N. C., R. Lewis, and D. Synder, "Measurement and Analysis of the Quality of Life," in N. C. Dalkey et al., eds., *Studies in the Quality of Life* (Lexington, Mass.: Heath, 1972), Ch. 4.
10. Debreu, G., *Theory of Value* (New York: Wiley, 1959).
11. Dolan, E. G., "Austrian Economics as Extraordinary Science," in E. G. Dolan, ed., *The Foundations of Modern Austrian Economics* (Kansas City: Sheed and Ward, 1976), pp. 3–15.
12. Drenick, R. F., "An Appraisal of the Status and Future of System Theory," in J. Fox, ed., *Proceedings of the Symposium on System Theory* (New York: Polytechnic, 1965), pp. 1–14.
13. Durkheim, E., *Suicide,* J. A. Spaulding and G. Simpson, trans. (Glencoe, Ill.: Free Press, 1951).
14. Easton, D., *A Framework for Political Analysis* (Englewood Cliffs, N.J.: Prentice-Hall, 1965).

15. Eckstein, A. (ed.), *Comparison of Economic Systems* (Berkeley, Cal.: University of California Press, 1971), Ch. 9.
16. Galbraith, J. K., "Power and the Useful Economics," *American Economic Review,* 63 (1973):1–11.
17. Gale, D., and H. Nikaido, "The Jacobian Matrix and Global Univalence of Mappings," *Mathematische Annalen,* 159, No. 2 (1965):81–93.
18. Georgescu-Roegen, N., *The Entropy Law and the Economic Process* (Cambridge, Mass.: Harvard University Press, 1971).
19. Goodenough, W. H., *Cooperation in Change* (New York: Wiley, 1966).
20. Goodman, N., *The Structure of Appearance,* 2nd ed. (Indianapolis: Bobbs-Merrill, 1966).
21. Gray, W., F. J. Duhl, and N. D. Rizzo, *General Systems Theory and Psychiatry* (Boston: Little, Brown, 1969).
22. Hagen, E., *On the Theory of Social Change* (Chicago: Dorsey, 1962).
23. Homans, G. C., "Contemporary Theory in Sociology," in R. E. L. Faris, ed., *Handbook of Modern Sociology* (Chicago: Rand McNally, 1964).
24. Hoos, I. R., *Systems Analysis in Social Policy* (London: Institute of Economic Affairs, 1969).
25. Hume, D., *The Philosphical Works,* vol. 1, T. H. Green and T. H. Grose, eds. (Darmstadt, Germany: Scientia Verlag Aalen, 1964).
26. Isard, W., *General Theory* (Cambridge, Mass.: MIT Press, 1969).
27. Kaplan, A., *The Conduct of Inquiry* (San Francisco: Chandler, 1964).
28. Keynes, J. M., Review of *A Method and Its Application to Investment Activity,* by J. Tinbergen, *Economic Journal,* 49 (1939):558–68.
29. Keynes, J. M., Comment on "On a Method of Statistical Business-Cycle Research. A Reply," by J. Tinbergen, *Economic Journal,* 50 (1940):154–6.
30. Kornai, J., *Anti-Equilibrium* (Amsterdam: North Holland, 1971).
31. Kuenne, R. E., "Quality Space, Interproduct Competition, and General Equilibrium Theory," in R. E. Kuenne, ed., *Monopolistic Competition Theory: Studies in Impact* (New York: Wiley, 1967), pp. 219–50.
32. Kuhn, T. S., *The Structure of Scientific Revolutions,* 2nd ed. (Chicago: University of Chicago Press, 1970).
33. Kuznets, S., "Modern Economic Growth: Findings and Reflections," *American Economic Review,* 63 (1973):247–58.
34. Liu, G., "Quality of Life: Concept, Measure and Results," *The American Journal of Economics and Sociology,* 34 (1975):1–13.
35. McKinney, J. C., *Constructive Typology and Social Theory* (New York: Appleton-Century-Crofts, 1966).
36. Mesarovic, M. D., and Y. Takahara, *General Systems Theory: Mathematical Foundations,* (New York: Academic Press, 1975).
37. Mill, J. S., *A System of Logic* (London: Longmans, 1970).
38. Ontell, R., *The Quality of Life in San Diego* (San Diego: The Urban Observatory of San Diego, 1973).
39. Orchard, R. A., "On an Approach to General Systems Theory," in G. J. Klir, ed., *Trends in General Systems Theory* (New York: Wiley, 1972), pp. 205–50.
40. Pareto, V., *The Mind and Society,* A. Bongiorno and A. Livingston, trans. (New York: Dover, 1935).

41. Parsons, T., *The Structure of Social Action,* 2nd ed, 2 vols. (New York: Free Press, 1968).
42. Rabow, G., *The Era of the System* (New York: Philosophical Library, 1969).
43. Riper, C. van, *Speech Correction,* 4th ed. (Englewood Cliffs, N.J.: Prentice-Hall, 1963).
44. Robinson, R., *Definition* (Oxford: Clarendon Press, 1962).
45. Rudin, W., *Principles of Mathematical Analysis,* 2nd ed. (New York: McGraw-Hill, 1964), Ch. 9.
46. Rudner, R. S., "Some Essays at Objectivity," *Philosophic Exchange,* 1 (Summer 1973):115-35.
47. Sorokin, P. A., *Social and Cultural Dynamics,* vol. 2 (New York: Bedminster, 1962).
48. Sorokin, P. A., *Fads and Foibles in Modern Sociology and Related Sciences* (Chicago: Henry Regnery, 1956).
49. Toulmin, S. E., *The Uses of Argument* (Cambridge: Cambridge University Press, 1959).
50. Weber, M., *The Protestant Ethic and the Spirit of Capitalism,* T. Parsons, trans. (New York: Scribner, 1956).
51. Weber, M., *The Sociology of Religion,* E. Fischoff, trans. (Boston: Beacon Press, 1963).
52. Winch, P., *The Idea of a Social Science* (London: Routledge & Kegan Paul, 1958).
53. Wymore, A. W., "A Wattled Theory of Systems," in G. J. Klir, ed., *Trends in General Systems Theory* (New York: Wiley, 1972), pp. 270-300.

CHAPTER 2

Notes on measurement

The purpose of this chapter is to outline briefly some of the important ideas relating to various forms of measurement. A complete survey is not intended. Only those notions relevant to determining the sorts of things that are required to have measurement (and hence must be absent without it) are discussed. The chapter begins with the most primitive form of measurement, namely, verbal classification by type or property. It then proceeds to the more precise and systematic characterization of properties on ordinal, interval (cardinal), and ratio scales. Problems arising from treating ordinal data as if they were interval data are also considered.

2.1 Types

Our world is so complex and diverse that raw, untempered observation of it produces only massive and hopeless confusion. To make any sense of the chaos at all requires abstracting from differences (based on properties or attributes) between things or objects that are seen. This furnishes a basis for making comparisons and hence for determining when two things are distinct or identical. Collections of identical things define groups. The process is one of categorization or delineation of type. Once categories are established, identification of a fresh object, that is, its assignment to one of the groups, becomes possible. Classification therefore emerges at the very core of human understanding. Implicitly, if not explicitly, it is a prerequisite to the modeling of any real phenomenon.

The fundamental character of categorization and types is easily illustrated. Language itself is a classification system. Each of its nouns and verbs describes a category (Landau [20, p. 82]). Although the words "tree" and "run" stand for a variety of like things, individuals use language to identify a tree as a tree or a running animal as an animal that is running. There are, to be sure, ambiguities and inconsistencies. But the expression and communication of categories is one of the primary functions of language. A second example arises in the analysis of human behavior. To comprehend mortal acts, "it is sufficient to find typical motives of typical actors which explain the act as a typical one arising out of a typical situation" (Schutz [27, p. 13]). The approach is thoroughly ingrained practically everywhere in behavioral science.

In view of the foregoing discussion, it is not surprising that man's efforts to classify date back (along with system ideas) to antiquity. Jung [15, pp. 510, 542], who devised the introvert–extravert scheme of psychological types [15], traces them to Greece five centuries before the birth of Christ. At that time nature was thought of as comprised of four elements: air, water, fire, and earth. Corresponding to these were four substances (humors) in the human body: blood, phlegm, and both yellow and black bile. Based on the latter categories, a system of four psychological temperaments was developed by Galen, a Greek physician in the second century A.D. Individuals in whom one of these humors was dominant belonged, respectively, to the sanguine, phlegmatic, choleric, or melancholic type. On the other hand, Sorokin, in addition to pointing out the appearance of Tönnies' *Gemeinschaft* and *Gesellschaft* societal forms in Plato, also mentions their existence in the writings of Confucius (Sorokin [30, p. ix]).

Three distinct notions of type are considered here (this approach follows Hempel [14]). Two require the explicit specification of a universe of discourse for their definition. To obtain them, various attributes are used to split up the universe into classes. Elements appearing in the same class have identical attributes and are of the same type. Such classification schemes are often called *typologies*. One typology is *finer* than another if every class of the former is contained in a class of the latter. A typology in which every class contains exactly one element (i.e., the finest possible typology) is *discrete*. These first two concepts of type, then, both depend on the identification of particular combinations of characteristics to define typologies. They and their typologies differ in that one requires a specific relationship to hold between the classes.

Of the two kinds of typologies thus generated, the simplest is based on ordinary classification procedures (see Lazarsfeld and Barton [21]). Experience and hunch are used to derive classes that will hopefully prove significant. The result is a *classificatory* typology. At the outset, only a few categories may be introduced. These could then be broken down into smaller and smaller classes as required, but at each stage, the universe of discourse is to be partitioned exhaustively into nonoverlapping sets. Finer and finer typologies are achieved. This successive reduction may be accomplished by superimposing new typologies on old ones, thereby subdividing the categories of the previous stage. As analysis continues, additional typologies could appear by combining classes in fresh ways. Relationships between types may be discovered, thus permitting unification of their respective classes, or supplementary groupings may be required to resolve issues involving certain combinations of types. In any case the categories employed should be adapted to the particular problem under investigation and should be capable of summarizing and exposing all relevant and appropriate information that may arise.

The ancient decompositions of natural matter and bodily substances described earlier are examples of classificatory typologies. Another illustration is provided by Kretschmer's physique types – pyknic, asthenic, and athletic – which also have their roots in Grecian antiquity (Kretschmer [18, Ch. 2] and Sheldon [28, pp. 10–22]). And, by contrast, Goodenough [11, p. 66] suggests that a society's customs may be classified as economic, religious, political, and so on, according to the ends they enable individuals to attain.

The second kind of typology entails a more formal structure (see, e.g., Rudner [26, pp. 35–8]). It requires an ordering relation that permits distinctions between gradations of types. In what follows it is referred to as an *ordering* typology. The ordering relation, ρ, is defined on the universe of discourse and taken to be reflexive, transitive, and symmetric, that is, an equivalence relation (see Section 3.1). Because any such relation partitions the universe into mutually exclusive and exhaustive subsets, a typology is automatically obtained. Furthermore, two elements in the same class are equivalent with respect to ρ (hence of similar type), and the type classes of the typology are themselves ordered according to certain specific gradations. In many cases "extreme" or "polar" types are present and all gradations fall in between.

Actually, it is not necessary to insist that ρ be an equivalence relation. If ρ is only transitive and reflexive, an equivalence relation can still be defined in terms of ρ (Section 3.1) and hence a typology with the same gradations of types as implied by ρ is obtained. Alternatively, if ρ is merely transitive, it can easily be extended to a transitive and reflexive relation. Once again, a typology reflecting the gradations of ρ emerges.

There are many examples of ordering typologies in nonphysical science. The introvert–extravert classification previously mentioned permits distinctions between individuals exhibiting these characteristics to a greater or lesser degree. Sheldon's [28] typologies of physiques categorize individuals according to the attributes endomorphy, mesomorphy, and ectomorphy – each measured on a seven-point scale. Rostow's [25] stages of economic development, Triffin's [31] market classifications by cross elasticities of sales, and Apter's [3, pp. 24, 25] categorization of political systems all serve to define ordering typologies.

Empirical typologies are typologies (classificatory or ordering) that are derived from data rather than from theory (see Winch [33, p. 68]). They are ad hoc constructions that function primarily to organize and summarize observations and that eventually may lead to theoretical construction or reformulation. Classifications of data by age, sex, occupation, and so on are commonplace. Other categorization schemes are often suggested by the data or the aims of the investigation. Mann [22], for example, groups industries according to barriers to entry. Kretschmer's and Sheldon's types, noted previously, are also of this variety. On a more sophisticated level, discriminant analysis (Section 13.2) is a statistical method for sorting data into categories. Adelman and Morris [2] have used it to assign countries to classes that reflect their potential for economic development. Factor and cluster analysis also provide a technique for defining typologies in that they permit interpretation of a collection of data in terms of "primary" factors or dimensions (Winch [33, p. 71] and Nunnaly [23, p. 346]). Considerable economy is achieved by grouping data into classes or clusters and using one variable to represent the entire group.

Implicitly or otherwise, typologies are employed analytically in many ways. A relation between variables may actually be a relation linking the classes of one typology to those of another. Obviously, if the general notion of relation itself were characterized in this manner, then when all typologies are discrete, the usual concept of relation (Section 3.1) would arise as a special case. Virtually all the results of Part I of this book apply to either situation. An alternative usage arises in the context of dummy variates (Section 13.2). Because they require the assignment of exactly one number to each type class, dummy variables cannot be defined without typologies. Indeed, provided that the number of type classes is not too large, specification of a typology is essentially the same as nominal measurement (Section 2.2). In another instance, statistical investigations of association (Section 12.4) are structured by the typologies appearing in contingency tables. Finally, mathematicians have developed a sophisticated theory of categories that provides a means for classifying abstract constructs (such as models) and for studying the relationships between them. An illustration appears in Section 6.5.

The third and last notion of type considered here, namely, the ideal or constructed type, is not necessarily associated with an ordering relation or typological class. In so far as its definition is concerned, the latter are irrelevant. Contrasted with the preceding approach to "type" as a collection of attributes, the ideal type is a theoretical system. To describe it requires specification of the elements with which the theory deals, as well as the hypotheses and propositions relating them. The concept further demands an empirical interpretation of the theory that, in turn, is to be thought of as a special case of a (perhaps eventually emerging) more comprehensive theory. Reality "approximates" the ideal type in one way or another and can be used to test its hypotheses. Examples include the standard vision of economic man, democracy, and feudal society (although the actual class of real phenomena these types are supposed to idealize is not clearly delineated).

In spite of the fact their definition does not require description of an overall classification scheme, ideal types may still be identified with the classes of an ordering or classificatory typological structure. Each type class in Triffin's market categories and in Rostow's previously cited stages of development refer to ideal types. Weber's [32, Ch. III] legal, traditional, and charismatic authority, Sorokin's [29, pp. 66–101] classification of cultures based on the ideational and sensate polar forms, and Wirth's [34] and Handman's [13, pp. 107–9] typologies of nationalism further illustrate the point.

As suggested earlier, employment of any typology (with or without ideal types) may be regarded as a form of measurement. The latter is considered now in some detail.

2.2 Numerical scales

All objects – both physical and conceptual – have properties (or, in the terminology of Section 1.3.4, qualities). Measurement is the association of numbers with these properties. Thus, for example, a plank has longness, heaviness, and hotness (or coldness). The property longness may be measured by length as inches, heaviness by weight as pounds, and hotness by temperature as degrees Fahrenheit. The plank may also provide its possessor with "utility." In theory, if not in practice, utility may be measured – say, as units of utils – but this concept of measurement is often quite different from that corresponding to longness, heaviness, and hotness. The distinction may be expressed in terms of scale.

These ideas can be made more precise. Consider first the philosophical viewpoint as represented by Ellis [9]. To develop a notion of measurement, Ellis begins with the concept of quantity. If it can be said that certain things have a particular quantity in common, then they must be comparable with respect to some property. The latter implies the existence of an ordering that enables comparisons to be made. To *measure* a quantity, as already suggested, is to assign numbers to things according to a rule. Each rule determines a *scale of measurement*. In practice there may be many independent procedures for measuring on a scale, but it is required that each associate "the same number to the same things under the same conditions."

According to Ellis, measurement of a quantity is possible whenever there exists a scale on which the quantity can be measured. This, in turn, rests on the fulfillment of three prerequisites: (i) A measuring procedure is available that permits the measurement of any object in the quantity ordering. (ii) Every thing that can be measured on the scale appears in the quantity ordering. (iii) The numerical ordering of objects on the scale exactly reflects the quantity ordering. A quantity ordering relative to a given property may therefore be thought of as an "underlying phenomenon" revealed by measurement.

More technically, mathematicians have also worried about the circumstances admitting measurement. The following is a brief outline of one approach. Only the most important definitions and propositions are presented. Many concepts taken for granted here are described later in Part I. The reader who is interested in proofs and further development is referred to Pfanzagl [24] and Krantz et al. [17].

Let A be a collection of objects and suppose some property such as longness orders the elements of A. The ordering, ρ, is taken to be a reflexive, transitive, and total binary relation (Section 3.1). Thus, in the case of longness, $a' \rho a''$ may mean "a' is at least as long as a''." It is ρ defined on A that is the underlying phenomenon to be, when possible, recorded by measurement. (Underlying phenomena may also include algebraic operations as described later.) Note that ρ induces an equivalence relation on A that partitions A into a collection, $\bar{A}$, of equivalence classes. It also defines an irreflexive and transitive relation, $\bar{\rho}$, on $\bar{A}$ in the natural way: For all distinct equivalence classes $[a]$ and $[b]$ in $\bar{A}$, $[a] \bar{\rho} [b]$ if and only if $a \rho b$. Thus an ordering typology is defined on A and the elements of $\bar{A}$ are type classes ordered by $\bar{\rho}$.

Let R be the set of real numbers ordered by "$\geqslant$." A *scale* is a function, f, mapping A into R such that

$$a' \rho a''$$

if and only if

$$f(a') \geqslant f(a'')$$

for all a' and a'' in A. Such a function is often called *order preserving* (see Section 3.1). The images of the elements of A under f are *scale values*. Scales are not, in general, unique. Furthermore, f can be viewed as mapping $\bar{A}$ into R according to

$$f([a]) = f(a)$$

for all a in A. In other words, a scale maps two elements of the same type class into the same number.

Along with preserving order, f may also be required (as it is subsequently) to preserve convergence. Before discussing convergence, however, one must have a topology (not to be confused with typology). Toward this end take as open intervals in $\bar{A}$ sets of the form

$$([a], [b]) = \{[x] : [a] \, \bar{\rho} \, [x] \, \bar{\rho} \, [b] \text{ and } [x] \text{ is in } \bar{A}\}$$

where $[a]$ and $[b]$ are in $\bar{A}$. The *interval topology* for $\bar{A}$ is the collection of all unions of open intervals in $\bar{A}$. Convergence of sequences of points of $\bar{A}$ is defined in the standard topological fashion (see Section 3.2). Because the interval topology is Hausdorff, convergence is unique.

The scale f is said to *preserve convergence* provided that for all sequences $\{[a_n]\}$ in $\bar{A}$ and all points $[a]$ in $\bar{A}$,

$$\lim_{n \to \infty} [a_n] = [a]$$

if and only if

$$\lim_{n \to \infty} f([a_n]) = f([a])$$

A convergence preserving scale is therefore continuous with respect to the interval topology and conversely.

Consider for a moment the special case in which ρ is an equivalence relation such that $\bar{\rho}$ is empty. (It is not necessary to assume that ρ is total.) Thus no ordering of the equivalence classes in $\bar{A}$ is induced by ρ, and consequently, the ordering typology described by ρ is merely a classificatory typology. Under these circumstances any scale mapping A into R is called *nominal*. A nominal scale therefore implies a 1–1 mapping of the equivalence classes of $\bar{A}$ into R. Nominal scale values are not unique, and the only information they can provide is whether two elements of A lie in the same equivalence class under ρ. All nominal scales based on ρ are equivalent representations of the underlying classificatory typology. They exist if and only if the cardinal number of the collection of all classes in $\bar{A}$ is at most the cardinal number of R.

Let g be a function mapping R into R. Then g is *increasing* whenever $y' \geqslant y''$ implies $g(y') \geqslant g(y'')$ for all y' and y'' in R. Moreover, g is a *positive linear transformation* if it can be written in the form

$$g(y) = \alpha y + \beta$$

where α and β are real numbers such that $\alpha > 0$. When $\beta = 0$, g is called a *positive dilation*. Positive dilations and linear transformations are clearly increasing. Now a scale is an *ordinal scale* if it is continuous and unique up to increasing and continuous maps of its range into R. The scale is an *interval* (*or cardinal*) *scale* if it is continuous and unique up to positive linear transformations of its range into R. And the scale is a *ratio scale* if it is continuous and unique up to positive dilations of its range into R. Longness and heaviness are measured on ratio scales of length and weight, hotness is measured on interval scales of temperature, and pleasure is usually measured on ordinal scales of utility. Conditions on the underlying phenomenon are now given that guarantee the existence of ordinal and interval scales.

The first proposition is easily stated: An ordinal scale representing ρ defined on A exists if and only if the interval topology for $\bar{A}$ has a countable base (Pfanzagl [24, pp. 75, 79]). Further concepts are needed to obtain the second.

A function $g : A \times B \to C$ is *continuous in its first* variable if for every b in B the map $g_b : A \to C$ defined by

$$g_b(x) = g(x, b)$$

is continuous. It is *continuous in its second variable* whenever $g_a : B \to C$ defined by

$$g_a(y) = g(a, y)$$

is continuous for all a in A. The function g is *cancelable* if and only if for all a in A and b in B both g_a and g_b are 1-1.

A (closed) *operation* "$\cdot$" on A is a function, say, g, mapping $A \times A$ into A. Provided

$$(a \cdot b) \cdot (c \cdot d) = (a \cdot c) \cdot (b \cdot d)$$

for all a, b, c, and d in A, the operation is called *bisymmetric*. It is *metrical* if and only if it is bisymmetric, continuous in each variable separately, and cancelable. An example of a metrical operation defined on $R \times R$ is

$$g^*(x, y) = \alpha x + \beta y + \gamma$$

where α, β, and γ are real numbers such that $\alpha \neq 0$ and $\beta \neq 0$.

The proposition asserting the existence of interval scales is as follows: Let A be connected and contain at least two elements. Then there exists an interval scale, f, such that for all a and b in A,

$$f(a \cdot b) = \alpha f(a) + \beta f(b) + \gamma$$

if and only if "$\cdot$" is metrical. The constants α and β are determined uniquely (Pfanzagl [24, p. 97]).

Additional properties that ensure the existence of ratio scales are not pursued here (see Pfanzagl [24, p. 101]). Suffice it to say, such properties express, in terms of the underlying phenomenon, the notion that all admissible transformations of scale leave scales having the same unchanged zero. Note also that ratio scales are interval scales, and ratio and interval scales are both ordinal scales. But the converse assertions do not hold.

An operation is *additive* if it is associative, commutative, cancelable, and continuous in each variable separately. Because associativity and commutativity imply bisymmetry, additive operations are metrical. It, therefore, follows that if an additive operation is defined on A, it is permissible to add units on the representing scale f. Thus it is meaningful in terms of the underlying phenomenon to add a 3-inch length and a 6-inch length to obtain a 9-inch length. A similar property cannot hold for ordinal scales.

These ideas are illustrated by considering the problem of comparing the heaviness of three objects. First, the objects may be ordered according to their heaviness as demonstrated by a balance. Next, any two objects may be placed on the same side of the balance and compared with the third. The combining of two objects in this way requires conceptually an additive operation. Measuring heaviness as weight transforms the ordering into "$\geqslant$" and the combination of two objects into "$+$."

The notion of meaningfulness in terms of an underlying phenomenon may be expressed in an alternative, equivalent way. For a statement or proposition involving numbers is clearly meaningful if and only if it is invariant under appropriate admissible transformations of the scale from which the numbers are taken. According to the foregoing definitions, the class of admissible transformations for ordinal scales consists of all increasing, continuous maps; that for interval scales contains only the positive, linear maps. Thus the sum of a 3-inch length plus a 6-inch length will always be a 9-inch length, regardless of whether the units of measurement are expressed in terms of inches or centimeters. But if, on a given scale, the ordinal utility of, say, one pear is one unit of utility, of two pears is four units, and of three pears is five units, then applying the admissible transformations of taking squares or square roots yields the data shown in Table 2-1. Upon squaring, one finds that the sum of the utilities of one and two pears is greater than the utility of three pears, whereas in the square root case it is less. The operation of addition is therefore not invariant under all ordinally admissible transformations of scale.[1]

The differences among the four scales as previously defined can be

---

[1] There are also assertions not meaningful with respect to interval scales. Although no problem arises with $x < y$, the statement $x < (1/2)y$ is meaningless because, upon changing each scale by adding b, the expression $x + b > (1/2)(y + b)$ occurs only when $b > y - 2x$. However, $x < (1/2)y$ is meaningful on ratio scales because the addition of b is not an admissible transformation of scale.

Table 2-1

Number of pears	Units of utility	Units of utility squared	Square roots of units of utility
1	1	1	1
2	4	16	2
3	5	25	$\sqrt{5}$

further illuminated by the example of, say, oldness. Suppose it is known that the age of person Γ is 20 years, whereas that of person Λ is 60 years. Consider the following statements: (i) Γ and Λ have different ages. (ii) Λ is older than Γ. (iii) Λ is 40 years older than Γ. (iv) Λ is three times as old as Γ. In fact, because oldness is measured on a ratio scale as age, all four statements are valid. The name "ratio" comes from the last because ratios like the 3 to 1 contained in statement (iv) are meaningful. The same 3 to 1 ratio would arise if oldness were expressed in terms of months rather than in years. If such ratios were to depend on the choice of scale (as in the case of Fahrenheit and Centigrade temperatures), this meaningfulness of ratios would be lost. But provided the first three statements remained meaningful, age would still be an interval measure of oldness.[2] If only (i) and (ii) were meaningful, then the scale on which oldness is recorded would be ordinal. With (i) alone it would be nominal, useful for classification purposes only.

It is important to emphasize that only on interval and ratio scales is the application of standard arithmetic operations to scale values meaningful in terms of an underlying reality. All techniques of analysis requiring arithmetic manipulation in this sense depend on at least interval measurement. On the other hand, when interval scales are not known, it may still be feasible and rewarding to use ordinal ones. In relation to utility theory, Edgeworth inadvertently suggested the same point:

> We cannot *count* the golden sands of life; we cannot *number* the "innumerable smile" of seas of love; but we seem to be capable of observing that there is here a *greater,* there is *less,* multitude of pleasure-units, mass of happiness; and that is enough. (Edgeworth [8, pp. 8, 9])[3]

[2] For statement (iii) to be meaningful, differences such as forty years must remain invariant across scales (even if expressed in different units) no matter where they arise on any particular scale. This property holds for temperature scales. If C and F denote, respectively, degrees Centigrade and Fahrenheit, it is well-known that $F = (9/5)C + 32$. Thus given two pairs of observations (F', C') and (F'', C''), each related by the preceding formula, $F'' - F' = (9/5)(C'' - C')$. Hence $C'' - C'$ is the same in degrees Fahrenheit regardless of whether $C'' = 30$ and $C' = 25$ or whether $C'' = 85$ and $C' = 80$.

[3] It is interesting that in spite of this remark and in spite of the fact that he was the inventor of indifference curve analysis (the basis of the modern, geometric approach to ordinal utility theory), Edgeworth always remained a firm believer in cardinal (interval) utility.

Economists have since gone on to develop a deep and sophisticated theory of demand dependent, to a considerable extent, on the notion of ordinal utility (see Katzner [16]).

Questions concerning the logical existence of scales are entirely different from the problem of finding procedures for measuring on them. Once an interval scale, say, is known to exist, it is necessary to have a standard with which to make comparisons and a test to determine the place of each object on the scale: Heaviness is measured by the position of a pointer on a balance; hotness is calibrated according to the length of a column of mercury. But to employ these tests with any confidence, one must further assume that they record only what is intended and nothing more. Thus assumptions must be made about the nature and behavior of variables other than that being measured. (This point has been emphasized by Blalock [6].) For example, weighing an object to obtain its heaviness requires the assumption that a single force revealing heaviness alone is operating on the object. A balance with a magnet underneath the side on which objects of unknown weight are to be placed does not meet this criterion, because the measurement of objects attracted or repelled by the magnet would not reveal their "true" heaviness. It follows that the underlying phenomenon must be specified to an extent greater than that which is required to prove the logical existence of scales.

In view of the fact that, for all practical purposes, nominal measurement is always possible, the adjective *nonquantifiable* will be reserved only for situations in which there does not seem to be any way of constructing ordinal, interval, or ratio scales. Thus a set of objects are nonquantifiable if there does not exist a generally acceptable underlying phenomenon satisfying the mathematical conditions that give meaning to such calibration. Criteria for acceptability necessarily depend on the norms and standards guiding analysis at the time of inquiry. These may vary from field to field. For example, someone could propose an interval scale for assigning numerical measurements to different manifestations of honesty. Given such a scale the associated underlying phenomenon is easily obtained. But acceptance of both scale and underlying phenomenon are unlikely: Most social scientists today would not agree that manifestations of honesty are, say, additive.

There is another distinction (apart from scale) between different types of measurement deserving attention. Measurement is called *fundamental* if it involves construction of scales to reflect an underlying phenomenon as previously described. Measurement is *derived* when new scales are obtained from others (fundamental or already derived). Thus the measurement of area may be thought of as derived from the multiplication of (fundamentally measured) length and "width." *Measurement by fiat* is measurement that is neither fundamental nor derived. It is used when both fundamental and derived scaling procedures are not available. All fiat measurement implicitly defines the property it quantifies. Examples include the intelligence test and Birkhoff's [5] ethical and aesthetic measures.

Because fiat measures are not constructed to reflect directly or indirectly an underlying phenomenon, they generally do not calibrate exactly what is wanted. Concepts formulated theoretically may be quite different from the operational proxies by which they are numerically gauged. Etzioni and Lehman [10] have called the result "fractional" measurement, because only a part of the concept in question is recorded on the scale. But because the precise relationship between what is supposed to be measured and what is in fact measured is seldom known, matters are probably much worse. Bauer [4, p. 37] has asked "Is it better to have a crude measure of a variable you are really interested in, or a precise measure of a variable which is only an approximation of what you are interested in?" Without resolution of this issue, empirical verification of theories by use of fiat constructions is highly questionable. Nevertheless, fiat measures have been and will continue to be important in prediction.

Perhaps with the idea of some sort of approximation in mind, numbers on ordinal scales have occasionally been used as if they were obtained from interval scales. Consider, for example, the Adelman and Morris [1] construction of scales on which countries can be identified according to such properties as the "character of basic social organization." Based on published statistics and surveys of knowledgeable opinion, Adelman and Morris begin by ranking countries according to these traits. Underlying phenomena are thus defined for each. Because there are only finitely many countries, ordinal scales are easy to find. However, no tests exist that determine the positions on the scales of newly obtained observations. Instead, the observations must first be fitted into the underlying rankings and then assigned numbers according to the particular scales already chosen. So far, so good. But Adelman and Morris then employ these numbers in a factor analysis (requiring their addition, etc.) to discover the significance of the characteristics for economic development. And because their scales are, in reality, ordinal rather than interval scales, there is no way to tell if the results secured are a true representation of reality or a manifestation of the properties of the particular scales chosen for computation. (The point was originally made by Brookins [7].)

To see what can go wrong with a factor analysis of ordinal data in general, consider the following data matrix containing three observations (rows) of two variables (columns):

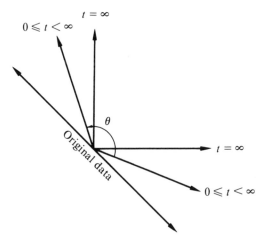

Figure 2-1

$$\begin{bmatrix} 1 & 3 \\ 2 & 2 \\ 3 & 1 \end{bmatrix}$$

Reflecting the fact that these points all lie on the same line, the associated correlation matrix,

$$\begin{bmatrix} 1 & -1 \\ -1 & 1 \end{bmatrix}$$

has eigenvalues $\lambda_1 = 2$ and $\lambda_2 = 0$. The variables are perfectly correlated and a single factor accounts for all their variation. Represented in terms of the correlation matrix, the data are shown as the two unit vectors in Figure 2-1 meeting at an angle of 180°.

Now apply the increasing transformation $h(x) = (x+t)^2$, where $t \geq 0$, to observations of the first variable. The data matrix becomes

$$\begin{bmatrix} 1 + 2t + t^2 & 3 \\ 4 + 4t + t^2 & 2 \\ 9 + 6t + t^2 & 1 \end{bmatrix}$$

and the correlation matrix is

$$\begin{bmatrix} 1 & -\dfrac{2\sqrt{2}}{S}(t+2) \\[4mm] -\dfrac{2\sqrt{2}}{S}(t+2) & 1 \end{bmatrix}$$

Table 2-2

	Regression with original data			Regression with transformed data		
	Original data	Deviation from mean	Regression results	Squared data (x only)	Deviation from mean	Regression results
x_1	1	−1		1	−3 2/3	
x_2	2	0		4	−2/3	
x_3	3	+1		9	+4 1/3	
x-mean	2			4 2/3		
y_1	1 2/3	−1 1/3		1 2/3	−1 1/3	
y_2	5 1/3	+2 1/3		5 1/3	+2 1/3	
y_3	2	−1		2	−1	
y-mean	3			3		
$\hat{\beta}$			1/6			−3/98
$\hat{\alpha}$			2 2/3			3 1/7
r^2			.007			.004

where

$$S = \frac{98}{3} + \frac{4}{3}t + 8t^2$$

The resulting eigenvalues are:

$$\lambda_1 = 1 + \frac{2\sqrt{2}}{S}(t + 2)$$

$$\lambda_2 = 1 - \frac{2\sqrt{2}}{S}(t + 2)$$

For any finite $t \geqslant 0$, since $\lambda_1 \neq \lambda_2$, two factors are required to span the data space. The data vectors appear in Figure 2-1 as the two unit vectors meeting at an angle θ of less than 180° but more than 90°. The correlation of the variables falls between 0 and −1. Furthermore,

$$\lim_{t \to \infty} \lambda_1 = \lim_{t \to \infty} \lambda_2 = 1$$

whence, by increasing t, the data can be made arbitrarily close to a situation in which there is no variable correlation at all. In the latter case the corresponding unit vectors in Figure 2-1 are those meeting at 90°. Computational procedures aside, in this illustration a legitimate transforma-

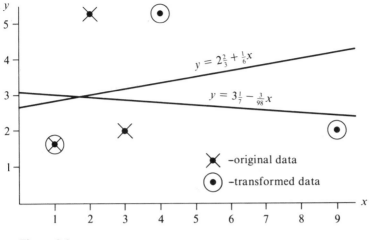

The lines shown are $y = 2\frac{2}{3} + \frac{1}{6}x$ and $y = 3\frac{1}{7} - \frac{3}{98}x$, with ✖ –original data and ⊙ –transformed data.

Figure 2-2

tion of the data modifies the picture emerging from factor analysis almost from one extreme to the other.

Factor analysis is not the only statistical technique that, upon use with ordinal data, depends on the choice of scale. The same is true of least-squares regression analysis, for in addition to altering the magnitude of estimated coefficients and the proportion of explained variance, increasing transformations of the data may further induce sign reversals. To be concrete, let three observations on variables x (exogenous) and y (endogenous) be given as in Table 2-2. Consider the regression equation

$$(2.2\text{-}1) \quad y^t = \alpha + \beta x^t + \epsilon^t \qquad t = 1, 2, 3$$

where α and β are parameters to be estimated, and ϵ^t is the random disturbance. Assume each ϵ^t is distributed independently as a normal variate with zero mean and the same variance. Deviations from means, estimates $\hat{\alpha}$ and $\hat{\beta}$, and the square of the correlation coefficient, r^2, are indicated in the table. Note $\hat{\beta} > 0$. Transforming just the x data by squaring provides new estimates as shown. Now $\hat{\beta} < 0$. The two regression lines are pictured in Figure 2-2.

The low values for r^2 in Table 2-2 should be marked: Little variance is explained by the regression. Clearly, as r^2 increases it will become harder to find a scale transformation that reverses sign. One would expect that beyond a certain point the monotonicity of the data would preclude any sign reversal of $\hat{\beta}$, although its magnitude would always be subject to change. Corroborating this expectation, Grether [12] has given necessary and sufficient conditions (on the original data) eliminating the possibility of a sign reversal of r no matter what increasing transformation is employed. Since r and $\hat{\beta}$ have identical signs, Grether's results apply to the latter. Thus if only signs of coefficients are of interest, and if the requisite conditions are met, least-squares regression would seem to be an appropriate statistical technique in spite of the ordinality of the data.

But still deeper problems arise. To confine attention to the simplest case, suppose $\alpha = 0$ and $x \geqslant 0$. Then the regression equation with neither error term nor subscripts (i.e., the "true" relation between y and x) becomes

(2.2-2) $y = \beta x$

Since x (not y) is measured ordinally, other legitimate specifications of equation (2.2-2) are, say,

(2.2-3) $y = \beta' x^2$

and

(2.2-4) $y = \beta'' x^3$

where β' and β'' are coefficients expressed in terms of the transformed scales. Now if (2.2-2) and (2.2-3) are to be valid simultaneously, then

$$x = \beta / \beta'$$

Similarly, putting together (2.2-2) and (2.2-4), one obtains

$$x = (\beta / \beta'')^{1/2}$$

and combining (2.2-3) and (2.2-4), one gets

$$x = \beta' / \beta''$$

Taken individually or collectively these conclusions do not make much sense. They arise because increasing transformations are applied to a variable x whose relation to y is required to be linear both before and after the transformation. This is generally impossible. Thus to employ least-squares regression analysis, one must not only assume the ordinary regression restrictions but also that the linear form of the relation between y and x holds only for the particular scales on which these variables are measured. Any increasing transformation of x, it must be supposed, alters the form of the relation. Of course, under such an assumption the Grether conditions are irrelevant because sign reversals cannot meaningfully arise. But the assumption still permits a logically consistent estimation of parameters, provided that the purpose of computing estimates is for use in prediction. These estimates, however, cannot yield any information concerning the nature of the true underlying relation. Alternative uses of regression analysis in the absence of even ordinal data are considered in Chapter 13.

It is, of course, possible to give further examples of statistical methods that become scale dependent upon application to ordinal data. The arguments that such procedures (a) can be tempered by experience and training and (b) are already enlisted to make important decisions (see Kuenne [19]), cannot validate their use. For the plain fact that arithmetic operations are not generally permissible with numbers obtained from ordinal scales is a serious drawback tending to impose important limitations. Many analytical propositions that are appropriate for interval scales simply cannot be applied. This is not surprising: Ordinal measurement can do no more than provide an equivalent, numerical representation of an ordering. It cannot legitimately add anything to the underlying phenomenon that does not already exist.

References

1. Adelman, I., and C. T. Morris, *Society Politics and Economic Development* (Baltimore: Johns Hopkins Press, 1967).
2. Adelman, I., and C. T. Morris, "Performance Criteria for Evaluating Economic Development Potential: An Operational Approach," *The Quarterly Journal of Economics,* 82 (1968):260–80.
3. Apter, D. E., *The Politics of Modernization* (Chicago: University of Chicago Press, 1965).
4. Bauer, R., "Detection and Anticipation of Impact: The Nature of the Task," in R. Bauer, ed., *Social Indicators* (Cambridge, Mass.: MIT Press, 1966), pp. 1–67.
5. Birkhoff, G. D., *Aesthetic Measure* (Cambridge, Mass.: Harvard University Press, 1933).
6. Blalock, H. M., Jr., "The Measurement Problem: A Gap Between the Languages of Theory and Research," in H. M. Blalock, Jr. and A. B. Blalock, eds., *Methodology in Social Science* (New York: McGraw-Hill, 1968), pp. 5–27.
7. Brookins, O. T., "Factor Analysis and Gross National Product: A Comment," *The Quarterly Journal of Economics,* 84 (1970):648–50.
8. Edgeworth, F. Y., *Mathematical Psychics* (London: Kegan Paul, 1881).
9. Ellis, B., *Basic Concepts of Measurement* (Cambridge: Cambridge University Press, 1966).
10. Etzioni, A., and E. W. Lehman, "Some Dangers in 'Valid' Social Measurement," *Annuals of the American Academy of Political and Social Science,* 373 (September 1967):1–15.
11. Goodenough, W. H., *Cooperation in Change* (New York: Wiley, 1966).
12. Grether, D. M., "Correlations with Ordinal Data," *Journal of Econometrics,* 2 (1974):241–6.

13. Handman, M. S., "The Sentiment of Nationalism," *Political Science Quarterly,* 36 (1921):104–21.
14. Hempel, C. G., "Typological Methods in the Social Sciences," in M. Natanson, ed., *Philosophy of Social Science, A Reader* (New York: Random House, 1963), pp. 210–30.
15. Jung, C. G., *Psychological Types* (*Collected Works,* v. 6), H. G. Baynes and R. F. C. Hull, trans. (Princeton, N.J.: Princeton University Press, 1971).
16. Katzner, D. W., *Static Demand Theory* (New York: Macmillan, 1970).
17. Krantz, D. H., R. D. Luce, P. Supes, and A. Tversky, *Foundations of Measurement,* vol. 1 (New York: Academic Press, 1971).
18. Kretschmer, E., *Physique and Character,* 2nd ed. revised, W. J. H. Sprott, trans. (London: Kegan Paul, Trench, Trubner, 1936).
19. Kuenne, R. E., "Interproduct Distances in a Quality-Space: Inexact Measurement in Differentiated Oligopoly Analysis," *Applied Economics,* 6 (1974):255–73.
20. Landau, M., *Political Theory and Political Science* (New York: Macmillan, 1972).
21. Lazarsfeld, P. F., and A. H. Barton, "Qualitative Measurement in the Social Sciences: Classification, Typologies, and Indices," in D. Lerner and H. D. Lasswell, eds., *The Policy Sciences* (Stanford, Ca.: Stanford University Press, 1951), pp. 155–92.
22. Mann, H. M., "Seller Concentration, Barriers to Entry, and Rates of Return in Thirty Industries, 1950–1960," *The Review of Economics and Statistics,* 48 (1966):296–307.
23. Nunnaly, J. C., *Psychometric Theory* (New York: McGraw-Hill, 1967).
24. Pfanzagl, J., *Theory of Measurement,* 2nd ed. (Würzburg-Vienna: Physica-Verlag, 1971).
25. Rostow, W. W., *The Stages of Economic Growth* (Cambridge: Cambridge University Press, 1960).
26. Rudner, R. S., *Philosophy of Social Science* (Englewood Cliffs, N.J.: Prentice-Hall, 1966).
27. Schutz, A., *Collected Papers,* vol. 2 (*Studies in Social Theory*), A. Brodersen ed. (The Hague: Martinus Nijhoff, 1964).
28. Sheldon, W. H., *The Varieties of Human Physique* (New York: Hafner, 1963).
29. Sorokin, P. A., *Social and Cultural Dynamics,* vol. 1 (New York: Bedminster, 1937).
30. Sorokin, P. A., in F. Tönnies, *Community and Society,* C. P. Loomis, trans. and ed. (E. Lansing, Mich.: Michigan State University Press, 1957), Preface.
31. Triffin, R., *Monopolistic Competition and General Equilibrium Theory* (Cambridge, Mass.: Harvard University Press, 1940).
32. Weber, M., *Economy and Society,* vol. 1, G. Roth and C. Wittich, eds. (New York: Bedminster, 1968).
33. Winch, R. F., "Heuristic and Empirical Typologies: A Job for Factor Analysis," *American Sociological Review,* 12 (1947):68–75.
34. Wirth, L., "Types of Nationalism," *American Journal of Sociology,* 41 (1936):723–37.

PART I

Theoretical methods

CHAPTER 3

Basic concepts

In much the same way as ordinary investigation of quantifiable experience rests on concepts such as set, relation, function, topology, and a multitude of others, so techniques for handling nonquantifiable phenomena may be built upon a similar foundation. To avoid confusion later, it is well to begin by specifying these fundamentals. The following discussion presents a brief outline of the basic set-theoretic and topological concepts and propositions that are required for subsequent use. It also illustrates the fact that a good deal of mathematical analysis does not depend on an ability to measure. Proofs that are well known and readily available are not repeated. The material is based, for the most part, on Halmos [4] and Kelley [5].

The results to be developed here have immediate application in social science. Consider, as one example, the dispute over whether the U.S. and Soviet economic systems are becoming more alike as time passes (see, e.g., Prybyla [6, Part V]). Many factors involved in the argument do not appear capable of measurement. To resolve this issue one clearly must know what it means for two economies to "come together." Provided general agreement can be reached concerning the relevant properties on which comparisons are to be based, Section 3.2 shows that a definition of closeness is indeed possible. This, then, furnishes a framework for probing the question of U.S.–Soviet similarity.

3.1   Sets, relations, and functions

A *set* is any collection, X, of well-defined objects. No assumptions of quantifiability are made. Each object, for example, might be a subjective value such as "fairness" or "honesty" held by an individual or a description of a particular environment (including physical, psychological, cultural, and social characteristics) in which a person lives. (The problems involved in defining these sorts of notions have already been explored in Section 1.3.3. Further discussion appears in Section 7.1.) Alternatively, the objects themselves might be collections of still other objects. Thus each object in X could be a list representing sets of values held by an individual or a list of environments facing each member of a group or it could consist of both lists combined. Objects could also be classes of a typology (Section 2.1). In any case the symbol x will denote the elements of X.

Two sets are *equal* if and only if they contain the same objects.

It is often possible to define particular sets by naming their elements. For example, X may be the collection of objects $x^1, \ldots, x^n$; that is,

$$X = \{x^1, \ldots, x^n\}$$

Alternatively, a set may be described by giving a property uniquely characterizing its elements. Thus X could be the collection of all objects, x, exhibiting property P, or, written symbolically,

$$X = \{x : x \text{ has property } P\}$$

The set containing no elements is called the *empty* set and denoted by $\varnothing$.

Sets may be compared and combined in various ways. Of interest here are *inclusion* ($\subseteq$), *union* ($\cup$), *intersection* ($\cap$), and *difference* ($-$). These are defined as follows: If A and B are sets, then

    i. $A \subseteq B$ or $B \supseteq A$ provided every x in A is also contained in B.
    ii. $A \cup B = \{x : x \text{ is in } A, \text{ or in } B, \text{ or in both}\}$.
    iii. $A \cap B = \{x : x \text{ is in both } A \text{ and } B\}$.
    iv. $A - B = \{x : x \text{ is in } A \text{ but not in } B\}$.

All standard properties of unions, intersections, and differences remain valid in the absence of measurement. Two sets A and B are *disjoint* or *mutually exclusive* when $A \cap B = \varnothing$. If $A \subseteq B$, then A is called a *subset* of B; it is a *proper subset* of B if, in addition, $A \neq B$. Every set contains the empty set as a subset. The *power set* of B, written $\mathcal{P}(B)$, is the class of all subsets of B:

$$\mathcal{P}(B) = \{A : A \subseteq B\}$$

Note $\varnothing$ is in $\mathcal{P}(B)$. The *complement* of A in B is $B - A$.

Consider two nonempty, but not necessarily disjoint, sets A and B. Following Halmos [4], an *ordered pair* whose first and second *coordinates* (or *components*) are, respectively, a in A and b in B is defined as:

$$(a, b) = \{\{a\}, \{a, b\}\}$$

The *Cartesian product, $A \times B$*, of A and B is a collection of ordered pairs:

$$A \times B = \{(a, b) : a \text{ is in } A \text{ and } b \text{ is in } B\}$$

Not all collections of ordered pairs are Cartesian products. More generally, when there are n sets, say, $X_1, \ldots, X_n$, the *n-tuple* or *vector* with coordinates x_i in X_i, where $i = 1, \ldots, n$, is

tion form) does not depend in any way on an ability to quantify the elements of its domain and range.

Consider any $f: X \to Y$, and suppose ρ and ζ order, respectively, X and Y. Whenever, for all x' and x'' in X,

$$x' \rho x''$$

if and only if

$$f(x') \, \zeta f(x'')$$

f is called *order preserving*. It is *order reversing* or *reciprocal* if

$$x' \rho x''$$

if and only if

$$f(x'') \, \zeta f(x')$$

for all x' and x''. When f is order reversing, the variables x and y are frequently referred to as *reciprocally* or *inversely related*.

Let $f: X \to Y$. If the range of f is identical to Y, then f is said to be *onto*. Also, f is *one-to-one* (or 1-1) provided distinct elements of X are mapped onto distinct elements of Y; that is, $f(x') = f(x'')$ implies $x' = x''$, for all x' and x'' in X. When f is both 1-1 and onto it is called a *1-1 correspondence*.

A set is *finite* if there exists a 1-1 correspondence between it and some subset of the positive integers of the form $\{1, \ldots, m\}$; *countably infinite,* if there is a 1-1 correspondence between it and the set of all positive integers; *countable,* if it is finite or countably infinite; and *uncountably infinite,* if it is not countable. Even with measurement unavailable, it is not difficult to conceive of uncountably infinite sets. For example, one may imagine, as does Apter [1, p. 34], two distinct political systems with a continuum of variation in between. In the same manner as one can visually distinguish a mere finite number of distinct colors out of the continuous spectrum, so it would be possible to list or observe only a finite number of political systems from such a continuum. The point is taken up again in Section 7.2.

Let I be a set and $\mathcal{Q}^*$ be a collection of subsets $A \subseteq X$. The map $f: I \to \mathcal{Q}^*$ defines a *family of sets $\mathcal{Q}$ indexed by I,* where $\mathcal{Q}$ is the range of f. Members of $\mathcal{Q}$ are written A_i when i is in I and $f(i) = A_i$. *Subfamilies* of $\mathcal{Q}$ are subsets of $\mathcal{Q}$. The union of all members of $\mathcal{Q}$ is denoted by

$$\bigcup_i A_i$$

No restrictions of countability are made on I.

Consider again $f: X \to Y$. The *inverse* of f, written f^{-1}, is a function mapping the power sets $\mathcal{P}(Y)$ into $\mathcal{P}(X)$, and defined by

$$f^{-1}(B) = \{x : f(x) \text{ is in } B \text{ and } x \text{ is in } X\}$$

for all $B \subseteq Y$. The set $f^{-1}(B)$ is referred to as the *inverse image* of B under f. It can be shown that for any $A \subseteq X$ and $B \subseteq Y$,

(3.1-1) $f(f^{-1}(B)) \subseteq B$

(3.1-2) $f(f^{-1}(B)) = B$ if and only if f is onto

(3.1-3) $A \subseteq f^{-1}(f(A))$

(3.1-4) $A = f^{-1}(f(A))$ if and only if f is 1–1

When f is both 1–1 and onto there exists an inverse function, also denoted by f^{-1}, mapping Y onto X, which is 1–1, and such that

$$f(f^{-1}(y)) = y$$
$$f^{-1}(f(x)) = x$$

for all y in Y and x in X.

The function $f: X \times Y \to X$ *projects* $X \times Y$ onto X whenever

$$f(x, y) = x$$

for all (x, y) in $X \times Y$. Similarly, if $g: X \times Y \to Y$, where

$$g(x, y) = y$$

for all (x, y) in $X \times Y$, then g is the projection of $X \times Y$ onto Y.

Situations postulating X and Y as sets of real numbers may be regarded as special cases of the preceding one in which additional properties of the elements are available for use. Thus, for example, it is permissible to add, subtract, multiply, and divide, and the relation "greater than or equal to" ($\geqslant$) linearly orders both X and Y. Under these circumstances a function $f: X \to Y$ is a (*strictly*) *increasing transformation* whenever $x' > x''$ implies $f(x') > f(x'')$, for all x' and x'' in X. It is a *linear transformation* if there exist real numbers α and β such that

$$f(x) = \alpha x + \beta$$

on X, and a *positive linear transformation* provided $\alpha > 0$. Note when $\beta \neq 0$, f does not satisfy

$$f(x' + x'') = f(x') + f(x'')$$

for all x' and x'' in X.

This section concludes with Zadeh's [11, 12] notion of a fuzzy set. The idea arises because the boundaries of many classes of objects in the real world are difficult to define precisely. The collection of all socialistic economic systems and the set of all honest people are two examples that could be approached in such a way. The fact that there is currently no accepted procedure for measuring "amounts" of socialism in economies or honesty in individuals is no hindrance.

Let X be a set of not necessarily quantifiable elements and denote the unit interval (with end points) of real numbers by $[0, 1]$. A *fuzzy set A* in X is defined by a "membership" function $f_A : X \rightarrow [0, 1]$, which determines the *grade of membership*, $f_A(x)$, in A of each x in X. Membership grades start at 0 and can not exceed 1. An element does not "belong" to a fuzzy set – the boundary is too blurred to permit such fine distinctions. Indeed, as previously indicated, the notion of fuzzy set itself stems from the difficulty of not knowing where a set begins and where it ends. On the other hand, a set $A \subseteq X$ of the sort originally imagined and used up until now, that is, one for which the boundaries are known and exact, is specified by the membership function

$$f_A(x) = \begin{cases} 1, & \text{if } x \text{ is in } A \\ 0, & \text{otherwise} \end{cases}$$

Inclusion, union, intersection, and difference can be extended to fuzzy sets.

A *fuzzy relation* on X is simply a fuzzy set in $X \times X$. Fuzzy orderings and fuzzy functions can also be defined.

3.2   Topology, convergence, and closeness

In order to deal with concepts such as convergence, stability, and continuity, it is necessary to have a topology. Although, in theory, any topology will do, in practice it is nice to have one that contributes as much as possible toward the goals of the analysis. The following topological construction attempts to preserve the intuitive meaning of the idea that two objects can be "close" or "similar" to each other. Section 3.3 will embed it into a more general framework. Some definitions are given first.

Let X be a set. A *topology* for X (distinct from the typologies of Section 2.1) is a family of sets, $\Im$, such that:

   i. $\varnothing$ is in $\Im$.
   ii. For each x in X there is a T in $\Im$ such that x is in T.
   iii. The intersection of any two members of $\Im$ is in $\Im$.
   iv. The union of any subfamily of $\Im$ is in $\Im$.

Sets together with their topologies are referred to as *topological spaces* and written $(X, \Im)$. The members of $\Im$ are called *open sets*. A subfamily $\mathcal{L} \subseteq \Im$ is a *base* for $\Im$ provided that each member of $\Im$ can be obtained as the union of members of $\mathcal{L}$. Bases with countable membership are said to be *countable*. The topology consisting of the family of all subsets of X, namely, $\mathcal{P}(X)$, is the *discrete topology* for X.

A *neighborhood* of x in X is a set $N \subseteq X$ for which there exists an open set T in $\Im$ containing x such that $T \subseteq N$. Not all neighborhoods are open, although every open set is a neighborhood of each of its points. Let A and B be subsets of X. Then A is *closed* whenever its complement $X - A$ is open; the *closure* of A (written $\bar{A}$) is the intersection of all closed sets in X containing A; A and B are *separated* provided

$$\bar{A} \cap B = \varnothing \quad \text{and} \quad \bar{B} \cap A = \varnothing$$

and A is *connected* if it cannot be written as the union of two nonempty, open, separated subsets of X. A *component* of the topological space $(X, \Im)$ is a connected subset of X, which is not contained in any larger connected subset of X. Components are always closed, whereas distinct components must necessarily be separated.

The topological space $(X, \Im)$ is *Hausdorff* if for all distinct x' and x'' in X there are disjoint neighborhoods of x' and x'' in $\Im$. It is *normal* provided that for every pair of disjoint closed sets A and B there exist disjoint open sets U and V for which $A \subseteq U$ and $B \subseteq V$.

A *pseudometric* on X is a function, d, mapping $X \times X$ into the non-negative real numbers, such that for all x', x'', and x''' in X,

   i. $x' = x''$ implies $d(x', x'') = 0$.
   ii. $d(x', x'') = d(x'', x')$.
   iii. $d(x', x'') + d(x'', x''') \geqslant d(x', x''')$.

If, in addition,

   iv. $d(x', x'') = 0$ implies $x' = x''$

for every x' and x'' in X, then d becomes a *metric*. For all x' and x in X and any $r > 0$,

$$S_r(x') = \{x : d(x', x) < r\}$$

is the *open sphere* of radius r about x'. When a pseudometric (or metric) exists, the family

(3.2-1) $\{S_r(x') : r > 0 \text{ and } x' \text{ is in } X\}$

is the base for a topology referred to as the *pseudometric (or, respectively, metric) topology* for X. A *pseudometric (or metric) space* consists of a set and a pseudometric (or metric) topology for it. Every pseudometric space is normal; every metric space is Hausdorff.

Let X be a set and $\mathfrak{I}$ a topology for X. Any subfamily of $\mathfrak{I}$, say, $\{T_\mu\}$, is an *open covering* of a set $A \subseteq X$ provided

$$A \subseteq \bigcup_\mu T_\mu$$

Every subcollection of $\{T_\mu\}$ that also covers A is called a *subcovering*. The set $A \subseteq X$ is *compact* if and only if every open covering of A by a subfamily of $\mathfrak{I}$ contains a finite subcovering.

Consider now what it means to assert that two objects, say, x' and x'', in X are "close" to each other. If the objects are capable of measurement, closeness could be taken to mean that the Euclidean distance $|x' - x''|$ is small. Even when quantification is not possible, a metric or pseudometric could still be defined on X and the concept of closeness (and for that matter, convergence) made to depend on it. Although there is no unique way to obtain one, it can be chosen to reflect the impression that certain elements appear to be closer together than others. For example, let the objects of X be ideologies of various societies. If it were felt that the ideology of the United States were closer to that of the Soviet Union than to that of mainland China, the metric (or pseudometric) should assign to the pair "ideology of the United States" and "ideology of the Soviet Union" a smaller number than to the pair "ideology of the United States" and "ideology of China." Note in the case of a pseudometric that distinct elements of X may be lumped into one (i.e., have no "distance" between them), since $d(x', x'') = 0$ does not ensure $x' = x''$. Such objects are as "close together" as they can become.

If, as is most certainly true of the previous example, there are uncertainties about the exact distances between pairs of points, Menger's notion of probabilistic metric could be used. It requires a function $F_{xy}(r)$ mapping the positive real line into the interval $[0, 1]$, which reflects the probability (see Chapter 12) that the distance between points x and y is less than r. Of course, F_{xy} must have certain properties such as $F_{xy}(r) = 1$ for all $r > 0$, if and only if $x = y$, and so on. The conception is similar in spirit to that of fuzzy sets and the basic ideas involved are summarized by Schweizer [9]. Still, in the absence of measurement, even a probabilistic metric rests on the same sort of subjective considerations as described earlier for the ordinary metric.

A third approach, and the alternative pursued here, turns on the definition of a topology for X. From this viewpoint, closeness and convergence will come to depend on which subsets of X are called open and which are not. Such a procedure will permit, in the ideology example, a more explicit statement of the "appearance of closeness" between ideologies.

One way to choose an appropriate topology for X is to think of closeness in terms of similarity of the "relative strengths" of exhibited properties. The more properties two objects of X have in the same relative strengths, the closer they will be considered to be. More precisely, it is assumed that each property induces a binary relation on X according to the degree to which objects exhibit that property. For the ith property, where i ranges over some not necessarily countable set I, write $x'\rho_i x''$ if and only if x' exhibits property i at least as strongly as x''. Thus if the objects of X consisted of various societies, it would be possible to rank them according to the degree to which each permitted individual freedom. Now ρ_i is taken to be both reflexive and transitive. Hence, as in Section 3.1, the relation $\hat{\rho}_i$ defined for all x' and x'' in X by $x'\hat{\rho}x''$ if and only if both $x'\rho_i x''$ and $x''\rho_i x'$, is an equivalence relation partitioning X into equivalence classes $[x]^i$. The assertion that two objects of X both exhibit property i to the same degree or in the same relative strengths, means that they are both in the same equivalence class as determined by $\hat{\rho}_i$.

Given i and v in I, let $\hat{\rho}_{iv}$ be the relation such that $x'\hat{\rho}_{iv}x''$ if and only if both $x'\hat{\rho}_i x''$ and $x'\hat{\rho}_v x''$, for all x' and x'' in X. Then $\hat{\rho}_{iv}$ is also an equivalence relation and two distinct objects can be in one of its associated equivalence classes $[x]^{iv}$ if and only if they satisfy both property i to the same degree and property v to the same degree. Clearly,

$$[x]^{iv} = [x]^i \cap [x]^v$$

for all i and v. These ideas can be generalized to accommodate any number of properties.

Suppose $\mathcal{E}$ to be the collection of all equivalence classes generated by all properties ρ_i. Let $\mathfrak{I}^0$ consist of all finite intersections and arbitrary unions of sets in $\mathcal{E}$. Then every object x in X is an element of some T in $\mathfrak{I}^0$, and hence $\mathfrak{I}^0$ is a topology for X. Letting $\mathcal{L}^0$ contain only finite intersections of sets in $\mathcal{E}$, one sees that $\mathcal{L}^0$ is a base for $\mathfrak{I}^0$. Note that the topology $\mathfrak{I}^0$ is obtained, in effect, from a family of ordering typologies (Section 2.1).

It is worth examining this topology in greater detail. Let E_j^i be the jth equivalence class obtained from the ith property, where j is in some possibly uncountable set J_i and i is in I. In terms of the preceding notation,

$$E_j^i = [x]^i$$

for some j and

$$\mathcal{E} = \{E_j^i : j \text{ is in } J_i \text{ and } i \text{ is in } I\}$$

The base $\mathcal{L}^0$ consists of finite intersections of the form

$$E_{j_1^{i_1}}^{i_1} \cap E_{j_2^{i_1}}^{i_1} \cap \cdots \cap E_{j_{n_1}^{i_1}}^{i_1} \cap E_{j_1^{i_2}}^{i_2} \cap \cdots \cap E_{j_{n_2}^{i_2}}^{i_2} \cap \cdots \cap E_{j_m}^{i_n}$$

for appropriate n and m. This expression may be abbreviated by

$$E_{j_1}^{i_1} \cap \cdots \cap E_{j_m}^{i_n}$$

Note also that because any two equivalence classes generated by the same $\hat{\rho}_i$ are disjoint, $\varnothing$ is in $\mathcal{L}^0$. The component of $(X, \mathfrak{I}^0)$ containing x is

$$C(x) = \{x' : x' \hat{\rho}_i x \text{ for every } i \text{ in } I\}$$
$$= \cap E_j^i$$

where the intersection is taken over all i and j, such that x is in E_j^i. The $C(x)$ are disjoint and

$$X = \bigcup_{x \text{ in } X} C(x)$$

Each element of the base is a union of appropriate $C(x)$.

If I is finite, every x in X is a member of a finite number of equivalence classes. Hence the foregoing intersection defining $C(x)$ is finite and

$$\{C(x) : x \text{ is in } X\} \subseteq \mathcal{L}^0$$

Furthermore, $C(x)$ is both open (because it is a part of the base) and closed (because it can be written as the complement of a union of base elements). When I is infinite, components are, of course, still closed. However, they are generally neither open nor contained in the base.

Consider now the idea of closeness among elements of X. Object x' is said to be *closer* to x than object x'' whenever x and x' appear together in numerically more equivalence classes than do x and x''. Thus x and x' have the relative strengths of at least one more property in common than do x and x''. Clearly, x' is closer to x than x'' if and only if x is closer to x' than x''. To illustrate, suppose X is the rectangle pictured in Figure 3-1. Let only two properties be given. Assume $\hat{\rho}_1$ partitions X into

$$E_1^1 = A \cup B \qquad E_2^1 = G \cup H$$

and $\hat{\rho}_2$ divides X similarly:

$$E_1^2 = A \cup G \qquad E_2^2 = B \cup H$$

Then h is closer to x than a, b, and g; both b and g are closer to x than a; and neither b nor g are closer to x than the other.

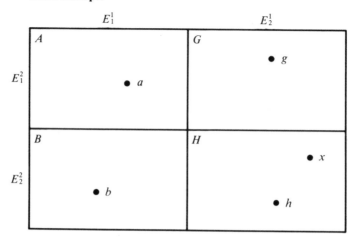

Figure 3-1

It is worth pausing briefly to note that these ideas are not entirely new to the nonphysical sciences. As the starting point for a theory of voting, for example, Riker and Ordeshook [7, Ch. 11] assume each voter orders candidates (with respect to personal preference) according to their positions on various dimensions associated with relevant policy issues. Different dimensions may give rise to distinct orderings of candidates. Voters' evaluation of candidates and hence their vote emerges from such orderings. Because they do not analyze the relationship between candidates implied by the orderings, Riker and Ordeshook need not be concerned with a topology or the notion of closeness. But it is clear that a foundation similar to that previously described has been provided.

A second example appears in certain methods for chronologically ordering archaeological deposits. A deposit is a collection of artifacts found together – presumably made at the same time and place. The frequency of any particular type of artifact (e.g., a style of pot) varies across deposits from different time periods according as that type gained and lost popularity by the people who used it. Thus deposits relatively close in time will have similar type frequencies, whereas those farther apart will not. Although similarity of frequencies is often given numerical characterization (see, e.g., Robinson [8]), it can also be expressed in terms of orderings. Divide the numbers between 0 and 100 into appropriate, exhaustive, closed intervals, A_k, where $k = 1, \ldots, K$, and such that if $k' \geqslant k''$ then the numbers in $A_{k'}$ are at least as large as in $A_{k''}$. If x and y are deposits and α is an artifact type, then consider the ordering, ρ_α, given by $x \rho_\alpha y$ whenever the percentage of artifacts of type α in x is in some A'_k, the percentage of artifacts of type α in y is in some A''_k, and $k' \geqslant k''$. The orderings ρ_α – one for each artifact type – can be used to construct the topology as previously described. Furthermore, the definition of closeness, suggested earlier, is identical to the archaeological concept of closeness over time: Deposit x is closer in time to y than to z whenever x and y have more equivalence classes in common than x and z. That is, the distributions of types over x and y are more similar than those over x and z.

Turning to convergence, a *sequence* is a function f defined on the nonnegative integers into a subset of X. Sequences are written either as $f(k)$, where $k = 1, 2, \ldots$, or as $\{x^k\}$. The obvious link between these notations is given by

$$x^k = f(k), \qquad k = 1, 2, \ldots$$

A sequence $\{x^k\}$ in X *converges* to x^* in X if and only if for all neighborhoods N of x^* there is a nonnegative integer k^0, such that x^k is in N for all $k \geqslant k^0$.

Suppose $\{x^k\}$ converges to x^*. Consider a neighborhood containing x^* of the form

(3.2-2) $\quad E_{j_1}^{i_1} \cap \cdots \cap E_{j_m}^{i_n}$

Since x^* is in $E_{j_1}^{i_1}$, and since the latter is also a neighborhood of x^*, there is a k^1 such that x^k is in $E_{j_1}^{i_1}$ for all $k \geqslant k^1$. Similarly, for each $\sigma = 2, \ldots, n$, there is a k^σ such that x^k is in $E_{j_\sigma}^{i_\sigma}$ when $k \geqslant k^\sigma$. Setting

$$K = \max_\sigma k^\sigma$$

it follows that x^k is in

$$E_{j_1}^{i_1} \cap \cdots \cap E_{j_m}^{i_n}$$

for all $k \geqslant K$. Thus, provided that the number of common equivalence classes in addition to $E_{j_1}^{i_1}, \ldots, E_{j_m}^{i_n}$ to which $x^1, \ldots, x^K$ belong does not decrease as k increases up to K, the first K objects of $\{x^k\}$ become closer to x^* at finite intervals. The argument remains valid for arbitrary large – but finite – n.

With I finite, x^* is in at most a finite number of equivalence classes. Hence there is a minimal neighborhood, U, of the form (3.2-2) containing x^*. Applying the preceding argument, not only is there a K such that x^k is in U for $k \geqslant K$, but every neighborhood of x^* must contain x^k when $k \geqslant K$. After K the sequence cannot become any closer to x^*. Furthermore, if $U = \{x^*\}$, then $\{x^k\}$, appears as:

$$x^1, \ldots, x^K, x^*, x^*, \ldots$$

In this last case, convergence occurs in "finite time" and is characterized by an absence of change after a finite number of steps. When all sequences in X converge to a single element as described here, $\Im$ is the discrete topology.

Convergent sequences, however, need not converge to unique objects. Suppose, for example, $X^* = \{x', x'', x'''\}$. Let only one property be specified and assume

$$[x'] = [x''] = \{x', x''\}, \qquad [x'''] = \{x'''\}$$

are the equivalence classes it generates. Then $\Im^0$ becomes

$$\Im^* = \{\varnothing, \{x', x''\}, \{x'''\}, \{x', x'', x'''\}\}$$

Note x' and x'' are *accumulation points* of X^* whereas x''' is not: Every neighborhood of, say, x' in $\Im^*$ contains elements distinct from x'. Consider the sequences:

$$f^1(k) = x' \qquad \text{all } k$$
$$f^2(k) = x'' \qquad \text{all } k$$
$$f^3(k) = x''' \qquad \text{all } k$$

Then f^1 converges to both x' and x'', as does f^2. Only f^3 converges uniquely – to x'''. In general, to guarantee that every convergent sequence in X converges uniquely, $\Im^0$ must be Hausdorff. The converse assertion is also true.

The approach to convergence and closeness developed in this section is more general and, perhaps, less arbitrary than the use of either a metric or a pseudometric. Considering generality first, note the preceding example provides an ordering-generated, topological space $(X^*, \Im^*)$ without unique convergence. Since every metric space is Hausdorff, and since $(X^*, \Im^*)$ is not Hausdorff, $(X^*, \Im^*)$ is not a metric space. Hence there is no metric with which closeness and convergence can be described.

There is, however, a pseudometric that, in this example, will do the job. To present it in a broader context, suppose some finite number, i^*, of orderings generates $\Im^0$. Let n be a function on $X \times X$ into the nonnegative integers associating with each (x', x'') the number of equivalence classes containing both x' and x''. Define d by

$$d(x', x'') = i^* - n(x', x'')$$

for all (x', x'') in $X \times X$. Then it is not hard to show that d is a pseudometric characterizing precisely the concepts of closeness and convergence described here.

A similar conclusion holds when there is an infinite number of orderings, provided that the number of objects in X is finite. That is, under these conditions all but a finite number of the ρ_i are redundant.

Nevertheless, the foregoing setting for closeness and convergence is still more general than the pseudometric alternative. Although rigorous proof is postponed to the next section, it is worth considering here an example that, along with illustrating many of the present ideas, also hints at the possibility of a similar conclusion. More specifically, the example shows that when neither the number of orderings, ρ_i, nor X is finite, $(X, \mathfrak{J}^0)$ need not be normal. Because every pseudometric space is normal, there is no pseudometric whose associated collection of open spheres (3.2-1) form a base for $\mathfrak{J}^0$. But it does not follow that the sets in $\mathfrak{J}^0$ cannot be characterized in terms of a pseudometric. As will become clear in Section 3.3, $\mathfrak{J}^0$ may still be a subtopology of the pseudometric topology defined by some pseudometric on X.

Let X be a countable set and enumerate its elements:

(3.2-3) $X = \{x_1, x_2, \ldots\}$

Suppose there are a countable number of orderings, ρ_i, each producing equivalence classes depicted along rows of the following:

$\rho_1 : E_1^1 = \{x_1, x_3, x_5, \ldots\}\, E_2^1 = \{x_2, x_4, x_6, \ldots\}$

$\rho_2 : E_1^2 = \{x_1, x_4, x_7, \ldots\}\, E_2^2 = \{x_2, x_5, x_8, \ldots\}\, E_3^2 = \{x_3, x_6, x_9, \ldots\}$

$\rho_3 : E_1^3 = \{x_1, x_5, x_9, \ldots\}\, E_2^3 = \{x_2, x_6, x_{10}, \ldots\}\, E_3^3 = \{x_3, x_7, x_{11}, \ldots\}\, E_4^3 = \{x_4, x_8, x_{12}, \ldots\}$

$\quad \vdots \qquad\qquad \vdots \qquad\qquad \vdots \qquad\qquad \vdots \qquad\qquad \vdots$

Because the intersection of any two of these equivalence classes is either empty or another equivalence class (e.g., $E_1^2 \cap E_3^2 = E_1^1 \cap E_3^3 = \varnothing$, while $E_1^1 \cap E_3^2 = E_3^5$, where $E_3^5 = \{x_3, x_9, x_{15}, \ldots\}$), the collection of all equivalence classes, $\mathcal{E}$, together with $\varnothing$, constitute a base for $\mathfrak{J}^0$. Hence every E_j^i in $\mathcal{E}$ is open.

Now each E_j^i in $\mathcal{E}$ is also closed, since

$$E_j^i = X - \bigcup_{\sigma \neq j} E_\sigma^i$$

and the union on the right is open. Similarly, since

$$\{x_\mu\} = X - \bigcup_{\substack{j \neq \mu \\ i \geq \mu - 1}} E_j^i$$

the single element sets $\{x_\mu\}$ are closed for every μ. Note the $\{x_\mu\}$ are not open, because they are not contained in $\mathfrak{J}^0$. Thus

$$A = \{x_1, x_4, x_7, \ldots\} \cup \{x_3\}$$

and

$$B = \{x_2, x_5, x_8, \ldots\} \cup \{x_6\}$$

are disjoint, closed subsets of X. However, any open sets U and V such that $A \subseteq U$ and $B \subseteq V$ cannot be disjoint (e.g., if $U = E_1^2 \cup E_3^3$ and $V = E_2^2 \cup E_2^3$, then $U \cap V$ contains x_{10}, x_{11} and more) and therefore $\mathfrak{I}^0$ is not normal.

With respect to arbitrariness, the underlying properties on which the construction of $\mathfrak{I}^0$ is based must be, to one degree or another, arbitrarily chosen. This cannot be escaped. Unlike the pseudometric (or metric) approach, however, at least the arbitrariness is clearly exposed by the list of properties. Furthermore, in any particular study of social phenomena, it would probably be easier to obtain agreement on suitable properties rather than on some not very transparent metric. And with properties specified, the temptation to think of closeness in terms of them would be hard to resist.

It is also true that the derivation of $\mathfrak{I}^0$ as previously described does not usually imply the possibility of interval, or even ordinal, measurement. As indicated in Section 2.2, to be able to obtain an ordinal scale from some ρ_i, one must require, in addition, that ρ_i be total and that the interval topology defined on the quotient $X / \hat\rho_i$ have a countable base. If X were finite or countably infinite, the latter restriction would be automatically satisfied, and thus, in that case, if ρ_i were also total, then the elements of X could be measured on an ordinal – but still not interval – scale.

Finally, it is necessary to comment briefly on sequences in general and introduce the idea of a continuous function. Let X be a set and $\mathfrak{I}$ be any topology for X. The statement that "$\{x^k\}$ converges to x' uniquely" is often abbreviated to

$$\lim_{k \to \infty} x^k = x'$$

This notation is only used when convergence is unique. Let X' be a second set with topology $\mathfrak{I}'$. A function $g: X \to X'$ is *continuous* if the inverse image of every open set of $\mathfrak{I}'$ is an open set in $\mathfrak{I}$. If $g: X \to X'$ is continuous, then for every uniquely convergent sequence $\{x^k\}$ in X,

$$\lim_{k \to \infty} g(x^k) = g\left(\lim_{k \to \infty} x^k \right)$$

The notion of continuity is independent of any ability to measure the elements of either X or X'.

3.3   Uniformities

The approach to closeness proposed in the previous section can be viewed as a special case of a more general analysis. By distilling a meaning for closeness from the properties of metrics that do not depend on the numerical identification of each point, one obtains a broader frame of reference. The fundamental concept is that of a uniformity.

Consider any collection, X, of arbitrary objects. Recall that a relation is a set of ordered pairs of elements of X, that is, a subset of $X \times X$. If U is such a relation, let U^{-1} denote its inverse. For any subsets U and V of $X \times X$ the *composition* $U \cdot V$ is the class of all pairs (x, z) for which there exists a y such that (x, y) is in U and (y, z) is in V. The diagonal, Δ, of X is defined by

$$\Delta = \{(x, x) : x \text{ is in } X\}$$

A *uniformity* for X is a nonempty family $\mathfrak{U}$ of subsets of $X \times X$ such that:

i. $\Delta \subseteq U$ for all U in $\mathfrak{U}$.
ii. If U is in $\mathfrak{U}$, then U^{-1} is in $\mathfrak{U}$.
iii. If U is in $\mathfrak{U}$, then there exists a V in $\mathfrak{U}$ such that $V \cdot V \subseteq U$.
iv. If U and V are in $\mathfrak{U}$, then $U \cap V$ is in $\mathfrak{U}$.
v. If U is in $\mathfrak{U}$ and there is a $V \subseteq X \times X$ such that $U \subseteq V$, then V is in $\mathfrak{U}$.

The pair $(X, \mathfrak{U})$ is called a *uniform space*.

The metric properties preserved in the notion of a uniformity are apparent in (i) to (iii). The first derives from the fact that the distance between a point and itself is zero; the second, from the symmetry condition requiring the distance between x and y to be the same as that between y and x; and the third is a form of the triangle inequality that asserts that the sum of the distances between x and y and y and z is always greater than the distance between x and z. Thus when U is in $\mathfrak{U}$ the statement that (x, y) is in U is sometimes interpreted as saying, "x and y are U-close," or "x is close enough to y." Furthermore, x may be said to be *closer* to y than to z provided there exists a U in $\mathfrak{U}$ such that U contains (x, y) but not (x, z).

An element U of a uniformity $\mathfrak{U}$ is pictured as the shaded subset of $X \times X$ in Figure 3-2. Of course, the identification of points on a line with objects of X is arbitrary and hence the shape of U depends on the particular identification chosen. But no matter what identification is used it will always be true that $\Delta \subseteq U$.

A subfamily, $\mathcal{S} \subseteq \mathfrak{U}$, is a *base* for $\mathfrak{U}$ if and only if for all U in $\mathfrak{U}$ there

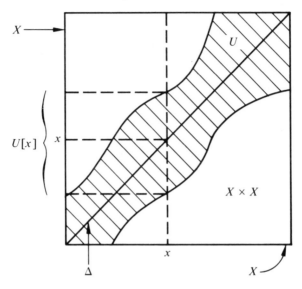

Figure 3-2

is an S in S such that $S \subseteq U$. Bases for uniformities are characterized by the following properties:

    i. $\Delta \subseteq S$ for every S in S.
    ii. If S is in S, then there is a V in S such that $V \subseteq S^{-1}$.
    iii. If S is in S, then there is a V in S such that $V \cdot V \subseteq S$.
    iv. If S and V are in S, then there is a W in S such that $W \subseteq S \cap V$.

This is entirely analogous to the notion of a base for a topology.

For each x in X and U in $\mathfrak{U}$, let

$$U[x] = \{ y : (x, y) \text{ is in } U \}$$

An example of a $U[x]$ appears in Figure 3-2. Given the uniformity $\mathfrak{U}$ for X, the family of all subsets T of X with the property that for each x in T there exists a U in $\mathfrak{U}$ where $U[x] \subseteq T$, forms a topology. It is called the *uniform topology* for X. In general, many distinct uniformities can generate the same uniform topology for any fixed X.

The topological construction of Section 3.2 is intimately related to a specific uniformity and uniform topology. To see this, consider the set, $\mathfrak{L}^0$, of all finite intersections of equivalence classes derived from the orderings, ρ_i, of that section. Let $\mathfrak{G}$ be the collection of all subclasses of $\mathfrak{L}^0$, which partition X into mutually exclusive and exhaustive subsets. Each ρ_i generates one such subclass of $\mathfrak{L}^0$; and various combinations of

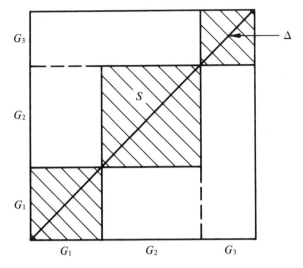

Figure 3-3

sets obtained by intersecting the sets secured from, say, ρ_i and ρ_j, yield many more. Thus if G is in $\mathcal{G}$ and the sets of G are indexed by α, then

$$X = \bigcup_\alpha G_\alpha$$

where $G = \{G_\alpha\}$ and

$$G_{\alpha'} \cap G_{\alpha''} = \varnothing$$

for all α' and α''. Define $\mathcal{S}^0$ as the collection of sets S of the form

$$S = \bigcup_\alpha (G_\alpha \times G_\alpha)$$

for some $G = \{G_\alpha\}$ in $\mathcal{G}$. Each G in $\mathcal{G}$, then, determines exactly one S in $\mathcal{S}^0$. An example with $G = \{G_1, G_2, G_3\}$ is illustrated in Figure 3-3.

To verify that $\mathcal{S}^0$ is a base for some uniformity $\mathcal{U}^0$ one must only note for any S and V in $\mathcal{S}^0$ that the preceding construction ensures

   i. $\Delta \subseteq S$.
   ii. $S = S^{-1}$.
   iii. $S \cdot S = S$.
   iv. $S \cap V$ is contained in $\mathcal{S}^0$.

All properties characterizing bases for uniformities are therefore satisfied.

It follows that the topology $\mathcal{T}^0$ of Section 3.2 is a subtopology of the uniform topology obtained from $\mathcal{U}^0$. Furthermore, the notion of closeness developed in Section 3.2 is a special case of that defined here. For if x is closer to y than z in the sense of Section 3.2, then x and y have more equivalence classes in common than do x and z. Hence an S in $\mathcal{S}^0$ can be found that contains (x, y) but not (y, z). In the sense of the present discussion, then, it is also true that x is closer to y than z.

Thus the more general approach to closeness is through specification of a uniformity and hence the associated uniform topology. But the question of why this is more satisfactory than the employment of a metric or pseudometric requires further clarification.

First of all, every pseudometric, d, on X determines a uniformity, $\mathcal{U}^d$, according to

(3.3-1) $\mathcal{U}^d = \{ U_r : r > 0 \}$

where

$$U_r = \{ (x, y) : d(x, y) < r \}$$

It is called the *pseudometric uniformity* with respect to d. The uniform topology arising from $\mathcal{U}^d$ is identical to the pseudometric topology for X derived from d. Thus whenever a pseudometric generates a particular uniformity, it must also generate the uniform topology obtained from that uniformity.

A uniform space $(X, \mathcal{U})$ is said to be *Hausdorff* provided that the intersection of all sets in $\mathcal{U}$ is exactly the diagonal Δ. It is *metrizable* (or *pseudometrizable*) if there exists a metric (or, respectively, pseudometric), d, such that $\mathcal{U}$ is the uniformity generated by d. The basic metrization theorems assert that (i) $(X, \mathcal{U})$ is metrizable if and only if it is Hausdorff and has a countable base, and (ii) $(X, \mathcal{U})$ is pseudometrizable if and only if it has a countable base.[1] It is clear that the uniformity, $\mathcal{U}^0$ (and hence $\mathcal{S}^0$), developed from the orderings ρ_i of Section 3.2 is not usually pseudometrizable when both X and the number of distinct ρ_i are

---

[1] In light of the discussion of measurement in Section 2.2, these propositions suggest a link between the existence of ordinal scales and the existence of metrics. As in Section 2.2, (A, ρ) is the underlying phenomenon to be revealed in measurement, $\bar{A}$ is the collection of equivalence classes under ρ, and $\mathcal{S}$ is the interval topology for $\bar{A}$. It is easily verified that the space $(\bar{A}, \mathcal{S})$ is T_1 (i.e., $\{y\}$ is closed for every y in $\bar{A}$) and regular (i.e., for each closed subset B of $\bar{A}$ and each y in $\bar{A}$ but not B, there are disjoint open sets S' and S'' in $\mathcal{S}$ such that $B \subseteq S'$ and y is in S''). Note the T_1 property implies that any pseudometric is also a metric. Combining Theorem 17 of Kelley [5, p. 125] with the results of Section 2.2 gives the following connection between the existence of ordinal scales and metrics: An ordinal scale representing ρ on A exists if and only if $(\bar{A}, \mathcal{S})$ is metrizable and separable (i.e., $\bar{A}$ contains a countable, dense subset). Any metric must surely characterize the same open intervals in $\bar{A}$ as defined by either ρ or the ordinal scale.

uncountably infinite. There can be no single pseudometric in terms of which the sets of $\mathcal{U}^0$ and $\mathfrak{I}^0$ are capable of definition. The specification of a uniformity for the purposes of analysis is therefore more general than that of a pseudometric.

Recall now the example of a non-normal $(X, \mathfrak{I}^0)$ based on (3.2-3). In the previous section it was argued that although $(X, \mathfrak{I}^0)$ could not be a pseudometric space, it might still be possible to derive the sets of $\mathfrak{I}^0$ from a pseudometric. That this is, in fact, the case can be seen from the following reasoning: The uniformity, $\mathcal{U}^0$, generated by the given equivalence classes surely has a countable base. There exists, therefore, a pseudometric, d, generating $\mathcal{U}^0$. Consequently, the uniform topology is identical to the pseudometric topology determined by d. Since $\mathfrak{I}^0$ is a subtopology of the uniform topology, the sets in $\mathfrak{I}^0$ may be defined with reference to d. Note it is property (v) in the original description of uniformities that provides the extra sets contained in the uniform topology. Lacking these sets $\mathfrak{I}^0$ cannot be normal. It is also clear that a similar argument applies whenever either X or the number of orderings is countable, for in both cases a countable number of equivalence classes is ensured. The only circumstance in which a single pseudometric might not exist is if both X and the number of orderings are uncountable.

The relationship between pseudometrics and uniformities, however, does not end here. Let $\mathfrak{D}$ denote a family of pseudometrics on X and

$$U_{r,d} = \{(x,y) : d(x,y) < r\}$$

for d in $\mathfrak{D}$ and $r > 0$. Then

$$\mathcal{U}^{\mathfrak{D}} = \{U_{r,d} : d \text{ is in } \mathfrak{D}, \text{ and } r > 0\}$$

is also a uniformity. In terms of the previous notation of (3.3-1),

$$\mathcal{U}^{\mathfrak{D}} = \bigcup_{d \text{ in } \mathfrak{D}} \mathcal{U}^d$$

Not only does every pseudometric on X generate a uniformity for X; the same is true of all families of pseudometrics on X. The interesting result for the present discussion is that all uniformities can be generated in this way: Corresponding to every uniformity, $\mathcal{U}$, for X, there exists a family of pseudometrics, $\mathfrak{D}$, on X such that $\mathcal{U}^{\mathfrak{D}} = \mathcal{U}$.

Thus in the end even the uniformity approach goes back to (a possibly uncountable number of) pseudometrics. In most cases, however, the derivation of $\mathfrak{I}^0$ from orderings ρ_i is more direct and simpler than obtaining a (perhaps more general) topology through $\mathfrak{D}$ and $\mathcal{U}^{\mathfrak{D}}$. As suggested in Section 3.2, it would also be more transparent. Because, in practice, a straightforward, uncomplicated topology is usually all that is needed anyway, the best route is likely to be the direct construction of $\mathfrak{I}^0$ from the ρ_i.

3.4   Fixed sets and points

It is sometimes useful in social science to know circumstances in which sets and points remain unchanged under functional transformation. Proofs of existence of equilibria in general Walrasian microeconomies are, perhaps, the best-known examples (see Arrow and Hahn [2]). In addition to the fact that propositions relating to fixed sets and points can be formulated without reliance on measurement, they also turn out to be relevant for subsequent discussion.

Three distinct theorems are presented here. The first is based on a generalization of the notion of function defined in Section 3.1. A *multivalued function g* from one set X to another set X' is a relation such that

$$g \subseteq X \times X'$$

and for every x in X there is at least one x' in X' with (x, x') in g. The symbol $g(x)$ now refers to the collection of all x' in X' associated with x under g, and for any $A \subseteq X$,

$$g(A) = \{x' : x' \text{ is in } g(x) \text{ and } x \text{ is in } A\}$$

When x' is unique for all x, g reduces to the ordinary (single-valued) function discussed earlier. Let topologies $\mathfrak{I}$ and $\mathfrak{I}'$ for X and X', respectively, be specified. Then the multivalued function g is *upper semicontinuous at x^0* in X if and only if for every open set T' in $\mathfrak{I}'$ containing $g(x^0)$, there is a neighborhood N of x^0 in $\mathfrak{I}$ such that $g(x) \subseteq T'$ for all x in N. If, for all x in X, both $g(x)$ is compact and g is upper semicontinuous at x, then g is called *upper semicontinuous on X*. Continuous functions are upper semicontinuous but not conversely. The following fixed set theorem is given by Berge [3, p. 113]. Its proof is omitted.

3.4-1   Theorem: Let $(X, \mathfrak{I})$ be a Hausdorff topological space such that X is compact. If g is any upper semicontinuous, multivalued function mapping X into itself, then there exists a nonempty compact subset A of X such that

$$g(A) = A$$

Note that to say $g(A) = A$ for some $A \subseteq X$, does not necessarily mean there is an x in X for which

$$g(x) = x$$

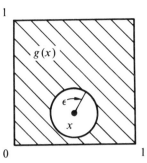

Figure 3-4

The existence of a fixed point is not implied by the existence of a fixed set. Let X be the closed unit square in the quantifiable Euclidean plane; $\mathfrak{J}$, the relative Euclidean topology; and ϵ, a positive real number.[2] Define the multivalued function $g : X \to X$ (Figure 3-4) by

$$g(x) = \{x : |x| \geqslant \epsilon \text{ and } x \text{ is in } X\}$$

for all x in X. Then $(X, \mathfrak{J})$ is a Hausdorff topological space, X is compact, g is upper semicontinuous, and

$$g(X) = X$$

But there are no fixed points under g.

The next result is entirely set theoretic in character. Continuity and other topological restrictions are not required. At issue is a single-valued function, f, mapping the power set of, say, X into itself. In spite of the fact that function values are now sets, f is not multivalued: the objects of the mapping are sets – not points – and f assigns to each A in $\mathcal{P}(X)$ exactly one B in $\mathcal{P}(X)$. Let

$$\mathcal{S} = \{A : f(A) \subseteq A \text{ and } A \text{ is in } \mathcal{P}(X)\}$$

$$\mathcal{L} = \{A : A \subseteq f(A) \text{ and } A \text{ is in } \mathcal{P}(X)\}$$

$$S = \bigcup_{\mathcal{S}} A$$

and

$$L = \bigcup_{\mathcal{L}} A$$

Clearly, both S and L are in $\mathcal{P}(X)$.

---

[2] I am indebted to Walter P. Heller for alerting me to this example and Theorem 3.4-2.

3.4-2   Theorem: Let $f: \mathcal{P}(X) \to \mathcal{P}(X)$ be a function such that $\mathcal{S} \neq \varnothing$, $\mathcal{L} \neq \varnothing$, and

(3.4-3) $A \subseteq B$ implies $f(A) \subseteq f(B)$

for all A and B in $\mathcal{P}(X)$. Then

$$f(S) = S \quad \text{and} \quad f(L) = L$$

Proof: Let A be in $\mathcal{S}$. Then $S \subseteq A$ and, by (3.4-3), $f(S) \subseteq f(A)$. But because A is in $\mathcal{S}$, $f(A) \subseteq A$, and hence $f(S) \subseteq A$. Since this is true for all A in $\mathcal{S}$, $f(S) \subseteq S$. On the other hand, applying (3.4-3) to $f(S) \subseteq S$ gives $f(f(S)) \subseteq f(S)$. Consequently, from the definition of $\mathcal{S}$, $f(S)$ is in $\mathcal{S}$. And since S is the intersection of all elements of $\mathcal{S}$, $S \subseteq f(S)$. Therefore $f(S) = S$.

Now let A be in $\mathcal{L}$. Then $A \subseteq L$ and, by (3.4-3), $f(A) \subseteq f(L)$. But with A in $\mathcal{L}$, $A \subseteq f(A)$ so that $A \subseteq f(L)$. Since this holds for all A in $\mathcal{L}$, $L \subseteq f(L)$. Again applying (3.4-3), $f(L) \subseteq f(f(L))$, implying $f(L)$ is in $\mathcal{L}$. Hence from the definition of L, $f(L) \subseteq L$, and thus $f(L) = L$.   Q.E.D.

It is clear that S in Theorem 3.4-2 can be empty – in which case the assertion $f(S) = S$ becomes $f(\varnothing) = \varnothing$.

By adding a little more set-theoretic structure, one can obtain a fixed point theorem in which the fixed points are indeed points instead of sets. Continuity properties still are not needed.

Let X be a nonempty set and ρ a binary relation on X, which is reflexive, transitive, and antisymmetric.[3] Let $A \subseteq S$. Then any x in X such that $x \rho a$ for all a in A is an *upper bound* for A. Similarly, x is a *lower bound* for A provided that $a \rho x$ for all a in A. Let A^* be the set of all upper bounds of A and A_* the collection of all lower bounds. When A^* has a lower bound or A_* an upper bound they are called, respectively, the *least upper bound* or *greatest lower bound* of A. The pair (X, ρ) is a *lattice* if every two-element subset of X has a least upper and greatest lower bound in X. It is a *complete* lattice if, in addition, all subsets of X have least upper and greatest lower bounds in X.

3.4-4   Theorem: Let (X, ρ) be a complete lattice and $f: X \to X$ be a function such that

[3] Let $\bar{\rho}$ be the equivalence relation generated by ρ. Then the notion of antisymmetry required here is that $x' \rho x''$ and $x'' \rho x'$ imply $x' \bar{\rho} x''$ for all x' and x'' in X. This is slightly different from the definition given earlier in Section 3.1.

(3.4-5) $\quad x\rho x'\quad$ implies $\quad f(x)\rho f(x')$

for all x and x' in X. Let

$$P = \{x : f(x) = x\}$$

Then P is not empty and (P, ρ) is a complete lattice.

Theorem 3.4-4 is due to Tarski [10]. Its proof is analogous to that of Theorem 3.4-2 and is not given here. Note also the similarity between conditions (3.4-3) and (3.4-5).

References

1. Apter, D. E., *The Politics of Modernization* (Chicago: University of Chicago Press, 1965).
2. Arrow, K. J., and F. H. Hahn, *General Competitive Analysis* (San Francisco: Holden-Day, 1971).
3. Berge, C., *Topological Spaces,* E. M. Patterson, trans. (New York: Macmillan, 1963).
4. Halmos, P. R., *Naive Set Theory* (Princeton, N.J.: van Nostrand, 1961).
5. Kelley, J. L., *General Topology* (Princeton, N.J.: van Nostrand, 1964).
6. Prybyla, J. S., *Comparative Economic Systems* (New York: Appleton-Century-Crofts, 1969).
7. Riker, W. H., and P. C. Ordeshook, *An Introduction to Positive Political Theory* (Englewood Cliffs, N.J.: Prentice-Hall, 1973).
8. Robinson, W. S., "A Method for Chronologically Ordering Archaeological Deposits," *American Antiquity,* 16 (1951):293–301.
9. Schweizer, B., "Probabilistic Metric Spaces – The First 25 Years," *New York Statistician,* 19 (1967):3–6.
10. Tarski, A., "A Lattice Theoretical Fixpoint Theorem and Its Applications," *Pacific Journal of Mathematics,* 5 (1955):285–309.
11. Zadeh, L. A., "Fuzzy Sets," *Information and Control,* 8 (1965):338–53.
12. Zadeh, L. A., "Similarity Relations and Fuzzy Orderings," *Information Sciences,* 3 (1971):177–200.

CHAPTER 4

Algebraic structure

Although, as clearly apparent by now, there are a considerable number of set-theoretic and topological concepts and propositions available for use, even in the absence of measurement, it is still not enough. The inclusion of nonquantifiable objects in an analytical framework obviously requires that addition, subtraction, multiplication, division, and so forth be dropped. These must be replaced with other manipulative tools before proceeding. In doing so, one naturally turns to algebraic operations on functions, several of which may be performed regardless of whether their variables can be measured.

This chapter develops an algebraic structure to serve as the basis for subsequent analysis. The general theory of semigroups of partial transformations is outlined first, followed by a discussion of the specific circumstance in which it is employed later on. Once again, because all results are, at worst, relatively minor deviants of well-known propositions, no proofs are given. They may be found in Birkhoff and MacLane [1] and Ljapin [2]. A more general and comprehensive development is provided by Schweizer and Sklar [3].

4.1 Semigroups of partial transformations

It is appropriate to begin with a few preliminaries. Let X and Z be sets. As suggested in Section 2.2, an *operation* on X is a function $g : X \times X \to Z$. Function values under g are often written as, say, $x' \cdot x''$ instead of $g(x', x'')$, where x' and x'' are in X and the "$\cdot$" replaces g as the operation symbol. An operation is *commutative* if

$$x' \cdot x'' = x'' \cdot x'$$

and *associative* when

$$(x' \cdot x'') \cdot x''' = x' \cdot (x'' \cdot x''')$$

for all x', x'', and x''' in X. It is *closed* on X provided that $x' \cdot x''$ is in X for every pair x' and x'' in X, that is, whenever $g : X \times X \to X$.

Suppose X and Y are sets with an operation defined on each. Although the two operations are, in general, distinct, confusion will not arise when representing both by "$\cdot$". A *homomorphism* from X to Y is a mapping $f: X \rightarrow Y$ such that for all x' and x'' in X,

$$f(x' \cdot x'') = f(x') \cdot f(x'')$$

Note the operation "$\cdot$" on the left is that defined on X, whereas the one on the right is defined on Y. *Isomorphisms* are 1-1 and onto homomorphisms whose inverse functions are also homomorphic.

A *semigroup* is a nonempty set on which a closed and associative operation has been defined.

Consider a nonempty set Y. Any mapping of one subset of Y into another, for example,

$$f: A \rightarrow B$$

where $A \subseteq Y$ and $B \subseteq Y$ is a *partial transformation* of Y. If either A or B is empty, then f is also referred to as empty and denoted by $\varnothing$. Let Q^* be the class of all partial transformations of Y. Arbitrary subclasses of partial transformations of Y are denoted by Q where $Q \subseteq Q^*$.

The successive application of two partial transformations serves to characterize an operation on any Q. Thus with $f: A \rightarrow B$ and $g: C \rightarrow D$ in Q, and with $D \subseteq A$ (making it possible to apply first g to C and then f to the range of g), define $f \cdot g$ as the partial transformation $h: C \rightarrow B$ such that

$$h(y) = f(g(y))$$

for all y in C. If D is not a subset of A, or if either f or g is empty, set $h = \varnothing$. This operation is called *composition*. Loosely speaking, when f and g appear in equation form as, say,

$$y^1 = f(y^2), \qquad y^2 = g(y^3)$$

composition permits the substitution of the second equation into the first, and hence the elimination of y^2 from the system:

$$y^1 = f(g(y^3))$$

on C. It is easily verified that Q^* is a semigroup under composition.

Consider, for the moment, any semigroup S with operation "$\cdot$". A *left identity* in S is an element ϵ_l in S such that

$$\epsilon_l \cdot s = s$$

for all s in S. A *right identity*, ϵ_r, requires

$$s \cdot \epsilon_r = s$$

for every s in S. An element, ϵ, which is both a left and a right identity is called an *identity*. Returning to the case of a semigroup, Q, of partial transformations of Y, let $A \subseteq Y$. The *partial identity* on A, written e_A, is the partial transformation $e_A : A \to A$ where

$$e_A(y) = y$$

for all y in A. If $Q = \{f, \varnothing\}$ where $f : A \to B$, then e_A would be the right and e_B the left identity were they added to Q. There could be no identity in Q unless $A = B$.

For $f : A \to B$ in any Q, the *left inverse* of f is the partial transformation $f_l^{-1} : B \to A$ such that

$$f_l^{-1} \cdot f = e_A$$

or

(4.1-1) $\quad f_l^{-1}(f(y)) = y$

for all y in A. Similarly, the *right inverse* is the partial transformation $f_r^{-1} : B \to A$ for which

$$f \cdot f_r^{-1} = e_B$$

or

(4.1-2) $\quad f(f_r^{-1}(y)) = y$

for all y in B. Conditions (4.1-1) and (4.1-2) may be regarded as special instances of, respectively, their set-theoretic counterparts (3.1-3) and (3.1-1). Furthermore, (3.1-4) and (3.1-2) imply that f has a left inverse if and only if it is 1–1, and a right inverse if and only if it is onto. These propositions can also be proved algebraically without any reference to set-theoretic concepts.

When f has both left and right inverses, it is said to have an *inverse*, f^{-1}. In this case

$$f^{-1} = f_l^{-1} = f_r^{-1}$$

and f^{-1} is identical to the inverse function of Section 3.1. Clearly, f has an inverse if and only if it is 1–1 and onto. There is, of course, no guarantee that Q contains any inverses of f.

These concepts of inverse carry over as previously defined to semigroups in general. Furthermore, any semigroup containing an identity and inverses for all of its elements is a *group*. If g is a group, then for all γ, γ', and z in G, the cancellation laws,

$$z \cdot \gamma = z \cdot \gamma' \quad \text{implies} \quad \gamma = \gamma'$$

$$\gamma \cdot z = \gamma' \cdot z \quad \text{implies} \quad \gamma = \gamma'$$

are valid, and the equations

$$\gamma \cdot z = \gamma', \qquad z \cdot \gamma = \gamma'$$

are uniquely solvable for z in G.

4.1-3   Theorem (Ljapin [2, pp. 30, 31]): A semigroup, Q, of 1-1 and onto partial transformations of Y forms a group if and only if Q contains the inverse of each of its elements and there exists a subset $\Omega \subseteq Y$ such that for all $f: A \to B$ in Q,

$$A = B = \Omega$$

One of the conditions required in Theorem 4.1-3 is that all elements of Q be (complete – not partial) transformations of the same subset of Y. (Note, however, they are still partial transformations of Y). If this were not the case – say, some functions are defined on Ω_1 whereas the remainder are defined on $\Omega_2 \neq \Omega_1$ – then, as suggested earlier, it would be impossible to have a (universal) identity in Q. There could be partial identities e_1 on Ω_1 and e_2 on Ω_2, but if f in Q were defined on Ω_2, then $f \cdot e_1$ would be empty and not equal to f. Therefore Q could not be a group. On the other hand, it may be that the sufficient conditions to have a group are satisfied by the two subsets of partial transformations, one defined on Ω_1 and the other, on Ω_2. Under these circumstances Q would be a semigroup consisting of the union of two groups.

Usually, a semigroup, Q, of partial transformations of Y, is neither a group nor the union of groups. Nevertheless, algebraic conditions on the structure of Q can still be given that guarantee the existence of an inverse for any particular f in Q. To do so, consider again the general semigroup S. For z in S define

$$zS = \{z \cdot s : s \text{ is in } S\}$$

and, when $I \subseteq S$ and $I \neq \varnothing$, set

$$IS = \{z \cdot s : z \text{ is in } I \text{ and } s \text{ is in } S\}$$

Now for any $A \subseteq Y$, let

$$Q_{d(A)} = \{f : \text{either } f \text{ is in } Q \text{ and the domain of } f \text{ is } A, \text{ or } f = \varnothing\}$$

$$Q_{r(A)} = \{f : \text{either } f \text{ is in } Q \text{ and the range of } f \text{ is } A, \text{ or } f = \varnothing\}$$

Then $Q_{d(A)}$ and $Q_{r(A)}$ are semigroups. Any function $f: A \to B$ in Q is *right invertible* provided that for all g in $Q_{r(B)}$ the equation

$$f \cdot z = g$$

has a solution for z in $Q_{r(A)}$; that is,

$$fQ_{r(A)} = Q_{r(B)}$$

Similarly, when

$$Q_{d(B)} f = Q_{d(A)}$$

f is *left invertible*. Naturally, f is referred to as *invertible* if and only if it is both left and right invertible.

4.1-4   **Theorem** (Ljapin [2, pp. 233, 234]): Let Q be a semigroup of partial transformations of Y. Then $f: A \to B$ in Q is invertible if and only if
   i. f has a right identity in $Q_{r(A)}$ and a left identity in $Q_{d(B)}$, and
   ii. f is not contained in any proper subset R of $Q_{r(B)}$ or any proper subset L of $Q_{d(A)}$ such that

$$RQ_{r(A)} \subseteq R, \qquad Q_{d(B)} L \subseteq L$$

In general, asserting that f is invertible reveals nothing about whether any of its inverses exist or, if they do, whether they are in Q. However, since condition (i) of Theorem 4.1-4 requires e_A to be in $Q_{r(A)}$ and e_B to be in $Q_{d(B)}$, and since the definition of these partial identities further implies that e_A is also in $Q_{d(A)}$ and e_B is also in $Q_{r(B)}$, the following result is obtained.

4.1-5   **Theorem:** Let Q be a semigroup of partial transformations of Y. Then $f: A \to B$ in Q has an inverse in Q (and hence is 1–1 and onto) if and only if
   i. f has a right identity in $Q_{r(A)}$ and a left identity in $Q_{d(B)}$, and
   ii. f is not contained in any proper subset R of $Q_{r(B)}$ or any proper subset L of $Q_{d(A)}$ such that

$$RQ_{r(A)} \subseteq R, \qquad Q_{d(B)} L \subseteq L$$

4.2   A particular specification

Because the semigroups of partial transformations used in subsequent chapters may include mappings such as $f: A \to B$ and $g: C \to D$, where

A, B, C, and D need not contain vectors with the same indexed components or even be of similar dimension, the necessary algebraic structure is somewhat more complex. It is therefore worth repeating the appropriate parts of Section 4.1 as applied to this case.

Thus suppose X is a set of objects that may or may not be capable of measurement. Let the elements of X be vectors and consider the components of $x = (x_1, x_2, \ldots, x_n)$. As x ranges over X each x_k assumes values in some set X_k. In general, X is a subset of the Cartesian product of the X_k, but little will be lost by assuming they are the same. Now excluding the empty combination, there are $2^n - 1$ distinct ways in which the variables $x_1, x_2, \ldots, x_n$ may be combined: x_1, x_2, x_4 and $x_1, x_2, \ldots, x_n$ are two illustrations. To each combination assign a number between 1 and $2^n - 1$ (the actual order of appearance is not important). Let C^i denote the set containing combination i, where $i = 1, \ldots, 2^n - 1$. For any i, C^i has k_i distinct components of x. These are thought of as a k_i-tuple, in which, whenever possible, the variables are listed with the smallest subscript coming first. Let D^i be the set over which the k_i-tuple of C^i is permitted to range; D^i is thus a Cartesian product of various X_k's. Let

$$D = \bigcup_{i=1}^{2^n - 1} D^i$$

Note that D contains vectors of different dimensionality. Clearly, $X \subseteq D$.

Let Q^* be the collection of all mappings of the form

$$f : D^i \to D^j$$

for some not necessarily distinct i and j. Include the empty transformation in Q^*. Then each element of Q^* is a partial transformation of D. Note that the partial identity transformations

$$e_{D^i} : D^i \to D^i$$

where $e_{D^i}(x^i) = x^i$ for all x^i in D^i are contained in Q^*. The symbol Q will refer to arbitrary subclasses of partial transformations of D.

To define composition on any Q, let $f : D^i \to D^j$ and $g : D^u \to D^v$ be two of its elements. Write

$$C^{i-v+u} = (C^i - C^v) \cup C^u$$

Note C^{i-v+u} contains a legitimate combination of one or more of $x_1, x_2, \ldots, x_n$. Let x^{i-v+u} be the k_{i-v+u}-tuple of C^{i-v+u}, x^{i-v} that of $C^i - C^v$, and x^u that of C^u. Write

$$x^{i-v+u} = (x^{i-v}, x^u)$$

even though the same x_k's may be components of both x^{i-v} and x^u. Define "·" as follows: When D^v is not contained in D^i set $f \cdot g = \emptyset$ (the empty transformation). If $D^v \subseteq D^i$ then $f \cdot g = h$ where

$$h : D^{i-v+u} \rightarrow D^j$$

and

$$h(x^{i-v+u}) = f(g(x^u), x^{i-v})$$

for all x^{i-v+u} in D^{i-v+u}.

As an example, consider the variables x_1, x_2, x_4, x_5, and partial transformations

$$f : D^i \rightarrow D^j, \qquad g : D^u \rightarrow D^v$$

where

$$x_5 = f(x_1, x_2), \qquad x_2 = g(x_1, x_4)$$

Then $C^{i-v+u} = \{x_1, x_4\}$ and

$$x^{i-v+u} = (x_1, (x_1, x_4))$$

Furthermore, the composition of f and g obtained by substitution of g for x_2 in f is

$$x_5 = h(x_1, x_4)$$

where

$$h(x_1, x_4) = f(x_1, g(x_1, x_4))$$

It is easily seen that Q^* is closed under "·" and that "·" is associative. Therefore Q^* is a semigroup.

Let $f : D^i \rightarrow D^j$ be in any Q and suppose $C^u \subseteq C^i$. Fix $\bar{x}^{i-u}$ in D^{i-u}. The *restriction of f to D^u for $\bar{x}^{i-u}$* is the partial transformation

$$f/_{D^u} : D^u \rightarrow D^j$$

such that

$$f/_{D^u}(x^u) = f(x^u, \bar{x}^{i-u})$$

for all x^u in D^u.

Consider $f : D^i \rightarrow D^j$ in any Q and let $C^u \subseteq C^i$. Now f has a *left inverse with respect to C^u for $\bar{x}^{i-u}$* whenever there exists a partial transformation

$$f^{-1}_{l, C^u} : D^j \times \{\bar{x}^{i-u}\} \rightarrow D^u$$

for which

$$f_{l,C^u}^{-1} \cdot f/_{D^u} = e_{D^u}$$

that is,

$$x^u = f_{l,C^u}^{-1}(f(x^u, \bar{x}^{i-u}), \bar{x}^{i-u})$$

on D^u. The right inverse f_{r,C^u}^{-1} is defined similarly. When f has both left and right inverses with respect to C^u for $\bar{x}^{i-u}$, it will be said to have an *inverse with respect to C^u for $\bar{x}^{i-u}$*. The inverse is written $f_{C^u}^{-1}$. It is clear that when they exist,

$$f_{C^u}^{-1} = f_{l,C^u}^{-1} = f_{r,C^u}^{-1}$$

To illustrate, suppose

$$x_3 = f(x_1, x_2)$$

Thus $f: D^i \rightarrow D^j$, where $C^i = \{x_1, x_2\}$ and $C^j = \{x_3\}$. If f has a left inverse with respect to $C^u = \{x_1\}$ for $\bar{x}_2$, then

$$x_1 = f_{l,C^u}^{-1}(\bar{x}_2, x_3)$$

where

$$x_1 = f_{l,C^u}^{-1}(\bar{x}_2, f(x_1, \bar{x}_2))$$

for all values of x_1.

Because inverses are used extensively later, it is important to know conditions under which they exist. The following theorems and corollary (all of which are straightforward extensions of results from Section 4.1) provide information of this sort.

4.2-1   Theorem: Let $f: D^i \rightarrow D^j$ be in any Q and $C^u \subseteq C^i$. Then for each value of x^{i-u}, f has a left inverse with respect to C^u if and only if $f/_{C^u}$ is 1-1. It has a right inverse with respect to C^u if and only if $f/_{C^u}$ is onto.

Corollary: $f: D^i \rightarrow D^j$ in any Q has an inverse with respect to $C^u \subseteq C^i$ for every x^{i-u} if and only if $f/_{C^u}: D^u \rightarrow D^j$ is 1-1 and onto for all values of x^{i-u}.

Let Q be a semigroup of partial transformations of D, which is neither a group nor the union of groups. Necessary and sufficient conditions are now given for the existence of particular inverses in Q. For $f: D^i \rightarrow D^j$ in Q, $C^u \subseteq C^i$ and each x^{i-u} in D^{i-u}, let

$$S_{d(D^u)}(x^{i-u}) = \{g : g \text{ is in } Q, \text{ and either the domain of } g \text{ is}$$
$$D^u \times \{x^{i-u}\}, \text{ or } g = \varnothing\}$$

$$S_{r(D^j)}(x^{i-u}) = \{g : g \text{ is in } Q, \text{ and either the elements of the}$$
$$\text{domain of } g \text{ include } x^{i-u} \text{ as a fixed}$$
$$\text{component and the range of } g \text{ is } D^j, \text{ or}$$
$$g = \varnothing\}$$

Call f *right invertible with respect to* C^u *for* x^{i-u} provided

$$f \cdot \theta = g$$

has a solution in $S_{r(D^u)}(x^{i-u})$ for all g in $S_{r(D^j)}(x^{i-u})$; that is,

$$fS_{r(D^u)}(x^{i-u}) = S_{r(D^j)}(x^{i-u})$$

where

$$fS_{r(D^u)}(x^{i-u}) = \{f \cdot g : g \text{ is in } S_{r(D^u)}(x^{i-u})\}$$

Similarly, f is *left invertible with respect to* C^u *for* x^{i-u} if

$$S_{d(D^j)}(x^{i-u})f = S_{d(D^u)}(x^{i-u})$$

It is *invertible with respect to* C^u *for* x^{i-u} if and only if it is both left and right invertible with respect to C^u for x^{i-u}.

4.2-2   **Theorem:** Suppose Q is a semigroup of partial transformations of D. Let $f : D^i \to D^j$ be in Q and $C^u \subseteq C^i$. For f to be invertible with respect to C^u for x^{i-u} it is necessary and sufficient that
i. f have a right identity in $S_{r(D^u)}(x^{i-u})$ and a left identity in $S_{d(D^j)}(x^{i-u})$, and
ii. f not be contained in any proper subset A of $S_{r(D^j)}(x^{i-u})$ or any proper subset B of $S_{d(D^u)}(x^{i-u})$ such that

$$AS_{r(D^u)}(x^{i-u}) \subseteq A$$

$$S_{d(D^j)}(x^{i-u})B \subseteq B$$

As in Section 4.1, the preceding conditions are also necessary and sufficient for the existence of inverses:

4.2-3   **Theorem:** Suppose Q is a semigroup of partial transformations of D. Let $f : D^i \to D^j$ be in Q and $C^u \subseteq C^i$. Then f has an inverse with respect to C^u at all x^{i-u} if and only if for each x^{i-u} conditions (i) and (ii) of Theorem 4.2-2 are met.

The results of this chapter provide the algebraic basis for everything that follows. Systems of partial transformations (i.e., subsets of some *Q*) are studied next in terms of particular forms in which they might appear, and all subsequent applications (Part II) are naturally viewed as models consisting of precisely these kinds of structures. The fundamental tool of algebraic manipulation in every case is function composition. And the existence of various inverses will emerge in Chapter 5 as an important condition in the methodological rules developed there for the conduct of analysis without measurement.

References

1. Birkhoff, G., and S. MacLane, *A Survey of Modern Algebra,* 3rd ed. (New York: Macmillan, 1965).
2. Ljapin, E. S., *Semigroups* (Providence, R.I.: American Mathematical Society, 1963).
3. Schweizer, B., and A. Sklar, "The Algebra of Functions," Parts I, II, and III, *Mathematische Annalen,* 139 (1960):366–82; 143 (1961):440–7; 161 (1965):171–96.

CHAPTER 5

Analysis of specific systems

Abstracting common elements from the theoretical systems of various fields of scientific inquiry in order to study the properties of systems in general, has always been one of the central aims of general systems analysis. As pointed out in Section 1.4, this approach has already borne considerable fruit because of an initially surprising commonality of technique and analytical viewpoint among a wide variety of disciplines. Thus, for example, equations of the form

$$y_i = f^i(x_1, x_2, \ldots, x_n) \qquad i = 1, \ldots, n$$

or

$$\frac{dx_i}{dt} = f^i(x_1, x_2, \ldots, x_n) \qquad i = 1, \ldots, n$$

appear frequently in the physical, biological, and in some areas of the social and psychological sciences. Systems such as these may be and have been investigated with respect to existence, uniqueness, and stability of solutions and many other properties. The general theorems so obtained apply to all instances in which the equations arise.

There are, however, many systems especially in the nonphysical sciences that appear similar to those previously described, except that one or more of the x_i or y_i seem to be incapable of measurement. Several examples have already been discussed; more are presented in Parts II and III. None of the known results concerning existence, uniqueness, and stability of solutions apply in these cases.

Of course, it is always possible to construct arbitrary scales on which nonquantifiable variables can be "measured." Each value of the variable "society's culture" could be assigned, say, a number between 0 and 1 on the real line. A "rationalization" could be found for such a scale if a researcher really believed that certain cultures are "closer together" than others. But, as suggested in Section 2.2, results obtained by using this technique tend to depend on the particular scales chosen, whereas the actual properties of the relationships between the variables – the substance of any theory – are obscured. The usefulness of such an approach is therefore open to serious question.

Based on the foundation of Chapters 3 and 4, the following develops general, analytical guidelines that do not depend on the assumption that all variables can be measured. The argument provides appropriate definitions of solution, stability, and so forth and makes assertions about such things as the existence of solutions and their properties. It is sufficiently general to include systems in which all variables are nonquantifiable, all are quantifiable, and some are quantifiable while others are not. When all variables are quantifiable, the known theorems on existence of solutions, and so forth are both consistent with and supplemental to it.

More precisely, this chapter is concerned with the analysis of three types of systems: simultaneous equations, periodic equations, and choice functions. Sufficient conditions for the existence of solutions in the first, for the existence of stationary paths and stability in the second, and for a general rationalization of choice in the third are given. Special attention is devoted to the case in which the number of variable values is finite. A discussion of the problem of maximization is also included.

The propositions developed here clearly imply that rigorous model building as it is practiced today need not be confined solely to the analysis of scalable phenomena. Many of the standard concepts and techniques currently employed to understand quantifiable reality turn out to be applicable to situations in which measurement is impossible. Furthermore, in addition to the provision of rules governing scientific inquiry in the absence of measurement, criteria for judging the analytical structures of previously completed work also emerge. Thus, for example, methods for testing the internal consistency of the models of Pareto and Parsons that were cited in Section 1.1 are obtained.

5.1   Simultaneous relations

Let X be any collection of well-defined objects and $\mathfrak{I}$ a topology for X. No assumptions of quantifiability are made. The symbol $x = (x_1, x_2, \ldots, x_n)$ will represent the elements of X as well as the variable ranging over them. When one or more of the x_i are held fixed while the remaining components of x are permitted to vary, the fixed x_i's are called *parameters*.

Recall that D is the collection of vectors of varying dimensions obtained by forming all possible combinations of values of $x_1, \ldots, x_n$. A system of *simultaneous relations* is defined to be any subset of a semigroup, Q, of partial transformations of D written in equation style. It is useful to begin by considering systems of the form

(5.1-1) $\quad x_j = f^j(x_1, \ldots, x_{j-1}, x_{j+1}, \ldots, x_K, \rho), \qquad j = 1, \ldots, L$

where $\rho = (x_{K+1}, \ldots, x_n)$ is a vector of parameters and f^j is in Q for all j. Note (5.1-1) maps a subset of D, call it Y, into itself. This type of system is abundantly illustrated in Part II. Most instances are special cases in which more variables than just x_j are missing from each equation.

A *solution* of (5.1-1) is a vector $(\bar{x}_1, \bar{x}_2, \ldots, \bar{x}_K)$ such that $(\bar{x}_1, \bar{x}_2, \ldots, \bar{x}_K, \rho)$ is in X and $(\bar{x}_1, \bar{x}_2, \ldots, \bar{x}_K)$ satisfies all equations of (5.1-1) simultaneously:

$$\bar{x}_j = f^j(\bar{x}_1, \ldots, \bar{x}_{j-1}, \bar{x}_{j+1}, \ldots, \bar{x}_K, \rho)$$

for all $j = 1, \ldots, L$. It is *unique* with respect to ρ if there is only one vector $(\bar{x}_1, \bar{x}_2, \ldots, \bar{x}_K)$ with this property.

A technique for obtaining solutions along with the conditions required for its application will now be derived when the number of equations and variables in (5.1-1) are the same, that is, when $K = L$. Suppose first that $K = L = 2$. Then (5.1-1) reduces to

(5.1-2) $\quad x_1 = f^1(x_2, \rho), \qquad x_2 = f^2(x_1, \rho)$

Let f^1 have an inverse, g^*, in Q with respect to at least one of the components of the parameter vector ρ for all values of x_2 and the remaining parameters. It is convenient to denote this parameter by π and to disregard all others. Thus

$$\pi = g^*(x_1, x_2)$$

Upon substitution from (5.1-2),

$$\pi = g(x_1, \pi)$$

where

$$g(x_1, \pi) = g^*(x_1, f^2(x_1, \pi))$$

Of course, g is in Q. Now let g have an inverse, α^*, in Q with respect to x_1 for all values of π. Then

(5.1-3) $\quad x_1 = \alpha(\pi)$

where

$$\alpha(\pi) = \alpha^*(\pi, \pi)$$

Once again, α is in Q. Substituting (5.1-3) into (5.1-2),

$$x_2 = \beta(\pi)$$

where

(5.1-4) $\quad \beta(\pi) = f^2(\alpha(\pi), \pi)$

and β is in Q. Although not explicitly indicated, α and β also depend on the components of ρ distinct from π. Thus (5.1-3) and (5.1-4) give unique solutions of (5.1-2) for each value of ρ. (Uniqueness arises because both α and β are single-valued functions.) The conditions that are sufficient to guarantee the existence of these functions are that f^1 have inverses with respect to at least one parameter and that g have inverses with respect to x_1. Alternative sufficient conditions are that f^2 have inverses with respect to at least one parameter and that a function analogous to g have inverses with respect to x_2.

As an example, let

$$x_1 = f^1(x_2, \rho) = x_2 + \rho$$

$$x_2 = f^2(x_1, \rho) = \rho x_1$$

where x_1, x_2, and ρ are real numbers with $\rho \neq 1$. Then

$$g(x_1, \rho) = x_1 - \rho x_1$$

$$\alpha(\rho) = \frac{\rho}{1 - \rho}$$

and

$$\beta(\rho) = \frac{\rho^2}{1 - \rho}$$

It is also easy to illustrate the argument for the nonquantifiable case. Let $X_1 = X_2 = \{a, b, c\}$, $X_3 = \{\rho^0, \rho'\}$ and suppose f^1 and f^2 are given in the following tabular form:

f^1: $x_1 = f^1(x_2, \rho)$	x_2	ρ	f^2: $x_2 = f^2(x_1, \rho)$	x_1	ρ
a	a	ρ^0	a	a	ρ^0
c	b	ρ^0	a	b	ρ^0
b	c	ρ^0			
			b	a	ρ'
c	a	ρ'	a	c	ρ'
b	b	ρ'			
a	c	ρ'			

There is one solution for each parameter value. When $\rho = \rho^0$ it is $x_1 = x_2 = a$ and for $\rho = \rho'$ it is $x_1 = c$, $x_2 = a$. The inverse of f^1 with respect to

ρ, that is, g^*, obviously exists for all values of x_2. Using f^2 to eliminate x_2 in g^* gives g:

g:	ρ	x_1	ρ
	ρ^0	a	ρ^0
	ρ'	c	ρ'

Note that the values of x_1 that do not "match up" in the substitution process are eliminated from the domain of g. The same thing happens in the previous, numerical example. Finally, g also has an inverse with respect to x_1 for each value of ρ, and hence α is

α:	x_1	ρ
	a	ρ^0
	c	ρ'

Similarly,

β:	x_2	ρ
	a	ρ^0
	a	ρ'

Unlike the last example, f^2 does not have an inverse with respect to x_1 for $\rho=\rho^0$. A third illustration may be found in Section 13.1.

Returning to the general system with $K=L$, namely,

$$(5.1-5) \quad x_j = f^j(x_1,\ldots,x_{j-1},x_{j+1},\ldots,x_K,\rho), \qquad j=1,\ldots,K$$

substitution of the Kth equation into the first $K-1$ gives

$$x_j = g^j(x_1,\ldots,x_{K-1},\rho) \qquad j=1,\ldots,K-1$$

where

$$g^j(x_1,\ldots,x_{K-1},\rho) = f^j(x_1,\ldots,x_{j-1},x_{j+1},\ldots,x_{K-1},f^K(x_1,\ldots,x_{K-1},\rho),\rho)$$

and g^j is in Q for all $j=1,\ldots,K-1$. Consider any j and suppose g^j has an inverse, g^*, with respect to at least one parameter or variable distinct from x_j - say, for example, x_1 - for all values of the remaining x_i's and parameters. Then

$$x_1 = h^*(x_2,\ldots,x_{K-1},\rho)$$

where

$$h^*(x_2,\ldots,x_{K-1},\rho) = g^*(x_j,x_2,\ldots,x_{K-1},\rho)$$

Provided h^* has an inverse, h^j, with respect to x_j for all values of the remaining x_i's and all values of ρ,

$$x_j = h^j(x_1, \ldots, x_{j-1}, x_{j+1}, \ldots, x_{K-1}, \rho)$$

where h^j is in Q. Arguing similarly for each $j=1, \ldots, K-1$, the original relations (5.1-5) are reduced to a system of $K-1$ equations in $K-1$ unknowns. Continuing in this manner, a two equation, two variable system is obtained, which may be solved under the appropriate conditions as previously indicated. Now, substituting the solution of the two-by-two system back into the three-by-three, then substituting these results into the four-by-four, and so on yields the solution of (5.1-5). The conditions required for the procedure to work are the existence of suitable inverses at each stage of the reduction process. As in the two-dimensional case the solution is unique.

Alternative sufficient conditions for the existence of solutions can be derived from one of the fixed point theorems of Section 3.4. Using the symbols y and z to denote the K-vectors of, respectively, arguments and function values of f, one can abbreviate (5.1-5) to

(5.1-6) $z = f(y, \rho)$

where y and z are both in Y (the domain of f). Thus solutions of (5.1-6) appear as fixed points of f; that is, y in Y is a solution whenever

$$y = f(y, \rho)$$

Now introduce a binary relation ζ on Y. The following result is an immediate consequence of Theorem 3.4-4.

5.1-7   **Theorem:** Let ρ be fixed. If (Y, ζ) is a complete lattice and f is order preserving; that is,

$y' \zeta y''$ implies $f(y', \rho) \zeta f(y'', p)$

for all y' and y'' in Y, then the set of solutions (given ρ) of (5.1-6) is not empty and, together with ζ, forms a complete lattice.

The nice thing about Theorem 5.1-7 is that all restrictions are expressed in terms of f and its domain Y. It is not necessary to check auxiliary functions derived from f in order to determine if solutions exist. On the other hand, merely knowing that there are solutions does not mean they are easily found. Theorem 5.1-7 also does not guarantee uniqueness of solutions and further requires additional hypotheses (which may be difficult to justify) concerning the existence of an ordering. These three disadvantages do not appear as shortcomings of the first approach as previously developed, but in that case the advantage of avoiding the use of auxiliary functions to state the sufficient conditions is absent.

Although there are numerous exceptions to the "rule," any system of simultaneous equations will not be uniquely solvable unless there are at least the same number of unknowns as there are equations. Both results that were obtained here apply only to this case. The exceptions arise first from the fact that a system with more unknowns than equations can still have a unique solution. In three-dimensional Euclidean space, for example, two uniquely tangent surfaces determine a single point. Secondly, systems with fewer unknowns than equations are also capable of having unique solutions. Three distinct straight lines in the Euclidean plane could all intersect at the same point. Similar illustrations in the nonquantifiable case are easily found. Thus many kinds of simultaneous equations can be resolved into a unique solution. However, the most common approach in the nonphysical sciences is to require systems to have the same number of equations as unknowns. Further results concerning the solutions of these systems appear in Section 5.2 and 5.3.

5.2   Periodic relations

The second class of systems to be examined are those that evolve over time. When all variables are capable of measurement these may be expressed as systems of either simultaneous differential or difference equations. In the absence of measurement, however, the meaning of differentiation and difference is not clear; changing systems are best represented in terms that are parallel to the latter. Illustrations of the use of such equations in the social sciences are provided in Chapters 9 and 10.

With discrete time identified here by the superscript t (elsewhere it is more convenient to locate t as a subscript), the simplest evolving system may be written as the first-order *periodic* relation or equation

(5.2-1) $x_1^t = f(x_1^{t-1}, \rho), \qquad t = 1, 2, \ldots$

where f is in a semigroup, Q, of partial transformations, the parameter vector $\rho = (x_2, \ldots, x_n)$, and (x_1^t, ρ) is in X for all t. A *stationary* path for (5.2-1) is a value, $\bar{x}_1$, such that $(\bar{x}_1, \rho)$ is in X and

$$x_1^t = \bar{x}_1,$$

for all t.

Sufficient conditions for the existence of unique, stationary paths are easily derived. Now stationarity requires

$$\bar{x}_1 = f(\bar{x}_1, \rho)$$

Suppose f has an inverse, g^*, in Q with respect to one of the parameters, say π, for all values of $\bar{x}_1$ and the remaining parameters. Disregarding all other parameters,

$$\pi = g(\bar{x}_1)$$

where

$$g(\bar{x}_1) = g^*(\bar{x}_1, \bar{x}_1)$$

If g has an inverse, h, in Q with respect to $\bar{x}_1$, then

$$\bar{x}_1 = h(\pi)$$

which gives, since h is implicitly dependent on ρ, a unique stationary value for each vector ρ. The sufficient requirements are, therefore, that f have inverses in Q with respect to at least one of the components of ρ and g have an inverse in Q with respect to $\bar{x}_1$. Sufficient conditions based on the fixed point Theorem 3.4-4 can be derived as in Section 5.1.

For any initial value x_1^0, equation (5.2-1) generates a path over time as follows:

$$x_1^1 = f(x_1^0, \rho)$$
$$x_1^2 = f(f(x_1^0, \rho), \rho)$$
$$\vdots$$
$$x_1^t = f(\ldots f(f(x_1^0, \rho), \rho), \ldots, \rho)$$

In general this path will not be stationary. But it is said to be *stable* if the sequence $\{x_1^t\}$ converges to a stationary value $\bar{x}_1$ with respect to the appropriate relative topology $\mathfrak{I}^*$ obtained from $\mathfrak{I}$. (Recall $\mathfrak{I}$ is the given topology for X that is fixed at the beginning of Section 5.1.)

It is possible to give sufficient conditions for a path $\{x_1^t\}$ to be stable along lines suggested by the "second method" of Lyapunov. (The idea is based on Mesarovic and Takahara [10, p. 166].) Let Z be a set of real numbers containing its greatest lower bound, z^0. A function $L : X \rightarrow Z$ will be called a *Lyapunov function* for f whenever both of the following conditions are met:

i. For all (x_1', ρ) and (x_1'', ρ) in X, if

$$x_1' = f(x_1'', \rho)$$

then

$$L(x_1'', \rho) \geqslant L(x_1', \rho)$$

ii. For all neighborhoods N of $\bar{x}_1$, which are contained in the topology $\mathfrak{I}^*$, there exists a number z_N in Z such that $z_N > z^0$, and

$$L(x_1, \rho) \begin{cases} < z_N, & \text{if } x_1 \text{ is in } N \\ \geqslant z_N, & \text{otherwise} \end{cases}$$

Consider a path $\{x_1^t\}$ and suppose a Lyapunov function for f exists. Assume further that for all neighborhoods N of $\bar{x}_1$ in $\mathfrak{I}^*$, there is a t^0 for which

$$L(x_1^{t^0}, \rho) \leqslant z_N$$

Then from condition (i)

$$L(x_1^t, \rho) \leqslant z_N, \qquad t \geqslant t^0$$

whence $\{x_1^t\}$ must converge to $\bar{x}_1$. Therefore the existence of a Lyapunov function for f, together with the restriction that going far enough out in the sequence $\{x_1^t\}$ provides an x_1^t with Lyapunov function value as small as required, is sufficient to guarantee the stability of $\{x_1^t\}$.

When there is more than one equation, for example,

$$x_1^t = f^1(x_1^{t-1}, x_2^{t-1}, \rho), \qquad t = 1, 2, \ldots$$
$$x_2^t = f^2(x_1^{t-1}, x_2^{t-1}, \rho), \qquad t = 1, 2, \ldots$$

where f^1 and f^2 are in Q, the vector of parameters is $\rho = (x_3, \ldots, x_n)$, and (x_1^t, x_2^t, ρ) is in X for all t, a *stationary path* is defined as a pair of values $(\bar{x}_1, \bar{x}_2)$ such that $(\bar{x}_1, \bar{x}_2, \rho)$ is in X and

$$x_i^t = \bar{x}_i$$

for $i = 1, 2$, and all t. To obtain $(\bar{x}_1, \bar{x}_2)$ as a function of ρ, the system of simultaneous equations

$$\bar{x}_1 = f^1(\bar{x}_1, \bar{x}_2, \rho)$$
$$\bar{x}_2 = f^2(\bar{x}_1, \bar{x}_2, \rho)$$

is solved as in Section 5.1. Time paths depend on pairs of initial values, (x_1^0, x_2^0), and stability is handled in the obvious way. The generalization to many equations is clear.

The Kth-order periodic equation:

(5.2-2) $\quad x_1^t = f(x_1^{t-1}, \ldots, x_1^{t-K}, \rho), \qquad t = K + 1, K + 2, \ldots$

where f is in Q, $\rho = (x_2, \ldots, x_n)$, and (x_1^t, ρ) is in X for $t = 1, 2, \ldots$, is analyzed by setting

$$v_1^t = x_1^t$$

$$v_i^t = x_1^{t-i+1}, \qquad i = 2, \ldots, K+1$$

and thus reducing (5.2-2) to the following system of $K+1$ first-order periodic relations:

$$v_1^t = f(v_2^{t-1}, v_3^{t-1}, \ldots, v_{K+1}^{t-1}, \rho),$$

$$v_i^t = v_{i-1}^{t-1}, \qquad i = 2, \ldots, K+1$$

The argument proceeds as previously indicated. Time paths are now generated by specifying K initial values. Systems with many equations of varying orders are handled similarly.

By translating systems of simultaneous equations such as (5.1-1) into a dynamic context, one can obtain additional propositions concerning the existence of their solutions. Accordingly, let $y = (x_1, \ldots, x_K)$, and Y be the set (obtained by appropriately projecting X) over which y varies. Denote by $\Im_y$ the topology of Y relative to $\Im$. As in Section 5.1, the map

$$f : Y \rightarrow Y$$

defined on Y for each ρ gives rise to the simultaneous equations system

(5.2-3) $z = f(y, \rho)$

where y and z are in Y. Note (5.2-3) is the same as (5.1-5) and (5.1-6). The fixed points of f are the solutions of the system.

Thinking of f as transforming values of y at time $t-1$ (written y^{t-1}) into values of y at time t (written y^t), (5.2-3) becomes a system of periodic equations

(5.2-4) $y^t = f(y^{t-1}, \rho)$

As before, (5.2-4) generates a sequence $\{y^t\}$ for every initial value y^0 in Y. A solution of (5.2-3) corresponds to a stationary path of (5.2-4). It is now possible to give entirely different sufficient conditions for the existence of solutions of simultaneous equations from those of Section 5.1.

5.2-5   **Theorem:** Let ρ be fixed, $\Im_y$ be Hausdorff and suppose f is continuous with respect to $\Im_y$. If there is a y^* in Y such that

$$\lim_{t \rightarrow \infty} y^t = y^*$$

for some sequence $\{y^t\}$ generated by (5.2-4), then y^* is a solution of (5.2-3) given ρ.

Proof: Since $\mathfrak{I}_y$ is Hausdorff, convergence is unique. Suppose

$$\lim_{t \to \infty} y^t = y^*$$

where

$$y^t = f(y^{t-1}, \rho), \qquad t = 1, 2, \ldots$$

Then, since f is continuous,

$$\lim_{t \to \infty} y^t = f\left(\lim_{t \to \infty} y^{t-1}, \rho\right)$$

whence,

$$y^* = f(y^*, \rho) \qquad\qquad\qquad \text{Q.E.D.}$$

A solution, y^*, of (5.2-3) is *stable* with respect to y^0 if the sequence generated by (5.2-4) whose initial value is y^0 converges to y^*. It is *globally stable* if it is stable with respect to all y^0 in Y. Thus if (5.2-3) has a globally stable solution, y^*, then all sequences generated by (5.2-4) converge to y^*.

A sequence $\{y^t\}$ is *cyclic* if there exist integers $\delta > 1$ and t^0 such that for all $t > t^0$,

$$y^t = y^{t+\delta}$$

In this case the *length* of the cycle is δ and $\{y^t\}$ is called a δ-*cycle*. The following results are concerned with the existence of solutions and cycles for the case in which Y has a finite number of elements. Because the proofs are trivial, they are omitted.

5.2-6 **Theorem:** Suppose Y has a finite number of elements. If (5.2-3) has no solution, then every sequence generated by (5.2-4) is cyclic.

Corollary: Suppose Y has a finite number of elements. If no sequence generated by (5.2-4) is cyclic, then (5.2-3) has at least one solution.

5.2-7 **Theorem:** Let Y have a finite number of elements and suppose (5.2-3) has at least one solution. Then every sequence generated by (5.2-4) that does not converge to a solution is cyclic.

Corollary: Let Y have a finite number of elements and suppose no solution of (5.2-3) is stable with respect to any nonsolution element y^0 in Y. Then every sequence generated by (5.2-4) whose initial value is not a solution is cyclic.

The next section pursues the finite case in greater detail. Before proceeding, however, consider a simple example that illustrates several of the preceding ideas. Let x be a not necessarily quantifiable variable ranging over the set $X = \{a, b, c, d, e\}$. Take the parameter-vector ρ to be fixed and define the function $f: X \rightarrow X$ by

x	$f(x)$
a	e
b	d
c	c
d	c
e	a

Using f as the basis for the periodic relation

$$x^t = f(x^{t-1}, \rho)$$

one sees that the time path starting at $x^0 = c$ is stationary since f implies that $x^t = c$ for all subsequent t. Moreover, the time path that begins with $x^0 = b$ converges to this stationary path since, again according to f,

$$x^1 = d$$

$$x^t = c, \qquad t \geq 2$$

Similarly, the time paths initiating at either $x^0 = a$ or $x^0 = e$ are 2-cycles.

5.3 The finite case

Several results concerning the existence of cycles and solutions of simultaneous equations have already been established in Section 5.2 for the case in which the number of values that the variables can assume is finite. This section presents further analysis of simultaneous equations in the finite case. An application is suggested in Chapter 8.

Recall, first, the original sufficient conditions producing solutions in Section 5.1 required certain inverses to exist. If X is finite and X_i is the set over which x_i varies $(i = 1, \ldots, n)$, then the existence of inverses implies that X_i and X_j must have equal numbers of elements for appropriate i and j. As illustrated by the second example of Section 5.1, it is not necessary that all X_i and X_j possess the same number of elements. However, in the course of defining a particular applied problem, if the proper X_i and X_j do not have like numbers of elements, there are at least two ways to rescue the proposition. One possibility is to add extra dummy elements to the sets that are short and extend the f^j accordingly. Trouble will not arise as long as one of the dummies does not appear in that part of the solution needed for analysis.

Alternatively, the argument could be rephrased for set-valued functions. Thus in the two-dimensional case, (5.1-2) would be replaced by

$$x_1 \in f^1(x_2, \rho), \qquad x_2 \in f^2(x_1, \rho)$$

where the symbol "$\in$" should be read "is an element of." Sufficient conditions for the existence of solutions are now quite simple. Given ρ, a solution exists whenever

$$\Delta_1 \cap \Delta_2 \neq \varnothing$$

where

$$\Delta_1 = \{(x_1, x_2) : x_1 \in f^1(x_2, \rho) \text{ and } x_2 \in X_2\}$$

$$\Delta_2 = \{(x_1, x_2) : x_2 \in f^2(x_1, \rho) \text{ and } x_1 \in X_1\}$$

There is, of course, no guarantee that any solution will be unique.

Even when the preceding patch-up techniques are inappropriate, Theorems 5.1-7, 5.2-5 to 5.2-7, and their corollaries can still be applied. In this context the possibility of multiplicities of solutions and cycles is now examined. The reader may wish to refer to the example at the end of the previous section for concreteness.

The system of simultaneous equations under consideration is that of Section 5.2, namely,

(5.3-1) $\quad z = f(y, \rho)$

where z and y are in Y, and Y consists of vectors $(x_1, \ldots, x_K)$. In dynamic form, (5.3-1) is expressed as

(5.3-2) $\quad y^t = f(y^{t-1}, \rho), \qquad t = 1, 2, \ldots$

Starting from any initial value y^0 in Y, (5.3-2) generates a sequence $\{y^t\}$ in Y. The stationary paths of (5.3-2) are solutions of (5.3-1).

Suppose Y contains M elements: $Y = \{y^1, \ldots, y^M\}$. Let p_{um} be the probability (the notion of probability is defined in Chapter 12) that $y^t = y^m$ when $y^{t-1} = y^u$ for $m, u = 1, \ldots, M$. These probabilities are taken as given. Assume the p_{um} do not depend on t and note

$$\sum_{m=1}^{M} p_{um} = 1$$

for all u. Generally the matrix of probabilities

$$P = \begin{bmatrix} p_{11} & \cdots & p_{1M} \\ \vdots & & \vdots \\ p_{M1} & \cdots & p_{MM} \end{bmatrix}$$

is called the *transition* matrix. Of course in this case, given (5.3-2), for each u there is an m^0 such that

$$p_{um^0} = 1$$

whereas

$$p_{um} = 0$$

for all $m \neq m^0$.

5.3-3   Theorem: A system of the form of (5.3-1) can have either $0, 1, \ldots, M-1$, or M solutions.

Proof: A solution is represented in the transition matrix P only by ones on the diagonal; that is, y^m in Y is a solution whenever $p_{mm} = 1$. Since there are M diagonal elements, there can be no solutions, one solution, ..., or at most, M solutions.   Q.E.D.

5.3-4   Theorem: If the columns of the transition matrix, P, also sum to unity, (5.3-1) cannot have $M-1$ solutions.

Proof: To have $M-1$ solutions requires $M-1$ ones on the diagonal, for example,

$$P = \begin{bmatrix} 1 & 0 & \cdots & 0 & 0 \\ 0 & 1 & \cdots & 0 & 0 \\ \vdots & \vdots & & \vdots & \vdots \\ 0 & 0 & \cdots & 1 & 0 \\ 1 & 0 & \cdots & 0 & 0 \end{bmatrix}$$

But the only way all columns can now sum to unity is if the last 1 is also on the diagonal.   Q.E.D.

Note that a sufficient condition for the columns of P to add up to 1 is that P be symmetric (i.e., $p_{um} = p_{mu}$ for all m and u).

Let $M \mid \gamma$ denote the (whole) number of times M is divisible by γ. Thus

$$M = (M \mid \gamma)\gamma + r$$

for some integer or remainder r where $0 \leqslant r < \gamma$.

5.3-5   **Theorem:** A system of the form (5.3-2) can generate either $0, 1, \ldots, (M \mid \gamma) - 1$, or $M \mid \gamma$ out of $\binom{M}{\gamma}[(\gamma-1)!]$ possible γ-cycles for each $\gamma = 2, \ldots, M$.

Proof: To have a γ-cycle among γ elements, one element can be mapped into any of the $\gamma - 1$ remaining elements. There are then only $\gamma - 2$ possibilities left for the next, and so on. Hence there are $(\gamma-1)!$ possible γ-cycles with γ elements. Furthermore, since the number of ways of choosing γ elements out of M elements is $\binom{M}{\gamma}$, there are $\binom{M}{\gamma}[(\gamma-1)!]$ possible γ-cycles with M elements.

On the other hand, any set of M elements can be divided up into at most $M \mid \gamma$ mutually exclusive subsets of γ elements. Therefore (5.3-2) can generate no more than $M \mid \gamma$ γ-cycles.

Q.E.D.

5.3-6   **Theorem:** If (5.3-1) has Λ_1 solutions and (5.3-2) generates Λ_γ γ-cycles for each $\gamma = 2, \ldots, M$, then

$$\Lambda_1 + \sum_{\gamma=2}^{M} \Lambda_\gamma \leqslant M$$

When $\Lambda_1 < M$ the inequality is strict.

Proof: It is clear from the structure of the transition matrix that any y^m in Y is a solution, is contained in exactly one cycle, or is an element of one or more sequences generated by (5.3-2) that converges to a solution. The conclusion is now evident.

Q.E.D.

The preceding discussion is suggestive of both the notion of a Markov chain and the fact that Markov theory is capable of application regardless of whether or not the elements of Y can be measured. In practice (especially in the nonphysical sciences), general transition matrices, that is, ones for which it is not necessarily true that to each u there corresponds an m^0 such that $p_{um^0} = 1$ frequently arise. Random disturbances in the real world may prevent (5.3-2) from being exact, or the process itself could be stochastic in nature. In either case, if $y^{t-1} = y^u$, outcomes other than y^{m0} are possible (with positive probability) at time t. A small portion of the theory of finite Markov chains is now outlined to illustrate the use of Markov analysis in the nonquantifiable context. Because all proofs are standard and easily found elsewhere, they are omitted. The development follows Kemeny et al. [8].

Consider an uncertain or stochastic process characterized by specifying the collection of states $Y = \{y^1, \ldots, y^M\}$ into which the process might enter along with a matrix of transition probabilities (i.e., a transition matrix) $P = [p_{um}]$ as defined earlier. In general, any square matrix $[p_{um}]$ such that for all u and m,

$$p_{um} \geq 0, \qquad \sum_{m=1}^{M} p_{um} = 1$$

can serve as a transition matrix. The term *probability vector* will refer to any row vector of nonnegative real numbers summing to one.

Suppose initial states y^m in Y arise with probability p_m^0, where $m = 1, \ldots, M$. Then

$$p^0 = (p_1^0, \ldots, p_M^0)$$

is a probability vector. For any m, let p_m^t be the probability that the process will be in state y^m after t steps. Then

$$p^t = (p_1^t, \ldots, p_M^t)$$

is also a probability vector. If, for all $t \geq 1$,

(5.3-7) $p^t = p^{t-1}P$

where P is a transition matrix, and if the transition probabilities of P are independent of time, then the process is called a *finite Markov chain*. Equation (5.3-7) implies:

$$p^t = p^0[P]^t, \qquad t \geq 0$$

where $[P]^t$ is P raised to the tth power.

Any exact process such as (5.3-2) may be transformed into a Markov chain merely by specifying p^0, for then P is determined according to the solutions and cycles of f and the p^t are obtained from (5.3-7). To illustrate, suppose $M = 3$ and f has one solution, y^1, and one 2-cycle so that

$$P = \begin{bmatrix} 1 & 0 & 0 \\ 0 & 0 & 1 \\ 0 & 1 & 0 \end{bmatrix}$$

Clearly, the probability at t of being in state y^1 is always the probability of starting there, whereas due to the cyclical oscillation between the remaining states y^2 and y^3, the probability at t of being in y^2 (or y^3) is the same as that of starting in y^2 (or y^3) if t is even, or of starting in y^3 (of y^2) if t is odd. All this is reflected in (5.3-7).

A transition matrix P is *regular* if there exists a $t \geq 1$ such that all entries of $[P]^t$ are positive.

A probability vector ω is a *fixed point* of P whenever $\omega = \omega P$. If $p^0 = \omega$, then from (5.3-7)

$$p^t = \omega$$

for all t. Thus the probability of being in any state is the same at all stages of the process.

5.3-8 **Theorem:** If P is regular, then:
　　　i. There exists a unique fixed point ω of P whose components are all positive.
　　　ii. For any probability vector p,

$$\lim_{t \to \infty} p[P]^t = \omega$$

　　　iii. If W is the matrix each of whose rows are ω, then

$$\lim_{t \to \infty} [P]^t = W$$

An element y^m in Y is an *absorbing state* whenever

$$p_{mm} = 1$$

A Markov chain is *absorbing* provided that it has at least one absorbing state, and from every state it is possible for the process to go to an absorbing state (not necessarily in one step). Upon reaching an absorbing state, the process is said to be *absorbed*. Applied to the Markov chain arising out of (5.3-1) and (5.3-2), y^m is a solution of the former if and only if it is an absorbing state. Furthermore, if the process is absorbing, then all sequences generated by (5.3-2) converge to some solution of (5.3-1). There can be no cycles.

5.3-9 **Theorem:** If a Markov chain is absorbing, then for any initial state, the probability that the process will be absorbed is 1.

Consider any absorbing Markov chain with φ absorbing and ψ non-absorbing states ($\varphi + \psi = M$). By appropriately arranging states, one can write its transition matrix in the form

$$P = \begin{bmatrix} I & 0 \\ R & Q \end{bmatrix}$$

where I is the φ by φ identity matrix, 0 is the φ by ψ matrix of zeros, and R and Q are, respectively, ψ by φ and ψ by ψ matrices. It can be shown that the ψ by ψ matrix

$$H = (I - Q)^{-1}$$

exists for all absorbing Markov chains. The following theorem gives an interpretation for the entries, h_{um}, of H.

5.3-10   Theorem: h_{um} is the average number of times the process enters each nonabsorbing state y^m when it begins in (initial) nonabsorbing state y^u.

Let β be a ψ by 1 column vector of 1's. Set

$$\theta = H\beta$$

and denote the components of θ by $\theta_u (u = 1, \ldots, \psi)$.

5.3-11   Theorem: θ_u is the average number of steps before absorption when the process starts in nonabsorbing state y^u.

Let g_{um} be the probability that the process will be absorbed into absorbing state y^m if it begins in the nonabsorbing state y^u. Denote the ψ by φ matrix of these probabilities by $G = [g_{um}]$. Then G may be computed as follows.

5.3-12   Theorem: $G = HR$

5.4   Maximization

The fundamental role played by maximization in the conduct of scientific inquiry is well documented. In economics, for example, maximizing behavior characterizes the notion of rationality, and hence lies at the very heart of economic theory (see, e.g., Intriligator [3]). For this reason and also because it is frequently linked to the choice systems of Section 5.5, a short discussion of maximization in nonquantifiable settings is a worthwhile digression.

Let X be a set and $\mathfrak{I}$ be a topology for X. The idea of maximization can be expressed directly in terms of a reflexive and transitive relation ξ

on X, or indirectly by recourse to a function f mapping X into a set, S, upon which a reflexive and transitive relation, ζ, has been defined. Thus x^0 is ξ-*maximal* in X if $x^0 \xi x$ for all x in X, and x^0 is f (*or* ζ)-*maximal* whenever $f(x^0) \zeta f(x)$ for all x in X. Frequently S is taken to be a subset of the real line and ζ to be $\geqslant$. Maximality is an ordinal property: The concept is defined by an ordering either on X or on S. Application of any order-preserving transformation to X or S (including increasing transformations when f is real-valued) yields the same ordinal information originally induced by, respectively, ξ or ζ. Maximal elements are left unchanged. Of course, under the circumstances sketched in Section 2.2, f could actually be a numerical, ordinal scale representing ξ. In any event, the presence of some kind of order is essential if the notion of maximization is to be meaningful.

The next issue concerns the conditions under which maximal elements can be said to exist. For the case in which ξ is defined on X, one set of sufficient restrictions is obtained by appeal to Zorn's lemma (Halmos [2, p. 62]).[1] Thus if,

   i. $X \neq \varnothing$,
   ii. ξ is antisymmetric (and hence a partial order), and
   iii. every chain in X has an upper bound,

then Zorn's lemma asserts the existence of at least one ξ-maximal element. An alternative approach is more topological in nature. A family of sets, $\mathcal{Q}$, has the *finite intersection property* provided that the intersection of each finite subfamily is nonempty. Let $\mathcal{Q}_\xi$ be the family of all sets of the form:

$$W_x = \{x' : x' \xi x \text{ and } x' \text{ is in } X\}$$

for all x in X. If ξ is total, then $\mathcal{Q}_\xi$ has the finite intersection property. Now assume the topology, $\mathfrak{I}$, on X has been specified in such a manner that all W_x are closed. Supposing, in addition, X is also compact, it follows that the intersection of all W_x in $\mathcal{Q}_\xi$ cannot be empty (Kelley [7, p. 136]). But x^0 in

$$\bigcap_{x \text{ in } X} W_x$$

implies x^0 is ξ-maximal over X. Therefore the appropriate choice of $\mathfrak{I}$ together with compactness of X and totality of ξ also guarantee the existence of ξ-maximal elements. Uniqueness of maximal elements cannot be ensured without further restrictions.

---

[1] Zorn's lemma is equivalent to the Axiom of Choice.

It is clear that the foregoing sets of sufficient conditions can each be applied to $f(X) \subseteq S$ when maximality is defined with respect to f and ζ. In these situations a collection of maximal elements $M \subseteq f(X)$ is obtained first. The f-maximal elements in X are then contained in the inverse image $f^{-1}(M)$. Interestingly enough, as long as ζ is total on $f(X)$ and the requisite topology has been assigned to S, the well-known theorem, "If f is continuous and X is compact, then f has a maximum value on X," is a direct consequence of the second of the results in the previous paragraph. That is, when X is compact, the continuity of f implies $f(X)$ is compact (Kelley [7, p. 141]), and hence the conclusion is immediate. Note that if S is a class of real numbers and ζ is $\geqslant$, then ζ is automatically total and assignment of the usual Euclidean topology to S is sufficient for the theorem to hold.

Continue, for a moment, with S as a subset of the real line ordered by $\geqslant$. If it were possible to discover a 1-1 correspondence, c, between another subset, S^0, of the real line and X so that

$$f \cdot c : S^0 \to S$$

turns out to be twice continuously differentiable, then the usual first and second order (quantifiable) differential conditions can be invoked to identify the f-maximal elements. Although there are many 1-1 correspondences between subsets of the real line and X, existence (and uniqueness) of maximal elements does not depend on the use of one correspondence or another to locate them. In fact, the employment of c in this manner (when possible) may provide a convenient and practical way of determining which elements of X are f-maximal. Reassignment of numbers by using alternative correspondences will merely "relocate" the maximal elements and may make them more difficult to find.

Returning to the general argument, it is conceivable that maximal elements could occasionally arise as solutions to a system of simultaneous equations.[2] In such a case sufficient conditions for existence of solutions are also sufficient for existence of maximal elements. On the other hand, solutions of simultaneous equations might further appear as maximal elements with respect to some ξ or f. Hence conditions sufficient for the existence of maximal elements could also become sufficient for the existence of solutions.[3]

---

[2] In quantifiable, differentiable circumstances, maximal elements may also satisfy a system of simultaneous first-order (differential) equations.

[3] In quantifiable economics, for example, the solutions of a Walrasian system of market-clearing equations have been expressed as constrained maximal elements of a community utility function. See Katzner [5].

5.5   Choice systems

The last kind of system considered here is a choice system. Both stochastic and nonstochastic varieties are discussed.

Let $\mathcal{A}$ be a collection of nonempty subsets, A, of X. A (nonstochastic) *choice function* is a mapping $h: \mathcal{A} \to X$ such that for all A in $\mathcal{A}$, $h(A)$ is contained in A. Thus h "chooses" elements from each A in $\mathcal{A}$. That such a function can always be defined is a consequence of the axiom of choice (Halmos [2, pp. 59–60]). A *choice system* consists of a collection of one or more choice functions.

Theoretical interest in choice systems stems from a desire to rationalize choice, that is, to explain the reasons for or definitions of choice functions. In the nonstochastic case, one approach begins with a binary relation ξ^* defined on X, sometimes referred to as a preference ordering, which is assumed to be both transitive and reflexive. Now, as described in Section 3.1, ξ^* gives rise to an equivalence relation that partitions X into equivalence classes $[x]$. Furthermore, ξ^* induces an ordering, ξ, on the collection, E, of all equivalence classes defined for all $[x']$ and $[x'']$ in E by $[x'] \xi [x'']$ if and only if $x' \xi^* x''$. It is clear that ξ partially orders E: ξ is reflexive, transitive, and antisymmetric.

For any A in $\mathcal{A}$, let

$$E_A = \{[x] : x \text{ is in } A\}$$

Since $A \neq \varnothing$ by assumption, $E_A \neq \varnothing$. Also, ξ partially orders E_A. Assume that every chain in E_A (a subset on which ξ is total) has an upper bound in E_A with respect to ξ. Thus if C is such a chain, there is an $[x^0]$ in E_A with $[x^0] \xi [x]$ for all $[x]$ in C. By Zorn's lemma, which is equivalent to the Axiom of Choice (Halmos [2, pp. 62–5]),[4] there exists an $[x]_A$ in E_A such that $[x]_A \xi [x]$ for all $[x]$ in E_A. A choice function h may therefore be defined by

$$h(A) = [x]_A$$

for all A in $\mathcal{A}$. Thus h chooses the ξ-maximal or "most preferred" class from E_A. The following properties of h are easily verified:

   i. $h(A) \neq \varnothing$ for all A in $\mathcal{A}$.
   ii. For A' and A'' in $\mathcal{A}$, suppose $A' \subseteq A''$ and x is in A'. If x is in $h(A'')$, then x is in $h(A')$.

Examinations of nonstochastic choice appear often in the nonphysical sciences usually under the assumption that the elements of X are capable

---

[4] The use of Zorn's lemma to secure the existence of ξ-maximal elements has been noted in Section 5.4.

of measurement.[5] In one common form there is a continuous function, μ, representing ξ^* such that $\mu(x') \geqslant \mu(x'')$ if and only if $x' \xi^* x''$ for all x' and x'' in X. Suppose that all A in $\mathcal{Q}$ are compact. Then for every A there exists a nonempty set $\{x\}_A$, each point of which maximizes μ over A (Section 5.4). Evidently $\{x\}_A$ is an equivalence class in E_A and an upper bound for every chain in E_A. Furthermore, $\{x\}_A = [x]_A$. Hence any rationalization of choice based on the maximization of a continuous function is a special case of that described here. An application of choice analysis to nonquantifiable phenomena is presented in Chapter 9.

Choice can also be viewed as an uncertain phenomenon. Thus with X a set and $\mathcal{Q}$ and $\mathcal{B}$ subsets of the power set $\mathcal{P}(X)$, let

$$\mathcal{B}\mathcal{Q} = \{(B,A) : B \subseteq A \text{ and } A \text{ is in } \mathcal{Q}\}$$

A *probability choice function* is a mapping $Q : \mathcal{B}\mathcal{Q} \to [0,1]$ such that for each A in $\mathcal{Q}$, $Q(B,A)$ as a function of B is a probability measure on A. (Probability measures are defined in Section 12.2.) The symbol $Q(B,A)$ may be interpreted as the probability of choosing the set B out of A. For single element sets $B = \{x\}$, write $Q(x,A)$ in place of $Q(\{x\},A)$. Then $Q(x,A)$ is the probability of choosing the point x from A. Usually $Q(x,A) = 0$ for all x in A. But if A is countable, then $Q(x,A)$ may take on any value inclusively between 0 and 1. Note $Q(x,\{x\}) = 1$ for all x in X.

As with nonstochastic functions, probabilistic choice can also be rationalized. All three alternatives sketched here ignore multiple-point choices (B is always taken to be a single element set) and confine themselves to countable or finite sets A in $\mathcal{Q}$.

Consider first a reflexive, transitive, and total preference ordering, ξ, on X. Set $W_x = \{y : y \xi x \text{ where } x \text{ and } y \text{ are in } X\}$. With A in $\mathcal{Q}$ countable, let Q be any function such that

    i. $Q(x,A) \geqslant 0$, for all x in A,
    ii. $\Sigma_{x \text{ in } A} Q(x,A) = 1$,
    iii. $\Sigma_{y \text{ in } W_x} Q(y,A) \geqslant \frac{1}{2}$ if and only if $x \xi z$, for all z in A.

Given ξ, such a Q can always be defined. Condition (iii) ensures that the probability of choosing a ξ-maximal preference point in A is at least $\frac{1}{2}$. If $A = \{x,y\}$ then

$$Q(x,\{x,y\}) \begin{cases} \geqslant \frac{1}{2}, & \text{if and only if } x \xi y \text{ (preference or indifference)} \\ = \frac{1}{2}, & \text{if and only if } x \xi y \text{ and } y \xi x \text{ (indifference)} \\ > \frac{1}{2}, & \text{if and only if } x \xi y \text{ and not } y \xi x \text{ (preference)} \end{cases}$$

[5] See, for example, Davidoff and Reiner [1] in urban and regional planning, Katzner [4] in economics, and Taylor [11] in political science.

This is the so-called constant utility model (Luce and Suppes [9, p. 333]). Although preferences are nonstochastic, the decision-making process is subject to error or other random disturbances.

In the random utility model (Luce and Suppes [9, p. 338]), uncertainty enters into preferences rather than the making of decisions. A *stochastic preference ordering* on X is a mapping $\mu : X \times X \to [0,1]$ such that

$$\mu(x, y) \geqslant 0$$

and

$$\mu(x, y) + \mu(y, x) = 1$$

for all x and y in X. Here $\mu(x, y)$ is the probability that x is preferred to y. Given μ, probabilistic choice may be defined for all $\{x, y\}$ in $\mathcal{C}$ by

$$Q(x, \{x, y\}) = \mu(x, y)$$

Note that the probability choice function Q is specified only for two-element sets, although in the constant utility case it may be obtained for any countable A in $\mathcal{C}$.

A third approach is based on the hypothesis that choices are made by eliminating alternatives (Tversky [12]). Let A be a finite set and $C_1, \ldots, C_n$ its nonempty subsets. For convenience set $C_1 = A$. One way of choosing a point from A is to eliminate elements of A successively by sequentially choosing smaller and smaller C_i's. After a finite number of steps a single element is left and chosen from A. The process can be described in terms of the Markov analysis developed earlier. Let p_{ij} be the probability that in the elimination procedure C_j is chosen from C_i, where $i, j = 1, \ldots, n$. Then

$$P = \begin{bmatrix} p_{11} & \cdots & p_{1n} \\ \vdots & & \vdots \\ p_{n1} & \cdots & p_{nn} \end{bmatrix}$$

is a transition matrix as defined in Section 5.3 and the choice process is a Markov chain. For any $i \neq j$, note that $p_{ij} > 0$ if and only if $C_j \subseteq C_i$ ($C_j \neq C_i$), and $p_{ij} = 0$ otherwise. Furthermore, $p_{ii} = 1$ if and only if C_i is a single-element set.

In general, there are many distinct subsequences of $C_1, \ldots, C_n$, which, by eliminating alternatives, end at the same x in A. Each C_i in every such sequence must contain x. Hence a probabilistic choice function, Q, is consistent with the elimination of alternatives process provided

$$Q(x, A) = \sum p_{ij} Q(x, C_j)$$

where the sum is taken over all i and j for which x is in C_j. Without further restrictions specification of P and Q is always possible.

Of course, additional structure could be required in any of these three models with ensuing implications for Q. The interested reader is referred to Luce [9] and Tversky [12].

References

1. Davidoff, P., and T. A. Reiner, "A Choice Theory of Planning," *Journal of the American Institute of Planners,* 28 (1962):103–15.
2. Halmos, P. R., *Naive Set Theory* (Princeton, N.J.: van Nostrand, 1961).
3. Intriligator, M. D., *Mathematical Optimization and Economic Theory* (Englewood Cliffs, N.J.: Prentice-Hall, 1971).
4. Katzner, D. W., *Static Demand Theory* (New York: Macmillan, 1970).
5. Katzner, D. W., "A Simple Approach to Existence and Uniqueness of Competitive Equilibria," *American Economic Review,* 62 (1972):432–7.
6. Katzner, D. W., "On the Analysis of Systems Containing Non-Quantifiable Elements," *Kybernetes,* 2 (1973):147–55.
7. Kelley, J. L., *General Topology* (Princeton, N.J.: van Nostrand, 1964).
8. Kemeny, J. G., A. Schleifer, Jr., J. L. Snell, and G. L. Thompson, *Finite Mathematics with Business Applications,* 2nd ed. (Englewood Cliffs, N.J.: Prentice-Hall, 1972), pp. 113–20, 215–32.
9. Luce, R. D., and P. Suppes, "Preference, Utility and Subjective Probability," in R. D. Luce, R. R. Bush, and E. Galanter, eds., *Handbook of Mathematical Psychology,* vol. III (New York: Wiley, 1965), pp. 249–410.
10. Mesarovic, M. D., and Y. Takahara, *General Systems Theory: Mathematical Foundations* (New York: Academic Press, 1975).
11. Taylor, M., "Mathematical Political Theory," *British Journal of Political Science,* 1 (1971):339–82.
12. Tversky, A., "Choice by Elimination," *Journal of Mathematical Psychology,* 9 (1972):341–67.

CHAPTER 6

General systems

Having studied several specific systems in some detail, it is now worth considering systems and their properties in general. This will provide a firm foundation for the results of Chapter 5, and at the same time, suggest further directions in which techniques for analyzing nonquantifiable phenomena have been and can be developed.

Of the various approaches to the notion of system, that associated with the name of Mesarovic is most confluent with the viewpoint expressed here. Without any formal structure in mind, Mesarovic thinks of a system simply as a relation on abstract sets. To analyze particular problems, however, structure must be added – but only that necessary for the given purpose. This is the approach adopted below. After an initial presentation of the general definition of system, the specific systems of Chapter 5 are derived as special cases. Next various forms of systemic causality are examined. Subsequent considerations relate to connections between systems, feedback, and the problem of control. The chapter concludes with a classification scheme for systems based on the theory of categories. Because the discussion is primarily definitional and provides little in the way of formal proof, the reader who is interested in rigorous argument may wish to refer to Mesarovic and Takahara [7].

6.1 Definition of a system

Let X and Y be abstract sets called objects.[1] (Any number of objects can be used but there is no need to consider more than two.) A *system, S,* is defined to be a collection of ordered pairs,

$$S \subseteq X \times Y$$

If S is a function it is referred to as a *functional system* and written

$$S : X \to Y$$

---

[1] The use of the word "object" to denote a set takes a slight but inconsequential liberty with earlier terminology referring to objects as the elements of sets. It is done to conform with the relevant parts of the system literature. The context in which the word is used should prevent confusion.

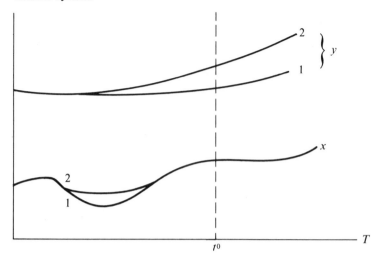

Figure 6-1

When S is not a function, a new set or object, Z, may be introduced in such a way that

$$S : Z \times X \to Y$$

is a function. In general, there are many sets, Z, that can accomplish this transformation. Once one is chosen it is called a *global state object* for S. If the elements of Z can be thought of as values assumed by a vector, say, $(z_1, \ldots, z_n)$, then the z_i are called *state variables*.

Frequently systems are considered over time. The latter is represented by any linearly ordered set, T. Let A and B be arbitrary sets and suppose A^T is the set of all functions mapping T into A. Define B^T similarly. Setting $X = A^T$ and $Y = B^T$, dynamic systems can then be characterized as

$$S \subseteq A^T \times B^T$$

(This conception is identical to that described in Section 1.3.) A global state object can also be specified so that S becomes a function.

To illustrate, two time paths for x and y in the Euclidean plane are pictured in Figure 6-1. Suppose S associates x-path 1 with y-path 1 and x-path 2 with y-path 2. At time t^0 both x-values are the same. The only way to know which is the appropriate y-value at t^0 is to know in which "state" the system is operating, that is, which path applies. This is the reason for introducing state variables and global state objects.

Two other important systems concepts are related to global state objects. When X alone depends on time (i.e., $X = A^T$), any global state object is called an *initial state object*. Suppose, however, that both X and Y depend on time (i.e., $X = A^T$, $Y = B^T$) and

$$S \subseteq X \times Y$$

For any x in X recall $x : T \to A$. Denote function values, $x(t)$, by x_t. Let X_t consist of all functions in X restricted from the origins of time up to some t in T:

$$X_t = \{\{(\alpha, x_\alpha)\} : x \text{ is in } X \text{ and } \alpha \leqslant t\}$$

Define Y_t similarly. Restricting S also up to and including t gives the restricted system S_t, where

$$S_t \subseteq X_t \times Y_t$$

Let Z_t be an (arbitrary) global state object for S_t, so that

$$(6.1\text{-}1) \quad S_t : Z_t \times X_t \to Y_t$$

Set

$$\bar{Z} = \bigcup_t Z_t$$

Define an equivalence relation η on $\bar{Z}$ to identify which states, if any, are the "same" at different times. Then the quotient

$$\bar{Z}/\eta$$

is called the *state space*. When time does not enter the system through both X and Y, the concept of state space is irrelevant.

Systems are specified in greater detail through at least three processes: (a) by introducing structure in the objects X and Y, (b) by listing the ordered pairs of S, and (c) by providing a rule for defining S. As an example of (a), topologies are often imposed on X and Y so that the system's stability properties can be defined and studied (Section 5.2). Topologies also appear in the subsequent discussion of control. The second method is only applicable for the limited number of circumstances in which S is finite. Approach (c) requires the specific definition of a correspondence associating elements of X with elements of Y (Chapter 5).

An alternative way of introducing structure by indicating rules is called the method of *constructive specification*. This requires the definition of two mappings:

$$(6.1\text{-}2) \quad F : Z \times X \to Z, \qquad G : Z \to Y$$

For example, when only X depends on time, F associates with each pair consisting of an initial state and x – time path, another initial state in Z.

The function G assigns a y-value to the latter. Taken together, the composition of F and G, namely,

(6.1-3) $G \cdot F: Z \times X \to Y$

is the original system with global state object Z; that is,

$$S = G \cdot F$$

A system may therefore be characterized by the quadruple (Z, X, F, G).

It is interesting to see how the specific systems of Chapter 5 can be obtained as special cases of a general system. Each is now considered in turn.

Simultaneous equations: Begin with the functional system

$$S: X \to X$$

where the elements of X are n-dimensional vectors. Suppose D^i and D^j are obtained from X as in Chapter 4 and consider partial transformations of the form

$$S_{ij}: D^i \to D^j$$

Choose a fixed vector x^0 in X. Where components of the vectors in X have been deleted to obtain points of D^i, replace them by the corresponding components of x^0. Thus with X two dimensional, $x = (x_1, x_2)$ in X, and x_1 in, say, D^1, such a reconstructed vector would be (x_1, x_2^0) where $x^0 = (x_1^0, x_2^0)$ is the fixed vector. Let Ω^{2^n-1-i} be the set containing the vector derived from x^0 by deleting components corresponding to those retained in the formation of D^i. In the preceding example, $\Omega^2 = \{x_2^0\}$. The set of all vectors reconstructed from D^i is written

$$D^i \times \Omega^{2^n-1-i}$$

A similar set may be obtained with respect to D^j. Denote it by

$$D^j \times \Omega^{2^n-1-j}$$

Extending S_{ij} to these enlarged sets in the obvious manner gives the new transformation

$$S_{ij}^*: D^i \times \Omega^{2^n-1-i} \to D^j \times \Omega^{2^n-1-j}$$

which is no longer partial. It is clear that S_{ij} can be chosen so that

$$S_{ij}^* \subseteq S$$

Focusing only on such S_{ij}'s, let

$$\bar{S} = \bigcup_{i,j} \{S_{ij}^*\}$$

Thus $\bar{S}$ or any of its subsets corresponds to a system of simultaneous equations generated by S. In other words, any system of simultaneous equations can be obtained from an appropriate general system S by projecting it onto suitable subspaces.

Simultaneous equations can also be derived as a special case of a general system by the method of constructive specification. Let

$$X = X_1 \times \cdots \times X_K$$

$$Y = X_1 \times \cdots \times X_L$$

$$Z = Z_1 \times \cdots \times Z_L$$

where $L \leqslant K$ and X_i (or Z_i) is the set over which the variable x_i (or z_i) may range. Suppose F and G are any functions specified by (6.1-2) such that

$$G(z) = (G^1(z), \ldots, G^L(z))$$

and

$$F(z,x) = (F^1(z_1, x_2, \ldots, x_K), F^2(x_1, z_2, x_3, x_4, \ldots, x_K), \ldots,$$
$$F^L(x_1, \ldots, x_{L-1}, z_L, x_{L+1}, \ldots, x_K))$$

Setting $f^i = G^i \cdot F^i$, for each i, and following (6.1-3),

$$(x_1, \ldots, x_L) = (f^1(x_2, \ldots, x_K, z_1), f^2(x_1, x_3, x_4, \ldots, x_K, z_2), \ldots,$$
$$f^L(x_1, \ldots, x_{L-1}, x_{L+1}, \ldots, x_K, z_L))$$

Finally, replacing each z_i by the scalar ρ gives the simultaneous system (5.1-1) of Section 5.1.

Periodic relations: To obtain the Kth-order periodic equation (5.2-2) of Section 5.2, let $X = A^T$ and $Y = B^T$ and set

$$x = (y_{t-1}, \ldots, y_{t-K}), \qquad y = y_t$$

where x varies over X and y over Y. In this case z is a scalar variable whose corresponding set is Z. Now from the equations of (6.1-2) with arbitrary F and G, namely,

$$G(z) = y_t, \qquad F(z,x) = z$$

is derived

$$y_t = f(y_{t-1}, \ldots, y_{t-K}, z)$$

where $f = G \cdot F$. The precise formulation of Chapter 5 is found by writing $z = \rho$. Systems of simultaneous periodic equations are derived in an analogous fashion.

is,

Choice functions: Let X be a family of sets indexed by Z; that

$$X = \{A_z : z \text{ is in } Z\}$$

Take

$$Y = \bigcup_z A_z$$

Define

$$G(z) = y$$

for some y in A_z and all z in Z, and

$$F(z^*, A_z) = z$$

for all z^* in Z and A_z in X. Then since F is independent of z^*,

$$y = f(A_z)$$

where $f = G \cdot F$. This is the choice function, h, of Section 5.5. The derivation of probability choice functions is left to the reader.

6.2   Causality

To achieve the purpose of many inquiries outside the physical sciences frequently requires establishing relationships between analytical factors. In a significant number of cases these relationships are elusive, and hence an assertion of probable causality linking the occurrence of one set of events to another would be an enormously important substitute.[2] But because the nonphysical sciences are often restricted to passive observation (as opposed to the controlled experimentation used in the physical sciences), it is generally impossible to discover which, if any, of the factors are "probable causes" and which are "probable effects." Under such conditions causality can be introduced only in terms of the formal structural relations that are employed (i.e., postulated) in the investigation. Although in this technical form definitions of causality are

---

[2] Exact causal propositions, even in the physical sciences, are incapable of empirical discovery. See Russell [8].

likely to be exact, any comparison of the structure with reality can suggest, at most, a probable causal connection.

Causality has to do with discerning a direction of cause and effect between factors. The statement that one variable, x_1 (ranging over X_1), *causes* another, x_2 (over X_2), is interpreted here as asserting that the values of x_1 and x_2 must occur in pairs (the idea is traceable to Hume [4, p. 377]); that is, causality imposes an ordering, C, on the Cartesian product of X_1 and X_2:

$$C \subseteq X_1 \times X_2$$

For various reasons it may be desirable to introduce further restrictions on causal orderings. Thus one may wish to require that C associate a unique value of x_2 to each value of x_1 or a single value of x_1 with each value of x_2 or perhaps even both. The first forces C to be a function on X_1; the second constrains its inverse to be a function on X_2. But because there is no logical reason why one effect could not have more than one cause, or one cause more than one effect, these properties are excluded from the preceding definition.

From the point of view of general systems at least four aspects of causality have arisen. These are as follows.

6.2.1 External causality

By thinking of X as a set of "inputs" and Y as a set of "outputs" in the formulation of any general system, S, namely,

$$S \subseteq X \times Y$$

one automatically implies a causal direction from X to Y. The ordering determined by S is called an *external* causal ordering and x is said to cause y. Furthermore, once a global state object, Z, is introduced, and once a particular state of the system, z in Z, is specified, S is reduced to a function on X. Hence there can be only one effect (y-value) for each cause (x-value).

6.2.2 Internal causality[3]

Consider a functional system, S, whose outputs are also used as inputs:

$$S : X \times Y \rightarrow Y$$

[3] The material of this subsection is based on Mesarovic [6], which generalizes the original idea of H. A. Simon [9].

If, for instance, S were an elementary system of simultaneous equations, as in (6.2-1) to (6.2-3) below, both so-called "dependent" (y) and "independent" (x) variables would appear on one side of the equality while only the dependent variables could appear on the other. A further example is provided by the system of simultaneous equations discussed in Section 5.1 when $K > L$.

Suppose each y in Y is a vector $(y_1, \ldots, y_n)$ whose components, y_i, range over some set Y_i. Then

$$Y \subseteq Y_1 \times \cdots \times Y_n$$

Without loss of generality consider the case in which

$$Y = Y_1 \times \cdots \times Y_n$$

Let Y' denote the Cartesian product of some subcollection of the Y_i and let y' be the variable that assumes as values the vectors of Y'. If S' is a subsystem of S (i.e., $S' \subseteq S$) such that

$$S' : X \times Y' \rightarrow Y'$$

then S' is called *self-contained*. A subsystem is self-contained, therefore, if only the output variables of y' are needed as inputs (along with x) to determine the value of y'.

To illustrate, let $y = (y_1, y_2, y_3)$, $y' = (y_1, y_2)$ and $x = x_1$, where all variables range over the set of real numbers. Consider the system

(6.2-1) $y_1 = x_1 + y_2$

(6.2-2) $y_2 = x_1 - y_1$

(6.2-3) $y_3 = x_1 + y_1 y_2$

For each value of x_1, unique values of y_1 and y_2 can be determined from (6.2-1) and (6.2-2) alone. Only after the latter have been so "solved" can the value for y_3 be found from (6.2-3). Equations (6.2-1) and (6.2-2) are a self-contained subsystem of (6.2-1) to (6.2-3).

Suppose S' and S'' are two self-contained subsystems of S:

$$S' : X \times Y' \rightarrow Y', \qquad S'' : X \times Y'' \rightarrow Y''$$

Let $Y^* = Y' \cap Y''$. Then the system, S^*, defined by

$$S^* = S' \cap S''$$

is also a self-contained subsystem of S:

$$S^* : X \times Y^* \rightarrow Y^*$$

Since the number of sets Y_i is finite, it follows that there exists at least one *minimal* self-contained subsystem (i.e., one that itself contains no self-contained subsystem). In the preceding example (6.2-1) and (6.2-2) constitute a minimal self-contained subsystem.

Once the collection of minimal self-contained subsystems of any given system are known, the *internal* causal ordering can be defined: First, if y' is the output vector of a minimal self-contained system S', then x is said to cause y'. This part of the internal causal ordering is given by S'. If y' then appears along with another output vector, y'', in a larger self-contained subsystem S'' containing S', that is,

$$S'' : X \times Y' \times Y'' \to Y' \times Y''$$

and if there is no other distinct self-contained system, S^0, such that

$$S' \subset S^0 \subset S''$$

then (x, y') causes y''. The second part of the internal causal ordering then appears as S''. But suppose, on the other hand, S'' were to contain an additional output vector, y''', from a second minimal self-contained system:

$$S''' : X \times Y''' \to Y'''$$

In symbols

$$S'' : X \times Y' \times Y''' \times Y'' \to Y' \times Y''' \times Y''$$

If there were also no self-contained system between S''' and S'', then (x, y', y''') would cause y'' as directed by S'', and so on. In the illustration given earlier, x_1 causes (y_1, y_2), and (x_1, y_1, y_2) causes y_3. An instance of internal causality when none of the variables are capable of measurement is provided by Chapter 8 in which the first four equations of (8.1-2) are a minimal self-contained subsystem of the political structure. The latter is also a self-contained (although not minimal) subsystem of a larger system that describes the general structure of society in Chapter 10.

6.2.3 Time causality

There are two types of time causality of interest here. Each is based on the dynamic system

(6.2-4) $S \subseteq X \times Y$

where $X = A^T$ and $Y = B^T$ as defined in Section 6.1. Recall that if x is in X,

$$x : T \to A$$

and the images of T under x are written

$$x_t = x(t)$$

For x in X and y in Y, let

$$x/_t = \{(\alpha, x_\alpha) : \alpha \leqslant t\}, \qquad y/_t = \{(\alpha, y_\alpha) : \alpha < t\}$$

In terms of the ideas and notation of (6.1-1), $x/_t$ is in X_t and $y/_t \cup \{(t, y_t)\}$ is in Y_t. With a global state object Z_t given at each t, the system (6.2-4) restricted up to t is

$$S_t : Z_t \times X_t \to Y_t$$

If for each z in Z_t and all t in T, there is a representation of S_t of the form

$$y_t = f^t(z, x/_t)$$

then S is called *nonanticipatory* and at each point in time a causal ordering from $x/_t$ to y_t given z is defined. Any nonanticipatory system can be decomposed so that its dynamic evolution over time can be described and studied entirely within the state space (Mesarovic [6, pp. 103–5]).

A better known form of time causality arises from the possibility of completely determining the present state of a system solely from past input and output observations. When occurring, the only additional information needed to obtain present output is present input. In fact, all future outputs of the system can be found without reference to states. This phenomenon is called past-determinacy. Formally, S is *past-determined* whenever there exists a t^0 such that for all $t \geqslant t^0$, where t and t^0 are in T, the restricted system S_t has a representation of the form

$$(6.2\text{-}5) \quad y_t = f^t(x/_t, y/_t)$$

Given $t \geqslant t^0$, the causal direction is from $(x/_t, y/_t)$ to y_t.

Past-determined systems are very common. For example, all periodic equations, including those in Section 5.2 and Chapters 9 and 10, may be expressed as in (6.2-5). To illustrate in the quantifiable case,

$$y_t = y_{t-1} + x_t$$

where x_t and y_t are scalar variables and $t > 0$, has as its solution

$$y_t = y_0 + \sum_{\alpha=1}^{t} x_\alpha$$

for $t \geqslant 1$. Therefore it, too, is past-determined.

6.2.4   *Irreversibility*

The definition of causal direction between x_1 and x_2 as given here requires only the specification of an ordering,

$$C \subseteq X_1 \times X_2$$

If it happens that $X_1 = X_2$, then the possibility of having, for each (x_1', x_2') in C, an (x_1'', x_2'') in C such that

$$x_1' = x_2'', \qquad x_2' = x_1''$$

cannot be ruled out. In such a case, that is, when C is symmetric, what can it mean to say that one variable is a cause and the other an effect? The same difficulty arises even if $X_1 \neq X_2$ provided

$$X_1 \cap X_2 \neq \emptyset$$

For this reason causal orderings are often compelled to exhibit an additional property, namely, asymmetry (see, e.g., Blalock [2, pp. 9, 10]). Given any causal ordering, C, causes always produce effects; but with C asymmetric, the direction of causality is irreversible. Note that even if both C and its inverse are taken to be functions, there is still no guarantee of the presence or absence of asymmetry. For with x a real, scalar variable,

$$f(x) = x$$

defined on the entire real line is symmetric, whereas

$$f(x) = x^2$$

is asymmetric for $x > 1$, and is neither symmetric nor asymmetric when considered over the set for which $x \geqslant 1$.

The irreversibility issue, however, does not arise with internal and time causality. In the former case the direction of causality depends on moving from systems with fewer variables to those with more, and in the latter, on the passage of time. Neither of these directions can be reversed. Asymmetry is therefore introduced in the very process of characterizing the causal ordering. This is not so with external causality. The easiest way to ensure asymmetry here is to have

$$X_1 \cap X_2 = \emptyset$$

But if X_1 and X_2 must overlap, and if observation refutes all asymmetric relational forms, then irreversibility cannot be a property of the external causal ordering.

6.3   Connection and feedback

Systems are connected by joining outputs of one to inputs of another. It is not necessary to require every output to be connected to a "succeeding" input or every input be connected to a "preceding" output. The question of which outputs may be connected to which inputs is determined according to the demands of the particular problem under consideration and taken as given in the following discussion.

To reflect the fact that certain inputs and outputs of a system,

$$S \subseteq X \times Y$$

are available for connection, let x_A denote those components of x that are available and x_N denote those that are not:

$$x = (x_A, x_N)$$

Partition y similarly. Corresponding to x_A, x_N, y_A, and y_N are value sets X_A, X_N, Y_A, and Y_N over which each vector, respectively, ranges. Thus

$$X = X_A \times X_N, \qquad Y = Y_A \times Y_N$$

and S may be described as

$$S \subseteq (X_A \times X_N) \times (Y_A \times Y_N)$$

It is now possible to define three basic connecting operations on the class of all connectable systems.

Consider first the *cascade* connection, "$\circ$". It is defined as follows: Write

$$S^1 \circ S^2 = S^3$$

whenever

$$S^1 \subseteq X^1 \times (Y_N^1 \times Y_A^1)$$
$$S^2 \subseteq (X_N^2 \times X_A^2) \times Y^2$$
$$S^3 \subseteq (X^1 \times X_N^2) \times (Y_N^1 \times Y^2)$$

where

$$Y_A^1 = X_A^2 = A$$

and $((x^1, x_N^2), (y_N^1, y^2))$ is in S^3 if and only if there exists an a in A such that

$$(x^1, (y_N^1, a)) \quad \text{is in } S^1$$

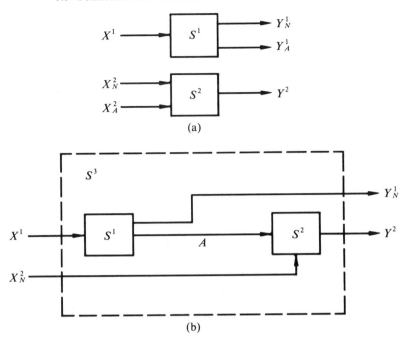

Figure 6-2

$$((x_N^2, a), y^2) \quad \text{is in } S^2$$

Using the "black box" diagram to represent systems as in Section 1.4, S^1 and S^2 are shown in Figure 6-2a and the cascade connection defining S^3 is pictured in Figure 6-2b.

An example will indicate how the cascade connection arises. Suppose S^1 represents the U.S. federal government (system) and S^2 represents the government of any state. Generally speaking, money flows to the federal government in the form of taxes and loans (x^1) and is either spent on services for the public (y_N^1) or given to the states. The amounts flowing to each state (in the case of S^2 it is y_A^1) are the connecting output components to state governments. Receiving income from the federal government (x_A^2) – its connecting input component – and from its own tax and loan sources (x_N^2), the state government S^2 converts money into public services and grants to local governments. These can either be lumped together (y^2) or the local governments can be thought of as connected in cascade to S^2. In either case it is clear that $y_A^1 = x_A^2$. Other illustrations are easily found in which the links between systems are not based on quantifiable data.

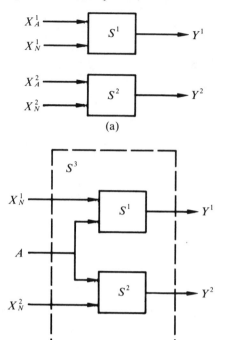

Figure 6-3

The second operation, "$*$", is defined by

$$S^1 * S^2 = S^3$$

whenever

$$S^1 \subseteq (X_A^1 \times X_N^1) \times Y^1$$
$$S^2 \subseteq (X_A^2 \times X_N^2) \times Y^2$$
$$S^3 \subseteq (A \times X_N^1 \times X_N^2) \times (Y^1 \times Y^2)$$

where

$$X_A^1 = X_A^2 = A$$

and $((a, x_N^1, x_N^2), (y^1, y^2))$ is in S^3 if and only if

$$((a, x_N^1), y^1) \quad \text{is in } S^1$$
$$((a, x_N^2), y^2) \quad \text{is in } S^2$$

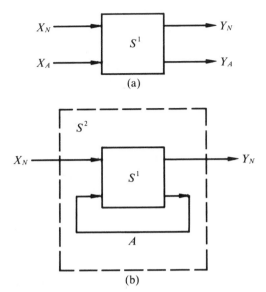

Figure 6-4

It is called the *parallel* connection and is illustrated in Figure 6-3. In the previous example all state governments are in parallel with each other. Their common input connecting component is money from federal sources.[4]

To define the *feedback* or third connection, F, set

$$F(S^1) = S^2$$

whenever

$$S^1 \subseteq (X_A \times X_N) \times (Y_A \times Y_N)$$
$$S^2 \subseteq X_N \times Y_N$$

where

$$X_A = Y_A = A$$

and (x_N, y_N) is in S^2 if and only if there exists an a in A such that

$$((a, x_N), (a, y_N)) \quad \text{is in } S^1$$

This operation is diagrammed in Figure 6-4. An example of feedback

[4] Strictly speaking, input a has to be chosen carefully in order for the definition of parallel connection to apply. If all states were receiving the same sum, then a could represent dollars per state. Otherwise a could be a vector indicating the funds going to each.

appears in Chapter 9. The planning system there is inserted in a feedback loop connecting some of the inputs and outputs of the environmental system (see Figure 9-1).

Most of the important cases in which systems interact can be built up by the use of these three connecting operators. They also provide the basis for system decomposition. If S is a system, its *components* are systems from which S can be obtained upon application of the connecting operators. It can be shown that every system with at least two inputs and outputs can be decomposed into two components joined by the cascade connection (Mesarovic and Takahara [7, Ch. 10, Sec. 2]). Every such system can also be decomposed into two other components that are tied together by a combination of the cascade and feedback operations (Mesarovic and Takahara [7, Ch. 10, Sec. 2]). Further decompositions are also possible.

6.4   Control

An important issue in the analysis of systems concerns the possibility of generating particular outputs within a fixed, specified structure. Indeed, the desire to govern outcomes of given systemic phenomena is often a prime motivating force behind investigative undertakings. It is clear, however, that when dealing with nonchangeable structures, the only way such control can be exercised is through the manipulation of one or more inputs. The idea that inputs may be employed to induce preferred outputs is the basis of the approach described here.

Formally, consider a given functional system of the form

(6.4-1) $S : Z \times X \to Y$

Let

(6.4-2) $E : Z \times X \times Y \to V$

be a function that evaluates the performance of S according to some predetermined criteria expressed in terms of the elements of some object V. Thus, for example, an ordering could be defined on V and, on application of E, the outputs of S evaluated with respect to their relative position in it. In any event, the composition of S and E, namely,

$$E \cdot S : Z \times X \to Y$$

is denoted by g, where

$$g(z, x) = E(z, x, S(z, x))$$

for all (z, x) in $Z \times X$.

An element v in V is *achievable* (reproducible) if it can be secured as an output of g when desired, that is, if there exists an x in X and z in Z for which

$$g(z, x) = v$$

Similarly, v in V is *controllable* provided that there is an x in X with

$$g(z, x) = v$$

for all z in Z. Controllability, then, means that v is achievable regardless of the values taken on by z. The vector (or scalar) of variables x is often referred to as a vector (or scalar) of control parameters. A subset of V is achievable or controllable whenever each of its points is, respectively, achievable or controllable. Note that any controllable point is also achievable but not conversely. Sufficient conditions for achievability and controllability have been given elsewhere (see Mesarovic and Takahara [7, Ch. 7]).[5] An example of the use of achievability in the nonphysical sciences appears in Section 9.3.

An especially interesting aspect of control is called "optimal" control. As usually formulated, it involves the solution to a problem arising for systems with controllable sets. Suppose, as suggested earlier, a reflexive and transitive ordering φ on V serves as the basis for evaluating the system described in (6.4-1) and (6.4-2). Let $\bar{V}$ be the subset of controllable points in V. Assume $\bar{V} \neq \varnothing$. The problem of optimal control is to choose the control parameters to obtain the best possible v in $\bar{V}$ with respect to φ. An *optimal choice* is an x^* such that

$$g(z, x^*) \, \varphi \, g(z, x)$$

for all x where $g(z, x)$ is in $\bar{V}$.

One property of optimal choice is Bellman's Principle of Optimality (Bellman [1, p. 83]). Viewing (6.4-1) and (6.4-2) in the dynamic terms of Section 6.1, z, x, and v all represent functions that map the time set T into other appropriate sets. Function values are written z_t, x_t, and v_t, respectively, for all t in T. Let the system start at $t = 0$ with initial values z_0 and x_0. Suppose that φ on V is defined by reflexive and transitive orderings φ^t on the collection of all function values v_t according to:

$$v' \varphi v'' \quad \text{if and only if} \quad v_t' \varphi^t v_t'' \quad \text{for all } t > 0$$

Denote the composite $E \cdot S$ at time t (i.e., the function relating z_t and x_t to v_t) by $g^t(z_t, x_t)$. Bellman's principle states that no matter what the values of z_0 and x_0, if x^* is an optimal choice, then for all $t > 0$,

---

[5] Sufficient conditions for achievability in a specific case are given in Section 9.3.

$$g^t(z_t, x_t^*) \, \varphi^t g^t(z_t, x_t)$$

for every x_t whose associated function x satisfies the condition that $g(z,x)$ is in $\bar{V}$. Thus optimal choice over T requires optimal choice at each t in T.

A second property of optimal choice, namely, Halkins's Principle of Optimal Evolution [3], necessitates the imposition of additional structure and the reformulation of the notion of system in a dynamic context. An *H-dynamical system*, $(W, \mathfrak{I}, \psi)$, consists of a set W, a topology $\mathfrak{I}$ for W, and a relation ψ on W such that

    i. ψ is reflexive and transitive.

    ii. For all a, b, and c in W, if $a\psi b$ and $a\psi c$, then either $b\psi c$ or $c\psi b$.

    iii. For all a and b in W and neighborhoods N_a containing a in $\mathfrak{I}$, if $a\psi b$, then there is a neighborhood N_b containing b in $\mathfrak{I}$ with $N_b \subseteq \{x : y\psi x \text{ and } y \text{ is } N_a\}$.

Interpreting $a\psi b$ to mean the appearance of b follows a in time, condition (ii) asserts that if b and c follow a, then either b follows c or c follows b. It is, of course, possible for b and c to follow each other, that is, for b and c to occur together. Similarly, condition (iii) says that given $a\psi b$ and any N_a, there is a neighborhood of b that is "small" enough to be a subset of the collection of all points following the elements of N_a. Clearly, many systems of the form (6.4-1), regardless of whether they are identified as dynamic in the sense of Section 6.1, can be thought of as H-dynamical by setting $W = Z \times X \times Y$ and introducing the requisite structure.

The relevant framework in which to develop the Principle of Optimal Evolution involves a collection of related H-dynamical systems. Specifically, an *H-dynamical polysystem* is a triple $D = (W, \mathfrak{I}, \Psi)$ such that

    i. $(W, \mathfrak{I}, \psi)$ is an H-dynamical system for every ψ in Ψ.

    ii. For all a, b, and c in W and all ψ' and ψ'' in Ψ, if $a\psi' b$ and $b\psi'' c$, then there is a ψ in Ψ for which $a\psi b$ and $b\psi c$.

If a is in W, then the set of points that are *reachable* from a is

$$R(a) = \{b : a\psi b \text{ for some } \psi \text{ in } \Psi\}$$

If A is a subset of W, then

$$R(A) = \bigcup_{a \text{ in } A} R(a)$$

is the reachable set from A. With a and b in W, ψ in Ψ, and $a\psi b$, the set

$$T(a, b, \psi) = \{x : a\psi x\} \cap \{x : x\psi b\}$$

is called the *trajectory* associated with ψ from a to b. The trajectory $T(a, b, \psi)$ is thus the collection of points "in between" a and b under ψ.

A *control problem* for D is the quintuple $C = (W, \mathfrak{J}, \Psi, A, B)$ where A is an initial subset and B is a terminal subset of W. A *solution* for C is a triple (a, b, ψ) such that a is in A, b is in B, ψ is in Ψ, and $a \psi b$. This solution defines an acceptable trajectory, $T(a, b, \psi)$, for C.

As indicated earlier, optimal control requires the evaluation of the elements of the terminal set B. Rather than introducing an evaluation function such as (6.4-2), let the ordering, φ, on which evaluations are based, be defined directly on B. Suppose φ on B is transitive and irreflexive (instead of transitive and reflexive as assumed before) and that for all a in B and all neighborhoods N_a containing a in $\mathfrak{J}$, there exists a b in $B \cap N_a$ with $b \varphi a$. In other words, for all a there is a b "near" a ranking higher with respect to φ than a. An *optimal control problem* for the H-dynamical polysystem D and control problem C is a sextuple $O = (W, \mathfrak{J}, \Psi, A, B, \varphi)$. An *optimal solution* for O is a solution (a, b, ψ) of C with the particularity that there is no other (i.e., "better") solution $(\bar{a}, \bar{b}, \bar{\psi})$ of C with $\bar{b} \varphi b$. The optimal solution (a, b, ψ) generates an optimal trajectory $T(a, b, \psi)$.

Halkin's Principle of Optimal Evolution is now stated without proof: If (a, b, ψ) is an optimal solution of O, then the optimal trajectory $T(a, b, \psi)$ lies on the boundary[6] of $R(A)$. Thus to locate an optimal trajectory, one must look on the boundary of the collection of points that are reachable from the initial set A.

Still further properties of optimal choices or solutions are given by the well-known Maximum Principle of Pontryagin (see, e.g., Intriligator [5, Ch. 14]). This principle, however, has little significance in the absence of measurement. It does not really apply to the nonquantifiable world.

6.5 Categories of systems

Loosely speaking, categories consist of sets of objects along with certain kinds of mappings. Functors transform categories into other categories. Taken together, these notions provide a basis for classifying systems and studying relationships between them.

Let Θ be a class of objects, θ_α, where α is an index, and suppose that to each pair of objects $(\theta_\alpha, \theta_\beta)$ in Θ there is associated a set $M_{\alpha\beta}$. The elements of $M_{\alpha\beta}$ are called *morphisms* and are denoted by $m_{\alpha\beta}$; they are functions from θ_α to θ_β:

---

[6] The point x is *on the boundary* of the set $G \subseteq W$ if every neighborhood of x in $\mathfrak{J}$ intersects both G and $W - G$. The *boundary* of G is the collection of all its boundary points. For a proof of the principle see Halkin [3, p. 381].

$$m_{\alpha\beta} : \theta_\alpha \to \theta_\beta$$

Let $\mathfrak{M}$ be the collection of all morphisms; that is,

$$\mathfrak{M} = \bigcup_{\alpha, \beta} M_{\alpha\beta}$$

A composition operation on $\mathfrak{M}$ is a function mapping

$$M_{\beta\gamma} \times M_{\alpha\beta} \to M_{\alpha\gamma}$$

for any α, β, and γ. The composite of $m_{\alpha\beta}$ and $m_{\beta\gamma}$ is written

$$m_{\beta\gamma} \cdot m_{\alpha\beta} = m_{\alpha\gamma}$$

for some element $m_{\alpha\gamma}$ of $M_{\alpha\gamma}$.

The triple $\mathcal{C} = (\Theta, \mathfrak{M}, \cdot)$ is a *category* whenever (a) composition is associative, that is, for all $m_{\alpha\beta}$, $m_{\beta\gamma}$, and $m_{\gamma\delta}$ in $\mathfrak{M}$,

$$m_{\gamma\delta} \cdot (m_{\beta\gamma} \cdot m_{\alpha\beta}) = (m_{\gamma\delta} \cdot m_{\beta\gamma}) \cdot m_{\alpha\beta}$$

and (b) for each α there exists an element I_α in $M_{\alpha\alpha}$ such that

$$I_\alpha \cdot m_{\beta\alpha} = m_{\beta\alpha}, \qquad m_{\alpha\beta} \cdot I_\alpha = m_{\alpha\beta}$$

for all β.

Let $\mathcal{C} = (\Theta, \mathfrak{M}, \cdot)$ and $\mathcal{C}' = (\Theta', \mathfrak{M}', *)$ be categories. A *functor, F,* is a function mapping objects into objects:

$$F : \Theta \to \Theta'$$

and morphisms into morphisms:

$$F : \mathfrak{M} \to \mathfrak{M}'$$

such that (a) for all α,

$$F(I_\alpha) = I'_{\alpha'}$$

where α' is obtained from

$$\theta'_{\alpha'} = F(\theta_\alpha)$$

and (b) for all α, β, and γ,

$$F(m_{\beta\gamma} \cdot m_{\alpha\beta}) = F(m_{\beta\gamma}) * F(m_{\alpha\beta})$$

Before applying these concepts to classify systems, one must have a notion of equivalence among them. This, in turn, requires some preliminary discussion of operations and homomorphisms. Take X and Y to be objects and let an operation be given on each. From now on, even though they are different, all operations will be denoted by the same symbol, "·". They are distinguishable notationally according to the sets on which they are defined. The operations on X and Y induce an operation on $X \times Y$ as follows: For all (x, y) and $(\bar{x}, \bar{y})$ in $X \times Y$, set

(6.5-1) $(x, y) \cdot (\bar{x}, \bar{y}) = (x \cdot \bar{x}, y \cdot \bar{y})$

Remember from Section 4.1 that a function, say,

$$h_x : X \to X'$$

is a *homomorphism* provided

$$h_x(x \cdot \bar{x}) = h_x(x) \cdot h_x(\bar{x})$$

for all x and $\bar{x}$ in X. Homomorphisms thus preserve algebraic structures. If h_x and

$$h_y : Y \to Y'$$

are both homomorphisms, then

$$h : X \times Y \to X' \times Y'$$

defined by

$$h(x, y) = (h_x(x), h_y(y))$$

for all (x, y) in $X \times Y$, is also a homomorphism. An isomorphism is a homomorphism that is 1–1 and onto, and whose inverse is also homomorphic.

Consider, now, two systems:

$$S \subseteq X \times Y, \quad S' \subseteq X' \times Y'$$

and the preceding homomorphism $h = (h_x, h_y)$ between $X \times Y$ and $X' \times Y'$. Suppose h_x is onto. Call S' a *model* of S provided that for all (x, y) in $X \times Y$, if (x, y) is in S, then $h(x, y)$ is in S'. Define S and its model S' to be *equivalent* whenever h is an isomorphism and for all (x', y') in $X' \times Y'$, if (x', y') is in S', then its inverse image $h^{-1}(x', y')$ is in S.

A model of S must therefore have an algebraic structure similar to S. The particular structure exhibited by S' depends on the homomorphism. Homomorphisms should be chosen according to the properties that are to be preserved for study in the model. The remaining details are suppressed. Since only h_x is assumed onto, the image of S is generally a proper subset of its model. Models, then, may contain additional implications that are not present in the original system. Two systems are equivalent only when the elements of their object sets correspond uniquely to each other and each system is a model of the other. The next few paragraphs present three examples of how systems may be classified into categories. Relationships among these categories are also discussed.

For given objects X and Y, let Θ be the class of all systems

$$S \subseteq X \times Y$$

Let $\mathfrak{M}$ be the collection of all homomorphisms $h = (h_x, h_y)$ that map object sets of one system in Θ into those of another such that the latter is a model of the former. With composition among the components of h taken to be the standard notion of Section 4.1,[7] define composition, "$\cdot$", on $\mathfrak{M}$ as in (6.5-1). Then it is easily seen that

$$\mathcal{C}_S = (\Theta, \mathfrak{M}, \cdot)$$

is a category – call it the *category of general systems* with respect to X and Y.

To obtain the second category, recall that a relation $R \subseteq X \times Y$ is a function whenever there do not exist two ordered pairs in R with the same x-value but with distinct y-values. Let $\mathfrak{M}'$ be that subset of $\mathfrak{M}$ whose elements, h, in addition to their other properties, *preserve functions,* that is, if

$$S \subseteq X \times Y,$$

$$h : X \times Y \rightarrow X' \times Y'$$

$$R \subseteq S$$

and, if R is a function, then $h(R)$ is also a function. Retaining the same class of models, Θ, of $\mathcal{C}_X$,

$$\mathcal{C}_S^f = (\Theta, \mathfrak{M}', \cdot)$$

is a subcategory of $\mathcal{C}_S$ called the *function preserving category of general systems* with respect to X and Y.

The last category classifies systems for which global state objects, Z, have been specified. Let

$$S : Z \times X \rightarrow Y$$

$$S' : Z' \times X' \rightarrow Y'$$

be systems and suppose $h = (h_x, h_y, h_z)$ is a homomorphism,

---

[7] In this context it is not necessary to define the composite of two (component) homomorphisms whose domain and range do not match up appropriately. However, the composite of such functions was defined as the empty function in Section 4.1.

$$h: X \times Y \times Z \rightarrow X' \times Y' \times Z'$$

$$h_x: X \rightarrow X', \quad h_y: Y \rightarrow Y', \quad h_z: Z \rightarrow Z'$$

such that h_x is onto, and for all x and z,

(6.5-2) $\quad h_y(S(z,x)) = S'(h_z(z), h_x(x))$

It is clear that if (x,y,z) is in S (i.e., $S(z,x)=y$) and $h_x(x)=x'$, $h_y(y)=y'$, and $h_z(z)=z'$, then from (6.5-2),

$$y' = S'(x', z')$$

and hence (x', y', z') is in S'. Therefore S' is a model of S. Equation (6.5-2) is nothing but a restatement of the "model condition" given earlier.

With

$$S: Z \times X \rightarrow Y$$

fixed, let Θ'' be the class of all models of S as defined by the homomorphism of the preceding paragraph. Let $\mathfrak{M}''$ be the collection of all such homomorphisms between the object sets of models of S. Define composition, "$\cdot$" on $\mathfrak{M}''$ as in (6.5-1). Then

$$\bar{\mathbb{C}}_S = (\Theta'', \mathfrak{M}'', \cdot)$$

is also a category. It may be referred to as the *category of global state general systems* with respect to X, Y, and Z.

Thus a category of systems is a class of systems that all have the same algebraic structure. All models of all its systems are contained in it. The associativity axiom for morphisms (a part of the definition of category) corresponds here to the idea that a model of a model of a system is also a model of the same system. But alternative specifications of the same system can have distinct nonalgebraic structures: The homomorphisms linking systems may or may not be function preserving, and the systems themselves may be described with or without global state objects. Such differences require separate categories. The fact that these categories still arise from the same base, however, means that functors may be defined between them. Algebraic structures are the same within categories, whereas categories based on different nonalgebraic structures are related by functors.

Given X, Y, and Z and two representations for the same system S,

$$S \subseteq X \times Y, \quad S: Z \times X \rightarrow Y$$

there are two important functors relating $\mathbb{C}_S$, $\mathbb{C}_S^f$, and $\bar{\mathbb{C}}_S$. One,

$$F: \mathcal{C}_S^f \to \bar{\mathcal{C}}_S$$

assigns to every system of $\mathcal{C}_S^f$ a global state representation in $\bar{\mathcal{C}}_S$; the other,

$$G: \bar{\mathcal{C}}_S \to \mathcal{C}_S$$

associates with each global state system of $\bar{\mathcal{C}}_S$ a general system in $\mathcal{C}_S$. The former increases nonalgebraic structure in the sense of adding global state objects and is called *constructive*; the latter reduces it by taking them away and is termed *forgetful*. It is not necessary at this point to provide detailed definitions of F and G (see Mesarovic and Takahara [7, Ch. 12, Section 2]). Suffice it to say, they preserve the "model relation" between S and its models: In the case of, say, F, if S' is a model of S, then $F(S')$ is a model of $F(S)$.

References

1. Bellman, R., *Dynamic Programming* (Princeton, N.J.: Princeton University Press, 1957).
2. Blalock, H. M., Jr., *Causal Inference in Nonexperimental Research* (Chapel Hill: University of North Carolina Press, 1964).
3. Halkin, H., "Topological Aspects of Optimal Control of Dynamical Polysystems," *Contributions to Differential Equations,* 3 (1964):377–85.
4. Hume, D., *The Philosophical Works,* vol. 1, T. H. Green and T. H. Grose, eds. (Darmstadt, Germany: Scientia Verlag Aalen, 1964).
5. Intriligator, M. D., *Mathematical Optimization and Economic Theory* (Englewood Cliffs, N.J.: Prentice-Hall, 1971).
6. Mesarovic, M. D., "Mathematical Theory of General Systems and some Economic Problems," in H. W. Kuhn and G. P. Szegö, eds., *Mathematical Systems Theory and Economics I* (Lecture Notes in Operations Research and Mathematical Economics, vol. 11) (Berlin: Springer, 1969), pp. 93–116.
7. Mesarovic, M. D., and Y. Takahara, *General Systems Theory: Mathematical Foundations* (New York: Academic Press, 1975).
8. Russell, B., "On the Notion of Cause," in *Mysticism and Logic and Other Essays* (London: George Allen & Unwin, 1959), pp. 180–208.
9. Simon, H. A., "Causal Ordering and Identifiability," in W. C. Hood and T. C. Koopmans, eds., *Studies in Econometric Method* (New York: Wiley, 1953), Ch. 3.

CHAPTER 7

Some epistemological considerations

The aim of Chapters 3 to 6 has been to develop a guiding methodology for analysis when measurement of at least one of the factors under investigation is not now and may never be possible. Variables and relations between them were defined and tools for manipulation were proposed. This led to the emergence of model-building techniques that are analogous to those often employed in the examination of scalable phenomena. A logical basis for the conduct of analysis without measurement has thereby been established.

Loose ends, nevertheless, remain. The translation of nonquantifiable concepts into nonquantifiable variables; the meaning of infinity in the absence of numerical calibration; and the representation of time, change, and evolution in such a context all require further explanation. In particular, it is necessary to explore the role these elements play in the conduct of inquiry and the resulting contribution to the understanding of reality that emerges from them. Attention is now turned to these kinds of issues.

The intent of the following discussion is clearly different from that of Section 1.3. The purpose of the latter was to illustrate the notion that what is most often referred to as "scientific analysis" does not – insofar as its philosophical underpinnings are concerned – depend on measurement. Thus organizational constructs (e.g., assumptions, laws, theories), guidelines for argument, and methods of definition, to name a few, retain their meaning and force in nonquantifiable circumstances. But the way in which various facets of reality are represented in analytical constructs, and the implications for the knowledge so obtained, have until now been ignored.

The problems that will presently be considered have already come up explicitly or implicitly on preceding pages. The reasons for postponing comment on them were twofold. First, they are largely philosophical in nature and, requiring lengthy digressions if discussed where they arose, would have interrupted the analytical development. Consequently, the suggestion of a sort of correspondence between analysis with and without measurement would have been more fragmented than it presently appears.

Second, and more important, is the close connection between many of these issues and those discussed by Georgescu-Roegen in his *The Entropy Law and the Economic Process* [13]. This interesting and insightful volume contains, in part, one of the few relatively recent attempts to present epistemological queries as they relate directly to economics in particular, and hence to social and behavioral science in general. Because so little effort has been expended on such matters in the past, the danger of increasing the gap between analysis and actuality has increased. Indeed, many areas of investigation have already become suspect in terms of usefulness and relevance: Their contribution to what is supposed to be knowledge is seriously in doubt (see, e.g., Sorokin [24], Georgescu-Roegen [13], and Ward [25]).

By reserving these epistemological questions for a single chapter, analysis without measurement can be placed in sharper relief against the philosophical foil of Georgescu-Roegen. Its role in obtaining knowledge can be more efficiently clarified and contrasted to that of standard, quantifiable methods. And its entanglement with reality is easier to expose.

7.1   Dialectical analysis

Concepts, as suggested in Section 1.3, are mental constructs that serve to organize our perceptions of reality into more or less abstract, but still understandable, elements. However, the nature of the process of human thought often imposes limitations on the analytical roles they can play. Based on these roles, Georgescu-Roegen [13, pp. 43–7] distinguishes two categories of concepts.

In certain cases the human mind is perfectly capable of sharply delineating the boundaries of an idea. The result is an *arithmomorphic* concept. Such concepts can be clearly dintinguished and separated from all others. They are distinctly discrete: There is no overlap between them and their opposites. The velocity of a moving object is an arithmomorphic concept as is the price of an apple at the supermarket and the temperature of a pot of water. In fact, the collection of real numbers as a whole provides uncountably many arithmomorphic concepts, for each number may be conceived as something smaller than all those that are larger than itself and larger than all those that are smaller than itself. Thus 3 is distinctly discrete from 4 or $\sqrt{2}$.

On the other hand, there are concepts whose boundaries human powers seem unable to define clearly and precisely. Exact characterizations are either arbitrary in that they do not conform to standard ideas or, in analytical contexts, extraordinarily difficult to employ. Where, for example, does one quality of experience leave off and another begin?

Democracy and nondemocracy are two different ideas, each with a variety of shades of meaning and, what is more important, with certain shades of one overlapping certain shades of the other. Georgescu-Roegen refers to these concepts as *dialectical*. Dialectical notions are distinct, although not, as their arithmomorphic counterparts, discretely so. Each is surrounded by its own penumbra of meanings. Any dialectical concept is distinguishable from all others (including its opposite), because no two penumbras can be identical. But, although impossible for arithmomorphic concepts, a country may be both a democracy and a nondemocracy at the same time.

The importance of dialectical notions arises from the limitations of arithmomorphic ones. No doubt the latter have led to momentous contributions to knowledge; no doubt, too, they provide the means for great efficiency and easy checking of thought. However, the nature of our world is such that they are often unable to encapsulate real-life phenomena (Georgescu-Roegen [13, p. 81]). Democracy, competition, intelligence, culture, social class – in short, many of the fundamental concepts of the social and behavioral sciences – are essentially dialectical in character.

Of course, the structure of analysis based on arithmomorphic concepts is well known. Discretely distinct (often "operational" or quantifiable) notions are defined, assumptions made, and propositions obtained by appeal to the rules of logic. Reasoning is usually checked and rechecked (the same result is derived in different ways), and hypotheses and propositions are often subjected to empirical tests. On the other hand, because a fundamental requirement is that something, say, z, cannot simultaneously be both A and not A, logic is not applicable when dealing with dialectical concepts. Neither arithmomorphic–theoretical nor arithmomorphic–statistical techniques are appropriate. Nevertheless, as will presently be argued, the arithmomorphic approach is an exceedingly useful and important tool in dialectical analysis.

It is also worth emphasizing that thinking with dialectical concepts, however mathematically inexact, need not be muddled. As Bridgeman put it, "Little Johnnie and I myself know perfectly well what I want when I tell him to be good, although neither of us could describe exactly what we meant under cross-examination..." (Bridgeman [6, p. 72]). And an excellent example of dialectical reasoning has been provided by Bertrand Russell:

Not only are we aware of particular yellows, but if we have seen a sufficient number of yellows and have sufficient intelligence, we are aware of the universal *yellow*; this universal is the subject in such judgements as "yellow differs from blue" or "yellow resembles blue less than green does." And the universal yellow is the predicate in such judgements as "this is yellow"... (Russell [23, p. 212])

In addition to being a legitimate mode of thought, dialectical reasoning can also be checked. The checks may not be so precise and sure as in the case of logic, but they are checks all the same. Georgescu-Roegen [13, pp. 52, 337] identifies two. The first is by application of the ancient Socratic method: systematic questioning of all aspects of the argument. The second employs arithmomorphic similes; that is, dialectical reasoning can be likened to various arithmomorphic arguments, although none of these test arguments are ever capable of replacing the original in its entirety. Clearly, error uncovered by either the Socratic method or the use of logic in an arithmomorphic simile casts doubt on the dialectical argument. However, although it provides a certain comfort and satisfaction, a lack of error does not imply correctness. Thus the modern mathematical approach to Marxian economics (see, e.g., Morishima [19]) can be seen as an arithmomorphic simile of dialectical Marxian dynamics. And, in fact, all economic models may be regarded as arithmomorphic similes of underlying dialectical reality.

The structure of dialectical analysis, then, also contains concepts, assumptions, and propositions. Its results may be checked by the Socratic method and arithmomorphic simile. Because the social and behavioral sciences are concerned solely with life phenomena, and because arithmomorphic concepts are unable to capture completely the essence of such ideas, the purpose of social and behavioral arithmomorphic models is to illustrate, facilitate, clarify, and check dialectical analysis. In addition, statistical rejection of an arithmomorphic simile would question the dialectical base from which it comes.

Without commitment to any metaphysical perspective, the methodology derived in preceding chapters may be recognized as an alternative technique for obtaining arithmomorphic similes that is parallel to the usual procedure of quantifiable investigation. Previous arguments indicate that rigorous arithmomorphic analysis does not require measurement. As long as appropriate concepts are distinctly discrete so that the rules of logic apply, arithmomorphic inquiry can be conducted in ways that are analogous to those permissible when numerical scales are available.

To expand the point, recall (Section 3.1) that variables are characterized by designating the sets over which they range. Although the idea underlying any variable may be either arithmomorphic or dialectical, the set of variable values must be arithmomorphically defined. The price of a hammer, for example, is an arithmomorphic concept whose associated variable ranges over a collection of (arithmomorphic) numbers. Similarly, to define the variable "culture," a collection of discretely distinct cultures must be verbally described. Cultures of, say, North American

Indian or African tribes as well as those found in modern Western society are a few of the many possibilities. Thus to express a dialectical concept as an arithmomorphic variable requires the delineation of suitable arithmomorphic "points."

The fact that certain concepts such as "freedom" and "justice" currently suffer from vagueness in characterization is no drawback. Various manifestations of freedom and justice are still capable of sufficiently precise and discrete description so as to distinguish each from all others. These manifestations may therefore be taken as the arithmomorphic elements comprising the sets by which the variables "freedom" and "justice," respectively, are defined. (A similar point has been made by Parsons [20, p. 255].)

All results developed in Chapters 3 to 6 can be seen in this light. Arithmomorphic similes are obtained from dialectical reality by concentrating on aspects that appear to be discretely distinct. It is also clear that the philosophical discussion of Section 1.3, although sound in the arithmomorphic context for which it was historically intended, needs modification to apply to a dialectical environment. There are, to be sure, dialectical laws, models, and the like (e.g., the Marxian model of dynamic, economic progression). But notions such as logic, which depend on discretely distinct elements, are relevant only in an arithmomorphic setting. Also, it is interesting that Carnap's (Section 1.3.2) idea of explication of prescientific into scientific concepts can be interpreted as the transformation from dialectical background to arithmomorphic simile.

Finally, it should be pointed out that even though the idea of a fuzzy set (Section 3.1) might seem to suggest accommodation of a dialectical penumbra of meanings, the notion is still wholly arithmomorphic. That is, the ability to assign a number (grade of membership) between 0 and 1 inclusive to all objects in the universe of discourse (higher numbers indicating "more within" the set in question) rests on the property of discrete distinctness of the elements involved. Either z has grade of membership α, or it does not. It cannot overlap an element with membership grade β. Fuzziness arises because the boundary of the set itself is blurred – not the boundaries of the arithmomorphic objects from which the set is built up.

7.2   Infinity

The definitions of finite, countably infinite, and uncountably infinite sets of objects given in Section 3.1 (in terms of the relationship of these sets to corresponding sets of real numbers) are standard mathematical notions. But they do not provide much insight into what it means to describe an infinite collection of nonquantifiable elements. Who, for example, could ever specify each item on an infinite list of distinct cultures? The finiteness of the human experience guarantees that no one, not even all of humankind put together, is capable of characterizing more than a finite number of them. Thus it is necessary to ask about the possibility of constructing infinite sets without naming every object.

There is, of course, a well-known answer to this question in the arithmomorphic case. When all objects under consideration are distinctly discrete, a specific (although not unique) progression of mathematical constructions leads first to countably and then uncountably infinite sets. (A more formal discussion of the subject may be found, e.g., in Wilder [26].) One starting point is Peano's axioms. Any two sets X and Y satisfying them are isomorphic, and, in turn, are isomorphic to the class of natural numbers $N = \{1, 2, 3, \dots\}$.[1] Thus X, Y, and N are all of the same (i.e., the smallest) order of infinity and are called countably infinite. Among other things (including the concept of mathematical induction), Peano's axioms call for the existence of a "successor function": a mapping that assigns to each element that object following it. In the case of N the successor function maps 1 into 2, 2 into 3, 3 into 4, and so on. Specification of an appropriate successor function is the main feature in Peano's construction of a countably infinite set.

Addition is universally possible with natural numbers – but not subtraction. The problem is that zero and the negative numbers are not available. To extend the natural numbers to the set of all integers requires expressing the idea of subtraction in terms of addition. An analogous construction yields the collection of rational numbers: Although multiplication of any two integers can be defined, due to the lack of fractions, their division generally cannot. The rationals are obtained by characterizing division in terms of multiplication. It turns out that extending the natural numbers to the integers and the integers to the rationals does not change the order of infinity of any of these sets. Each remains countably infinite.

The rationals do not comprise a "complete" collection of numbers because, for example, the length of the diagonal of the unit square is not contained among them. A higher order of infinity is generated by plugging up the "holes" between the rationals. One method is to divide the rationals into two disjoint sets, such that all elements of one are smaller than all elements of the other. Each such division or (Dedekind) cut is identified as a real number. Alternatively, convergent (Cauchy) sequences of rationals may be considered. Some will converge to rationals; others

---

[1] This does not mean that the elements of X and Y are quantifiable (see Section 2.2).

will not. Regardless, the real numbers are defined to be the limits of these sequences. Both the Dedekind and Cauchy approaches lead to the same thing: a set having a higher order of infinity than the rationals. It is called the linear or arithmetic continuum and is uncountably infinite.

Before even arriving at the point where the Dedekind and Cauchy constructions can be employed, it is necessary to first build up the rationals from the natural numbers. The latter, however, demands use of arithmetic operations that may not make sense with nonquantifiable objects. Nevertheless, it is still possible to obtain a set whose order of infinity is at least as high as that of the linear continuum independently of the measurement issue, for the power set (the class of all subsets) of any countably infinite set is, in fact, uncountable. Although it remains a matter of conjecture as to whether the order of infinity of both sets is identical, it is known that the order of infinity of such a power set cannot be less than that of the linear continuum. Hence the only thing needed to secure an uncountably infinite set is a countably infinite collection of objects. Neither ordinal nor interval measurement is required. Thus the problem of constructing countably and uncountably infinite sets with arithmomorphically defined and not necessarily quantifiable elements reduces to the specification of a successor function.

At first glance this unfortunate result may seem difficult to live with. In the absence of numerical scales the obstacles to be overcome in the construction of infinite sets are formidable indeed. By what means can a successor function over a collection of, say, discretely distinct cultures be defined? Surprisingly, perhaps, the escape lies in that these kinds of questions turn out to be irrelevant. As will become clear momentarily, it is not necessary for the conduct of analysis actually to be able to describe how infinite sets are formed.

Historically, the linear continuum arose as the product of an effort to give useful and mathematically accurate meaning to the worldly continuum as it was perceived by human intuition (Hobson [16, pp. 53–5]). To formalize the idea that a body in continuous motion passes through every "position" on its path, one could replace the inexactness of "position" by the exactness of "indivisible point" (real number). These sharply delineated units could be strung up alongside each other, leaving no gaps in between. It would then become possible to say at any moment precisely where the moving body was. Thus a standard for what was thought to be continuous would be provided and, at the same time, the intuitive continuum could be given a rigorous and exactly defined (arithmomorphic) representation.

By the very nature of the abstracting process, however, important properties of the intuitive continuum are lost in this representation.

Also, the relationship between the intuitive continuum and its representation, namely, the arithmomorphic linear continuum, is not very clear. As Aristotle held and Hobson, an eminent mathematician, admitted, human perceptions of reality preclude a continuity from being composed of indivisible points (Aristotle [3, 231^a lines 24-5, 231^b lines 15-16], Hobson [16, p. 89]). A continuous line can only be broken up into things that themselves are infinitely divisible. It would not come as a shock, therefore, if someday it were "discovered" that the linear continuum did, in fact, contain "holes." A "larger" continuum made up of "smaller" points would then replace the linear continuum as the arithmomorphic representation of the intuitive continuum. Such a transition would not take place until the uses to which numbers are put require a smaller indivisible unit than the reals (Georgescu-Roegen [13, p. 368]).

And what is the intuitive continuum? According to Georgescu-Roegen [13, p. 66]), it is one of those special concepts "about which we can discourse... without being able to define." That no one has yet provided a definition does not refute its validity. It was a perfectly sound concept before Dedekind and Cantor abstracted the linear continuum, and the fact of this abstraction can in no way diminish its reliability. One view of the intuitive continuum is as follows: It is not composed of discretely distinct, indivisible units, but rather of "dialectically overlapping elements leaving no holes" (Georgescu-Roegen [13, p. 67]).

Thus in the absence of measurement, infinity can be understood with reference to the intuitive continuum: Both countably infinite and uncountably infinite sets of discretely distinct objects are extractable from it. To illustrate, a theoretical discussion may, for one reason or another, employ a linearly ordered set of nonquantifiable objects. It may also postulate a "least" and a "greatest" element, that is, two extremes or end points (with respect to the ordering) taken as Weberian ideal types. All other nonideal entities fall in between (see, e.g., Rudner [22, pp. 32-8, 54-6]). To ensure an infinity in such a context, it is only necessary to suppose that (again, with respect to the ordering) between every pair of points there lies a third. (According to Section 2.2, this structure by itself does not imply the existence of either ordinal or interval scales.) In any case, although human limitations may prevent the description of more than a finite number of, say, cultures, for the purposes of arithmomorphic simile, no difficulty exists in thinking of the variable "culture" as ranging over an infinite set derived from the intuitive, cultural continuum. The actual method of construction of this arithmomorphic abstraction is totally inconsequential.

Infinite collections of discretely distinct, nonquantifiable objects appear repeatedly throughout scholarly literature. Accompanied by neither explanation nor apology, the only way to interpret these sets is as intuitive continua or arithmomorphic extractions from them. Apter [2, p. 34], for example, speaks of a "continuum of political systems." Downs postulates a continuum of variation between a free market economy and one subject to full government control. A similar continuity is supposed for the possible positions a political party might take on any issue (Downs [8, pp. 116, 132]). Miner [18] provides an extensive discussion of the "folk-urban continuum." And the notion (from the comparative economic systems literature) that the U.S. and Soviet economies might be "converging" suggests the possibility of an infinity of intermediate economic systems (see, e.g., Prybyla [21, Part V] and Bornstein [5, Chs. 28-30]).

Several illustrations emerge in like manner from the idea of continuous evolution. Spencer's definition has been applied to social development by Durkheim [9, pp. 41, 262] and [10, p. 105] and to cultural progression by Carneiro [7, p. 835]. Continuous change is also suggested by Bolinger's [4, p. 87] discussion of evolving languages and by Heilbroner [15, pp. 624, 630] in the context of economic development (see also Heilbroner's map [15, on the inside, back cover]). The fact that evolution is thought of as continuous necessarily implies the existence of a continuum in the minds of these writers. Thus social, cultural, linguistic, and economic continua are fundamental to this literature.

Georgescu-Roegen [12, p. 243] has also pointed to several instances of nonquantifiable infinity. One consists of qualities of human expectations. An expectation is a state of mind in reference to any (usually) uncertain matter. It depends on the individual, the evidence available to him, and on an assertive proposition concerning the matter in question. Georgescu-Roegen argues that the class of all expectations is larger than the linear continuum. A similar conclusion is reached for collections of qualities in general:

There is no reason why the cardinal power of all of the qualities we can think of even in a simple set-up should not exceed that of the arithmetical continuum... In other words, the manifold of our thoughts differs from the arithmetical continuum not only by its indivisible continuity but also by its dimensionality. (Georgescu-Roegen [13, p. 76])

Note that the continuua in these latter two examples do not (as in some previous cases) have their constituent points lined up between two extremes. A third illustration of this sort is the collection of all possible inkblots.

Granted, then, that infinite sets of distinctly discrete objects are capable of conception and use, the problem of defining relations (Section 3.1) between them remains. When numbers are available, relations are often characterized by articulating a rule: "square each number and add it to 10," illustrates the idea. But in the absence of measurement, how could anyone provide a rule for relating, say, an arithmomorphic continuum of cultures to one of economies when there is no way of knowing anything about most of the "points" in either? The only recourse would seem to be to list all the ordered pairs of the relations involved. Once again, the finiteness of human experience utterly stymies any attempt to write down a complete description. Hence an actual specification of relations between nonquantifiable, infinite sets is not possible.

But as is the case with the arithmomorphic continuum, cogent analysis does not require complete specification. In the same intuitive way that nonscalable continua arise, a relation between nonquantifiable infinite sets can be conceived, although only a finite portion of it is ever capable of recognition. The additional supposition that these relations exhibit special properties (e.g., those developed in Chapter 5) poses no further difficulty unless facts are identified to the contrary. Furthermore, it is also clear that a lack of full description of postulated relations has not prevented scholars from making good and reasonable use of them. That is, in context, many of the previous examples of uncalibrated continua appear in such relations. A specific illustration is given by, say, equation (8.1-1) of the next chapter. It is extracted from Apter [2] and expresses a functional relation between two nonquantifiable variables that Apter asserts is reciprocal (Section 3.1) and whose domain and range, although not explicitly stated, are most likely taken by him to be infinite. Thus even without measurement, the properties of incompletely delineated relations, along with the relations themselves, have customarily played a role in social science.

The point, of course, is that regardless of whether relations can be explicitly defined in their entirety, a claim of occurrence of relations (and functions) between nonquantifiable, infinite sets as well as particular properties these relations might exhibit are perfectly acceptable hypotheses for the conduct of inquiry. This conclusion should not be surprising: Similar approaches are quite common throughout standard, quantifiable analysis. To mention but one example, when talking of demand "curves" or functions, economists express a continuum of quantities in relation to a continuum of prices in spite of the fact that, in practice, only a finite number of each can ever be observed. Even if the relation is defined by explicating a rule, how are economists to know if they have the right rule? An infinite number of distinct curves can always be drawn through any finite number of points. The assumption here of a particular rule rests on the same foundation as the assumption of an incompletely described relation between two nonquantifiable, infinite sets – the only difference is that one is more extensively specified than the other.

The comparison is worth amplification. Suppose a finite number of "points" have been observed. In the scalable world, gaps between observations are often filled by interpolation (e.g., postulating a single straight line or convex surface on which all points lie). However, because there is no way of knowing the true missing points, any interpolation is necessarily arbitrary. Certainly interpolation permits more complex and sophisticated theory than would otherwise be allowed. But to the extent that a particular theory is based on specific interpolations, it inherits the latter's capriciousness. The corresponding technique in the absence of measurement confronts the same obstacle. To fill in the missing points by supposing that a relation with certain properties exists, even if it cannot be exhaustively described, enhances theory construction. Nevertheless, caprice still enters to the degree that the theory depends on the unobserved parts of the relation and their properties. Except for numbers and the power they provide, analysis with and without measurement, approach incompleteness in essentially the same way.

Thus unless finiteness is explicitly demanded, the propositions of Chapter 5 are relevant for both finite and infinite sets of variable values. In either case, to use these results requires the same epistemological base upon which ordinary numerical analysis rests. As is customary, subsequent applications in Part II will not indicate the "size" (cardinality) of individual sets except when necessary for the correctness of argument.

7.3   Change

When a phenomenon can be measured, change through time is easy to analyze and observe. By comparing scale values of two distinct time periods one can clearly detect the occurrence of change, at least in principle. Often the direction, magnitude, and rate of change (the latter two being meaningful only in terms of numbers) are studied. Because change is so frequently thought of as "quantifiable change," the present discussion focuses on those aspects that do not rely on calibration. Nevertheless, much of what is said also applies to the numerical world.

The following is intended to be sketchy and brief. The reader interested in detailed argument is referred to Georgescu-Roegen [13].

Consider, first, the notion of "time." As far as human capacity to sense Nature is concerned, there is no such thing as an "instant of time." Time is, rather, a series of imprecise and overlapping durations in which the future becomes an inexactly felt duration and then slips into the past. It is a dialectical concept (Georgescu-Roegen [13, pp. 69–72]). The idea of instants of time (or discretely distinct time periods) all lined up one after the other is an arithmomorphic abstraction. It permits identification of the linear continuum as the standard reference for keeping track of the movement of time. The use of differential and difference equations in quantifiable analysis as well as periodic relations when measurement is impossible (Chapters 5 and 6) depend on it. But the fact that the abstraction differs fundamentally from the dialectical conception cannot be ignored.

Time and change are tightly interwoven; one can hardly be discerned without the other. Furthermore, change, unobservable at an instant of time, is capable of detection only over durations. Although the distinction between sameness and qualitative change rests ultimately in the beholder, judgments as to whether a change has actually occurred turn on the relation of the thing in question to "its other." Change can only appear in contrast to the environment in which it is set. And because there are no clear-cut boundaries delineating where it begins and ends, qualitative change, like time, is dialectical in character (Georgescu-Roegen [13, pp. 63, 69]).

One result of change is novelty or newness. Novelty can be classified according to the manner in which it is detected. Some phenomena are discovered by deductions from existing knowledge. Future eclipses of the sun fall into this category. Others cannot be known until they are seen. Without divine guidance, no Martian could have prophesied the emergence of human beings on the face of the earth. Nor could man's arrival have upset any of Nature's laws familiar to the Martian at the time. Still a third kind of phenomenon defies prediction, even after the appearance of one or more observations. "From the same basis...a multiplicity of novel forms may spring up" (Georgescu-Roegen [13, p. 117]), and the particular form to arise is unknowable beforehand. Thus it is impossible to determine in advance what type of society a given national class of people will mold, even though considerable information concerning the biological, social, and political properties of human beings as well the emergence of many previous societies is available.

Evolution is the historical development of irrevocable change (Georgescu-Roegen [13, p. 198]). It is quite possible that there are no universal laws of evolution as such, but rather that distinct classes of phenomena change according to their own peculiar laws. Reflecting the second and third kinds of novelty previously described, evolutionary disorderliness appears because the repeated instances in which A is

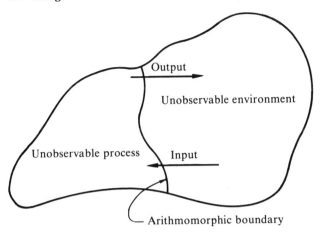

Figure 7-1

observed to follow *B* occur, in actuality, for only a single category of events.

Regardless of whether interest centers on novelty or evolution, change remains a dialectical idea. But dialectical analysis, remember, may still employ arithmomorphic simile to illustrate, clarify, and check its content. Thus a way of abstracting arithmomorphic counterparts from dialectical change is needed. One approach, which uses the notion of process (Georgescu-Roegen [13, pp. 211–15]), is schematically diagrammed in Figure 7-1.

Suppose reality can be divided into two pieces: the process in question and its environment. All occurrences in reality are either a part of one or the other. Assume further that there is an arithmomorphic boundary between them. The boundary sets the (finite) time duration of the process and, at any moment, also serves to contrast the process against its environment. Events within the process as well as those without (i.e., in the environment) remain hidden from view. Only objects crossing the arithmomorphic boundary are capable of observation. Thus the arithmomorphic description of what happens in any process consists of the record of boundary crossings. Elements crossing from the environment to the process may be called inputs; those crossing in the opposite direction are outputs.

The arithmomorphic description of a process therefore reduces to a general system as described in Section 1.4 and Chapter 6. (Recall especially the "black box" of Section 1.4.) It follows that because they are special types of systems (Section 6.1), periodic or (when measurement is possible) differential equation models may serve as arithmomorphic similes for the dialectical analysis of change.

7.4   The geometry of space

The first three sections of this chapter have dealt with particular problems in achieving understanding from scientific analysis. Questions concerning the nature of concepts, the construction of infinite sets, and the interpretation of change have been discussed. Now it is worth stepping back from isolated specifics to look at the setting as a whole in which understanding takes place.

Understanding, of course, can occur on many levels. In its more primitive form it is mostly descriptive and involves little interrelationship between concepts. Abstraction is possible but severely limited. For example, the notion "height of a tree" (ordinally measured by observing one tree taller than another) may be perceived as having nothing in common with the concept "distance between villages" (also ordinally measured perhaps in terms of walking time). Both concepts require some disassociation from reality. But deeper understanding is reached through greater abstraction. That is, the more abstract notion of "length" lies behind both these concepts and provides a link between them: Each can be measured in the same units on the same scale. It is the relatively sophisticated understanding provided by significant abstraction that is of interest here.

In reference to scientific inquiry the term "space" has at least two distinct meanings. First is real or actual space in which events happen and phenomena occur: A society evolves, a government raises taxes, magnets attract, and the sun sets. It is in real space that human beings live. It is in real space that they interact with others and with their physical, social, and cultural environment. And it is real space that they, through their senses, are able to observe. But as already indicated, man obtains understanding by abstracting from real space. The fulfillment of this process requires that he create a second, abstract space for his thoughts. Assumptions, propositions, theories, models, and the like being mental constructs, exist in abstract space – not in the real world. Depending on the discreteness with which relevant concepts can be described, abstract space is either arithmomorphic or dialectical (Section 7.1).

Because numbers are abstractions, real space is not, by itself, quantitative. However, sometimes it may be interpretable in terms of a quantifiable abstract space. It is also possible that certain facets of the abstract space could be scalable while others are not. Even within scalable parts, both ordinal and interval calibrations could arise. There are obviously a multitude of possibilities. Naturally, the particular abstract space employed will depend on the segment of real space that is involved, along with the purpose and scope of the inquiry. To illustrate, questions about physical phenomena, say, the tides, are questions about real physical space. The relevant abstract space is (abstract) four-dimensional physical space based on three quantifiable spatial location coordinates and quantifiable time. The so-called real space of colors can be analyzed in an abstract three-dimensional space of numerical intensities (see, e.g., Aleksandrov [1, pp. 151–3]). And Parson's mostly non-quantifiable abstract space of social action [20] reflects the real space of social activity.

One of the central themes of earlier chapters has been that abstract arithmomorphic space may be considered mathematical in character. Hence ideas are represented symbolically and subject to the rules of logic. Any assumption may be made as long as it is not known to contradict other assertions or properties of the abstract space; and any proposition is valid as long as it can be logically proved. To say that something exists in abstract space, therefore, is quite different from claiming its existence in real space. That is, in the former case existence may be either proved or, provided no contradictions are introduced, assumed. In the latter, existence can only be certified by observation in the real world (Hahn [14, pp. 1600–5]). Thus, for example, although the notion of a finite or infinite set of objects is an element of abstract space, only finite numbers of the objects themselves can be seen in real space.

Many of the important properties of abstract (arithmomorphic) space may be described by the adjective "geometric." Objects, events, phenomena, or states serve to determine the points of such a space. A "figure" is an arbitrary aggregate of points. The geometry of the space consists of those spatial relations (e.g., congruence, similarity, distance, continuity, etc.) between figures and points singled out for the purpose of analysis (Aleksandrov [1, p. 155]). In this sense a topological space may also be viewed as a geometric space in which the spatial relation of neighborhood of one point to a set of points is defined. Among other things, the latter relation may be used to express the idea that a point can lie arbitrarily close to a set.

The most common abstract space appearing in analysis today is Euclidean space. It consists of a collection of quantifiable objects together with axioms that elucidate various spatial relations (see, e.g., Aleksandrov [1, pp. 122–4, 167]). For example, one of the more famous axioms asserts that through a point not lying on a given line, only one parallel to the given line can be drawn. Distance between points $x = (x_1, \ldots, x_n)$ and $y = (y_1, \ldots, y_n)$ in the space is defined from the Pythagorean theorem by

$$(7.4\text{-}1) \quad \left[\sum_{i=1}^{n} (x_i - y_i)^2 \right]^{1/2}$$

and this formula does not depend on the particular points x and y under consideration. The geometric properties of Euclidean space are known to every high school student: The sum of the angles of a triangle is 180°, the ratio of the circumference of a circle to its radius is 2π, and so on.

It is not surprising that Euclidean space has emerged as the most important abstract space in current use. Euclidean properties have evolved through many centuries of painstaking experimentation. They appear as reasonable and fundamental laws of nature that reflect observed features of the real physical space of everyday life. Nevertheless there are serious difficulties with Euclidean space. First of all, it contains lines of arbitrarily long length. It is thus, in Hahn's [14] terminology, a space of infinite extension. But it is questionable if real space, even real physical space, can be associated with this characteristic (Hahn [14, p. 1610]). What precludes the possibility of a real space being viewed as a space of finite extension, that is, a space in which the length of all lines is less than some finite number? Such a property holds for the geodesic lines (the counterpart of lines in Euclidean space) on any three-dimensional sphere.

A more significant challenge to the supremacy of Euclidean space arises in that spheres are also non-Euclidean in other ways. The sum of the angles of a triangle on the surface of a sphere is more than 180°, and the larger the surface area of the triangle is, the greater the discrepancy will be. A similar assertion holds for the ratio of the circumference of a surface circle to its surface radius: In this case the ratio is less than 2π. The intuitive plausibility of Euclidean geometry notwithstanding, it only approximates the geometry on the sphere (and hence on earth) in small areas on the spherical surface.

The importance of these non-Euclidean peculiarities is magnified by the fact that, as a result of the theory of relativity, similar properties have been found to hold in real four-dimensional physical space. Thus the geometry of the real (interstellar) physical world is more like that of a surface in Euclidean space than that of Euclidean space itself. Of course, if analysis is to be useful, these properties must be represented in abstract space. Therefore although Euclidean space may be a valuable approximation of our small earthly world, the plain truth is that it simply does not correspond to reality in the large. Abstract physical space must be supposed to have a form other than Euclidean space. The emergence of this new vision of real space has forced modification of Newtonian laws of mechanics and other propositions in abstract space that were originally conceived in Euclidean terms.

One possible substitute for Euclidean space is called Riemannian space. In general, the space obtained from any smooth surface in Euclidean space is Riemannian. A converse proposition is also valid: Any Riemannian space can always be represented in terms of a surface in Euclidean space of sufficiently large dimensionality (Aleksandrov [1, pp. 166, 168]). Furthermore, the notion of distance in Riemannian space may be viewed as Euclidean distance (7.4-1) corrected for the fact that the two spaces are not identical:

$$(7.4\text{-}2) \quad \left[\sum_{i=1}^{n} (x_i - y_i)^2 \right]^{1/2} + \epsilon$$

where $x = (x_1, \ldots, x_n)$, $y = (y_1, \ldots, y_n)$, ϵ becomes small as x and y move closer (in terms of Euclidean distance) together, and the expression (7.4-2) is dependent on the coordinate system in which it is expressed (Aleksandrov [1, pp. 167, 168]). Thus Riemannian space is approximated by Euclidean space in small regions. The theory of relativity makes use of a variant of Riemannian space as abstract physical space. An alternative approach is based on the ideas of Lobačevskiĭ (Aleksandrov [1, pp. 101–22, 188]).

The meaning of the development of the theory of relativity for the present discussion is clear: Understanding is profoundly affected by the abstract space in which ideas and relationships are organized and expressed. It is exceedingly important therefore that abstract space at least reflect all of the known relevant properties of real space as completely as possible. This is not to suggest that only one abstract space is ever consistent with real space: There will usually be many ways of looking at the same thing. But it does ensure that the error (above and beyond that by which any particular analysis might be flawed) introduced by the unknown inaccuracies of the abstract space itself is held to a minimum.

Although the preceding argument has been stated primarily with respect to physical space, it is surely applicable outside the realms of physics and astronomy. Certainly its conclusion applies to all inquiry. Regardless of the specific problem under consideration, the abstract space in which it is analyzed must reflect all relevant properties of the appropriate segment of real space. If the relevant characteristics of real space are unknown, efforts ought to be undertaken to discover them. Should the abstract space be assumed quantifiable? If so, should it be Euclidean, Riemannian, or take some other form? Ought it be of finite or infinite extension?[2] In the nonquantifiable case or when certain facets of the abstract space are scalable while others are not, what should its geometric properties be? Without answers to these questions the chance of faulty understanding increases. Moreover, as Hofstadter [17, pp. 611–13] has suggested, the proper choice of an abstract space and its properties may be crucial to the solution of many real problems.

In the nonphysical sciences at least three kinds of abstract spaces implicitly, if not explicitly, have appeared. The first, Euclidean space (or some generalization or variant of it), is frequently used whenever all elements seem to have appropriate numerical characteristics. The second, nonquantifiable space, has seldom been geometrically specified to any significant extent in any context. (One method of geometric specification using topologies and uniformities has been proposed in Sections 3.2 and 3.3.) The third type of space, composed of both scalable and nonscalable segments is often assumed Euclidean in its quantifiable part, with little mention made of the remainder. In all three cases not much thought has gone into determining the properties of real space that have to be geometrically incorporated in abstract space. In many instances the relevance of the abstract space employed is an open question.

References

1. Aleksandrov, A. D., "Non-Euclidean Geometry," in A. D. Aleksandrov, A. N. Kolmogorov, and M. A. Lavrent'ev, eds. and K. Hirsch, trans., *Mathematics, Its Content, Methods, and Meaning,* vol. 3 (Cambridge, Mass.: MIT Press, 1963), pp. 97–189.

2. Apter, D. E., *The Politics of Modernization* (Chicago: University of Chicago Press, 1965).

3. Aristotle, *Physics,* in W. D. Ross, ed., *The Works of Aristotle,* vol. II (Oxford: Oxford University Press, 1930).

4. Bolinger, D., *Aspects of Language* (New York: Harcourt Brace and World, 1968).

5. Bornstein, M., *Comparative Economic Systems: Models and Cases* (Homewood, Ill.: Irwin, 1974).

6. Bridgeman, P. W., *The Intelligent Individual and Society* (New York: Macmillan, 1938).

---

[2] Note that the property of finite extension does not preclude the existence (in abstract space) of infinite sets of points. This is illustrated by any spherical surface in three-dimensional Euclidean space.

References   155

7. Carneiro, R. L., "Scale Analysis, Evolutionary Sequences, and the Rating of Cultures," in R. Naroll and R. Cohen, eds., *A Handbook of Method in Cultural Anthropology* (Garden City, N.Y.: Natural History Press, 1970), pp. 834–71.

8. Downs, A., *An Economic Theory of Democracy* (New York: Harper, 1957).

9. Durkheim, E., *The Division of Labor in Society,* G. Simpson, trans. (Glencoe, Ill.: Free Press, 1933).

10. Durkheim, E., *The Rules of Sociological Method,* 8th ed., S. A. Solway and J. H. Mueller, trans. (New York: Free Press, 1938).

11. Georgescu-Roegen, N., "Mathematical Proofs of the Breakdown of Capitalism," in *Analytical Economics* (Cambridge, Mass.: Harvard University Press, 1966), pp. 398–415.

12. Georgescu-Roegen, N., "The Nature of Expectation and Uncertainty," in *Analytical Economics* (Cambridge, Mass.: Harvard University Press, 1966), pp. 241–75.

13. Georgescu-Roegen, N., *The Entropy Law and the Economic Process* (Cambridge, Mass.: Harvard University Press, 1971).

14. Hahn, H., "Infinity," in J. R. Newman, ed., *The World of Mathematics,* vol. 3 (New York: Simon & Schuster, 1956), pp. 1593–611.

15. Heilbroner, R. L., *The Economic Problem* (Englewood Cliffs, N.J.: Prentice-Hall, 1968).

16. Hobson, E. W., *The Theory of Functions of a Real Variable and the Theory of Fourier's Series,* vol. 1 (New York: Dover, 1957).

17. Hofstadter, D. R., *Gödel, Escher, Bach: An Eternal Golden Braid* (New York: Basic Books, 1979).

18. Miner, H., "The Folk-Urban Continuum," in P. K. Hatt and A. J. Reiss, Jr., eds., *Cities and Society,* 2nd ed. (New York: Free Press, 1957), pp. 22–34.

19. Morishima, M., *Marx's Economics* (Cambridge: Cambridge University Press, 1973).

20. Parsons, T., *The Structure of Social Action,* vols. 1, 2 (New York: Free Press, 1968).

21. Prybyla, J. S., *Comparative Economic Systems* (New York: Appleton-Century-Crofts, 1969).

22. Rudner, R. S., *Philosophy of Social Science* (Englewood Cliffs, N. J.: Prentice-Hall, 1966).

23. Russell, B., "Knowledge by Acquaintance and Knowledge by Description," *Mysticism and Logic and Other Essays* (London: Allen & Unwin, 1959), pp. 209–32.

24. Sorokin, P. A., *Fads and Foibles in Modern Sociology and Related Sciences* (Chicago: Henry Regnery, 1956).

25. Ward, B., *What's Wrong with Economics* (New York: Basic Books, 1972).

26. Wilder, R. L., *Introduction to the Foundations of Mathematics,* 2nd ed. (New York: Wiley, 1965).

Applications to theoretical problems

Prologue

Part II is concerned solely with the application of the methodology developed in Part I to selected theoretical discussions. The static, simultaneous relations model is used in Chapter 8 to distinguish between political structure and political system by thinking of the former as a system of simultaneous relations and the latter as a solution of it. In Chapter 9 a planner's view of the making of sequential decisions by society's decision-making units is modeled with a system of periodic relations. Time paths are examined with respect to the logic of their potential for manipulation by the planner. Chapter 10 again utilizes a system of simultaneous relations to describe the general structure of society. Society itself is defined as a solution of the system dependent on certain parameter values. Change over time also occurs as parameters modulate according to specific periodic relations.

It should be emphasized that in all three cases, claims of originality are strictly limited. No outstanding problem is solved, no conclusion is extended, no new proposition is proved, and no new question is raised in any of the fields that these chapters represent. In fact, practically all approaches, concepts, hypotheses, and propositions are lifted directly from the references cited. Thus the models presented are at least as deficient as the original sources. Nevertheless, the contribution of these chapters is to show how the methodology of Part I can be applied to existing ideas. The result is an infusion of fresh rigor, precision, and mathematical-type argument into work that has already been completed. It is hoped that this will lead eventually to solutions for problems not yet resolved, extensions of old conclusions, proofs of new propositions, and the raising of new questions. Here, however, it is enough to illustrate the employment of analyis without measurement in the theoretical modeling of real phenomena.

Chapter 11 is somewhat more ambitious. It deals with the social interactions of individuals within a firm and their impact on the firm's efficiency (Pareto optimality) and profitability. The chapter is a reproduction of a paper published elsewhere and provides a modest example of new analytical structures and propositions that are possible in the absence of measurement. The basic model is a simultaneous relations system.

159

Upon perusal of the chapters of Part II, the reader will find that many of the results of Part I are not directly employed. In most cases only certain propositions of Section 3.2 and Chapter 5 are needed. This should not be surprising. After all, ideas from set theory, algebra, systems theory, and so on constitute the foundation on which much formal inquiry rests. The same basis also supports Section 3.2 and Chapter 5. Thus Part I is concerned with developing a broad methodological setting in which analysis without measurement can take place. To investigate any particular phenomenon, one reaches into this background solely for those specific analytical techniques that are relevant for the purpose at hand. All else is usually ignored. The reader will discover further that Chapter 11 is on a higher intellectual level than Chapters 8 to 10. Although the primary purpose of the latter is merely to give some insight into the construction of models in the absence of measurement, that of Chapter 11 is to show how scientific investigation can be pursued within such models once they are actually built.

CHAPTER 8

Political systems

Political life, according to Easton [3], is a "system of behavior." At the same time that its elements are interacting with each other, the system as a whole is influenced by and exerts pressure on its environment. Stress is constantly arising within the system and out of its surroundings, and efforts to deal with it result in parametric and even structural variation. The ability of the system to survive depends on the kind of information feedback it receives from its environment, for this is the only channel through which political decision makers can discover which parametric and structural changes are necessary.

More precisely, a political system is a collection of certain kinds of human interactions. These are social in nature and involve both individuals and groups. The distinguishing feature of political interactions is that they are directed toward the authoritative allocation of things that are considered of value within society. Authoritative allocations are accomplished, for example, by physically taking away valued possessions, erecting barriers to prevent their procurement, and providing some individuals or groups with the means for their acquisition. The allocations are authoritative in that individuals and groups consider themselves bound by them. Observing that political interactions as described here appear in many parapolitical groups (such as the family, business firms, and religious and social groups), Easton reserves the term "political system" only for those sets of interactions that are relevant for allocating valued things to a society as a whole.

Although this chapter treats the concept of a political system in a grosser way, it is quite similar in method and spirit to Easton's view. Rather than emphasizing collections of allocative interactions, political systems are taken to be the outputs of a more general system of different interactions, called the political structure. Political systems are still, to be sure, systems, but the collections of interactions Easton uses to characterize them are not the primary ones of interest here. Instead, the interactions of the political structure are the focal point; and these, in turn, produce the interactions Easton designates as a political system.

An advantage of such an approach is that it easily permits distinctions between political elements that are common to all societies and those peculiar to each. Given a political structure, the political system may

161

vary without necessitating revision in the basic definition. Many different kinds of political systems may, therefore, be analyzed within the same structural framework. Furthermore, by obtaining knowledge of structure and parameters, it becomes possible to predict (assuming that the structure remains relevant) the type of political system that should emerge from any particular society.

The analysis is presented in a formal, mathematical way. This is desirable for several reasons: Precision is added to definitions of concepts, statements of propositions, and proofs. The structure of argument becomes more transparent and unnecessary elements, such as unused assumptions are less difficult to detect. Finally, the logical consistency of models is openly exposed and hence easily examined. The approach used here would be fully recognizable as a standard mathematical treatment were it not for the fact that none of the variables is capable of measurement in the usual sense (see Section 2.2). Thus it is natural to ask in what ways can analysis proceed and propositions be checked against reality. A theoretical technique, however, has already been developed in Part I; references to it are provided subsequently. The empirical issue – that is, the testing of nonquantifiable hypotheses – is postponed to Part III.

Discussion begins by defining political structure as a system of simultaneous equations or relations among particular variables (see Chapter 5). Political system is then introduced as a solution of the political structure that is dependent on parameter values. When solutions do not exist the possibility of cycles of political systems arises. No effort is made to argue that the variables and relations chosen are in any sense "correct" or reflect the views of large numbers of political scientists. The specific model that is presented is based on Apter [1]. However, it is merely intended as an illustration of a general, analytical technique that is applicable in a wide variety of circumstances.[1]

It should also be emphasized that neither the importance nor significance of Apter's work is in question. But by not paying scrupulous attention to formal considerations, Apter leaves himself open to the possibility of both contradictions and incompletely specified structures. Certain relations may logically be incapable of holding in force simultaneously and the structure of his system may be insufficient to support his argument. The following material is extracted from a small portion of Apter's study so as to illustrate and resolve these issues and is not

---

[1] An earlier version of this model [4] has been used to illustrate the notion of logical consistency or completeness. It is revised here so as to simplify argument, exemplify the internal causality of Section 6.2, and adhere more faithfully to Apter's original presentation.

intended as a comment on the consistency and completeness of his entire volume.

8.1 Political structure

Before describing relations of the political structure, consider first the variables on which they are based. As a start take ideology. There is, of course, no known way to describe ideologies numerically so that numbers assigned to different ideologies can be manipulated (i.e., added, multiplied, etc.) with the same meaning as that possessed by ordinary computation. What, for example, can the sum of numbers assigned to ideologies mean? But it is still possible to give a verbal description of any particular ideology which distinguishes it from everything else. Let $\mathcal{I}$ be the set containing all such descriptions. In spite of the fact that only a finite number of ideologies are ever capable of delineation, $\mathcal{I}$ may still be regarded as either finite or infinite (Section 7.2). The variable "ideology" can now be characterized as that variable that assumes as values those and only those elements of the set $\mathcal{I}$. Denote the ideology variable by the symbol I.

This is a perfectly general way of obtaining nonquantifiable variables and is used extensively here. The set of variable values is initially identified verbally and the variable itself is defined as that which ranges over the specified value set. In presenting the remaining variables, it is implicitly assumed that such a procedure has been executed, although only an intuitive description of each variable is provided. Thus v is to represent values and goals of society; the value set defining v contains all admissible lists (of varying lengths) of possible values and goals. To carry out their responsibilities, maintain authority, and operate efficiently, all governments use some sort of coercion, which is denoted by c. Information, such as the bounds within which the public will accept government action, is needed by any government to resolve problems. This comes from various sources, including the specific groups to which the government considers itself to be accountable. Suppose z varies over types and quantities of information flowing between government and those governed.

Government policies are made and implemented in response to particular situations. A situation, Y, is a comprehensive statement of a circumstance in which government and society may find themselves. One situation, for example, might include the threat of war with another country, high domestic unemployment, and considerable pressure from the agricultural community for financial aid. Generally there are many policies with which the government may respond to a given situation.

The variable r symbolizes a list of policies – one for every conceivable situation. Thus each value for r is a complete program for meeting all possible contingencies. Finally, let d be patterns and processes for making authoritative decisions; a, ways in which governments may be held accountable to groups outside itself; and Q, the psychological needs, values, and cognitions (perceptions of reality) of all individuals in society (see Section 10.1).

The first part of the political structure to be considered is a functional relation between coercion and information. Apter [1, p. 238] believes it is reciprocal: Greater coercion (defined in terms of some ordering) corresponds to less information and conversely. (See Section 3.1 for a general definition of reciprocal functional relations.) But whatever the form, it may be written symbolically as

$$(8.1\text{-}1) \quad c = f^1(z)$$

Equation (8.1-1) means that to each value of z, the relation f^1 assigns a unique value of c. (Apter, of course, neither uses this notation nor presents his argument symbolically.) The property of being reciprocally related, if true, is naturally expressed in terms of this correspondence. Note an (external) causal direction (Section 6.2.1) is implied by placing c on the left side of the equation and z in the brackets following f^1. Although (8.1-1) says something different from

$$z = g(c)$$

it does not matter here whether f^1 or g is used. The former is arbitrarily chosen. At the theoretical level it is enough merely to assume that (8.1-1) exists; on the empirical plane it becomes necessary to determine if evidence for it can actually be found in reality (see Part III).

A second functional relation is assumed to exist between decision making and accountability:

$$d = f^2(a)$$

Here, again, Apter [1, p. 244] argues for reciprocity between d and a.

These same variables are also involved in more complex relations, namely,

$$c = f^3(a, d), \qquad z = f^4(a, d)$$

Apter [1, p. 244] also suggests a special form for f^3 and f^4, but it is not necessary to pursue his description here.

Three further relations complete the picture (these are in part also suggested by Apter [1, pp. 250–2]):

$$r = f^5(v, c, z, I, Y)$$

$$v = f^6(r, I)$$

$$I = f^7(v, Q)$$

Their meaning and verbal interpretation are analogous to those of previous equations. The middle one, for example, asserts the existence of a functional relation f^6 among values and goals of society, government policies, and ideologies. The precise form of these relations is unimportant for present purposes.

Thus the political structure consists of the seven equations,

$$(8.1\text{-}2) \quad c = f^1(z), \quad d = f^2(a)$$

$$c = f^3(a, d), \quad z = f^4(a, d)$$

$$r = f^5(v, c, z, I, Y)$$

$$v = f^6(r, I), \quad I = f^7(v, Q)$$

in nine variables: c, z, d, a, r, v, I, Y, and Q. The notion of political system is now characterized within this framework.

8.2   Solutions and cycles

Before describing a political system, it is necessary to decide which variables, if any, are to be taken as parameters, that is, determined by forces wholly outside and independent of the political structure. There are two parameters here: general situations, Y, and the needs, values, and cognitions of all members of society, Q. It is assumed that at any point in time, values for Y and Q are given; values for the remaining variables are yet to be found. Note that the political structure (8.1-2) has now been reduced to a system of seven equations in seven variables.

A political system may be defined as a specification of one variable value for each variable. The possible candidates for political systems depend on the value sets over which the variables range. Any combination of elements, one taken from each value set, depicts a political system. Thus political system itself may be thought of as a variable; it is written (c, z, d, a, r, v, I) and abbreviated by the symbol, p; that is,

$$p = (c, z, d, a, r, v, I)$$

So far only definitions of variables and relations among them have been identified. But at this point two analytic questions arise. The first, concerned with the internal or logical consistency of the political structure, inquires if it is possible to conceive of all relations of (8.1-2) in force simultaneously. Might not the satisfaction of some subset of equations preclude or contradict the satisfaction of others? The second issue is closely related (in fact, it is mathematically equivalent) to the first: Does the political structure determine political systems in the sense that designating parameter values requires acceptance of certain political systems as the only ones consistent with the simultaneous occurrence of the equations of (8.1-2)? In other words, does (8.1-2) have solutions – are there values for the variables that satisfy all equations simultaneously? If so, the model is clearly internally consistent. Furthermore, when solutions do, in fact, exist it is also useful to know if they are unique, that is, if each pair of parameter values generates through (8.1-2) a single political system.

One answer to these questions has been provided by Section 5.1 under the conditions that (i) the number of variables and equations is identical, and (ii) $f^1, \ldots, f^7$, and certain auxiliary relations have appropriate inverses. These conditions imply that a solution of (8.1-2) exists and is unique. With the designation of Y and Q as parameters, (8.1-2) already satisfies condition (i). For the moment, making the additional hypothesis (ii) thus ensures the political structure is internally consistent and determines a unique political system. In words parallel to those describing the tabular example on pages 92–3 of Section 5.1, from the variety of possible values of the component variables making up political systems, all but one value for each variable are eliminated by the simultaneous occurrence of the relations of the political structure.

As also pointed out in Section 5.1, the solution of (8.1-2) depends on the given values of parameters Y and Q. Generally speaking, changes in parameters alter solutions. In fact, (8.1-2) defines a new relation between solution values of the variables and given parameter values. This may be expressed as

(8.2-1) $p = \psi(Q, Y)$

where p is the political system that satisfies all equations of (8.1-2) simultaneously. Apter [1, pp. 34–6] suggests that varying parameter values may yield a continuum of political systems ranging from the "reconciliation" to the "mobilization" type. (The notion of continuum in the absence of measurement is discussed in Section 7.2.) Political systems can therefore modulate within a given political structure or, put another way, the same structure can be common to many political systems whose distinguishing features are determined by the nature of the specific parameter values given at the time. Any change in structural relations is reflected in ψ. Once ψ and the parameter values are known, political systems can be predicted as long as the structure remains intact. This particular structure, that is, equation (8.2-1), is embedded in a general model of society in Chapter 10.

It is interesting that the specific example chosen here also illustrates the notion of internal causality as described in Section 6.2.2. Because the first four equations of (8.1-2) constitute a minimal self-contained subsystem of the political structure, once the parameter values are specified a direction of causality from (c, z, d, a) to (r, v, I) is implied.

It may also be useful to point out that economists have, for some time, employed a similar technique to describe the perfectly competitive (Walrasian) economy (see, e.g., Arrow and Hahn [2]). A simultaneous equations model incorporating the assumptions that all consumers maximize utility subject to their budget constraints, that all firms maximize profits, and that supply equals demand in all markets serves as the economic structure. Solutions (called equilibria) are sought because the "real world" is studied in relation to them. Of course, in this context, the ability to measure prices, quantities, and so forth is put to good use, but it is clear that the method of analysis is analogous to that previously described.

Supppose, however, that condition (ii) is violated and hence (8.1-2) need not have solutions. This does not imply a lack of internal consistency. Noncompliance with (ii) merely means that there may be no political system that satisfies all equations simultaneously (i.e., the political structure might not determine any political system); it cannot by itself signify a contradiction between the satisfaction of two or more subsets of the equations of (8.1-2).

To illustrate simply the kind of analysis that can be developed in these circumstances consider a slight modification of Apter's model, namely, the substitution of

$$a = h(z)$$

for f^1. All other relations remain unchanged. This is not the place to argue whether h can be a meaningful part of a political structure. It is only introduced as a pedagogical device.

Given parameter values for Q and Y, think of the modified model as a system (Section 1.4) accepting inputs

$$p^{t-1} = (c^{t-1}, z^{t-1}, d^{t-1}, a^{t-1}, r^{t-1}, v^{t-1}, I^{t-1})$$

and producing outputs

$$p^t = (c^t, z^t, d^t, a^t, r^t, v^t, I^t)$$

where t represents any integer $t = 1, 2, 3, \ldots$ The superscripts t and $t-1$

may be interpreted as denoting time periods or merely used to distinguish between inputs and outputs. The revised model becomes

$$a^t = h(z^{t-1}), \quad d^t = f^2(a^{t-1})$$

$$c^t = f^3(a^{t-1}, d^{t-1}), \quad z^t = f^4(a^{t-1}, d^{t-1})$$

$$r^t = f^5(v^{t-1}, c^{t-1}, z^{t-1}, I^{t-1}, Y)$$

$$v^t = f^6(r^{t-1}, I^{t-1}), \quad I^t = f^7(v^{t-1}, Q)$$

and is abbreviated symbolically by

(8.2-2) $\quad p^t = f(p^{t-1}, Q, Y)$

With an initial political system p^0 specified, repeated application of (8.2-2) generates a sequence of political systems $p^1, p^2, p^3, \ldots$ Note the equations behind (8.2-2) are internally consistent.

When (8.2-2) has a solution it appears as a political system $\bar{p}$ such that

$$\bar{p} = f(\bar{p}, Q, Y)$$

Theorems 5.1–7 and 5.2–5 of Chapter 5 provide conditions, distinct from (i) and (ii) previously cited, under which (8.2-2) must have solutions. But independently of whether solutions exist, (8.2-2) may still generate "cycles" of political systems. That is, in the sequence $p^0, p^1, p^2, \ldots$ there could be a finite number of distinct political systems, and these could repeat themselves over and over again in the same order as the sequence progresses. Such cycles have been studied in Sections 5.2 and 5.3 under the condition that the value sets of all variables contain only a finite number of elements. Thus with or without solutions (but still in the presence of internal consistency) it may be possible to predict political systems in sequence, oscillating among particular types.

The idea of cyclical behavior is not new to the political science literature. Klingberg [5], for example, identifies a cyclical pattern of moods in American foreign policy. Further illustrations analyzed by others, including the swings between liberal and conservative periods, war cycles, and the rise and fall of civilizations are cited by him (Klingberg [5, pp. 260, 261]). More recently, Lenski [6, pp. 59–62] has observed cycles of political evolution, beginning with the seizure of power by a new elite and progressing through the violent suppression of opposition to (in attempting to increase legitimacy) the gradual reduction in the use of force until the regime is overthrown by another elite. Many of these cycles could be viewed as the outcome of a process like that described by (8.2-2). And the construction of this kind of formal structure would be a useful aid in the understanding of the forces operating behind these phenomena.

As a third alternative for obtaining internally consistent structures, (8.2-2) could describe a process in which the outputs p^t are not known with certainty. Given input p^{t-1}, all outputs are possible – each with a designated probability. In such situations, development could proceed along the lines of the theory of Markov chains as demonstrated at the end of Section 5.3.

To summarize, the techniques of analysis proposed here are all based on the construction of internally consistent models. In the first instance, political structures determine political systems as solutions to specified simultaneous equations. One way to accomplish this requires the use of political structures with the same number of relations as variables. Frequently, if there are more equations than variables, the system is "overdetermined" and a solution satisfying all relations cannot exist. The political structure lacks internal consistency. Likewise, if there are fewer equations than variables, it is "underdetermined." Solutions may exist but not uniquely; each class of parameter values will generally correspond to more than one political system. When the system is "exactly determined" (i.e., the number of variables and relations is the same), and when condition (ii) on inverses is also satisfied, the political system is uniquely obtained. In the exactly determined case with (ii) violated, cycles of political systems are a possibility; or if random elements interfere with the specification of an exact system of equations, the Markov approach may be employed. Regardless of the appropriateness of any particular line of argument, however, ignoring questions relating to internal consistency can only leave possible contradictions and underspecifications hidden within its fabric.

References

1. Apter, D. E., *The Politics of Modernization* (Chicago: University of Chicago Press, 1965).
2. Arrow, K. J., and F. H. Hahn, *General Competitive Analysis* (San Francisco: Holden-Day, 1971).
3. Easton, D., *A Framework for Political Analysis* (Englewood Cliffs, N.J.: Prentice-Hall, 1965).
4. Katzner, D. W., "Political Structure and System and the Notion of Logical Completeness," *General Systems,* 4 (1969):169-71.
5. Klingberg, F. L., "The Historical Alternation of Moods in American Foreign Policy," *World Politics,* 4 (1951-2):239-73.
6. Lenski, G. E., *Power and Privilege* (New York: McGraw-Hill, 1966).

CHAPTER 9

Planning

Planning, as defined by Ozbekhan [6], is an activity designed to operate on the present environment for the purpose of changing it into a more desirable state. Individual values determine which states are preferable. Given a particular environment and the configuration of values perpetuating it, fundamental change (i.e., that which creates a distinct future as opposed to an extension of the present) is introduced only through alterations of values. The latter can be varied by individuals alone. If and when specific value changes become socialized and widely accepted, movement from the original state to that implied by the new values is thought of as "progress." Stated in these terms, planning is the "organization of progress."

Ozbekhan also conceives of planning as a system that interacts in relation to another system – the environment. The environmental system takes the output of the planning operation as one of many inputs and produces environmental states. The latter also serve as inputs for planning. In this context the "planning system" is a relation as defined in Chapter 6. It may be considered in a static or dynamic framework and is capable of exhibiting various forms of causality, control, and feedback mechanisms. Ozbekhan endows it with a three-level structure: at the highest level, norms and guidelines are sought and general policy decisions are made; on the middle tier, specific goals are set and strategies devised; at the lowest level, decisions taken on the higher two are made operational and implemented. An example of such a system, in which it is assumed that inputs from the environment enter at each level, is diagrammed in Figure 9-1. Note the planning system appears in a feedback loop (Section 6.3) of the environmental system.

At the operational level a detailed model of the environment is an essential prerequisite. In particular, it is necessary to know which factors are capable of bringing about change, which subset of these can be controlled and manipulated, and how change occurs and in which directions it proceeds. Without this information it would be impossible to determine if a plan is capable of achieving its goals. Harris [3] has made a similar point in another context.

The purpose of what follows is to present the notion of operational planning in a mathematically formal context. This is desirable for many

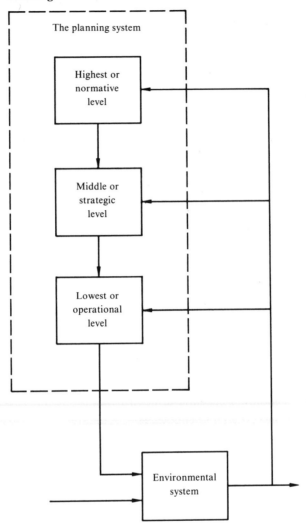

Figure 9-1

reasons. Concepts can be given exact meanings; logical or internal consistency can be easily checked; and assumptions, propositions, and proofs can be precisely formulated. Not only is such accuracy an end in itself but it also tends to make generalizations and unnecessary elements (such as unused assumptions) easier to detect. Thus, for example, the mathematical approach has enabled economists to learn that a complete account of the perfectly competitive microeconomy at equilibrium does not consist of descriptions of all markets. One of the markets can be omitted because it only duplicates information already contained in those remaining.

The demonstration in the preceding example that not all markets are needed to describe equilibrium is based on such facts as the sum of expenditures on all consumable commodities purchased by each consumer must be the same as the amount of money spent. Each of the elements in this statement (expenditures – prices times quantities – and amounts of money) are quantifiable. But to study a society and the means to control it from a planner's point of view requires consideration of many variables that are not, at least at present, capable of measurement. Many standard mathematical tools, therefore, are rendered useless. It makes no sense to add and multiply items that are nonquantifiable. One thing cannot be said to be "larger" than another nor can two elements be called "close together" in the usual way. Nevertheless, as has been described in Part I, it is still possible to define closeness, to talk about relations both between variables and over time, to manipulate these relations, and to use them to define and examine the properties of important concepts. These techniques will be applied in this chapter.

To illustrate the power of formal analysis as employed here, two aspects of subsequent argument may be mentioned. First, the issue of whether society's (or the planner's) goals can, in fact, be achieved emerges in exceedingly sharp and precise focus. Approachable only by understanding the dynamic structural interrelationships and parameters that describe how society functions, the answer hinges on the logical consistency (within the structure) of particular goals and appropriate parameters. It turns out that formal conditions on the structure can be provided to guarantee such consistency. Secondly, a meaningful plan can be based only on the parameters capable of control from outside the structure and must take into account the impact of changes in these parameters on society as dictated by the structure itself. In the absence of the former a plan cannot succeed; without the latter its chances of success are impossible to determine. Failure to heed these directives may be at the root of, for example, Wildavsky's [7, p. 104] comment that one of the reasons national economic planning does not work is the inability of a complex society to figure out how to get things done.

Thus the present concern is with logical and theoretical foundations. (Empirical verification and statistical issues are taken up in Part III). The idea is to construct an environmental system consisting of simultaneous periodic equations that are dependent on parameter values. An equilibrium or stationary path is found and assumed unique and stable; that is, all other paths converge to it. Society is viewed as following one of these stable paths. When parameters are modified the equilibrium shifts and society's path eventually veers in the direction of the new equilibrium. Although at any instant society is converging toward equilibrium, over time parameter variation may be so rapid as to give no impression of convergence at all. Nevertheless, if planners wish to know where society is headed (i.e., where it will wind up) at any particular moment, they need only discover the current equilibrium. To plan operationally, they must pursue those activities that transform the desired position (as dictated from the normative and strategic levels) into a stable equilibrium. If they can then maintain this as the equilibrium, the passage of time will do the rest.

It is appropriate, in passing, to note an analogy with the multiplier analysis of macroeconomic theory. Given a consumption function, specification of autonomous investment, government expenditure, and (exogenous) government tax receipts determine an equilibrium national income. Actual income is assumed to converge to the equilibrium as time passes. Generally, variation in any of these three specifications modulates equilibrium. The path of actual income then changes in the direction of the new equilibrium. In this simplified framework, to see where the economy is going requires location of the equilibrium. Furthermore, by manipulating its expenditure and tax receipts, the government is able to exercise some control over the system.

Until now it has not been necessary to direct attention toward any of the many specific forms in which planning may appear (e.g., socialist market planning, planning for economic development, urban planning). The foregoing considerations apply in general. But to carry out the proposed presentation, one must choose a concrete situation. For that purpose focus will be narrowed to the concern of a particular land-use planner. However, the model of society and the description of operational planning to be analyzed are intended only as an illustration of a general technique that is applicable to a variety of planning problems. It is the technique that is important – not necessarily the specific application. The latter, based on material that comes from McLoughlin [5], is not expected to appeal to everyone and no claims are made for it. Alternative models of the identical phenomenon could be developed with the same method.

An overall evaluation of McLoughlin's volume is not intended. Nevertheless, by ignoring the formal properties of his argument, potential contradictions and incomplete specifications are not ruled out. Thus the simultaneous occurrence of certain structural relations may not logically be possible and the postulated structure itself may be insufficient to support his argument. The material of Section 9.1 is chosen from McLoughlin's study so as to illustrate and resolve these difficulties and is not meant to be a statement about the general consistency and completeness of his entire work.

In succeeding pages a formal structure is first developed that describes a society capable of manipulation by varying the exogenous controls (parameters) that planners want to use. Next, with the controls inoperative, the evolution over time of the society is considered. Operational planning is then introduced as the use of these controls to achieve desired ends. The chapter concludes with a general discussion of the ways in which planning can influence society.

One final, preliminary point: It is interesting that in the planning literature there is a precedent for the formal use of nonquantifiable variables. Lowry [4, p. 125], in fact, has written down a functional equation relating the offer price for a parcel of land to various characteristics of both the buyer and the land, and to other variables, none of which need be capable of measurement.

9.1　A planner's view of society

The initial task is to construct a model of society that is useful for planning purposes. That described here consists of a group of decision-making units each choosing, in part, activities they perform in various spaces, that is, locations. The spaces themselves are selected from those available along with the quality of the spaces as well. Decisions are reached by surveying the existing environment and then acting so as to further particular goals. If left alone, the interaction of behavior among the decision-making units of society leads to an equilibrium.

More precisely, the subscript i is taken to run over decision-making units. These consist solely of individuals, firms, and government agencies. The way in which decisions are made by each type of unit will be considered later on; for the moment it is sufficient to note that at any time t there are n_t units. Thus $i = 1, \ldots, n_t$. Time as used in this context is discrete: It is divided into hours, days, weeks, or any other convenient interval. The value $t = 0$ may be thought of as designating the initial period. Subsequent periods are numbered consecutively.

With these conventions in mind, the variables may now be introduced. Let s_{it} vary over collections of spaces (locations) that unit i can use at time t. Single spaces (collections containing a single element) are possible values for s_{it}. Because multistoried buildings often house different activities on different floors, spaces include locations above and below ground as well as those at surface level. Although any space may be uniquely identified on a three-dimensional "map" by listing appropriate coordinates, this does not constitute measurement: The sum of any two spaces, for example, is certainly not the sum of their coordinates. For the purposes at hand the fact that any given space can be so identified merely means that the values that s_{it} can take on, and hence the variable itself, are well defined. Let S_t be the set of all spaces (map locations) available to the society in question at time t both currently in and out of use. It does not matter to unit i that one space may already be in use by another unit because i could still possibly take over that space by purchase or some other means. The values of s_{it} may be regarded as subsets of S_t. Thus the set of all subsets of S_t characterizes the variable s_{it}.

Depending on what is done with it, each space can exhibit a variety of structural qualities. Retail stores, living quarters, and factories all require distinct facilities and there are many different kinds of facilities that can serve each function. Because there is no difficulty in giving precise descriptions of structural qualities, they can be used to define a second variable: q_{it} will vary over collections of qualities that unit i is able to procure at time t. The symbol Q_t will be used to denote the set of all possible qualities of all possible spaces that are obtained at time t. Values of q_{it} are again subsets of Q_t.

Within spaces, activities are performed. There are economic, recreational, political, administrative, cultural, educational, and many more activities. Let A_t be the set of all possible activities in which any decision-making unit may engage: Each element of A_t is a uniquely describable activity. The values of the next variable, a_{it}, are subsets of A_t. Thus a_{it} varies over collections of activities in which unit i may engage at time t.

Activities interact and connect with each other through various forms of physical and nonphysical communication. Communication flows through channels (highways, railroads, telephones, etc.) and each channel can assume a variety of qualities. Thus three more variables and corresponding sets can be defined: M_t is the set of all possible kinds of communication that can exist between activities, C_t is the set of all available channels through which communications can flow, and P_t is the set of all existing qualities in which each channel may be used. Correspondingly, m_{it} is the variable ranging over subsets of M_t, c_{it} is that ranging over subsets of C_t, and p_{it} is the one over subsets of P_t.

To simplify notation, write

$$b_{it} = (a_{it}, s_{it}, q_{it}, m_{it}, c_{it}, p_{it})$$

and B_t for the set over which b_{it} ranges. In the terminology of Section 3.1, B_t is the Cartesian product of the power sets of A_t, S_t, Q_t, M_t, C_t, and P_t. Because decision-making units are assumed to make decisions and take actions only with respect to the preceding six variables – that is, they choose their activities, space, space quality, communication among their own and outside activities, and the channels and channel qualities they use – b_{it} is a variable that completely describes the actions taken by unit i at time t. Over time the unit may elect to remain as in the past or change one or more of the values of the components of b_{it}. The alternatives for action open to it at time t are B_t. As suggested in Section 7.2, the individual sets comprising B_t, as well as B_t itself, may be either finite or infinite. A further convenience will be to use the lowercase letters without the subscript i to denote the vectors of corresponding variables taken across all decision-making units. Thus $a_t = (a_{1t}, \ldots, a_{n_t t})$, $b_t = (b_{1t}, \ldots, b_{n_t t})$, and so on.

Now there are many elements of each set B_t that are not feasible and can be eliminated from consideration. Not all spaces are capable of being modified to assume every quality, nor do they permit all activities to occur within their boundaries. Iron ore, for example, cannot be mined from the top floor of a multistoried apartment building and so all values of b_{it} with

$$a_{it} = \text{iron mining}$$
$$s_{it} = \text{top floor of a particular, multistoried building}$$

can be discarded. In addition to these technological restrictions, there may be political or legal reasons for ruling out elements of B_t. Some private activities may be illegal in certain spaces, whereas some government activities may be politically unwise at a particular time. In any case, let B_t^* be the set of feasible alternatives (finite or infinite) that remain after all others are eliminated.

It is now possible to define the concept of environment. An environment, E_t, at time t, consists of a value for each variable together with the set of feasible alternatives:

(9.1-1) $\quad E_t = (b_t, B_t^*)$

Thus the term "environment" refers to the setting in which the individual decision maker makes decisions. Let $\mathcal{E}_t$ be the set of all feasible environments; thus E_t varies over $\mathcal{E}_t$.

Decisions, as indicated earlier, are thought of as the result of a process that takes both the environment and goals of the units into account. Let g_{it} denote the goals of unit i at time t; a value for g_{it} consists of a verbal list of goals. Goals are assumed to be exogenously determined by the unit at every point in time. Although each unit may act during any period t, the definition of environment indicates that the environment at time t cannot be determined until all actions by every unit that is going to act are completed. Because a unit cannot, therefore, observe the current environment before its actions, its decisions must be based on its current goals and last period's environment. Furthermore, for all feasible last period environments, the unit is assumed capable of deciding on some sort of current, feasible action independently of the current decisions made by all other units. In other words, there is a functional relation between last period's environment E_{t-1} and current actions b_{it} in B_t^* given current goals g_{it}:

$$(9.1\text{-}2) \quad b_{it} = f^{it}(g_{it}; E_{t-1}), \qquad i = 1, \ldots, n_t$$

The semicolon is used to separate the parameter g_{it} from the variable E_{t-1}, and the symbol f^{it} is the name of the relation. (Of course, b_{it} also depends on B_t^*, but it will do no harm to subsume B_t^* in the functional symbol f^{it}.) Thus with fixed g_{it}, f^{it} is a function mapping $\mathcal{E}_{t-1}$ into B_t^* which completely describes all contingent actions that a unit can take. In principle, the f^{it}'s are observable through experimentation: Given g_{it} it is only necessary to place the unit in different environments and watch it react.

One way in which a unit may make decisions, and hence determine its f^{it}, is as follows: Based on a survey of last period's environment, suppose the unit is able to order all alternatives of B_t^* according to its goals – one element ranks higher up in the order than another if it enables the unit to come closer to reaching its goals. A person might order the elements according to personal preferences; a firm, according to the profits each element produces; and a government agency, according to cost-benefit analyses. Certain alternatives in B_t^* will be irrelevant to various units and will rank very low in their ordering. For example, an individual will not have as much interest in renting space to use for collecting taxes as the revenue-collecting agency of a government. But regardless of whose ordering it is or how it has been obtained, if the ordering has certain specific properties, then, as indicated in Sections 5.4 and 5.5, the unit will always be able to choose at least one element from every B_t^* that is ranked no lower than any other element. If, in addition, these "best" alternatives are always unique, the process can be used to define f^{it} in the obvious way: For each g_{it}, let f^{it} associate with each E_{t-1} the best b_{it} in the ordering.

The equations of (9.1-2) constitute a system of first-order periodic relations. But before they can be taken as a description of an evolving society, a basic difficulty must be overcome. Consider a unit that has just chosen an element from B_t^*. It has thus decided at time t on a collection of activities, spaces, space qualities, communications, channels, and channel qualities. Suppose, however, the space it has chosen is not available – either another unit is using it and does not want to give it up, or during the period an unknown unit has also decided to use the same space and obtained it first. In still another instance, suppose due to decisions made by other units at time t, the channel quality that one unit chose is unable to transmit further communications. In either case, regardless of which units are currently using the space or channel, more units want to use it than is possible. Thus it is necessary to add to (9.1-2) a description of how such conflicts of interest are resolved.

There are, of course, many ways of resolving conflicts of interest. The market mechanism allocates space, channels, and the like to the highest bidder. When the market process is absent or breaks down, these items may be given to the most politically influential unit or to that unit with the strongest financial backing, or they may be allocated as directed by a plan. For the present purpose, however, such issues are not relevant. The method of analysis this chapter attempts to illustrate will best be served by using a highly simplified, if somewhat artificial, approach. The following requirement is therefore introduced: It is assumed that sufficient space, space qualities, channels, and channel qualities are available so that units do not have to compete to obtain them. Whatever a unit wants it can get. Under this stipulation the simultaneous equations of (9.1-2) provide a logically complete way of viewing society.

It is also clear that (9.1-2) is an internally consistent structure: Satisfaction of no subset of equations can preclude the satisfaction of others.

The society under consideration thus consists of activities taking place in spaces and communications between activities flowing through channels. All activities, communications, spaces, space qualities, and so on are chosen by decision-making units. Each new set of decisions, however, alters the existing environment and results in still further decisions. Before studying the meaning and impact of planning in this society, it is first necessary to prescribe how it evolves if left alone.

9.2 Change over time

One way of thinking about change over time is in relation to equilibrium. Besides the fact that the path followed by a system can move "toward" or "away" from an equilibrium, the equilibrium itself can change, thereby causing still further variations in the system's evolution. At the outset, then, it is necessary to specify what the parameters are. In the present case these are taken to be the goals of each unit (as indicated earlier) and the feasible sets over which the variables range. The parameters are "fixed" over time and denoted by setting $t = 0$. Thus

$$g_{it} = g_{i0}, \qquad i = 1, \ldots, n_t$$

$$B_t^* = B_0^*$$

for all t.

As a further simplification it will be assumed that both the behavior functions and the number of units are also "fixed":

$$f^{it} = f^{i0}, \qquad i = 1, \ldots, n_t$$

$$n_t = n_0$$

for all t. Using these conventions and (9.1-1), one may write the equations of (9.1-2) in the form

$$b_{it} = f^{i0}(g_{i0}, B_0^*; b_{t-1}), \qquad i = 1, \ldots, n_0$$

or, still more compactly, as

$$(9.2\text{-}1) \quad b_t = f^0(g_0, B_0^*; b_{t-1})$$

where $g_0 = (g_{10}, \ldots, g_{n_00})$, and f^0 is short for the vector of functions $(f^{10}, \ldots, f^{n_00})$. To trace the path that society follows over time is to know the values $b_0, b_1, b_2, \ldots$ These are easily obtained once the initial value b_0 is specified. For then

$$b_1 = f^0(g_0, B_0^*; b_0)$$

$$b_2 = f^0(g_0, B_0^*; f^0(g_0, B_0^*; b_0))$$

and so on. The following discussion of such "actual" paths and of equilibrium paths is illustrated in simplified form by the tabular example appearing on page 100 of Section 5.2.

An equilibrium or stationary path of (9.2-1) is defined as a position in which there is no tendency, over time, to change. Thus at equilibrium,

$$b_t = b_{t-1}$$

for every t. If $\bar{b}$ is such an equilibrium vector, then with $b_t = b_{t-1} = \bar{b}$, it must be so that

$$\bar{b} = f^0(g_0, B_0^*; \bar{b})$$

In spite of the fact that there is little hope of measuring any of the variables, several distinct sets of conditions have been given in Chapter 5 that guarantee the existence of at least one $\bar{b}$. Without further specification, one of these is assumed to be met. Furthermore, only cases in which equilibrium is unique (i.e., when there is a single vector $\bar{b}$ with the equilibrium property) are considered.

There are many possible relationships between the equilibrium path and the actual path followed by society (determined by b_0). The latter can converge to the equilibrium over time; that is,

$$\lim_{t \to \infty} b_t = \bar{b}$$

it can form cycles (Section 5.2), or do neither. To speak meaningfully about convergence, however, one must know what it means for b_t to "approach" $\bar{b}$ as t becomes large. This is not difficult to define even for nonquantifiable variables, although in the latter case there is an element of arbitrariness involved (see Section 3.2). Furthermore, sufficient conditions ensuring convergence have been developed in Section 5.2. It is therefore logically permissible to assume, as is done here, that actual time paths followed by society always converge to the stationary path; that is, the equilibrium is stable.

Thus regardless of where it begins, society, if left alone, will wind up in the same place. But, of course, society is never really "left alone" for very long. Suppose, for example, it is converging toward an equilibrium when the goals of one of the decision-making units changes. With a new g_{i0} equilibrium must change and the stability assumption then requires society's path sooner or later to slide toward it. Such variation in parameters may, in fact, occur frequently enough so that society never really seems to approach any equilibrium. Nevertheless, as long as it is possible to determine its actual position relative to the equilibrium, the "direction" in which society is moving can always be found.

9.3 Operational planning

To introduce operational planning, it is necessary to take into account the goals of society as perceived and handed down from the normative and strategic levels of the planning system. These may be expressed as aesthetic, health, economic, and many other aims. In one way or another, however, they can all be reduced to the vocabulary of environment as previously defined. To desire physical beauty is to want certain structural qualities and relationships among them to exist in the material world. To aim for economic development is to facilitate the arrangement of particular activities and channels in highly specialized ways. It follows that the goals of society may be viewed as a directive to strive for a specific vector in B_0^*.

The determination of society's goals is an interesting question. They may be imposed by a dictator or dictorial group, left up to a political voting mechanism in which the majority rules, emerge from custom and tradition, and so on. In the case of voting, the aims of government agencies (i.e., the appropriate g_{i0}) are inconsequential. Only the preferences of the voters, reflecting the goals of individuals, firms (the remaining g_{i0}), and other politically powerful groups have weight. There is considerable literature relating to the translation of individual into social preferences and much of it is relevant here. (A good starting point is with Arrow [1].) Thus supposing all persons have preferences among the points of B_0^*, under certain conditions there will be a social ordering of B_0^* with appropriate properties. The goals of society could be taken as the "best" point in that social order. The existence of such a point has been remarked on in another context (Sections 9.1, 5.4, and 5.5). However, the derivation of society's goals is not important for present purposes. And it does not matter how these goals are interpreted and evaluated at the normative and strategic levels. All that counts are the goals as they are passed on to the operational level, and these are assumed to be expressed as a particular point, z, in B_0^*.

Note in order to achieve goals z in B_0^*, there must be a set of parameters such that z is an equilibrium of equation (9.2-1). Only when this is so can the currently existing parameters be adjusted so that z becomes an equilibrium and society's path converges to it. More will be said on achievability later – for the moment assume it to hold.

Consider now an idealized world in which the only way that parameters can change is through the implementation of a plan. It is easiest to think of the planning system as operating completely outside the model of society (9.2-1), that is, as pictured in Figure 9-1, although it is not difficult to handle the case in which the things it produces are regarded as an output of one of the f^{i0}. An operational plan can then be characterized as a prescription for adjusting existing parameters so as to achieve z. Stability ensures that society will move toward it. Because of the difficulties experienced by society and its members during transition, it may not be appropriate, even if possible, to turn z immediately into the equilibrium point. More often a plan will call for a step-by-step sequence of small changes taken one at a time. A plan as conceived here is not unique: There will usually be an infinity of ways to change the existing equilibrium into z. An evaluation of these alternatives must be based on the relative merits of the transitional societies that evolve from the process of shifting the direction of society's path. A way to choose between them has been suggested by Davidoff and Reiner [2].

The analysis developed here suggests that there are many different types of controls (i.e., the parameters of relation (9.2-1)) available to a planner. First, the sets of alternatives making up B_0^* may be changed. General legislation as well as specific zoning adjustments can modify the availability of unused space, and channels can be improved, lengthened, and increased in number. Secondly, the b_{it} for any government agency may be varied by changing its goals, g_{i0}. This is accomplished by executive decree or legislation. A third approach is to alter the goals of individuals and firms through public advertising, the restriction of private advertising, and by the creation of tax and other incentives. Advertisments pointing out the dangers of cigarette smoking and a ban on all cigarette advertising by manufacturers attempting to sell cigarettes are examples of the first two.

Combining the second and third controls yields a case – namely, the influencing of the goals of all decision-making units – in which it is easy to be more precise. The problem of whether society's goals, z, can be achieved,[1] reduces to the question of when does there exist a vector of goals, g_0, that makes the relation

$$z = f^0(g_0, B_0^*; z)$$

hold for the given B_0^*. According to Section 5.1, existence is guaranteed if, for example, appropriate inverses are present. Let $\bar{g}$ be the goals that produce equilibrium at z. An operational plan in this context is a finite sequence of parameters $g^1, \ldots, g^K, \bar{g}$, where g^1 reflects the existing goals of society. Denote by $b^1, \ldots, b^K, z$, the corresponding sequence of associated equilibria (b^1 is the current one) obtained from (9.2-1). In general, there is no logical reason why the g^k or b^k should become "closer" to, respectively, $\bar{g}$ or z as k increases from 1 to K, but there may be strong practical reasons why the plan should exhibit increasing closeness for the latter. (See Section 3.2 for a definition of closeness of nonquantifiable elements.) For example, the closer together the b^k are, the easier the transition from one state to another may become. Furthermore, the members of society may want to know how well their planners are doing, and the nearness of the b^k to z is an obvious test. From this point of view the choice of $g^1, \ldots, g^k$ becomes a problem in optimal control (Section 6.4).

It is now possible to drop some of the assumptions of the idealized world as previously hypothesized and consider planning in a more realistic context. As a start, suppose z is not achievable; that is, there do not exist parameters g_0 and B_0^* that position equilibrium at z. The difficulty lies with the functions f^{i0}, which reflect the unwillingness of decision-making units to behave in a manner that is consistent with the achievement of society's goals. The obvious solution is to attempt to change f^0. Altering the operation of government agencies is accomplished, in principle, by decree. They can be told, say, to switch from previously used rules to cost-benefit analysis to determine their b_{it}. The decision-making processes of individuals and firms are harder to influence. This may require educational programs as well as incentives to reinforce new procedures, and even then the outcome is far from certain.

The planning problem becomes still more complex when population, other parameters, and the behavioral relations (9.2-1) are permitted to

---

[1] A more general conception of achievability appears in Section 6.4. Because in the present case the vector z is specified in advance, the stronger notion of controllability in Section 6.4 does not apply.

vary, as they must certainly do, independently of the planning agency. Technological advances, wars, and riots all change activities, communications, spaces, and channels and the qualities available of the latter (i.e., B_0^*). They can also cause profound moral and morale shifts that affect the behavioral relations and the goals of individuals and firms as well as of society. In a world as dynamic as ours, the best of planning systems still does not appear good enough. The highways planned yesterday for tomorrow are no longer wanted today. Last year's highly prized sounds, smells, and sights of economic "progress" are now despised as intolerable pollutions. In such a setting planners must constantly revise their estimates and guesses of the model of society and the values of its parameters. By determining the current equilibrium, they know from the stability hypothesis where society is headed. Plans must involve the creation of future equilibria that reflect where they think society wants to go. Then the planners can only wait and watch as the events of the day intrude before the stability property can get them there.

All this, of course, presupposes that in addition to parameters, planners are capable of specifying at any point – past or present – the behavioral relations, f^0, and that they can project these relations into the future. Only when f^0 is known can the impact of varying a control be determined. Furthermore, to repeat an earlier remark, the model itself may be open to question. Future research, therefore, should be directed toward developing the appropriate model and revealing the precise nature of its behavioral relations. If planners are unable to keep ahead of changes in society, such a strategy will at least help to prevent them from falling too far behind.

References

1. Arrow, K. J., *Social Choice and Individual Values,* 2nd ed. (New York: Wiley, 1963).
2. Davidoff, P., and T. A. Reiner, "A Choice Theory of Planning," *Journal of the American Institute of Planners* 28 (1962):103–15.
3. Harris, B., "Plan or Projection," *Journal of the American Institute of Planners* 26 (1960):265–72.
4. Lowry, I. S., "Seven Models of Urban Development: A Structural Comparison," *Urban Development Models,* Highway Research Board, Special Report 97 (Washington, D.C.: National Academy of Sciences, 1968), pp. 121–46.
5. McLoughlin, J. B., *Urban and Regional Planning* (New York: Praeger, 1969).
6. Ozbekhan, H., "Toward a General Theory of Planning," in E. Jantsch, ed., *Perspectives of Planning* (OECD Working Symposium on Long-Range Forecasting and Planning, Bellagio, Italy, 1968), pp. 47–155.
7. Wildavsky, A., "Does Planning Work?" *The Public Interest* 24 (Summer 1971):95–104.

CHAPTER 10

Simultaneous change and modernization

Modernization is a process of change. Economic development is only one of many interdependent aspects of the modernizing process. This is hard to dispute and yet there are practically no current theories of economic development that include sociological, cultural, and political change as a part of their dynamic fabric.[1] Nor, for that matter, are there noneconomic theories that explicitly account for impact on and feedback from economic variables. Either, it would seem, one believes that economic development causes sociological, cultural, and political modulation, and hence is only concerned with economics, or one feels that sociological, cultural, and political modifications are preconditions for economic change, and therefore only the noneconomic factors are important. The obvious truth of the matter is that economic, sociological, cultural, and political transformations are all occurring simultaneously and any theory that does not explicitly allow for this is subject to rather severe limitations.

The purpose of this chapter is to illustrate a way of constructing models in which both economic and noneconomic change may be analyzed simultaneously. The examples presented are syntheses of the efforts of several authors, each writing from the point of view of his own discipline. No claims of comprehensiveness or correctness are made for the results. Because each author has his own concept of what is important, and because he may leave out elements that others regard as essential, the works upon which the following is based cannot be regarded as representative of the thinking within their respective disciplines. Furthermore, any synthesis necessarily retains much of the restrictiveness and many of the failures of the sources from which it is drawn. Thus, as a structure within which to analyze society and its evolution, subsequent models will probably not satisfy everyone. They are

---

[1] Important steps in the direction of accounting for both economic and noneconomic forces in development have been taken by (a) Myrdal [11] with a broad outline suggesting how the principle of circular causation might be applied, (b) Adelman and Morris [1] who have attempted to determine which noneconomic variables substantially influence economic development, and (c) Hunter [9] who describes the development process in considerable detail.

185

intended, however, only as illustrations of ways to discuss change within a general – social, psychological, economic, political, and cultural – framework.

The method proposed for conceptualizing society is analogous to the Walrasian general equilibrium technique of microeconomic theory. In the Walrasian model the microstructure of a perfectly competitive economy consists of a system of demand and supply functions that reflect, respectively, the assumptions that for every set of input and output prices (a) consumers buy those commodities and sell those resources that maximize utility, subject to their budget constraints, and (b) firms produce those outputs and hire those inputs that maximize their profits. General equilibrium is then defined as a point that satisfies all demand and supply functions simultaneously. Similarly, in the model presented here the general structure of society consists of all persons together with economic, social, cultural, and political substructures. Each part is described as a set of relations between appropriate variables. Society is thought of as determined by the simultaneous occurrence of all structural relations or, equivalently, as a "point" that satisfies every one concurrently.

The idea of using concomitant interrelationships to characterize society is not new. As far back as the eighteenth century Hume wrote:

An analyst or historian who should undertake to write the history of Europe during any century, would be influenced by the connexion of contiguity in time and place. All events, which hapened in that portion of space, and period of time, are comprehended in his design, tho' in other respects different and unconnected. They have still a species of unity, amidst all their diversity. (Hume [8, p. 19, n. 3])

According to Ruskin, who lived in the following century, "Great nations write their autobiographies in three manuscripts – the book of their deeds, the book of their words, and the book of their art. Not one of these books can be understood unless we read the two others..." (Ruskin [13, p. 3]). And recently Kenneth Clark's interpretation of civilization [3], with its heavy emphasis on the "book of art," still rests on this underlying simultaneity.

To introduce change, the relations of the social structure, and hence society, are considered to be dependent on parameters. As parameters shift, society modulates. It is argued that certain parameters vary from generation to generation in prescribed endogenous ways. The result is a dynamic system that traces out "paths" for society over time. All paths are assumed stable: In time they approach an equilibrium or stationary state. Furthermore, the stationary state itself depends on additional parameters whose exogenous movements force modifications in the equilibrium. With a new equilibrium, society's time path eventually changes direction and is pulled toward it. Thus transformation occurs by approaching one stationary state after another.[2] Such is the process of change; under certain circumstances its consequences are modernization.

As in the previous chapter, an analogy with economists' multiplier analysis is easily drawn: Once the level of autonomous investment is fixed the equilibrium level of national income is determined by the constant in the consumption function and the marginal propensity to consume. The actual time path of income is assumed to converge toward the equilibrium level. But vary the level of investment, and the equilibrium level of income changes. The time path of actual income now moves toward the new equilibrium level and the speed of convergence depends on the marginal propensity to consume.

The use of simultaneous structural relations to characterize society and of dynamic relations to express change needs some vindication, for all the relations considered here involve variables that cannot be measured. In a sense, this is nothing new; analyses of nonquantifiable phenomena are common throughout the social sciences. In what follows, however, some rather specific rules and concepts are relied upon: As is customary, nonquantifiable variables are specified in terms of the linguistic conceptual primitives that are acceptable to the disciplines from which they come. But to determine society, subsequent argument insists on the same number of relations as variables and assumes that their simultaneous occurrence is both possible and, for each set of parameter values, unique. In the dynamic context it supposes a stationary state also exists uniquely, and its stability stipulation (as with all such requirements) necessarily rests on a meaningfully defined concept of convergence. The parallel with standard mathematical tools often used in quantitative studies is obvious; their use in the absence of measurement has been justified in Part I.

Employment of such a formal mathematical approach has obvious advantages. In addition to enforcing rigor and precision in definitions, propositions, and argument (e.g., a very precise definition of the notion of stationary state emerges in Section 10.2), the logical or internal consistency of the entire structure is openly exposed and easily checked. Internal consistency is not to be taken lightly: There is little to analysis without it.

It might be thought that the presence of nonquantifiable variables does not lend itself to the derivation of empirically testable hypotheses.

---

[2] This is entirely consistent with Georgescu-Roegen's view that "growth cannot be conceived otherwise than as a passage from one stationary state to another" [4, p. 228].

But this is inaccurate because a substantial number of familiar statistical techniques also remain valid when measurement is impossible. The issues involved are discussed in Part III.

By way of summary, then, the first section defines the concept of society. The second introduces change over time, the reasons for it, and the notion of traditional society. Because there are observable phenomena that cannot be explained within the specific framework that is developed, an alternative approach is discussed in Section 10.3. Section 10.4 is concerned with the special kind of change called modernization and concludes with a comparison of the models presented and of the government policies they suggest to encourage modernization.

10.1   Society

Because the fundamental units of any society are individuals, it is natural to begin with a description of human behavior. Only two among many "models of man" suitable for this purpose are considered: A "psychodynamic" model that explains behavior in terms of man's psychological state, and a "behavioral" one, which views it as a result of learning. The discussion here is confined to the former; in later sections the learning approach is introduced as an alternative.

From the psychodynamic standpoint, behavior is unintelligible except in relation to personality. (See Hagen [6, Ch. 6] for a more detailed analysis.) The latter, in fact, may be defined as a mixture of nonphysical qualities that determine the behavior of individuals in every situation. These qualities are the relative strengths of their psychological needs (such as the need to be independent or the need to be respected by others), values, and cognitions (i.e., perceptions of the nature of reality). Intelligence and energy level are also important constructs of personality but it is assumed that the distributions of these factors are more or less identical in every society of the world.[3] As such they will not help to explain why some countries have modernized whereas others have not and may therefore be ignored.

Each variable involved in this notion of personality is assumed to take on values in some well-defined, perhaps infinite (Section 7.2), set. For example, any given situation in which individuals behave has certain unique characteristics distinguishing it from all others. It can also be described verbally. A value for the variable "situations," then, is one of these verbal descriptions. Similar ideas lie behind the variables "behavior patterns," "relative strength of needs," "relative strength of values,"

[3] With some documentation, Hagen argues that there is no reason for not making such an assumption [6, pp. 101, 102, especially footnotes 8–10].

and "relative strength of cognitions." However, once a list of appropriate needs, values, and cognitions is agreed upon, the strength of any one of them could conceivably be measured on an ordinal or even interval (cardinal) scale.[4] Indeed, necessary and sufficient conditions permitting the construction of such scales are known (Section 2.2). But it would be unreasonable to require these conditions to be satisfied for situations and behavior patterns. Although the values of the latter variables can be compared with historical situations and behavior, they cannot yet be quantified. It is always possible, of course, to assign to each situation a number on some scale, but the validity of any computation or conclusion based on such an artifice is entirely lost in the extreme arbitrariness of the original numerical assignment.

Thus a personality relation is postulated for each person of each generation: Behavior depends on the relative strengths of needs, values, and cognitions and on the particular situation in which behavior is demanded.

The preceding discussion may be conveniently summarized using mathematical notation. Let b_t^i vary over possible behavior patterns of individual i in generation t (sometimes referred to as individual i-t) and let x_t^i range over situations in which he may find himself. Denote the relative strengths of his needs, values, and cognitions by Q_t^i. Person i-t's personality, then, may be thought of as a function $\hat{\pi}_t^i$ that depends on Q_t^i and which shows for each situation x_t^i his unique behavior pattern b_t^i in it. This is written

(10.1-1) $\quad b_t^i = \hat{\pi}_t^i(Q_t^i, x_t^i)$

If n_t represents the number of persons in generation t, then the population of that generation is defined by (10.1-1), where $i = 1, \ldots, n_t$. Also, generations will be consecutively numbered with the first generation under consideration, designated as $t = 0$.

It is useful to think of the various groups formed by individuals as comprising the social substructure of society. Although as independent units, groups differ from one another, the behavior patterns of the membership within any group is relatively uniform. Personalities (i.e., the personality relations along with the relative strengths of needs, values, and cognitions), as well as many of the situations in which the members find themselves, are likely to be similar. Emphasizing the latter, take a group to consist of those individuals who face, for the most part,

---

[4] To define the notion of, say, relative strengths of a particular need, neither interval nor ordinal scales are required. It is only necessary that an appropriate ordering be specified on the value set of the variable that represents the need. Thus one value will exhibit greater (relative) strength than another according to the relationship between them given by the ordering. Ordinal measurement is not implied (see Section 2.2).

the same particular collection of situations in their daily lives. Farmers, business executives, persons with identical religious beliefs, and academicians often form such groups. Once all collections of these shared situations are known the social substructure is determined.

Formally, let X_t^i be the class of most prevalent, everyday situations in which person i-t finds himself. Clearly, if

$$X_t^i = X_t^j$$

then i and j are members of the same group. For subsequent discussion it is now convenient to redefine relation (10.1-1) so that b_t^i represents collections of behavior patterns for possible X_t^i. Hence the personality functions become:

(10.1-2) $b_t^i = \pi_t^i(Q_t^i, X_t^i),$ $i = 1, \ldots, n_t$

where, to indicate the new meaning of π_t^i, the circumflex over it in (10.1-1) has been dropped.

Another important aspect of society is its culture. Culture has been defined as consisting of standards for deciding what actually exists, what might exist, how one feels about it, what to do about it, and how to go about doing it, that is, standards for perception, judgment, and action (Goodenough [5, pp. 263–70, 358–9]). As such, individuals, groups, and societies all have cultures. The individual's culture is determined, to a large extent, by his own needs, values, and cognitions. That of society (or a group within it) is thought of as a general consensus of standards arrived at by its members through the interaction of their personal cultures with others and influenced by political and economic pressures that are imposed institutionally. More precisely, the culture of society; that is, the list of prevailing standards, c_t, in generation t is assumed to be a function, γ_t, of the strengths of the needs, values, and cognitions of all its members (abbreviated by the symbol Q_t); the political system p_t; and the degree to which investment decision making, d_t, is a part of economic life. Thus

(10.1-3) $c_t = \gamma_t(Q_t, p_t, d_t)$

Investment decision making and the political system are discussed momentarily. Culture, of course, is the determinant of traditions and customs that frequently appear as obstacles to economic development.

For the present purposes an appropriate political substructure has already been described in equations (8.1-2) of Chapter 8 and there is no need for repetition here. (The source, recall, is Apter [2].) Suffice it to say, in each generation this substructure consists of a system of relations among variables such as ideology, government policies, and information flowing between government and those governed. The unique simultaneous occurrence (assumed to exist) of all relations is taken to determine the political system, p_t. It emerges as dependent on the strengths of needs, values, and cognitions of all members of society, together with the general situations, Y_t, (e.g., a state of war with inflation) in which government policies are made. Adding the subscript t to equation (8.2-1) gives the formal statement that characterizes political systems for present use:

(10.1-4) $p_t = \psi_t(Q_t, Y_t)$

The economic relations within society may be more or less sophisticated depending on the degree to which development has progressed. More advanced economies have a well-organized price or communications system that announces shortages and surpluses to would-be investors. Investors, in turn, channel idle resources into areas where they are needed, thus increasing the efficiency and productive capacity of the economy. The investment decision-making process is therefore well established and heavily relied on. However, in underdeveloped economies there may not be many entrepreneurial personalities who are willing to make investment decisions, the political system or the culture may exert pressures against investment, and investment opportunities may not exist or go by undetected because the communication system is ineffective. Hence investment decision making may be almost nonexistent in such a society.

The extent to which investment decision making occurs will be thought of as reflecting the degree to which economic development has taken place. The foregoing argument suggests that investment decision making, d_t, in generation t depends on the needs, values, and cognitions of the members of society, the political system, the culture, and the existence of investment opportunities, E_t, in that generation. Denoting this function by δ_t:

(10.1-5) $d_t = \delta_t(Q_t, p_t, c_t, E_t)$

The general structure of society in any generation is composed of the cultural, political, investment decision making, and all personality relations, together with a social substructure recorded in similarities between the X_t^i's. It thus consists of equations (10.1-2) to (10.1-5). For convenience the model is reproduced here:

(10.1-6) $b_t^i = \pi_t^i(Q_t^i, X_t^i),$ $i = 1, \ldots, n_t$

$$c_t = \gamma_t(Q_t, p_t, d_t)$$

$$p_t = \psi_t(Q_t, Y_t)$$

$$d_t = \delta_t(Q_t, p_t, c_t, E_t)$$

This may be regarded as a system of $n_t + 3$ equations in $n_t + 3$ variables $b_t^1, \ldots, b_t^{n_t}, c_t, p_t, d_t$, and $2n_t + 2$ parameters $Q_t^1, \ldots, Q_t^{n_t}, X_t^1, \ldots, X_t^{n_t},$ Y_t, E_t. Each variable ranges over a possibly infinite set (Section 7.2). The functions $\pi_t^1, \ldots, \pi_t^{n_t}, \gamma_t, \psi_t, \delta_t$ are assumed to be known. Also assumed are the appropriate conditions described in Section 5.1, so that once the values of the parameters are specified, unique values of the variables are determined. All other variable values are eliminated, as in the tabular example on pages 92–3 of Section 5.1, by the simultaneity of the relations in (10.1-6). The structure of society is therefore internally consistent: Satisfaction of any subset of equations of (10.1-6) cannot rule out the satisfaction of others.

Society itself is defined to be the vector

$$s_t = (b_t^1, \ldots, b_t^{n_t}, c_t, p_t, d_t)$$

Under the preceding hypotheses, relations (10.1-6) uniquely determine society according to parameter values; that is,

(10.1-7) $s_t = \sigma_t(Q_t, X_t, Y_t, E_t)$

where $X_t = (X_t^1, \ldots, X_t^{n_t})$ and σ_t is the name of the functional dependence between parameters and societies. To each set of parameter values, σ_t assigns that society conforming to all structural relations simultaneously; that is, s_t is the solution of (10.1–6).

The next task is to introduce change.

10.2   Evolution

The following discussion of change begins, somewhat paradoxically, with a definition of the equilibrium or stationary state. Before proceeding, however, observe that even if none of the relations $\pi_t^i, \gamma_t, \psi_t, \delta_t$ change over time, the number of persons in society n_t does. Hence σ_t will usually be at least slightly different from σ_{t+1} and σ_{t-1} and the general structure of society (10.1-6) should not be the same from generation to generation. This sharply contrasts with the types of models that are often used by social scientists today. For example, in the two-sector growth model of economic theory the structure of the model is assumed to remain fixed over time and the analysis focuses, in part, on the stability or convergence properties of time paths generated within that structure. But in (10.1-6) the structure itself varies over time and thus the analysis of change is an entirely different problem.

Nevertheless, it is still possible to give meaning to the concept of a society in equilibrium independently of structural variations. Let m_i and f_i be superscripts denoting, respectively, the mother and father of individual i-t. Of course, the parents of i-t are of generation $t-1$. A society is said to be in equilibrium if and only if for every t and $i=1,\ldots,n_t$,

$$Q_t^i = \begin{cases} Q_{t-1}^{m_i}, & \text{if person } i\text{-}t \text{ is female} \\ Q_{t-1}^{f_i}, & \text{if person } i\text{-}t \text{ is male} \end{cases}$$

$$b_t^i = \begin{cases} b_{t-1}^{m_i}, & \text{if person } i\text{-}t \text{ is female} \\ b_{t-1}^{f_i}, & \text{if person } i\text{-}t \text{ is male} \end{cases}$$

$$E_t = E_{t-1}$$

$$c_t = c_{t-1}$$

$$p_t = p_{t-1}$$

$$d_t = d_{t-1}$$

Thus equilibrium exists if none of the variables and parameters are changing over time. The population may be expanding or contracting but the needs, values, and cognitions of parents; the situations they face, and their behavior patterns in those situations are passed on to their children without alteration. The latter thus appear as carbon copies of the former.

Of course, history has yet to produce a society in which every one of the equilibrium conditions is satisfied. Many societies, however, have gone through periods that seem to be good approximations of the stationary state. These are often called periods of traditionalism. They exhibit features such as overpowering customs, rigid social class systems, inheritance of social position, and little economic progress. No two traditional periods through which a society may go at different times are ever alike, because the burst of activity and development that occurs in between is reflected in the later state. For the last four centuries the Western world has been experiencing such a period of expansion. How much longer this will last (if, indeed, it will ever cease) is still an open question. But if an end comes, once again some approximation of the equilibrium state will prevail. And future scholars may someday refer to it as a traditional state.

Note that the concept of stationarity does not depend on quantification. To say that the relative strengths of needs, values, and cognitions are passed on from generation to generation without alteration does not require that unique numbers be assigned to them and then to assert that these numbers remain fixed over time. It is only necessary verbally to describe the relative strengths of the needs, values, and cognitions in question and to insist on the constancy of these descriptions.

Uniqueness and stability of equilibria may also be considered in such a context. Thus an equilibrium is unique if there is only one set of values of the variables that has the equilibrium property. Stability, on the other hand, requires the values of variables that are moving along time paths to converge to values on the equilibrium path. (The idea of convergence has been given precise meaning in Section 3.2.)

To analyze specifically the impact of change over time, one must study the links between successive generations. The first is concerned with the relationship between parent and child. (The following ideas are discussed in great detail by Hagen [6, Ch. 7].) It is assumed that a child's personality is formed from experiences during his earliest years. These experiences are the result of his parents' efforts to care for his growing needs. Every child suffers some frustration and its persistence or how it is relieved profoundly affects his personality. Therefore the behavior patterns of parents to a large extent determine the needs, values, and cognitions of their offspring. Furthermore, as the child grows and interacts more and more with the world outside the family, the basic impressions he has received at home are reinforced or contradicted by the political, cultural, and economic aspects of his parents' society, which he encounters. Hence this bond between generations may be expressed by a periodic relation: The relative strengths of a person's needs, values, and cognitions depend on his parents' personality functions and situation sets, and on the culture, political system, and extent of investment decision making emerging from his parents' generation; that is,

$$(10.2\text{-}1) \quad Q_t^i = \alpha_t^i(\pi_{t-1}^{m_i}(Q_{t-1}^{m_i}, X_{t-1}^{m_i}), \pi_{t-1}^{f_i}(Q_{t-1}^{f_i}, X_{t-1}^{f_i}), c_{t-1}, p_{t-1}, d_{t-1})$$

where $i = 1, \ldots, n_t$ and the symbol α_t^i represents the link between child i of generation t and his parents.

Another tie between successive generations has to do with the existence of opportunities for investment (Hirschman [7, Chs. 4–6]). Every generation must live with shortages of some goods and surpluses of others. The process of eliminating them may cause shortages and surpluses of different commodities due to the effects of forward and backward linkage and construction (or lack thereof) of social overhead capital. Thus the resolution of one generation's "imbalances" creates new ones for the next. The existence of imbalances, however, means that there are opportunities for investment. Hence investment decision making in one generation creates investment opportunities for the next. The presence or absence of investment opportunities is also subject to the state of technical knowledge. A second link between generations, then, asserts that the existence of investment opportunities in any generation depends on the technology available to that generation, written K_t, and on investment decision making during the previous one:

$$(10.2-2) \quad E_t = \beta_t(K_t, d_{t-1})$$

Equations (10.1-7), (10.2-1), and (10.2-2) characterize the evolution of society over time.

Assume now that all situation sets in the social structure, the general situation in which government policy is made, and the state of technical knowledge are determined exogenously and independently of time. They are, therefore, not affected by other variables and relations. Symbolically, write

$$(10.2-3) \quad X_t^i = X_*^i, \quad Y_t = Y_*, \quad K_t = K_*$$

for every i and t. It follows, as in Section 5.2, that once initial values for the relative strengths of each person's needs, values, and cognitions, along with the starting points for culture, political system, and investment decision making are specified, a time path for society can be traced out. It is further required that for all social structures, general situation sets, and states of technology, a unique equilibrium society exists and is stable. (Conditions ensuring existence and stability for the special case in which n_t is constant over time are given in Section 5.2. Again, the simplified tabular example on page 100 of Section 5.2 is relevant.) Thus the natural tendency of any society, when left undisturbed, is to become traditional. However, if for some reason any individual, general situation set, or the technology varies, a new stationary state will exist and the time path of society will eventually be diverted toward it.

The only task now remaining to complete the model is to explain how the exogenous parameters in equations (10.2-3) might change. Modifications in the state of technology and general situations are not given much emphasis here. Suffice it to say, it might be advantageous to eliminate the exogeneity of the former and think of it as depending on, say, last generation's technology; the strengths of all persons needs, values, and cognitions; and the political system (in particular, on government policy toward education). But adding the extra relation at this point is an unnecessary complication and so no special explanation of changes in technology is given. On the other hand, general situations will change if, for example, a society is conquered by or wins independence from a foreign power.

By far the most interesting changes occur in individual situation sets.[5] Recall that for each person X_*^i is indicative of his niche or group identification in the social substructure. Membership in the group places certain obligations on him but in return his values and activities are respected not only by fellow members but outsiders as well. Thus by identifying with a group, the individual finds a place for himself in society; lacking this, his life can be neither satisfying nor meaningful. The trouble begins when members of some group feel that society in general and those whose esteem they value in particular no longer respect their aims and purposes.[6] Without such respect it becomes impossible for group members to achieve satisfaction in life and consequently they find themselves in entirely new situations.

The effects of these variations in individual situation sets will be pursued because they also shed light on the nature of the personality link (relation (10.2-1)) between successive generations. Withdrawal of respect leaves the individual in the position of desiring esteem from those who will not give it. He tends to retreat by suppressing his plight from his consciousness. But the pain still leads to frustration and rage that can only be vented on objects, such as his children, permitted by society. Thus changes in situations lead to changes in behavior patterns. Of course, children perceive the conflict and pain of their fathers through the latter's behavior toward them. Children learn to deny that they have expectations for satisfaction in life in order to avoid that pain. They also learn to repress their rage. But their needs, values, and cognitions are bound to be different from their parents because the latter were not reared under such circumstances. The process continues with repression becoming greater and personalities changing from generation to generation. Eventually, innovative and creative personalities emerge who are prepared to break with tradition in order to regain the respect withheld from their fathers. They endeavor to make themselves powerful enough to force acceptance and respect by others. When this is accomplished, society once again becomes "traditional." Such an evolution of the innovative personality finds illustration in Japanese history as has been described at the beginning of Section 1.1. (Further examples are provided by Hagen [6] in the second half of his book.)

---

[5] The sequence of change described subsequently is due to Hagen [6, Chs. 9–11]. Although already outlined in Section 1.1, a more detailed presentation is worthwhile here.

[6] Hagen [6, Ch. 9] suggests four types of events that can cause the withdrawal of respect: changes in the holders of political power, the degrading of existing institutionalized activity, the perception of contradictions among status symbols, and nonacceptance of expected status upon migration to a new society.

10.3 An alternative perspective

It is characteristic of the psychodynamic approach that at least a few generations must pass after the initial withdrawal of status respect before innovative personalities begin to appear. Although realistic enough in Japan, the Japanese experience is by no means universal. In Pakistan, for example, there emerged quickly and seemingly out of nowhere, an entrepreneurial class that led the way to a truly remarkable economic development between 1947 and 1960 (see Kunkel [10, pp. 269–74]). This phenomenon cannot be inferred from a prior declassing of particular social groups. And variations in the other exogenous parameters (general situations in which government policies are made and the state of technology) do not furnish a very satisfying source of explanation. Rather, it seems more appropriate to abandon the psychodynamic basis of the analysis and to reformulate it with an alternative model of man.

The so-called learning or behavioral framework provides a convenient substitute. (A detailed exposition of the learning model of man may be found in Kunkel [10, Ch. 3].) In adopting it, the earlier behavior and situation variables as well as the definition of social substructure in terms of shared situations may be employed without change. Now, however, in all activities the individual is assumed to be rewarded or punished for his behavior according to the way in which his family, the group to which he belongs, and society as a whole react to it. The impact of rewards and punishments on behavior appears in conjunction with his current state of psychological deprivations and satiations. A reward may or may not be appealing according to the particular values of these variables. The individual's behavior is also influenced by his learning history (i.e., what he has learned from past experience and the norms and values derived from it) and his awareness of existing possible behavior patterns with which to respond in the situations he faces.

Putting these factors together results in a learning function to replace the personality relation (10.1-2) for the individuals of every generation: Behavior depends on situations, reward–punishment schedules r_t^i, deprivations and satiations v_t^i, learning history l_t^i, and awareness of possible behavior responses a_t^i, or

$$b_t^i = \mu_t^i(r_t^i, v_t^i, l_t^i, a_t^i, X_t^i), \qquad i = 1, \ldots, n_t$$

A description of the structure of society in this context may be completed by substituting each person's reward–punishment schedule, state of deprivations and satiations, learning history, and awareness of possible behavior responses for the relative strengths of each person's needs, values, and cognitions in the culture, political system, and investment decision-making functions of Section 10.1. Thus

$$(10.3\text{-}1) \quad c_t = \gamma_t'(r_t, v_t, l_t, a_t, p_t, d_t)$$

$$p_t = \psi_t'(r_t, v_t, l_t, a_t, Y_t)$$

$$d_t = \delta_t'(r_t, v_t, l_t, a_t, p_t, c_t, E_t)$$

where

$$r_t = (r_t^1, \ldots, r_t^{n_t}), \quad v_t = (v_t^1, \ldots, v_t^{n_t})$$

$$l_t = (l_t^1, \ldots, l_t^{n_t}), \quad a_t = (a_t^1, \ldots, a_t^{n_t})$$

and the symbol " ' " has been added to distinguish the functions γ_t', ψ_t' and δ_t' from their analogues in Section 10.1. The parameters in this model are $r_t, v_t, l_t, a_t, X_t, Y_t$, and E_t. The variables, the definition of society, and the determination of society from its structure are the same as in Section 10.1. Hence

$$s_t = \sigma_t'(r_t, v_t, l_t, a_t, X_t, Y_t, E_t)$$

where σ_t' is a function similar to σ_t in relation (10.1-7). Note that s_t still depends on the same parameters as in the psychodynamic approach, except that needs, values, and cognitions give place to their learning model counterparts.

The previous discussions of stationary and traditional society and uniqueness and stability of equilibria apply here with obvious modifications. Given initial values, society follows a time path that converges to some equilibrium until at least one exogenous parameter shifts. At that point a new equilibrium emerges and society's time path slides toward it. To study the way in which society changes over time, therefore, one must examine the endogenous and exogenous reasons for variations in the parameters: reward–punishment schedules, deprivations and satiations, learning histories, awarenesses of behavior patterns, existence of investment opportunities, general situations, and the social substructure. As before, no systematic internal force is assumed to operate on the last two. The same tranformation in the existence of investment opportunities as described in equation (10.2-2) is assumed here. The first four remain to be considered.

It seems natural that deprivations and satiations, learning histories, and awarenesses may be modified in the process of day-to-day living. Even in the absence of external effects an individual's behavior may vary as his experiences become richer. The model, however, does not break up time into small enough units to handle such phenomena. Once the parameters of a particular generation are set, the behavior of each person is fixed. In this sense the variable "behavior" reflects the "typical" pattern of an individual during his lifetime. But within a given generation, exogenous factors can alter deprivations and satiations, learning histories, and awarenesses, and the new "typical" behavior resulting from the change will cause a shift in equilibrium. Thus across time these parameters may be treated analogously to general situations and the social substructure.

Schedules of rewards and punishments, on the other hand, are assumed to vary internally: They depend on last generation's culture and on a control parameter Z_t, which is available to the government should it wish to intervene; that is,[7]

$$r_t = \varphi_t(c_{t-1}, Z_t)$$

The value of the control parameter would change, for example, if a government initiated policies to increase entrepreneurial incentives. In fact, successful governmental use of it provides an explanation for the striking progress in Pakistan previously mentioned. This link between generations is a periodic equation that is similar to those developed earlier. Although not pursued here, it may be given a more detailed analysis as with the intergenerational personality relation (10.2-1) of the psychodynamic model (see Kunkel [10, Ch. 9]). A conclusion analogous to that of Section 10.2 results: Variation in any exogenous parameter may produce "deviate" behavior that modulates equilibrium and results in changes in society's time path which, as it converges, could modify the norms defining "acceptable" behavior to include the deviates. Therefore customs and traditions blocking economic development can be overcome by applying pressure through appropriate exogenous channels.

10.4 Modernization

Whether based on personality formation or learning, the process of change described here is neutral. In principle it can be applied to dynamic patterns as diverse as the fall of the Roman Empire, the Italian Renaissance period, and the Industrial Revolution. In all of these, and for that matter, in almost any evolving situation, there are certain components

---

[7] The general problem of control has been discussed in Section 6.4. For simplicity, Z_t is taken here to be independent of the government policies that are a part of the definition of political system. It is not difficult, however, to make Z_t endogenous.

that could be regarded as a step in the direction of modernization, even though the end result might not be what one would want to call a modernized society. The relevance of any one depends on the definition of modernization accepted.

It is axiomatic that there will never be any general agreement among scholars as to which changes constitute the modernizing process, for any definition of modernization explicitly or implicitly involves the introduction of value judgments by the person giving it. Modernization, after all, is the means to an end – a "modernized society." Although several modernized societies may have particular characteristics in common, there will usually be many other equally important characteristics that are unique to each separately. Thus there can be no single, correct way to give the concept of a modernized society precise meaning. Researchers must necessarily use their own judgment to determine the appropriate definition for the purposes of their work. This choice can only reflect their values. Once made, however, the definition of modernization is simple. *Modernization* is any process of change leading toward the modernized society.

In terms of the models developed here, if $\bar{s}$ is designated the modernized society, and if it is also the equilibrium or stationary state, then by the stability hypothesis the actual path of society is modernizing. Even when $\bar{s}$ is not the equilibrium it may still be feasible as an equilibrium in the sense that there exist parameter values that center it there. If so, the actual path generated by any sequence of exogenous parameter changes ending up with $\bar{s}$ as the target equilibrium may also be considered modernizing.

A most important aspect of the preceding approach to modernization is that it can only be meaningful in terms of a specified dynamic explaining how change takes place. Two possible interpretations of movement over time have been presented. Lacking something of this sort, the concept of modernization provides little more than a sterile abstraction, for it contains nothing to indicate how the phenomenon is to be observationally identified. Even if one knows where society is and what the term modernized society means, without understanding the process of change there is no way of determining if the current direction of society's path is, in fact, modernizing.

By contrast, in the view of Nettle and Robertson [12, p. 129], modernization consists of "attempts on the part of international actors (being *effectively* the dominant political elites in national societies) to enhance the quality of their societies in relation to other societies." Thus the notion of modernized society is determined for each society by the political elites who direct it according to what they believe to be important in the outside world. The modernizing process consists of their efforts, successful or not, to attain the modernized society.

On the other hand, the concept of development proposed by Adelman and Morris [1] may be regarded as a special case of the approach taken here. They implicitly identify modernized society with "modern" Western society. Achievement of the modernized society requires separating "the economic sphere, first from the complex of social organization and the norms that govern it, and, subsequently and to a lesser extent, from the political environment by which it is constrained" (Adelman and Morris [1, p. 267]). The emergence of this separation is easily thought of in terms of transformations of exogenous parameters as previously described, because variations in the latter cause personality, social, cultural, and economic alterations that most probably are those observed by Adelman and Morris.

The older notions of modernization defined entirely within the isolated disciplines of sociology, political science, and economics are also special cases of the preceding approach. To sociologists, modernization has frequently meant structural differentiation, that is, the splitting up of social institutions by function (religious, economic, political, etc.). Political scientists have often thought of modernization as the development of a flexible and adaptable political system that becomes increasingly more capable of handling rapid social and economic modulation. Economists have tended to associate modernization with one or more of the following: (a) rising, real per capita output, (b) falling percentage of the labor force in agriculture, (c) falling percentage of the value of exports accounted for by one or two raw materials, (d) declining inequality in the distribution of income, and so on. All these ideas can be interpreted in terms of a model similar, if not identical, to the one proposed here. All involve value judgments concerning the nature of modernized society, and all suffer from the fact that they are "partial" rather than "general equilibrium" concepts. Thus, for example, any of the four economic viewpoints implicitly assume that all social, cultural, psychological, and political variables are held fixed over the period of time under consideration while society "modernizes" only in its economic sphere. This weakness explains the well-known difficulty that when countries are classified according to any one of these four economic measures in order to determine which is more "developed," inconsistencies usually appear. There are always exceptions whose actual state of economic development warrants a different relative position on the scale.

To conclude, the two models of Sections 10.1 to 10.3 will be compared in terms of both structure and the types of policies they recommend to encourage modernization.

Perhaps the major advantage of these models is their emphasis on the simultaneity of sociological, cultural, political, and economic transformation. Change in one area does not occur without adjustment in and resulting feedback from others. Economic development cannot proceed too far ahead of noneconomic modification. Thus social, cultural, and political resistances to economic progress are built into the models themselves. It is also true that economic development need not be the major thrust of the modernization process. Cultural innovation, for example, could turn out to be far more significant.

The two models proposed here contain striking similarities in structure. Both consist of a system of simultaneous relations defining society and periodic relations linking generation to generation. Once the various parameters and starting values are specified, the natural tendency for society – in either case – is to approach the stationary state. Change is explained by resort to an initial, unexplained phenomenon: In the psychodynamic approach an elite group may somehow lose its status whereas the learning model would require, say, the shift of a group's deprivations and satiations.

Nevertheless, there are enormous differences between them. From the psychodynamic viewpoint, underdeveloped countries lacking entrepreneurial personalities have an almost insurmountable problem. Most governments are unwilling to ostracize groups from society in order to create innovative personalities. Even if they were, the process is long and the results are not guaranteed, for if creative individuals do emerge they may not direct their energies toward modernizing pursuits. If the description of personality formation is correct, then attempts to educate adults (and even children past a critical age) in entrepreneurial ways are likely to fail. It will be extremely difficult to induce in them the required change in needs, values, and cognitions. Perhaps the best that can be hoped for is that changes in the equilibrium culture, extent of investment decision making, and political system caused by other exogenous means (i.e., shifts in (10.2-3)) will eventually have the desired effects on personalities over a few generations.

If the learning approach is accepted, however, a variety of additional and formerly nonexistent parameters become available for manipulation. These include individual states of deprivations and satiations, learning histories, awareness of behavior patterns, and the control. Thus better schools can alter learning histories and behavior awareness. Mass media can communicate new deprivations. And a government can modify rewards and punishments by, for example, creating an atmosphere in which the potential gains from taking advantage of opportunities for entrepreneurial activity are both obvious and substantial.

Finally, just as the innovative persons emerging from psychodynamic evolutions of withdrawal need not channel their energies in directions appropriate for modernization, so might deviational behavior resulting from learning appear as ritualism, apathy, or crime. Furthermore, the rationalization that each approach provides seems to give a plausible explanation of change in some situations but not in others. If, in fact, different societies change for different reasons, this conclusion is not surprising. One could hardly expect more.

References

1. Adelman, I., and C. T. Morris, *Society, Politics and Economic Development* (Baltimore: Johns Hopkins Press, 1967).
2. Apter, D. E., *The Politics of Modernization* (Chicago: University of Chicago Press, 1965).
3. Clark, K., *Civilisation* (London: BBC and John Murray, 1969).
4. Georgescu-Roegen, N., *The Entropy Law and the Economic Process* (Cambridge, Mass.: Harvard University Press, 1971).
5. Goodenough, W. H., *Cooperation in Change* (New York: Wiley, 1966).
6. Hagen, E. E., *On the Theory of Social Change* (Chicago: Dorsey, 1962).
7. Hirschman, A. O., *The Strategy of Economic Development* (New Haven: Yale University Press, 1958).
8. Hume, D., *The Philosophical Works,* vol. 4, T. H. Green and T. H. Grose, eds. (Darmstadt, Scientia Verlag Aalen, 1964), essay on the association of ideas.
9. Hunter, G., *Modernizing Peasant Societies* (London: Oxford University Press, 1969).
10. Kunkel, J. H., *Society and Economic Growth* (New York: Oxford University Press, 1970).
11. Myrdal, G., *Rich Lands and Poor* (New York: Harper, 1957).
12. Nettle, J. P., and R. Robertson, *International Systems and the Modernization of Societies* (New York: Basic Books, 1968).
13. Ruskin, J., *St. Mark's Rest* (Chicago: Donohue, Hennebery, 1890?).

CHAPTER 11

Profits, optimality, and the social division of labor in the firm

WITH H. GINTIS

Neoclassical theory has traditionally taken the production function as an exogenous datum reflecting the technical structure of production (Samuelson [12], Ferguson [5]). Hence little effort has been expended on the analysis of the production process itself. (Two notable exceptions, Coase [4] and Simon [13], are discussed subsequently.) Yet surprisingly powerful theorems follow from this hypothesis according to the microeconomic logic of profit maximization. Certainly the most central of these theorems is that the profit-maximizing firm will choose Pareto-optimal production under normal conditions.

But in general, there is no reason to suppose that profit-maximizing entrepreneurs will make profit-maximizing decisions that are also in the best interests of their workers. In any given circumstance, therefore, it may be possible to make workers better off without reducing profits. Such a situation cannot be Pareto optimal, and there is no obvious mechanism, such as competition, operating within the firm that automatically leads it to optimality. Indeed, by modeling the firm as a complex collection of social relationships, we shall suggest that the neoclassical assertions concerning optimality in the firm hold only under restrictive and highly unrealistic assumptions. Specifically, profit maximization need not always result in the optimal allocation of human resources.

This observation calls into question a number of derivative but socially critical propositions often expressed as follows. First, the structure of authoritarian relations in the firm will be Pareto optimal. Secondly, wage differentials will reflect differences in the marginal productivity of workers in specified jobs. Thirdly, worker sovereignty will obtain in the same sense, and under the same conditions, as the more traditional consumer sovereignty (Gintis [7]). That is, the overall constellation of jobs in the economy will reflect the trade-off of workers between wages and job satisfaction, given an initial distribution of talents, skills, and

This chapter is reproduced (with minor changes) from *Sociological Economics,* L. Lévy-Garboua ed. (London: Sage, 1979), pp. 269–97. © Sage Publications Ltd., London, 1979. Reprinted by permission of Sage Publications.

material wealth. From these propositions arise some of the most fundamental perspectives on modern society that are gleaned from neoclassical economics. The first implies that production is socially neutral in
the sense that it is independent of property relations, class structure, and
the mode of social control of economic life. The social relations of the
enterprise are technologically determinate and ensure high productivity.
From the second, it is deduced that wage inequality results from the
differences in technically relevant attributes of individuals. In particular,
capitalism exhibits a strong tendency toward "meritocracy," whereby
individuals attain economic positions based on their "achievements"
alone, independently of such ascriptive characteristics as race, sex, social
class background, and ethnic origin. Thus persistent differences in economic outcomes across ascriptively distinct groups are imputed to differences in tastes, abilities, or opportunities of skill-acquisition. The
third implies that the historical development of work corresponds,
within the limits imposed by science and technology, to the preferences
of workers. If work is less than satisfying, it is because most workers
prefer higher incomes to more satisfying jobs. These views are not part
of the picture that emerges here.

We start by supposing that the firm relies on authoritative rather than
on market allocations of human activity. Coase [4] and Simon [13] also
introduce authority into the operation of the firm but argue that optimality would result provided the entrepreneur (a) lets the market allocate those elements that it does so efficiently, and (b) allocates through
entrepreneurial authority those that it cannot. This approach, however,
assumes that once the contract between entrepreneur and worker is
settled, the former tells the latter exactly what to do. The worker either
does it or finds another job. But contracts are not explicit enough, nor
are capitalists' powers sufficiently encompassing to dictate workers' attitudes; their values; their relations with their superiors; subordinates, and
co-workers; the manner in which they discharge their responsibilities;
and so on. Yet all these factors influence the output and hence profits of
the firm. Thus our analysis differs from Coase and Simon in that
workers are permitted to choose these factors for themselves, subject to
the constraints imposed by authority. Market allocations are not considered.

More precisely, this chapter develops an alternative model of the hierarchical division of labor within the firm. At its heart is the commitment
to treat all actors in the enterprise, not only the capitalist, as maximizing
an objective function subject to constraints. The model is then used to
investigate the conditions under which profit maximization leads to
Pareto optimality. Theorems also are developed that relate profit levels

to preference orderings and skills among workers. The beginnings of a mathematical theory of organizational structure in the firm are obtained thereby. (All of this draws heavily on Gintis [8].)

It is clear that many of the questions to be addressed subsequently cannot be discussed in a totally quantifiable setting. Variables such as human attitudes and human values seem to defy numerical representation. Values of these variables, that is, realizations of specific human attitudes and human values that might arise, have to be handled in abstract set-theoretic terms. Furthermore, we must be sure that even in the absence of measurement, the structural relations of the model are internally consistent and determinate. The methodological investigations in Part I of this volume have pointed the way toward handling these kinds of technical problems and our analysis rests squarely on them.

11.1 A model of the production process

We define the *job set* of the firm as $J = \{1, \ldots, n\}$ for a specified integer $n \geq 1$. The *job structure* of the firm represents the organizational hierarchy of authority within the firm and will be described in terms of a relation ρ on J where $j_1 \rho j_2$, for j_1, j_2 in J, should be interpreted as j_1 lies not below j_2 in authority. The job set and the job structure are taken as given. We also require ρ to be reflexive and transitive, and to possess the pyramidal property: For any j_1, j_2, j_3 in J, if $j_2 \rho j_1$ and $j_3 \rho j_1$, and if it is not the case that $j_1 \rho j_2$ and $j_1 \rho j_3$ then either (a) $j_2 \rho j_3$ and not $j_3 \rho j_2$, or (b) $j_3 \rho j_2$ and not $j_2 \rho j_3$.

Consider a collection of *workers* $W = \{1, \ldots, n\}$. An *assignment function* $K : J \to W$, 1-1 and order preserving, is assumed as given. K then associates each worker with a particular job and induces a hierarchical relation $\geq$ on W such that $K(j_1) \geq K(j_2)$ if and only if $j_1 \rho j_2$. If w and z are in W and $w \geq z$ but $z \not\geq w$, we write $w > z$. If $w > z$, we say w *is (directly or indirectly) superior to z in authority,* and z *is (directly or indirectly) subordinate to w.* If $w \geq z$ and $z \geq w$, we write $w \sim z$ and say w *and z are co-workers.*

Let w be in W. Define

$$\underline{S}_w = \{z \text{ in } W : w > z\}$$

and

$$\bar{S}^w = \{z \text{ in } W : z > w\}$$

Let S_w be the set of maximal elements of $\underline{S}_w$ and S^w the minimal elements of $\bar{S}^w$. Thus S_w is the set of immediate subordinates of w, and S^w is the set of immediate superiors of w. Now set

$$C_w = \{z \text{ in } W : z \sim w\}$$

that is, C_w is the set of co-workers of w. It is clear from the pyramidal property that although every worker has at most a single immediate superior, he may have more than one immediate subordinate.

Assume each worker w possesses a nonempty act set A_w contained in an act space $\mathcal{C}$, such that for any a_w in A_w, w is capable of performing act a_w and performance falls within the terms of the worker's contract with the employer. We do not require the elements of A_w to be in any way quantifiable. Define

$$A = \underset{w \text{ in } W}{\times} A_w$$

and assume a *production function f* such that $q = f(a)$, where output q results from each worker w choosing a_w in A_w, and $a = (a_1, \ldots, a_n)$.[1]

With the choice of a in A unknown, output will be indeterminate since A_w will not normally reduce to a single element for all w in W. Indeed, a broad range of behaviors are available to the worker at any time, all of which are legitimate in terms of the employment contract. Within this range we view the worker as acting to pursue his own goals subject only to the direct and indirect constraints the capitalist can place on the worker's choices, and the "moral influence" he can exercise over these choices within the constraint set. To formalize the notion of "constraint" we define *rules* of the organization as restrictions on A_w imposed upon workers by their superiors. Thus for any z in $\bar{S}^w$, suppose z is capable of imposing a *rule set* $R_{wz} \subseteq A_w$ on w. Let

$$R_w = \underset{z \text{ in } \bar{S}^w}{\bigcap} R_{wz}$$

Thus R_w is a collection of restrictions imposed on w by all of his superiors.

Note we are not assuming that a superior can choose the rule set R_{wz} at will. Whereas in principle z's choices may vary over the power set of A_w, in fact, z may be restricted contractually or legally to some subset of this power set. The subset to which z is so restricted is called the collection of *w-admissible rules*. In addition, z must also take into account the possibility that different rule sets may incur different costs to the firm in implementation.

Not all workers necessarily have superiors. If w in W has no superior in the sense already defined, the *director* of the firm (the capitalist or top management) is taken as his superior. For any worker w, the rule set imposed by the director is written $R_{w*} \subseteq A_w$. Let

---

[1] We have abstracted from nonhuman production inputs in order to simplify subsequent argument.

$$R_* = \underset{w \text{ in } W}{\times} R_{w*}$$

and take R_* as given by the director. For any worker w with $\bar{S}^w \neq \varnothing$, set $R_w^* = R_w \cap R_{w*}$. If $\bar{S}^w = \varnothing$ so that the only superior is the director, set $R_w^* = R_{w*}$.

Now consider any worker w. Let $\mathfrak{R}_z^w$ be the collection of z-admissible rule sets R_{zw} that w can impose on z in $\underline{S}_w$ and write

$$\mathfrak{R}^w = \underset{z \text{ in } \underline{S}_w}{\times} \mathfrak{R}_z^w$$

Denote the elements of $\mathfrak{R}^w$ by r^w. If $\underline{S}_w = \varnothing$, set $\mathfrak{R}^w = \varnothing$. We take $\mathfrak{R}^w$ as given for our purposes. In a larger model $\mathfrak{R}^w$ would depend on legality, as well as on feasibility and the cost of formulation and enforcement (Simon [13], Barnard [2], Gintis [8]). We assume for the time being that workers obey all rules. The contingent status of this assumption will be mentioned later.

We are now in a position to define a *decision* of an individual w in the organization. This will consist of two components: an act and a z-admissible rule for each subordinate z in $\underline{S}_w$. Formally, we define the *decision space* of w as $D_w = A_w \times \mathfrak{R}^w$ and call elements of D_w, namely, $d_w = (a_w, r^w)$, *decisions of* w. Let $D = \times_{w \text{ in } W} D_w$ and denote the elements or decisions of D by $d = (d_1, \ldots, d_n)$. Since output depends only on the acts of each worker and since $d_w = (a_w, r^w)$, for $w = 1, \ldots, n$, and $a = (a_1, \ldots, a_n)$, we write $f(d) = f(a)$.

It is assumed that workers base their choices of decisions on a real-valued utility function $p_w = P_w(d_w, \alpha_w)$ defined on D_w for each vector of parameters α_w. The nature of these parameters, as well as their ability to be altered through the actions of the entrepreneur, affect the worker's decisions within the rule restrictions imposed on him. We shall specify four components of α_w in ways that reflect the major lines of influence of members of the organization on the choices of a particular worker. First, the director may provide monetary incentives for worker performance. More precisely, for each w in W there is a nonnegative real-valued *incentive function* $y_w = Y_w(d_w)$ defined over D_w, where y_w, the actual component of α_w, is interpreted as the income w receives upon taking decision d_w. Subject to certain admissibility constraints that will not be specified, Y_w is chosen by the director.

According to the Weberian model of bureaucracy, no further elements are necessary to explain organizational behavior. The incentive structure will induce workers to obey rules, and adhering to rules is sufficient to ensure adequate worker performance. But there are at least two difficulties with this perspective. On the one hand, whether rules are obeyed

depends not only on their substance but also on the perceived authority
of the superior (Barnard [2, p. 168]). A superior appearing to be weak
may obtain relatively less cooperation from subordinates in following
the rules he issues and may also be reluctant to prescribe certain rules
that are in the interests of the firm if they might tend to decrease cooperation still further. On the other hand, even finely articulated rules are
insufficient to provide for all possible contingencies arising in production. Thus unless supported by other forms of influence, authority is not
enough to ensure that the worker will always make the "correct" decisions in unforeseen circumstances (Simon [12, p. 227]). To avoid these
pitfalls, we follow Simon in supposing that a worker's immediate
superior not only imposes rules upon him, but also provides *goals and
premises* (the second component of α_w) to guide the worker's choices. In
other words, for each w in W whose immediate superior is z in $\bar{S}^w$, there
is a real-valued *premise function* $g_w = G_w(d_w)$ defined over D_w. We take
G_w as an attribute of z, in the sense that it reflects a property of the
behavior of z, but G_w is given and not chosen through utility maximization. Moreover, G_w is an expression of the preferences of z over possible
decisions by w. It is independent of the incentive function and likely to
be received differently by w from the latter. In case w has no superior,
G_w is an attribute of the director. Of course, not all real-valued functions on D_w can serve as premise functions. But the characteristics such
functions should possess are not discussed here.

Once it is acknowledged that workers are influenced by their superiors,
it should also be admitted that they are influenced by their co-workers as
well (Gintis [8]). Like the former, the latter too may have a significant
impact on worker behavior. We capture the influence of co-workers on
their mutual performance by assuming each worker has a set of *value
orientations* (the third component of α_w) arising from the decisions of
his co-workers and these, in turn, affect the actions of each. Thus let $\mathcal{V}$
be the class of all possible value orientations. For any co-worker z (in
C_w) of w, let V_{wz} be a function transforming decisions of z into value
orientations v_{wz} (in $\mathcal{V}$) of w, where $z \neq w$. Thus

$$v_{wz} = V_{wz}(d_z)$$

Enumerating the elements of C_w distinct from w as $k_1, \ldots, k_{n_w}$, we have
n_w such functions. These are abbreviated as

$$V^w(d_{k_1}, \ldots, d_{k_w}) = (V_{wk_1}(d_{k_1}), \ldots, V_{wk_w}(d_{k_w}))$$

As with incentive and premise functions, we note but do not dwell on the
presence of admissibility requirements for the V^w.

The fourth and last component of α_w is based on the observation that decision making in the organization depends on the types of information at hand. Following Hurwicz [9], we introduce communications among individuals consisting of (possibly empty) strings of alphanumeric characters, blueprints, and so on. Let $*$ represent the profit-maximizing director, and define $W^* = W \cup \{*\}$. The space of all possible communications among individuals is written $\mathfrak{M}$. For w, z in W^*, and $z \neq w$, let m_{wz} be an element of $\mathfrak{M}$ that denotes the information passed from w to z. The *information received by* w (and the fourth component of α_w) is thus the vector $m_w = (m_{zw})$, where z is in W^* and $z \neq w$, and the *information transmitted by* w is the vector $m^w = (m_{wz})$, where z is in W^* and $z \neq w$. We suppose that m_{wz} is a function M^{wz} of d_w; that is,

$$m_{wz} = M^{wz}(d_w)$$

for all w in W and $z \neq w$ in W^*. Each M^{wz} is assumed to satisfy certain undescribed admissibility criteria. Information transmitted by the director is taken as given. The vector of functions indicating the information transmitted by w is abbreviated by

$$m^w = M^w(d_w)$$

where $M^w(d_w)$ is the vector $(M^{wz}(d_w))$, the components of which vary over $z \neq w$ in W^*. Similarly, the information received by w is shortened to

$$m_w = M_w(d_{(w)})$$

where

$$M_w(d_{(w)})$$
$$= (M^{1w}(d_1), \ldots, M^{w-1w}(d_{w-1}), M^{w+1w}(d_{w+1}), \ldots, M^{nw}(d_n), m_{*w})$$

and m_{*w} is the information transmitted to w from the director.

Worker w's utility function now is specified as

$$p_w = P_w(d_w, Y_w(d_w), G_w(d_w), V^w(d_{k_1}, \ldots, d_{k_w}), M_w(d_{(w)}))$$

where $d_{k_1}, \ldots, d_{k_w}$ and $d_{(w)}$ are determined by workers other than w. We assume that given $d_{k_1}, \ldots, d_{k_w}$ and $d_{(w)}$, worker w chooses d_w so as to maximize P_w over D_w, subject to the constraint that the chosen a_w component of d_w lies in the set R_w^* of restrictions imposed by his superiors. Note that the definition of D_w ensures that the chosen r^w components of d_w are z-admissible for every subordinate z of w.

In spite of the lack of quantifiability of d_w, conditions on D_w and P_w

Table 11-1

Variable	Number
a_w	n
q	1
R_{wz}	$\sum_w \beta_w$
m_{wz}	n^2
p_w	n
y_w	n
g_w	n
v_{wz}	$\sum_w (\gamma_w^2 - \gamma_w)$

that are sufficient to guarantee the existence of a constrained maximizer of P_w are known. (Recall Section 5.4. It is enough, for example, that P_w be continuous and D_w be compact.) These are assumed here without further discussion. However, because some parameters in each worker's utility function are the result of the decisions of others (namely, $d_{k_1}, \ldots, d_{k_w}$ and $d_{(w)}$), we are still not assured that a solution exists when all workers maximize utility simultaneously. Thus it is necessary to investigate the internal consistency of the model as a whole. The first step is to show that it is not underspecified. Let β_w be the cardinality of $\underline{S}_w$, and let γ_w be the cardinality of C_w. Then a breakdown of the number of variables is as shown in Table 11-1. Thus there are a total of

$$n^2 + 4n + 1 + \sum_w \beta_w + \sum_w (\gamma_w^2 - \gamma_w)$$

variables.[2] The equations line up as shown in Table 11-2. There are $n^2 + 3n + 1 + \sum_w (\gamma_w^2 - \gamma_w)$ of them, or a deficit of

$$n + \sum_w \beta_w$$

equations with respect to the unknowns. But each worker chooses d_w to maximize P_w, thus specifying $\beta_w + 1$ variables as functions of parameters in the utility function. Hence the maximization process determines an additional

$$\sum_w (\beta_w + 1) = \sum_w \beta_w + n$$

equations that cover the deficit.

---

[2] There are n^2 variables m_{zw} since each of n workers sends out information to each of $n-1$ workers plus the director. The director's communication to each worker is taken as given.

Table 11-2

Equation	Number
$q = f(a)$	1
$p_w = P_w(d_w, \alpha_w)$	n
$y_w = Y_w(d_w)$	n
$g_w = G_w(d_w)$	n
$v_{wz} = V_{wz}(d_z)$	$\Sigma_w(\gamma_w^2 - \gamma_w)$
$m_{wz} = M^{wz}(d_w)$	n^2

Therefore the model is exactly determined. The next step is to obtain solutions. Of course it could happen that some equations are derivable from others, or even if all equations are independent, there may still be no vector of variable values that satisfy all equations simultaneously. Fortunately, further conditions on the equations of the model (beyond those already required) are known that, without relying on quantification, ensure the existence of solutions. (See Chapter 5. Recall, one collection of such conditions is based on the existence of appropriate inverses.) These too are assumed. Additional restrictions could be imposed to obtain uniqueness. However, the latter are not necessary for subsequent argument and consequently are not postulated.

The last step is to ensure that all components of solutions of the equations are consistent with those requirements of the model that are not expressed in equation form. Consider a vector $d = (d_1, \ldots, d_n)$ in D that is not necessarily a solution. Then d may also be written as $d = (a, r)$, where $a = (a_1, \ldots, a_n)$ and $r = (r^1, \ldots, r^n)$. Now each r^w consists of a vector of rule sets R_{zw} chosen by w. We say that d is admissible whenever

$$R_w^* \neq \varnothing$$

for $w = 1, \ldots, n$, where here R_w^* is defined as it was earlier except that the rule sets that make it up now have been specifically chosen by superiors and the director. In other words, d is admissible as long as the choices of rules leave each worker with at least one act in his act set to choose from. We call d feasible provided that d is admissible and a_w is in the R_w^* chosen by the superiors of w, for each w. That is, d is feasible if each worker actually chooses from decisions remaining in his act set after all rules are imposed. Although feasibility depends on the director's rules R_*, the incentive functions $Y_w(d_w)$, indeed, on all parameters and functions of the model, in what follows we only identify for emphasis those parameters and functions that at the time seem to be most relevant. It is clear that there can be feasible points d in D that are not solutions. But for the model not to be vacuous, it is necessary to assume, as we do here, that feasible solutions exist.

To simplify some rather difficult arguments below, we employ a truncated version of the preceding model in the remainder of this chapter. With one exception to be noted later, all communication variables, and all value orientation and premise functions hereafter are discarded. Thus utility functions reduce to

$$p_w = P_w(d_w, Y_w(d_w))$$

for each w in W. It is assumed that if $Y_w(d_w)$ is an incentive function that satisfies the admissibility constraints alluded to (but not specifically described) earlier, then the incentive function $Y_w(d_w) - \epsilon$ also satisfies the same admissibility constraints for all sufficiently small real numbers $\epsilon > 0$. Furthermore, as a function of two variables, each $P_w(d_w, Y_w)$ is taken to be continuous on its domain. (It is possible to define continuity in the absence of measurement. See Section 3.2.)

Profits, π, are defined by

$$\pi = q - \sum_w y_w$$

or, in functional form, as

$$\pi(d) = f(d) - \sum_w Y_w(d_w)$$

where $d = (d_1, \ldots, d_n)$ and output price is set at unity. All costs not contained in the incentive functions Y_w, including those associated with the implementation of rules, are assumed to be zero. Finally, throughout subsequent discussion, proofs of the theorems are relegated to the appendix.

11.2   Conditions for Pareto optimality

We now proceed to investigate conditions under which profit maximization leads to Pareto optimality.

A collection of n incentive functions $\{Y_w(d_w): w \text{ is in } W\}$ is an *incentive system*. The incentive system $\{Y_w(d_w)\}$ is *efficient* with respect to the director's rules R_* whenever there is no other system $\{Y'_w(d_w)\}$ such that with d feasible given $\{Y_w(d_w)\}$ and R_*, and d' feasible given $\{Y'_w(d_w)\}$ and any R'_*,

$$P_w(d'_w, Y'_w(d'_w)) \geq P_w(d_w, Y_w(d_w))$$

for every w in W,

$$P_w(d'_w, Y'_w(d'_w)) > P_w(d_w, Y_w(d_w))$$

for at least one w in W, and

$$f(d') - \sum_w Y'_w(d'_w) \geqslant f(d) - \sum_w Y_w(d_w)$$

In other words, efficient systems have the property that at any feasible d they cannot be modified so as to increase profits without lowering the utility of at least one worker. Efficiency is defined with respect to R_* because the latter, in part, determines which decisions in D are feasible. The same incentive system could be efficient under one R_* but not under another.

Let B be a subset of D. A decision d in B is *Pareto optimal over B* if d is feasible for some R_* and incentive system $\{Y_w(d_w)\}$, and there is no other d' in B, feasible for some R'_*, such that for all w in W,

$$P_w(d'_w, Y_w(d'_w)) \geqslant P_w(d_w, Y_w(d_w))$$

where

$$P_w(d'_w, Y_w(d'_w)) > P_w(d_w, Y_w(d_w))$$

for at least one w, and

$$f(d') - \sum_w Y_w(d'_w) \geqslant f(d) - \sum_w Y_w(d_w)$$

Thus at a Pareto-optimal d, no feasible reorganization of production can make one worker better off (and no one else worse off) without lowering profits. Recall, with $d = (a, r)$ and $d' = (a', r')$, only when $a' \neq a$ is $f(d') \neq f(d)$. If there were a feasible d' in B satisfying the preceding inequalities (so that d could not be Pareto optimal), then d' would be called *Pareto superior* to d in B. When d is Pareto optimal over D, it is referred to as simply *Pareto optimal*.

Let $D^* = \{d = (a, r) : d$ is in D and $R_* = \{a\}\}$, that is, D^* is the collection of decisions constrained by the director choosing the acts of each worker. Our first result asserts that if the director chooses each worker's act, and if the incentive system is efficient, then any feasible solution is Pareto optimal. Roughly speaking, this makes precise the conditions ensuring optimality in the authoritarian (nonmarket) portion of the Coase–Simon model described earlier. Recall, in their approach the capitalist chose the specific task each worker was to perform.

11.2-1 Theorem: Let $d^0 = (a^0, r^0)$ in D^* be a feasible solution for $R^0_* = \{a^0\}$ and the incentive system $\{Y_w(d_w)\}$ employed by the director. If $\{Y_w(d_w)\}$ is efficient with respect to R_*^0, then d^0 is Pareto optimal over D^*.

Note that although d^0 may be Pareto optimal over D^*, it need not be Pareto optimal over the larger set D.

Even without the director choosing the acts of each worker, it is still possible to have Pareto-optimal solutions. An incentive system $\{Y_w(d_w)\}$ is said to be *act-stable* on D if for each $d=(a,r)$ in D, feasible given $\{Y_w(d_w)\}$ and some R_*, there is an $\epsilon>0$ and an r' such that $d'=(a,r')$ is feasible given some R_*' and the modified incentive system

$$\{Y_w(d_w) - \epsilon : w \text{ is in } W\}$$

Alternatively put, the act component of a feasible decision remains the component of some feasible decision in the face of slight variations in incentives. Neither d nor d' are necessarily solutions.

11.2-2 Theorem: If the incentive system $\{Y_w(d_w)\}$ employed by the director is act-stable and efficient with respect to some R_*, then any solution in D, feasible given R_* and $\{Y_w(d_w)\}$, is Pareto optimal.

As we know, at any feasible solution d^0, efficient incentives cannot be modified so as to obtain a new feasible decision d that yields increased profits without, at d, lowering the utility of at least one worker. Thus it is not surprising that efficient incentives lead to Pareto optimality. But Theorems 11.2-1 and 11.2-2 indicate that for the argument to go through, additional conditions are needed. These are required to ensure the feasibility of decisions being compared to d^0. This feasibility is achieved through the restriction that the director choose each worker's act in Theorem 11.2-1, and through act stability in Theorem 11.2-2.

A decision d^0 in $B \subseteq D$ *maximizes profit over* B given $\{Y_w(d_w)\}$ whenever

$$f(d^0) - \sum_w Y_w(d_w^0) \geqslant f(d) - \sum_w Y_w(d_w)$$

for all d in B. When $B=D$, we say simply that d^0 maximizes profit. If d^0 is profit maximizing over B and if d^0 is also one of the feasible solutions given $\{Y_w(d_w)\}$ to which Theorem 11.2-2 (or Theorem 11.2-1) applies, then d^0 is Pareto optimal. There are, however, further special circumstances in which profit-maximizing solutions are Pareto optimal. Several of these are now considered in turn.

In the first case, workers are motivated exclusively by monetary incentives, and as long as these incentives are chosen "properly" by the director, optimality prevails.

We say w in W is *incentive motivated* if for any $d^0 = (d_1^0, \ldots, d_n^0)$ and $d' = (d_1', \ldots, d_n')$ in D and any incentive function $Y_w(d_w)$ such that d^0 is feasible given $Y_w(d_w)$ and some R_*^0, and d' is feasible given $Y_w(d_w)$ and some R_*', if

$$Y_w(d_w') \geqslant Y_w(d_w^0)$$

then

$$P_w(d_w', Y_w(d_w')) \geqslant P_w(d_w^0, Y_w(d_w^0))$$

Thus, an incentive motivated worker cares about decisions only in so far as they affect his income.

An incentive system $\{Y_w(d_w)\}$ is *profit efficient* whenever $f(d') > f(d)$ implies

$$f(d') - \sum_w Y_w(d_w') > f(d) - \sum_w Y_w(d_w)$$

for all $d = (d_1, \ldots, d_n)$ and $d' = (d_1', \ldots, d_n')$ in D such that d and d' are feasible with respect to $\{Y_w(d_w)\}$ and some (not necessarily the same) R_*. In other words, profit efficiency means the incentive system is such that an increase in output is always accompanied by an increase in profit. With profit-efficient incentives, maximum profit can only occur at feasible decisions where output is maximal.

11.2-3 Theorem: Let $\{Y_w(d_w)\}$ be profit efficient. If all workers are incentive motivated, then any profit-maximizing solution, feasible given $\{Y_w(d_w)\}$ and some R_*, is Pareto optimal.

Further situations in which we would expect profit maximization to yield Pareto optimality arise when workers' preferences are constituted so that, of their own free will, workers choose decisions that conform perfectly to the profit-maximizing needs of the director or to the premises and goals provided by their superiors. To formalize these ideas requires the specification of ordering relations on decisions and rules.

Consider any worker w in W. Let d_w be distinct from d_w' in D_w. When

$$f(d_1, \ldots, d_{w-1}, d_w', d_{w+1}, \ldots, d_n)$$
$$> f(d_1, \ldots, d_{w-1}, d_w, d_{w+1}, \ldots, d_n)$$

for all d_z in D_z such that $z \neq w$ and both $(d_1, \ldots, d_{w-1}, d_w', d_{w+1}, \ldots, d_n)$ and $(d_1, \ldots, d_{w-1}, d_w, d_{w+1}, \ldots, d_n)$ are feasible, then we say d_w' domi-

nates d_w and write $d_w' > d_w$. Here it is not necessary to single out for emphasis specific functions and parameters with respect to which feasibility holds. Dominance thus requires output to rise upon substitution of d_w' for d_w in d, regardless of the values of the remaining components of d. We write $d_w' = d_w$ if under the preceding conditions output remains unchanged, and $d_w' \geqslant d_w$ if either $d_w' > d_w$ or $d_w' = d_w$. Clearly, $>$ on D_w is irreflexive, asymmetric, and transitive, and $\geqslant$ is reflexive, antisymmetric, and transitive. Assume $\geqslant$ is total on D_w.

11.2-4   Theorem: Let $d^0 = (d_1^0, \ldots, d_n^0)$ and $d' = (d_1', \ldots, d_n')$ be in D. If $d_w' \geqslant d_w^0$ for all w in W, then $f(d') \geqslant f(d^0)$. If, in addition, $d_w' > d_w^0$ for at least one w in W then $f(d') > f(d^0)$.

The definition of dominance among rule sets is more complicated. For any w, let $\mathfrak{R}_w$ be the collection of all admissible intersections R_w of rule sets imposed by the superiors of w. Consider first a worker w in W who has no subordinates. We say R_w' *dominates* R_w provided that R_w' and R_w are in $\mathfrak{R}_w$, $R_w' \subset R_w$, and for any a_w' in R_w' and a_w in $R_w - R_w'$, we have $d_w' > d_w$, where a_w' is the first component of d_w', and a_w is the first component of d_w. Confusion will not arise by using the same symbol ">" to denote both dominance on $\mathfrak{R}_w$ and dominance on D_w. Write $R_w' \geqslant R_w$ when $d_w' \geqslant d_w$, and $R_w' = R_w$ when $d_w' = d_w$. If w has subordinates, dominance on $\mathfrak{R}_w$ is defined only after dominance on $\mathfrak{R}_z$ is defined for every z in $\underline{S}_w$. In this case R_w' is said to *dominate* R_w if, in addition to the foregoing conditions, $R_{zw}' > R_{zw}$ for all z in $\underline{S}_w$, where R_{zw}' (and R_{zw}) is the rule set imposed by w on z in decision d' (and, respectively, d).[3] Again, $R_w' \geqslant R_w$ when both $d_w' \geqslant d_w$ and $R_{zw}' \geqslant R_{zw}$ for all z in $\underline{S}_w$, and $R_w' = R_w$ when both $d_w' = d_w$ and $R_{zw}' = R_{zw}$ for all z in $\underline{S}_w$. Thus $>$ is defined recursively over $\mathfrak{R}_w$ for every w in W.

For each w, dominance of rule sets ($>$) on $\mathfrak{R}_w$ is clearly irreflexive and asymmetric because dominance on D_w has these properties. To see that $>$ on $\mathfrak{R}_w$ is also transitive, it suffices to consider only the circumstances in which w has no subordinates. Suppose $R_w'' > R_w' > R_w$. Then $R_w'' \subset R_w' \subset R_w$. Hence $R_w'' \subset R_w$. Let a_w'' be in R_w'' and a_w be in $R_w - R_w''$. Now either a_w is in R_w' or it is in $R_w - R_w'$. In the former case $d_w'' > d_w$ (where a_w'' is the first component of d_w'') since $R_w'' > R_w'$. In the latter case choose any a_w' in $R_w' - R_w''$. Then $d_w'' > d_w' > d_w$ because $R_w'' > R_w' > R_w$. Since $>$ is transitive on D_w, we have $d_w'' > d_w$. Therefore $>$ is transitive on $\mathfrak{R}_w$. Except for totality, $\geqslant$ on $\mathfrak{R}_w$ has the same properties as $\geqslant$ on D_w. Assume $\geqslant$ is total on $\mathfrak{R}_w$.

---

[3] In terms of earlier notation, $d_w = (a_w, r^w)$ and $r^w = (R_{1w}, \ldots, R_{\beta_w w})$, where β_w denotes the number of elements in $\underline{S}_w$.

The last dominance relation is defined on D_w. Let d'_w and d_w be in D_w. If $d'_w > d_w$ and $R'_{zw} > R_{zw}$ for all z in $\underline{S}_w$ where R'_{zw} and R_{zw} are components of d'_w and d_w, respectively, we write $d'_w \ominus d_w$ and say that d'_w *strongly dominates* d_w. Both $\geqslant$ and $\ominus$ are defined in the obvious way. Since $\geqslant$ is reflexive, antisymmetric, transitive and total on D_w and on $\mathcal{R}_w$, so is $\;$ on D_w. Similarly $\oslash$ is irreflexive, asymmetric, and transitive.

We say that a worker, w, *internalizes the values of the firm* whenever $d'_w \ominus d_w$ implies

$$P_w(d'_w, Y_w(d'_w)) \geqslant P_w(d_w, Y_w(d_w))$$

for all incentive functions $Y_w(d_w)$ and all d'_w and d_w that are respective components of decisions d and d' in D, feasible given some (not necessarily the same) $\{Y_w(d_w)\}$ and R_*.

11.2-5 Theorem: Let $\{Y_w(d_w)\}$ be profit efficient. If all workers internalize the values of the firm, then any profit-maximizing solution, feasible given $\{Y_w(d_w)\}$ and some R_*, is Pareto optimal.

At this point it is worth illustrating how the foregoing analysis can be applied in a more general setting. To do so we enlarge our truncated model by reinstating the premise functions $G_w(d_w)$ that were introduced in the first section. We continue to ignore value orientations and message transmissions. Utility functions are therefore written

$$p_w = P_w(d_w, Y_w(d_w), G_w(d_w))$$

for each w. Earlier definitions are revised accordingly. Thus the notion of Pareto optimality remains unchanged, except that utility functions now are written as indicated here and it is emphasized that decisions are feasible with respect to three items (instead of two), namely, an incentive system $\{Y_w(d_w)\}$, a system of premise functions $\{G_w(d_w)\}$, and the director's rule sets R_*. On the other hand, internalization of the values of the firm requires not only the more general utility function, but it also must be strengthened so that the statement "$d'_w \ominus d_w$ implies $P_w(d'_w, Y_w(d'_w), G_w(d'_w)) \geqslant P_w(d_w, Y_w(d_w), G_w(d_w))$" now holds for all premise functions, G_w, in addition to everything else. Incentive motivation is treated analogously to internalization of the values of the firm by generalizing utility functions and extending the definition to hold for all premise functions. The only change necessitated in the definitions of incentive efficiency, act stability, profit efficiency, and the orderings among decisions and rule sets is the substitution of the revised emphasis in the notion of feasibility. Obvious modifications of the theorems and their proofs correspond.

Parallel to the concept of incentive motivation, worker w is called *vertically influenced* provided that for any incentive function $Y_w(d_w)$ and premise function $G_w(d_w)$, if $G_w(d'_w) \geqq G_w(d_w)$, then

$$P_w(d'_w, Y_w(d'_w), G_w(d'_w)) \geqslant P_w(d_w, Y_w(d_w), G_w(d_w))$$

for all d'_w and d_w that are respective components of decisions d and d' in D, where the latter are feasible given some (not necessarily the same) $\{Y_w(d_w)\}$, $\{G_w(d_w)\}$ and R_*. In addition, G_w is referred to as *nondecreasing with respect to* $\circledS$ on D_w when $d'_w \circledS d_w$ implies $G_w(d'_w) \geqslant G_w(d_w)$, for all d'_w and d_w subject to the preceding feasibility restriction.

11.2-6 Theorem: Let $\{Y_w(d_w)\}$ be profit efficient and $\{G_w(d_w)\}$ nondecreasing with respect to $\circledS$ for each G_w. If all workers are vertically influenced, then any profit-maximizing solution, feasible given $\{Y_w(d_w)\}$, $\{G_w(d_w)\}$, and some R_*, is Pareto optimal.

These theorems provide several illustrations of the circumstances in which profit maximization gives rise to Pareto optimality. In each case the conditions demanded are quite restrictive. For a variety of reasons optimality cannot be expected to obtain in general. In the first place, if (as is likely to be the case) the director does not know the preferences of his workers, then he is unable to select efficient incentives. He can still make sure incentives are profit efficient, but his workers may be neither incentive motivated nor vertically influenced. They also may not internalize the values of the firm. Reinstating value orientations and message transmissions magnifies the possibility of nonoptimal solutions considerably. In general, then, there may be no internal mechanism within the firm that guarantees that the process of profit maximization combined with utility maximization subject to rule constraints will produce a Pareto-optimal solution. Of course, the process may still yield solutions that are Pareto superior to other "attainable" modes of work organization, but this question can be resolved only through a more detailed analysis than that given above.

Our story, however, does not end here. Beyond the efficient allocation of human resources, the director of the firm surely is interested in the means by which profits can be increased. The next section examines some of the issues involved.

11.3   Conditions for profitability

What are the attributes of a good worker? Economic theory has been traditionally quite indisposed to broach this question. Indeed, were profit maximization Pareto optimal, the problem would reduce to one of the technical conditions of production; as such, it would not be an "economic" issue per se. But we have seen that in general this is not the case. Hence an answer is needed in order to have a theory of the labor market proper, as well as to evaluate alternative economic institutions and social policies (Bowles and Gintis [3]).

In our model a worker's attributes can affect profitability through (a) his possession of skills (i.e. the nature of A_w), (b) his preferences and hence choices among decisions, (c) his susceptibility to being motivated by incentives, (d) the way he imposes rules on his subordinates, (e) the nature of the premises he presents to his subordinates, (f) the weight he places on the premises of his superior, (g) the role played by his value orientations, (h) the way he receives and transmits information, and so on. Several of these possibilities are examined now in the context of our truncated model that was described at the end of Section 11.1 and explored extensively in Section 11.2.

Consider any worker w with act set $A_w \subseteq \mathfrak{A}$. Let $\bar{A}_w \subseteq \mathfrak{A}$ be a second act set such that $A_w \subset \bar{A}_w$, and write $d_w = (a_w, r^w)$ and $\bar{d}_w = (\bar{a}_w, \bar{r}^w)$ when, respectively, a_w is in A_w and $\bar{a}_w$ is in $\bar{A}_w - A_w$. If $\bar{d}_w \ominus d_w$ for all such $\bar{d}_w$ and d_w in D_w, and if $\bar{A}_w$ is substituted for A_w, then we say that w has *become more skilled*. Thus increasing skills means that potential output rises. But there is no guarantee that w will use his new skills (i.e., choose an act from $\bar{A}_w - A_w$) and that jealous co-workers will not attempt to subvert them so that output can, in fact, rise. The firm is *receptive to new skills of w* if in arriving at a new feasible solution after w has become more skilled and $\bar{A}_w$ has been substituted for A_w, the constrained set out of which w chooses his acts always contains at least one element of $\bar{A}_w - A_w$. Sufficient conditions under which more skills increase the value of the worker to the firm are as follows.

11.3-1   Theorem: Let $\{Y_w(d_w)\}$ be profit efficient. Suppose w internalizes the values of the firm and the firm is receptive to new skills of w. Given a feasible solution d, if w becomes more skilled and, at the same time, no other worker $z \neq w$ alters his chosen act, then profits are greater at the new feasible solution $\bar{d}$.

The restriction concerning internalization of the values of the firm in Theorem 11.3-1 can be replaced by incentive motivation provided that the incentive function chosen by the director for w exhibits an additional property. The incentive function $Y_w(d_w)$ is referred to as *nondecreasing with respect to* $\geqslant$ on D_w whenever $d'_w \geqslant d_w$ implies $Y_w(d'_w) \geqslant Y_w(d_w)$ for all d'_w and d_w in D_w.

11.3-2   Theorem: Let $\{Y_w(d_w)\}$ be profit efficient. Suppose w is incentive motivated, $Y_w(d_w)$ is nondecreasing with respect to $\geqslant$ on D_w, and the firm is receptive to new skills of w. Given a feasible solution d, if w becomes more skilled and, at the same time, no other worker $z \neq w$ alters his chosen act, then profits are greater at the new feasible solution $\bar{d}$.

Yet a third set of sufficient conditions can be expressed with the aid of premise functions in the context of the slightly enlarged model discussed at the end of Section 11.2.

11.3-3   Theorem: Let $\{Y_w(d_w)\}$ be profit efficient. Suppose w is vertically influenced, $G_w(d_w)$ is nondecreasing with respect to $\geqslant$ on D_w, and the firm is receptive to new skills of w. Given a feasible solution d, if w becomes more skilled and, at the same time, no other worker $z \neq w$ alters his chosen act, then profits are greater at the new feasible solution $\bar{d}$.

These theorems codify the sense in which workers with more skill are preferred by the director to those with less. The reader should note that the conditions under which the propositions are true are not always met and are certainly not trivial.

Discarding premise functions once again, we now formulate a proposition describing circumstances under which certain worker utility functions are more valuable to the firm than others. Let $P_w(d_w, Y_w(d_w))$ and $Q_w(d_w, Y_w(d_w))$ be two utility functions defined on D_w for a worker w in W. Let $\hat{d}_w$ be chosen under P_w, and $\bar{d}_w$ under Q_w. We say P_w *dominates* Q_w and write $P_w > Q_w$ if for any incentive function $Y_w(d_w)$ and all $\hat{d}_w$ and $\bar{d}_w$ in D_w, we have $\hat{d}_w > \bar{d}_w$.

11.3-4   Theorem: Let $\{Y_w(d_w)\}$ be profit efficient, $\hat{d}$ a feasible solution given utility functions P_z for every z in W, and $\bar{d}$ a nonprofit-maximizing feasible solution given utility functions Q_w for some worker w, and P_z for $z \neq w$. If $P_w > Q_w$ and the chosen act of each $z \neq w$ is the same for both $\hat{d}$ and $\bar{d}$, then profits are greater at $\hat{d}$ than at $\bar{d}$.

This theorem illustrates one of the major ways in which the employer-employee relation differs from a true market relationship. In a true market exchange the participants are concerned only with the properties of the entities exchanged and not with the personal attributes of each other (Arrow and Hahn [1, p. 23]). Indeed, this observation is the crux of the purported "performance orientation" of a capitalist economy that abjures all ascriptive and particularist valuations (Parsons [10], Friedman [6]). Yet we see that the employer cares very much about the preference structures of his employees and not only about their skills. (This point has also been documented empirically by Bowles and Gintis [3, Ch. 5].)

Our last proposition relates increased incentive motivation on the part of workers to greater profitability for the firm. Consider any worker w and two utility functions $P_w(d_w, Y_w(d_w))$ and $Q_w(d_w, Y_w(d_w))$ on D_w. Again, suppose $\hat{d}_w$ is chosen under P_w and $\bar{d}_w$ under Q_w. If for all incentive functions $Y_w(d_w)$,

$$Y_w(\hat{d}_w) > Y_w(\bar{d}_w)$$

then we say w is *more highly motivated by incentives* under P_w than under Q_w.

11.3-5 Theorem: Let $\{Y_w(d_w)\}$ be profit efficient, $\hat{d}$ a feasible solution given utility functions P_z for every z in W, and $\bar{d}$ a nonprofit-maximizing feasible solution given utility functions Q_w for some worker w and P_z for $z \neq w$. If w is more highly motivated by incentives under P_w than under Q_w, if $Y_w(d_w)$ is nondecreasing with respect to $\geqslant$ on D_w, and if the chosen act of each $z \neq w$ is the same for both $\hat{d}$ and $\bar{d}$, then profits are greater at $\hat{d}$ than at $\bar{d}$.

11.4 Conclusion

The fundamental observation emerging from the preceding analysis is that except under highly restrictive conditions, the pursuit of profit maximization by the firm may not allocate internal human activity Pareto optimally. The reason for this has to do with the manner in which we view the production process. In neoclassical theory, once technology and preferences are given, all that matters are the "neoclassical quantities," that is, the number of labor hours that flow through markets in conjunction with quantities of nonlabor inputs, and outputs that are consumed by the worker. Optimality follows from the constraints of competition and the postulates of rationality (maximization). But in our approach, even if labor hours and other neoclassical quantities could be determined independently, the worker would still have to choose acts, rules, value orientations, premises, and messages in order to carry out the responsibilities of his job. At the same time, he would also be subject to other rules, value orientations, premises, messages, and incentives that are thrust upon him. Now because incentives are defined over worker decisions, acts and rule sets may be viewed as "market-type" elements. After all, the director can reward certain acts and rules over others and, as we have seen, in certain cases, workers respond to these incentives as the director would like them to. Thus it is possible to speak of the "demand and supply" of acts and rule sets in much the same way as one speaks of the demand and supply of labor hours. However, even with rationality remaining the guiding hand of human behavior, it is clear that premises, value orientations, and messages do not flow through markets, and they are not constrained by the institutional mechanism of competition. Rather, in our model they serve as the basis for the formation of social relations among people that are crucial to the production process. Thus there is no reason to expect that the allocation of human activity within the firm would lead to Pareto optimality – even if it manages to maximize profits.

In a larger sense, the only proper conclusion to this study is a plea for further research. Although our model is quite complex, we have shown it to be amenable to rigorous analytical investigation. Our major propositions barely scratch the surface in understanding the complex interaction of acts, rules, incentive systems, preference structures, and patterns of influence involving values, premises, and information. At least three important problems stand out. First, the model needs to be integrated into a more expansive framework in which wage rates and labor market conditions bear on internal decisions and structures. Ideally one would also want to include interaction with consumers, other firms, labor unions, and the government. Second, a general model of organizational structure should be developed of which hierarchical organization is but one form. This model should be capable of determining, on the basis of profitability or efficiency, the precise conditions under which the hierarchical form will be chosen. Third, the situation that arises when workers do not necessarily obey the rules imposed by their superiors requires investigation.

The last of these issues deserves a final word. Organizational experience indicates that the cost of enforcing rules imposed by superiors rises rapidly as the number of violators increases. An individual who does not follow rules can be threatened or dismissed, but mass violations based on collusion between superiors and subordinates, and among co-workers, can swiftly destroy the downward transmission of rules and render inoperative certain necessary transmissions of information, value orientations, and premises. The solidarity of a worker coalition depends on such things as the commonality of interests, the benefits accruing to a worker upon withdrawal from it, and whatever penalties the coalition can impose on deviant members. On the other hand, the capitalist can discourage coalition formation by fragmenting work groups, increasing the "social distance" between superiors and subordinates, and routing important decision-making power through higher levels to minimize the degree of control that a group of workers may exercise over a co-worker.

To integrate these insights into our model requires that our analysis of interpersonal behavior be enlarged to include game-theoretic and bargaining elements. The difficulties associated with such an approach are well known. The benefits, however, should prove substantial.

Appendix

Proof of Theorem 11.2-1: Let $d^0 = (a^0, r^0)$ be a feasible solution in D^* for R_*^0 and $\{ Y_w(d_w) \}$. If d^0 were not Pareto optimal over D^*, then there would be a feasible $d' = (a', r')$ in D^*, where $R_*' = \{ a' \}$ and

$$(11.\text{A-1}) \quad P_w(d_w', Y_w(d_w')) \geq P_w(d_w^0, Y_w(d_w^0))$$

for each w in W,

$$(11.\text{A-2}) \quad P_z(d_z', Y_z(d_z')) > P_z(d_z^0, Y_z(d_z^0))$$

for some z in W, and

$$(11.\text{A-3}) \quad f(d') - \sum_w Y_w(d_w') \geq f(d^0) - \sum_w Y_w(d^0)$$

Define the incentive function

$$Y_z'(d_z) = \begin{cases} Y_z(d_z), & \text{if } d_z \neq d_z' \\ Y_z(d_z) - \epsilon, & \text{if } d_z = d_z' \end{cases}$$

for some $\epsilon > 0$, and consider the incentive system $\{ Y_w'(d_w) \}$ obtained as

$$Y_w'(d_w) = \begin{cases} Y_w(d_w), & \text{if } w \neq z \\ Y_w'(d_w), & \text{if } w = z \end{cases}$$

This is permissible according to the assumptions listed at the end of Section 11.1. Since $R'_* = \{a'\}$, d' is also feasible with $\{Y'_w(d_w)\}$. Hence from (11.A-1),

(11.A-4) $P_w(d'_w, Y'_w(d'_w)) \geqslant P_w(d^0_w, Y_w(d^0_w))$

for each w in W. With ϵ sufficiently small, the continuity of preferences and (11.A-2) imply

(11.A-5) $P_z(d'_z, Y'_z(d'_z)) > P_z(d^0_z, Y_z(d^0_z))$

Lastly, from (11.A-3),

(11.A-6) $f(d') - \sum_w Y'_w(d'_w) > f(d^0) - \sum_w Y_w(d^0)$

But (11.A-4) to (11.A-6) contradict the efficiency of $\{Y_w(d_w)\}$ with respect to R^0_*.   Q.E.D.

Proof of Theorem 11.2-2: The proof is the same as that of Theorem 11.2-1, except that both feasibility under the modified incentive system and the fact that $f(d')$ does not change when the incentive system is modified, now follow from act-stability.

Q.E.D.

Proof of Theorem 11.2-3: Let d^0 be a profit-maximizing solution that is feasible with respect to $\{Y_w(d_w)\}$ and R_*. Then

$$f(d^0) - \sum_w Y_w(d^0_w) \geqslant f(d) - \sum_w Y_w(d_w)$$

for all d in D. If $d^0 = (d^0_1, \ldots, d^0_n)$ were not Pareto optimal, then there would be a $d' = (d'_1, \ldots, d'_n)$ in D, feasible given $\{Y_w(d_w)\}$ and some R'_* such that,

(11.A-7) $P_w(d'_w, Y_w(d'_w)) \geqslant P_w(d^0, Y_w(d^0_w))$

for each w in W,

(11.A-8) $P_z(d'_z, Y_z(d'_z)) > P_z(d^0_z, Y_z(d^0_z))$

for some z in W, and

(11.A-9) $f(d') - \sum_w Y_w(d'_w) = f(d^0) - \sum_w Y_w(d^0_w)$

Note that (11.A-9) cannot be an inequality since d^0 is profit maximizing. Now from (11.A-7) and (11.A-8), because all workers are incentive motivated,

(11.A-10) $\sum\limits_{w} Y_w(d'_w) > \sum\limits_{w} Y_w(d^0_w)$

Combining (11.A-9) and (11.A-10), we obtain

(11.A-11) $f(d') > f(d^0)$

Applying profit efficiency to (11.A-11), we have

$$f(d') - \sum\limits_{w} Y_w(d'_w) > f(d^0) - \sum\limits_{w} Y_w(d^0_w)$$

contrary to (11.A-9). Q.E.D.

Proof of Theorem 11.2-4: Consider the sequence of vectors:

$$b^0 = d^0$$
$$b^1 = (d'_1, d^0_2, \ldots, d^0_n)$$
$$b^2 = (d'_1, d'_2, d^0_3, \ldots, d^0_n)$$
$$\vdots$$
$$b^{n-1} = (d'_1, \ldots, d'_{n-1}, d^0_n)$$
$$b^n = d'$$

When $d'_w \geqslant d^0_w$ for all w,

(11.A-12) $f(b^0) \leqslant f(b^1) \leqslant \cdots \leqslant f(b^n)$

so that $f(d^0) \leqslant f(d')$. If $d'_w > d^0_w$ for some w, then the corresponding inequality in (11.A-12) is strict. Hence in the latter case, $f(d^0) < f(d')$. Q.E.D.

Proof of Theorem 11.2-5: Let d^0 be a profit-maximizing solution that is feasible with respect to $\{Y_w(d_w)\}$ and R_*. Then profit efficiency implies

(11.A-13) $f(d^0) > f(d)$

for all feasible d in D distinct from d^0. If $d^0 = (d^0_1, \ldots, d^0_n)$ were not Pareto optimal, then there would be a $d' = (d'_1, \ldots, d'_n)$ in D, feasible given $\{Y_w(d_w)\}$ and some R'_* such that

(11.A-14) $P_w(d'_w, Y_w(d'_w)) \geqslant P_w(d^0_w, Y_w(d^0_w))$

for each w in W,

(11.A-15) $P_z(d'_z, Y_z(d'_z)) > P_z(d^0_z, Y_z(d^0_z))$

for some z in W, and

$$f(d') - \sum_w Y_w(d'_w) \geq f(d^0) - \sum_w Y_w(d^0_w)$$

Because each worker internalizes the values of the firm, (11.A-14) and (11.A-15) imply $d'_w \ominus d^0_w$ for all w, and $d'_z \ominus d^0_z$. Hence from Theorem 11.2-4 and the definitions of $\ominus$ and $\ominus$,

(11.A-16) $f(d') > f(d^0)$

But (11.A-13) applies to all feasible decisions, including d'. This contradicts (11.A-16).   Q.E.D.

Proof of Theorem 11.2-6: The proof is similar to that of Theorem 11.2-5.   Q.E.D.

Proof of Theorem 11.3-1: Write $d = (d_1, \ldots, d_n)$ and $\bar{d} = (\bar{d}_1, \ldots, \bar{d}_n)$, where d and $\bar{d}$ are the feasible solutions appearing in the statement of the theorem. Set $d_z = (a_z, r^z)$ and $\bar{d}_z = (\bar{a}_z, \bar{r}^z)$ for every z in W.

Because the firm is receptive to w's new skills, upon becoming more skilled and substituting $\bar{A}_w$ for A_w, w will always be able to choose at least one decision $\hat{d}_w = (\hat{a}_w, \hat{r}^w)$ such that $\hat{a}_w$ is in $\bar{A}_w - A_w$. But since w has become more skilled, $\hat{d}_w > \tilde{d}_w$, where $\tilde{d}_w = (\tilde{a}_w, \tilde{r}^w)$ is any decision with $\tilde{a}_w$ in A_w and the appropriate feasibility constraints are satisfied. Now w also internalizes the values of the firm so

$$P_w(\hat{d}_w, Y_w(\hat{d}_w)) \geq P_w(\tilde{d}_w, Y_w(\tilde{d}_w))$$

Therefore $\hat{d}_w$ will always be chosen over $\tilde{d}_w$. The same must also be true of the respective components $\bar{d}_w$ and d_w of the feasible solutions $\bar{d}$ and d. Hence $\bar{d}_w \ominus d_w$, from which we have $\bar{d}_w > d_w$. Since we have assumed a_z and $\bar{a}_z$ are identical for each $z \neq w$, it follows that $\bar{d}_z = d_z$ for $z \neq w$. By Theorem 11.2-4, $f(\bar{d}) > f(d)$. Profit efficiency now implies that profits are greater at $\bar{d}$.

Q.E.D.

Proof of Theorem 11.3-2: The proof is similar to that of Theorem 11.3-1, with the role of internalization of the values of the firm now being played by the hypotheses of incentive motivation and the nondecreasing property of $Y_w(d_w)$.   Q.E.D.

Proof of Theorem 11.3-3: The proof is similar to that of Theorem 11.3-1, with the role of internalization of the values of the firm now being played by the hypotheses of vertical influence and the nondecreasing property of $G_w(d_w)$.   Q.E.D.

Proof of Theorem 11.3-4: Write $\hat{d} = (\hat{d}_1, \ldots, \hat{d}_n)$, and $\bar{d} = (\bar{d}_1, \ldots, \bar{d}_n)$, where $\hat{d}$ and $\bar{d}$ are the feasible solutions appearing in the statement of the theorem. Let $\hat{d}_z = (\hat{a}_z, \hat{r}^z)$ and $\bar{d}_z = (\bar{a}_z, \bar{r}^z)$ for all z in W.

Now, since it is assumed that $P_w > Q_w$ and that $\hat{a}_z$ and $\bar{a}_z$ are identical for $z \neq w$, we have $\hat{d}_w > \bar{d}_w$, and $\hat{d}_z = \bar{d}_z$ for all z in W distinct from w. By Theorem 11.2-4, $f(\hat{d}) > f(\bar{d})$, so from profit efficiency, profits are greater at $\hat{d}$.   Q.E.D.

Proof of Theorem 11.3-5: The proof is the same as that of Theorem 11.3-2, except here $\hat{d}_w > \bar{d}_w$ follows from the facts that w is more highly motivated by incentives under P_w than under Q_w, and $Y_w(d_w)$ is nondecreasing with respect to $\geqslant$.   Q.E.D.

References

1. Arrow, K. J., and F. H. Hahn, *General Competitive Analysis* (San Francisco: Holden-Day, 1971).
2. Barnard, C. I., *The Functions of the Executive* (Cambridge, Mass.: Harvard University Press, 1966).
3. Bowles, S., and H. Gintis, *Schooling in Capitalist America: Educational Reform and the Contradictions of Economic Life* (New York: Basic Books, 1976).
4. Coase, R., "The Nature of the Firm," *Economica,* new series, 4 (1937): 386–405.
5. Ferguson, C. E., *The Neoclassical Theory of Production* (Cambridge: Cambridge University Press, 1971).
6. Friedman, M., *Capitalism and Freedom* (Chicago: University of Chicago Press, 1962).
7. Gintis, H., "Consumer Behavior and the Concept of Sovereignty," *American Economic Review,* 62 (May 1972):267–78.
8. Gintis, H., "The Nature of the Labor Exchange and the Theory of Capitalist Production," *Review of Radical Political Economics,* 8 (1976):36–54.
9. Hurwicz, L., "Optimality and Informational Efficiency in Resource Allocation Processes," in K. J. Arrow, S. Karlin, and P. Suppes, eds., *Mathematical Methods in the Social Sciences 1959* (Stanford: Stanford University Press, 1960), pp. 27–46.
10. Parsons, T., *The Social System* (New York: Free Press, 1951).
11. Samuelson, P. A., *Foundations of Economic Analysis* (Cambridge, Mass.: Harvard University Press, 1947).
12. Simon, H. A., *Administrative Behavior,* 2nd ed. (New York: Free Press, 1957).
13. Simon, H. A., *Models of Man* (New York: Wiley, 1957).

PART III

Empirical verification

CHAPTER 12

Statistical background

So far attention has been directed primarily toward the achievement of two major goals. First, a general methodology was developed to handle variables that seem incapable of measurement. Rules and guidelines enabling construction and manipulation of relations among such variables are thus available. These relations are basic components of the modern systems approach to analysis in social and behavioral science. Simultaneous equations systems, systems of periodic equations, and models of choice have received particular emphasis. The inescapable conclusion is that, except for measurement, nonquantifiable experience may be approached and understood in much the same way as is traditionally realized when the standard quantitative yardsticks are available.

The second goal was to demonstrate, at least at theoretical levels, how this methodology could be applied. Four examples were given: Political structure was defined as a system of simultaneous equations that may determine political systems or cycles. A dynamic model for planning purposes was presented along with a more complex account of society's process of social, political, cultural, economic, and psychological evolution. Lastly, the firm was modeled and analyzed in terms of the social interactions of the individuals it employs. In all instances, knowledge of structural relations and parameter values would, as in the quantifiable case, permit prediction.

Scientific inquiry, however, involves not only the creation of structure, theoretical propositions, predictions and the like, but also the determination of whether the structure, propositions, and predictions manifest themselves empirically. Accordingly, here in Part III, focus shifts to ways of obtaining specific knowledge of parameters and relations for the purpose of prediction or "empirical verification." The aim is to show that there are a variety of statistical methods available for checking against reality the hypotheses and conclusions obtained from theoretical investigations of nonquantifiable phenomena. Analysis without measurement, therefore, is something more than a mental exercise.

There is, in fact, historical precedent in the statistics literature for the study of procedures dealing with nonquantifiable observations. Some of it, namely that concerned with the idea of association between categorized variables, is discussed subsequently in its simplest form. At less formal levels there have been attempts to test nonquantifiable propositions with "casual" empiricism and by the tracing of historical events. Examples of these are also mentioned. But the main effort is reserved for statistical techniques, most often applied in the world of numbers, that remain valid even if measurements cannot be taken. Only a few illustrations are given; it is hoped they are suggestive of the kinds of statistical tools that are generally available.

More precisely, this chapter is concerned mostly with the statistical background that is frequently employed for empirical verification. Probability, random variable, distribution, and related concepts are developed first. Attention then turns to hypothesis testing, estimation, and tests for statistical relations between variables. Chapter 13 focuses on determination of the empirical nature of relations among variables. Among other topics, identification, the use of dummy variables in regression analysis, and prediction are discussed. An example of an empirical study of a "nonquantifiable phenomenon" appears in Chapter 14.

12.1   Preliminaries

Empirical verification is the process of discovering whether there is support for an hypothesis that something is, in fact, really so. To verify, one must both observe reality and interpret the theoretical implications of the observations. Interpretation, in turn, requires rules for understanding what is observed and criteria of admissibility. These rules and criteria determine which observations will establish the correctness of any hypothesis or prediction (Holt and Turner [3, pp. 2–4]).

One point of view has been formalized by Randall and Foulis [9] in an attempt to analyze mathematically the logic of empirical verification. Only a brief description of their approach is repeated here. Randall and Foulis define an operation as a set of instructions for carrying out a procedure. Sets of instructions have the property that for every execution of them, a unique outcome is obtained. Primitive operations are the basic ones and compound operations are built up from them. The set of all possible outcomes of any operation is its outcome set. Because there is a 1–1 correspondence between outcome sets and operations, the former may be taken as a definition of the latter. Certain subsets of each outcome set are identified as events; and it is the events that are subjected to empirical verification. An event is "validated" only when particular outcomes are observed from the operation that defines the event. Otherwise the event is "refuted."

The term "validation" should be used carefully. Under no circumstances is it ever possible to assert that, say, Newton's laws or the economist's hypothesis of utility maximization are "established" by affirmative observation. Certainly observations of happenings contrary to theoretical propositions refute the propositions. But, even in the face of identical outcomes from numerous repetitions of experiments, observations consistent with a theoretical proposition still do not confirm it as a fact of reality. They merely provide the comfort of harmony with nature.

This limitation holds for all forms of empirical verification, including the informal historical tests so often used in the social sciences. Two examples of these tests have already been described in Section 1.1: Weber's link between the Protestant Ethic and the spirit of capitalism is checked by observing the overwhelming numbers of Protestants (as compared with their percentage in the population) engaged in Western European capitalistic activity at the turn of the century. Hagen's sequence (recall also Section 10.2) beginning with the declassing of a social group, followed by the withdrawal, retreatism and repression of its members and their children, and concluding with the emergence of innovative personalities is compared with Japanese and other histories. That such procedures are legitimate (albeit, weak) forms of empirical verification is quite clear.

The historical approach, then, does provide a way of testing theoretical results. If a proposition asserts that condition A implies outcome B, then by looking back in experience for situations in which A obtains, one can discover if, in fact, it is accompanied by B. The historical circumstances in which the proposition might apply can, therefore, be determined. Empirical refutation – not proof of its factual correctness – remains a distinct possibility.[1]

On the other hand, the historical method does not provide objective criteria for deciding when a proposition or hypothesis might be accepted with some confidence as an "empirical reality". Out of one hundred historical situations in which A is observed, if B accompanies A in, say, eighty-five of them, is it safe to conclude that the proposition is a universal law in which some irregular outside disturbance prohibited concurrence 15 percent of the time? Only with more formal and powerful tools can such conclusions be reached. To these we now turn.

12.2 Probability

A *sample space,* Ω, is a set of not necessarily quantifiable objects that represent all possible outcomes from the performance of an operation

---

[1] Similarly, it is possible to determine historically whether B can appear in the absence of A. If so, then A cannot be the only condition implying B. See, for example, Gerschenkron [1, p. 53].

under specified conditions. The rules for manipulating subsets of Ω have been detailed in Section 3.1. A *σ-field*, $\mathcal{E}$, over Ω is a nonempty collection of subsets $E \subseteq \Omega$, which includes the complement relative to Ω of each of its elements, together with all countable unions and intersections of them. The sets in $\mathcal{E}$ are called *events*. A *probability measure*[2] is a function.

$$P: \mathcal{E} \rightarrow [0,1]$$

such that

    i. $P(E) \geqslant 0$, for all nonempty E in $\mathcal{E}$.

    ii. For any countably infinite sequence $\{E_i\}$ of mutually disjoint sets in $\mathcal{E}$,

$$P\left(\bigcup_{i=1}^{\infty} E_i\right) = \sum_{i=1}^{\infty} P(E_i)$$

    iii. $P(\varnothing) = 0$ and $P(\Omega) = 1$.

Recall the notion of probability has already been used to characterize the transition matrices of Section 5.3.

All the standard properties of probability measures follow (Wilks [11, pp. 10–16]). To illustrate without proof: For each E in $\mathcal{E}$,

$$P(E) + P(\bar{E}) = 1$$

where $\bar{E}$ is the complement of E. Also, for every E_1 and E_2 in $\mathcal{E}$,

$$P(E_1 \cup E_2) = P(E_1) + P(E_2) - P(E_1 \cap E_2)$$

And finally, if $\{E_i\}$ is a countable sequence of events in $\mathcal{E}$ such that either $E_1 \subseteq E_2 \subseteq \cdots$ or $E_1 \supseteq E_2 \supseteq \cdots$ then

$$\lim_{i \to \infty} P(E_i) = P(\lim_{i \to \infty} E_i)$$

where

$$\lim_{i \to \infty} E_i = \begin{cases} \displaystyle\bigcup_{i=1}^{\infty} E_i, & \text{when } E_1 \subseteq E_2 \subseteq \cdots \\ \displaystyle\bigcap_{i=1}^{\infty} E_i, & \text{when } E_1 \supseteq E_2 \supseteq \cdots \end{cases}$$

Convergence in $[0, 1]$ is with respect to the Euclidean topology relative to $[0, 1]$.

The *conditional probability* of E_1 given E_2 is defined by

---

[2] Use of the technical term "measure" here should not be confused with the notion of measurement as described in Chapter 2.

$$P(E_1/E_2) = \frac{P(E_1 \cap E_2)}{P(E_2)}$$

for any E_1 and E_2 in $\mathcal{E}$ such that $P(E_2) \neq 0$. Events E_1 and E_2 are said to be *independent* whenever

$$P(E_1 \cap E_2) = P(E_1)P(E_2)$$

Consider another space of objects, X. Choose a reference collection of subsets of X and call it $\mathcal{C}$. The *Borel field* over $\mathcal{C}$ is the minimum σ-field containing $\mathcal{C}$ and is denoted by $\mathcal{B}$. A function

$$V: \Omega \to X$$

is a *random variable* if and only if the inverse image of any set in $\mathcal{B}$ is contained in $\mathcal{E}$. It induces a probability measure, Q, on $\mathcal{B}$ according to the formula

(12.2-1) $Q(B) = P(V^{-1}(B))$

for all B in $\mathcal{B}$. In general, Q can be observed – not P. Given Q, it is always possible to find a P and a V satisfying (12.2-1), but they will not be unique.

To illustrate, let there be k societies under consideration. Suppose each element, ω, of Ω to be a list (k-vector) of k cultures – one for each society. Let $V(\omega)$ be the number of societies that have the same culture. Then with $x=10$, $Q(10)$ is the probability that ten societies have the same culture. It is the same as $P(V^{-1}(10))$ or the probability of the event consisting of all cultures that are common to exactly ten societies. Although in this example the range, X, of the random variable is the collection of nonnegative integers, in general, X need be neither numerical nor quantifiable.

Suppose a linear ordering, ρ, can be identified among the elements x of X; that is, X is a chain. (Such an assumption is generally not strong enough to permit measurement – see Section 2.2.) Let the reference collection $\mathcal{C}$ consist of sets of the form

$$C_x = \{x' : x\rho x' \text{ and } x' \text{ is in } X\}$$

for all x in X. Since $\mathcal{C}$ is contained in $\mathcal{B}$, and since Q is defined on the elements of the latter, a (cumulative) *distribution function, F,* may be obtained on X from

(12.2-2) $F(x) = Q(C_x)$

It is clear that

(12.2-3) $x'\rho x''$ implies $1 \geqslant F(x') \geqslant F(x'') \geqslant 0$

Furthermore, if there exists a b in X such that

$$b \rho x$$

for all x in X, then

$$F(b) = 1$$

Focus for a moment on the case in which there is no a and b in X such that $b \rho x \rho a$ for every x in X. Assign the interval topology, $\Im$, to X (Section 2.2). That is, with distinct x' and x'' in X, let

$$(x', x'') = \{x : x'' \rho x \rho x' \text{ where } x \text{ is in } X, \ x \neq x', \text{ and } x \neq x''\}$$

and take $\Im$ to be the collection of all unions of sets $(x', x'') \subseteq X$, together with $\varnothing$. Assume the following Archimedean property: For any nonconvergent sequence $\{x_n\}$ in X such that $x_{n+1} \rho x_n$ (or $x_n \rho x_{n+1}$) for all n, and any object x^* in X, there exists an $\bar{n}$ such that $x_{\bar{n}} \rho x^*$ (or $x^* \rho x_{\bar{n}}$). Now if $\{x_n\}$ is a nonconvergent sequence in X for which

$$x_{n+1} \rho x_n, \qquad n = 1, 2, \ldots$$

then

(12.2-4) $\lim\limits_{n \to \infty} F(x_n) = 1$

When

(12.2-5) $x_n \rho x_{n+1}, \qquad n = 1, 2, \ldots$

there obtains

(12.2-6) $\lim\limits_{n \to \infty} F(x_n) = 0$

The distribution function F is also continuous from the right: If $\{x_n\}$ is a sequence satisfying (12.2-5) and if

$$\lim\limits_{n \to \infty} x_n = x^0$$

then

(12.2-7) $\lim\limits_{n \to \infty} F(x_n) = F(x^0)$

Without the Archimedean condition, (12.2-4) and (12.2-6) need not hold. This is true even when the objects of X are numbers. Suppose

$$X = A \cup B$$

where

$$A = \{\dots, -\tfrac{5}{2}, -\tfrac{3}{2}, -\tfrac{1}{2}, 1, 2, 3, \dots\}$$
$$B = \{\dots, -3, -2, -1, \tfrac{1}{2}, \tfrac{3}{2}, \tfrac{5}{2}, \dots\}$$

and the linear order ρ is given by:

$$x'\rho x'' \quad \text{if and only if} \quad \begin{cases} x' \geqslant x'', \text{ when either } x' \text{ and } x'' \text{ are} \\ \quad \text{in } A \text{ or } x' \text{ and } x'' \text{ are in } B \\[6pt] x' \text{ is in } B \text{ and } x'' \text{ is in } A \end{cases}$$

for all x' and x'' in X. Arranged in order from left to right, the elements of X are

$$X = \{\dots, -\tfrac{3}{2}, -\tfrac{1}{2}, 1, 2, \dots, \quad \dots, -2, -1, \tfrac{1}{2}, \tfrac{3}{2}, \dots\}$$

Let Q_A and Q_B be probability measures on the subsets of, respectively, A and B. Then setting, for all $D \subseteq X$,

$$Q(D) = \tfrac{1}{2}Q_A(D \cap A) + \tfrac{1}{2}Q_B(D \cap B)$$

Q is a probability measure on the subsets of X. Clearly, the sequence $\{x_n\}$ where $x_n = n$ is a nonconvergent sequence in X, which does not satisfy the Archimedean restriction. Furthermore

$$\begin{aligned} \lim_{n \to \infty} F(n) &= \lim_{n \to \infty} Q(C_n) \\ &= \lim_{n \to \infty} \tfrac{1}{2}Q_A(C_n) \\ &= \tfrac{1}{2} \end{aligned}$$

contradicting (12.2-4).

Adding the Archimedean assumption to that of the existence of a linear ordering on X is still not strong enough to provide ordinal measurement when X is an uncountably infinite set. Certainly F is a natural candidate for an ordinal scale, but to be one would require (Section 2.2)

(12.2-8) $\quad x'\rho x'' \quad$ if and only if $\quad F(x') \geqslant F(x'')$

for all x' and x'' in X. Although the implication from left to right is supplied by (12.2-3), without further constraints its converse does not follow. There is nothing thus far that can prevent the occurrence of zero probability mass "between" objects of X. Should this happen, that is, if $F(x') = F(x'')$ for some distinct x' and x'' in X, there would be no way to tell if $x'\rho x''$ or $x''\rho x'$. On the other hand, it is possible for F to be an ordinal scale in the absence of the Archimedean property: the distribution function in the foregoing example could be chosen to satisfy (12.2-8).

(The role of Archimedean assumptions in the theory of measurement has been discussed by Krantz et al. [5].)

Thus it has been shown that the function F defined by (12.2-2) satisfies (12.2-3), (12.2-4), (12.2-6), and (12.2-7), provided ρ is linear and the Archimedean condition holds. Furthermore, the existence of an ordinal scale on X is generally not implied. By ruling out the chance of zero probability mass between the points of X, a converse proposition is obtained: Any function $F: X \rightarrow [0, 1]$ and associated linear ordering, ρ, satisfying (12.2-3), (12.2-4), (12.2-6), (12.2-7), and in addition, (12.2-8), determine a unique probability measure Q on the subsets of X according to (12.2-2) (Wilks [11, pp. 31–3]). The hypothesis of the latter proposition requires that F be an ordinal (but not necessarily interval) scale and also guarantees that the Archimedean restriction is met.

In general, F will depend on the choice of ρ. Once there is good reason to believe a particular ρ is valid, however, then the arbitrariness in the distribution function arising from the selection of ρ disappears. For example, if the elements of X are taken to be various societies, and if V is the random variable that assigns to each the degree of individual freedom it permits, then nonstatistical considerations may lead to a linear ordering of X according to the extent of individual freedom. On the other hand, in the absence of such criteria, the notion of distribution function is all but useless.

When the sample space is a Cartesian product of two or more components, and when the random variable under consideration can be broken up into corresponding components, construction of the joint distribution function (see Section 12.4) requires only that each of the component parts of the range of the random variable be a chain under some specified order. The argument is analogous to that previously given. For the remainder of this section and the next, however, interest centers on the one-dimensional case.

To obtain a probability density function from Q, one must introduce a second measure, μ, on $\mathcal{B}$. In this case, μ, mapping $\mathcal{B}$ into the nonnegative real line, has all the characteristics of a probability measure, except that $\mu(\Omega)$ need not be unity. Under certain conditions, not to be pursued here (see, e.g., Loève [7, p. 132]), the *probability density function, f,* may be defined as the Radon–Nikodym derivative of Q with respect to μ. Thus for all B in $\mathcal{B}$,

$$(12.2\text{-}9) \quad Q(B) = \int_B f \, d\mu$$

and hence, from (12.2-2),

(12.2-10) $F(x) = \int_{C_x} f d\mu$

for all x in X. When X is uncountable and exceptional points are excluded,

$$f(x) = F'(x)$$

where F' is the derivative of F as given by

$$F'(x) = \lim_{x' \to x} \frac{F(x') - F(x)}{\mu(C_{x'} - C_x)}$$

for $x'\rho x$.

Clearly, f depends on the selection of μ. Again, if there were no good criteria for making a choice, the result would be arbitrary indeed. However, when X is countable and all single element sets $\{x\} \subseteq X$ are in $\mathfrak{B}$, an obvious solution presents itself. In this case the probability density function becomes

$$f(x) = Q(\{x\})$$

on X, and

$$F(x) = \sum_{x\rho x'} f(x')$$

is the distribution function. These may be derived as special cases of (12.2-9) and (12.2-10) by picking μ to be the discrete measure; that is, for all B in $\mathfrak{B}$, $\mu(B)$ is the number of objects in B. Note a probability density function can be defined by (12.2-9) regardless of whether a linear ordering ρ is specified, but the definition of F and hence any relationship between F and f is meaningless without it. In general, given ρ, μ, and a probability density function f that admits integration, the distribution function is obtainable from (12.2-10).

Now suppose B is in $\mathfrak{B}$ so that $V^{-1}(B)$ is in $\mathcal{E}$. Let R denote the real line and $\mathcal{S}$ the minimal σ-field over the class of all open intervals in R. Consider any function

$$g: X \to R$$

such that for all S in $\mathcal{S}$ the set $g^{-1}(S)$ is contained in $\mathfrak{B}$. Then

(12.2-11) $\int_B g(x) \, dF(x) = \int_{V^{-1}(B)} g(V(\omega)) \, dP(\omega)$

where, recall, ω varies over the elements of Ω (Wilks [11, p. 72]).

If $X = R$ and ρ is identical to $\geqslant$, a familiar situation arises. Taking $\mathcal{C}$

to be the collection of all half-closed intervals $(-\infty, x]$ in X, the distribution function is given by

$$F(x) = P(\{\omega : V(\omega) \leqslant x\}) = Q((-\infty, x])$$

When it exists, the ordinary derivative of F (the Radon–Nikodym derivative with respect to Lebesgue measure) is the probability density function. The moments of V may also be computed using (12.2-11). In fact, all statistical theory in general may now be applied to analyze V.

The employment of real-valued random variables to transform non-quantifiable elements of a sample space into real numbers is a common technique. It nicely eliminates the difficulties arising when measurement is impossible.[3] An example is provided by the investigation of Mosteller and Wallace [8] into the disputed authorship question involving several of *The Federalist* papers. *The Federalist* is a series of seventy-seven essays that were written about 1787 by Alexander Hamilton, John Jay, and James Madison to persuade the people of New York State to ratify the federal Constitution. Authorship of all but twelve of the papers is more or less established; the controversy over those remaining centers around whether they were written by Hamilton or Madison. Mosteller and Wallace's approach is to identify frequencies of appearance of certain "marker" words in the known writings of each man. These are then used as the basis for analysis of the controversial twelve. In the foregoing context, set

Ω = all nonoverlapping 1,000-word passages written by Hamilton.

P = probability of occurrence defined for each event in the appropriate $\mathcal{E}$. (All elements of Ω are assumed equally likely.)

X = numbers of times a designated word can appear in each 1,000-word passage.

Thus $V : \Omega \to X$ maps nonquantifiable entities into quantifiable ones. There is a similar random variable for every marker word and a corresponding collection of random variables for Madison. Each induces a probability measure on the minimal σ-field over all closed intervals in the nonnegative real line and generates a probability density function (giving the probability of individual frequencies) on X. With the problem shifted to a numerical base, Mosteller and Wallace use Bayesian, regression, and other numerical methods to arrive at their conclusions.

---

[3] It is tempting to call such transformations a form of quantification in which properties of the sample space objects are calibrated. But it should be pointed out that this is quite different from the notion of measurement as defined in Section 2.2.

12.3   Hypothesis testing and estimation

Even in the absence of measurement, probability density functions can still depend on numerical parameters. To illustrate, with $X = \{x', x''\}$ and neither x' nor x'' quantifiable, the density function

(12.3-1) $f(x', \theta) = \frac{1}{2}(1 + \theta)$

$\qquad\quad f(x'', \theta) = \frac{1}{2}(1 - \theta)$

where $0 \leqslant \theta \leqslant 1$, depends on θ. A form of the Neyman–Pearson lemma is developed now, which leads to the standard hypothesis testing procedures to determine values for θ.

Suppose a random variable $V : \Omega \to X$ is known to have a probability density function belonging to the class

$\qquad \{ f(x, \theta) : \theta \text{ is in } \Theta \}$

for some set of real numbers Θ. Let Q denote the associated probability measure on $\mathscr{B}$ where $\mathscr{B}$ is the Borel field over the reference collection of subsets of X. A *statistical hypothesis* is an assumption about the value of θ. Only simple hypotheses are considered; that is, the *null* hypothesis

$\qquad H_0 : \theta = \theta_0$

is tested against the alternate

$\qquad H_1 : \theta = \theta_1$

Let A be a subset of X such that if an observation x falls in A, the null hypothesis is rejected. Suppose X is countable. Then the probability of a *type I error* (rejecting H_0 when true) is

$$Q(A/\theta_0) = \sum_{x \text{ in } A} f(x, \theta_0)$$

Writing $Q(A/\theta_0) = \alpha$, A is called a *critical region* or *test* of size α. The *power* of the test is

$$Q(A/\theta_1) = \sum_{x \text{ in } A} f(x, \theta_1)$$

and the probability of a *type II error* (accepting H_0 when false) is one minus its power:

$\qquad 1 - Q(A/\theta_1)$

If A and A^* are two tests of size α for which

(12.3-2) $Q(A/\theta_1) \geqslant Q(A^*/\theta_1)$

then A is at least as powerful as A^*. When strict inequality holds, A is more powerful than A^*. Any test A of size α with the property that (12.3-2) is valid for all other tests A^* of size α is called a *most powerful test* of size α.

When X is uncountable further assumptions are needed. Thus let a measure μ be specified on $\mathcal{B}$, and suppose integration of f with respect to μ is permissible. It is not necessary to have a linear ordering or distribution function. Redefining $Q(A/\theta_0)$ and $Q(A/\theta_1)$ for A in $\mathcal{B}$ as

$$Q(A/\theta_0) = \int_A f(x, \theta_0) \, d\mu$$

and

$$Q(A/\theta_1) = \int_A f(x, \theta_1) \, d\mu$$

the remaining notions of the preceding paragraph do not change. In either case the following version of the Neyman–Pearson lemma can be demonstrated. (Its proof is the same as that given by Wilks [11, p. 399].)

12.3-3   Theorem: If there exists a test A of size α and a constant $k > 0$ such that

$$f(x, \theta_1) \geq kf(x, \theta_0)$$

for x in A, and

$$f(x, \theta_1) \leq kf(x, \theta_0)$$

for x outside of A, then A is a most powerful test of size α.

Returning to the example of equations (12.3-1), consider the hypotheses

$$H_0 : \theta = \tfrac{1}{2}, \qquad H_1 : \theta = \tfrac{1}{4}$$

Letting $A = \{x''\}$ and choosing any k such that

$$\tfrac{5}{6} < k < \tfrac{3}{2}$$

satisfies the hypotheses of the theorem. Here the size of the critical region is $\tfrac{1}{4}$; the power of the test, $\tfrac{3}{8}$; and the probability of a type II error, $\tfrac{5}{8}$.

If a probability density function does not exist, there is still the probability measure Q on $\mathcal{B}$. As in (12.3-1), it may also depend on one or more parameters. Thus

$$H_0 : \theta = \theta_0$$

say, can still be tested against

$$H_1 : \theta = \theta_1$$

Critical regions are, as before, elements of $\mathcal{B}$ and all definitions that were given earlier (probability of a type I error, power, etc.) carry over in the obvious way. But without the probability density function there is no analogue of the Neyman–Pearson lemma. A most powerful test of size α exists only if it is possible to find a set in $\mathcal{B}$ with the requisite properties stated in the definition.

For situations in which it is inappropriate to represent the determination of θ as a choice between two hypotheses, (point) estimation procedures may be used. As in the previous discussion, suppose the probability density function of the random variable $V : \Omega \to X$ is of the form $f(x, \theta)$ for some θ in Θ. The problem is to associate with every set of, say, m observations in X a value for θ from Θ. The function mapping observations into Θ is called an *estimator* of θ, whereas its function values are possible *estimates*.

Each observation is thought of as a value of a random variable V^j mapping some underlying sample space Ω^j into X:

$$V^j : \Omega^j \to X, \qquad j = 1, \ldots, m$$

Function values (observations) of V^j are written $x^{(j)}$. The probability density function of V^j is taken to be $f(x^{(j)}, \theta)$, where θ is still to be determined and $j = 1, \ldots, m$. Thus all observations derive from the same density.

To illustrate the idea of estimation, interpret the V^j as independent random variables (see Section 12.4) and consider the likelihood function, L, defined by[4]

$$L(\theta) = \prod_{j=1}^{m} f(x^{(j)}, \theta)$$

for all θ in Θ. Note the observations $x^{(j)}$ are treated as fixed parameters subsumed in the functional symbol L. A *maximum likelihood* estimator is one that, for each set of observations $x^{(1)}, \ldots, x^{(m)}$, chooses θ so as to maximize the likelihood function with respect to it. Thus if $\hat{\theta}$ is such a maximizing value and if L is differentiable on Θ, then

(12.3-4)
$$\frac{dL(\hat{\theta})}{d\theta} = 0$$

In practice, (12.3-4) can be used to obtain $\hat{\theta}$. Maximization of the likeli-

---

[4] In general, $L(\theta) = g(x^{(1)}, \ldots, x^{(m)}, \theta)$ where g is the joint distribution of $x^{(1)}, \ldots, x^{(m)}$, as described in Section 12.4.

hood function means that θ has been selected to maximize the probability of observing $x^{(1)}, \ldots, x^{(m)}$.

Turning back once again to the example of (12.3-1) earlier in this section, suppose $m = 2$, $x^{(1)} = x'$, and $x^{(2)} = x''$. Then

$$L(\theta) = \tfrac{1}{4}(1 - \theta^2)$$

and the maximum likelihood estimate $\hat{\theta} = 0$. Thus the likeliest way of observing both x' and x'' when only two observations are taken is if the probability of each is $\tfrac{1}{2}$.

Because estimators map observations into estimates, if the observations are assumed to have a joint probability measure (see Section 12.4), and if an estimator has properties similar to those defining random variables, then as in (12.2-1), a probability measure is induced on an appropriate Borel field containing subsets of Θ. Suppose a probability density function is derivable from it. Because Θ is a set of real numbers, it is legitimate to speak of moments (such as the expected value of θ) obtained from the density function. Hence the familiar properties of unbiasedness, consistency, and efficiency of estimators may be defined in the usual manner (see, e.g., Lindgren [6, pp. 213–20]), and estimators in general can be analyzed in relation to these properties. For instance, it can be shown that, under appropriate conditions, if an unbiased, efficient estimator of θ exists, then the maximum likelihood method produces it. (Lindgren's proof [6, pp. 225–6)], with minor modifications, applies here.)

The subject of estimation arises again in Chapter 13.

12.4   Dependence

This section focuses on tests for the existence of statistical relations between variables. The approach is to adapt known methods for determining independence. For, if the hypothesis of independence between two random variables is rejected, it follows that there must be some sort of statistical relation between them.

Consider two sample spaces Ω_1 and Ω_2 with probability measures P^1 and P^2. Let P be a joint probability measure on $\Omega_1 \times \Omega_2$. The random variables

$$V^1 : \Omega_1 \rightarrow X_1, \qquad V^2 : \Omega_2 \rightarrow X_2$$

and

$$V : \Omega_1 \times \Omega_2 \rightarrow X_1 \times X_2$$

where $V = (V^1, V^2)$, induce probability measures Q^1, Q^2, and Q on, respectively, X_1, X_2, and $X_1 \times X_2$ according to equation (12.2-1). It is not necessary for X_1 and X_2 to be quantifiable. Call V^1 and V^2 *statistically independent* if and only if for all subsets $S = S_1 \times S_2$ of $\Omega_1 \times \Omega_2$,

(12.4-1) $Q(S) = Q^1(S_1)Q^2(S_2)$

If F^1 and F^2 are the respective distribution functions on X_1 and X_2, and if F is the joint distribution on $X_1 \times X_2$, then (12.4-1) is equivalent to

$$F(x_1, x_2) = F^1(x_1)F^2(x_2)$$

for all x_1 and x_2. (Wilks' proof [11, p. 43] applies with $\geqslant$ replaced by the orderings on X_1 and X_2.)

Only three of many possible tests for dependence (independence) are described here.[5] Consider, first, a random sample of n pairs, (x_1^i, x_2^i) for $i = 1, \ldots, n$, taken from $X_1 \times X_2$. Suppose ρ_j orders X_j, where $j = 1, 2$. Let π_j^i denote the sample rank of x_j^i with respect to ρ_j. Complications that arise by permitting ties in the rankings π_1^i or π_2^i are ignored. One measure of agreement between rankings is the ordinary correlation coefficient computed on them. It is called the (Spearman) *rank correlation coefficient* and reduces to (Hays and Winkler [2, pp. 245-7]):

$$r = 1 - \frac{6}{n(n^2 - 1)} \sum_{i=1}^{n} (\pi_1^i - \pi_2^i)^2$$

An alternative index of similarity is based on comparing the way ρ_1 orders the elements of (x_1^i, x_1^k) with the way ρ_2 orders those of (x_2^i, x_2^k). The pairs (x_1^i, x_1^k) and (x_2^i, x_2^k) are identically ordered provided, say, both

$$x_1^i \rho_1 x_1^k \quad \text{and} \quad x_2^i \rho_2 x_2^k$$

or, equivalently,

$$\pi_1^i > \pi_1^k \quad \text{and} \quad \pi_2^i > \pi_2^k$$

Since there are $\binom{n}{2}$ of these comparisons, a second measure of agreement is given by the (Kendall) *τ-statistic:*

$$\tau = \frac{\xi - \zeta}{\binom{n}{2}}$$

where ξ is the number of identically ordered pairs and ζ is the number of remaining pairs. Note if ρ_1 and ρ_2 are the same, then $r = \tau = 1$. When ρ_1 is exactly the "reverse" of ρ_2, $r = \tau = -1$. A discussion of the differences

---

[5] Other examples of tests that do not require measurement of the elements in the range of the random variable involved may be found in Walsh [10].

between r and τ may be found in Hays and Winkler [2, pp. 250, 252, 253]).

Both r and τ can be used to construct tests of statistical dependence. (Hays and Winkler [2, pp. 245–52] and Kendall and Stuart [4, pp. 473–7]). Under the null hypothesis H_0, namely, V^1 and V^2 are independent, the distribution of the test statistic

$$z_r = \frac{r(n-2)^{1/2}}{(1-r^2)^{1/2}}$$

is, for large n, approximately t with $n-2$ degrees of freedom. On the other hand,

$$z_\tau = \tau \left[\frac{9n(n-1)}{2(2n+5)} \right]^{1/2}$$

is distributed, for large n, approximately normally (also with H_0 in force). Thus if z_r or z_τ, as computed in the sample, fall in the critical region, H_0 is rejected.

As an illustration, suppose it is desired to test whether there is a statistical relation between the extent of individual freedom in a society and the extent to which investment decision making occurs. Then set

$$\Omega = \text{the collection of all possible societies}$$
$$X_1 = \text{possible extents of individual freedom}$$
$$X_2 = \text{possible extents of investment decision making}$$

and let

$$V^1 : \Omega \to X_1, \qquad V^2 : \Omega \to X_2$$

The definitions of X_1 and X_2 suggest that appropriate orderings might be found for each. Let this be done, sample the population, and compute r or τ. Note that if H_0 is rejected and hence the existence of a statistical relation accepted, a direction of causality (Section 6.2) between the variables is still not established. A more sophisticated and detailed application of the τ-statistic to test for functional dependence between variables may be found in Chapter 14.

On the other hand, suppose the purpose was to discover if there is a statistical relation between society's values and its culture, between peoples' religious beliefs and the kinds of economic activity in which they are engaged, or between social class and personality type. Orderings in such cases, even if known, are not usually unique and so choosing one merely to be able to apply the foregoing tests cannot lead to significant results. A more appropriate tactic is based on the notion of association. Consider a population classified according to the presence or absence

Table 12-1

	Exhibits B	Does not exhibit B	
Exhibits A	n_{11}	n_{12}	n_{1a}
Does not exhibit A	n_{21}	n_{22}	n_{2a}
	n_{b1}	n_{b2}	n

of characteristics A and B. If, for example, the population consists of the people living in Japan, the characteristics might be:

A = descendant of a samurai
B = innovative personality

Each observation in a sample of size n must fall into one and only one category in Table 12-1, where n_{11}, say, is the number of elements of the sample exhibiting both A and B, and

$$(12.4\text{-}2) \quad n_{ia} = n_{i1} + n_{i2}$$

$$(12.4\text{-}3) \quad n_{bj} = n_{1j} + n_{2j}$$

$$(12.4\text{-}4) \quad n = \sum_{i,j} n_{ij}$$

for $i, j = 1, 2$.

Characteristics A and B are said to be *unassociated* in the sample if there is the same proportion of observations exhibiting A among those exhibiting B as among those not exhibiting B, that is, if

$$(12.4\text{-}5) \quad \frac{n_{11}}{n_{b1}} = \frac{n_{12}}{n_{b2}}$$

There are three other equivalent ways of defining lack of association:

$$(12.4\text{-}6) \quad \frac{n_{21}}{n_{b1}} = \frac{n_{22}}{n_{b2}}, \quad \frac{n_{11}}{n_{1a}} = \frac{n_{21}}{n_{2a}}, \quad \frac{n_{12}}{n_{1a}} = \frac{n_{22}}{n_{2a}}$$

In any case, (12.4-2) to (12.4-5) imply

$$\frac{n_{11}}{n_{b1}} = \frac{n_{1a}}{n}$$

and hence unassociation also means that the proportion exhibiting A among B is the same as in the entire sample. If

$$\frac{n_{11}}{n_{b1}} > \frac{n_{12}}{n_{b2}}$$

Table 12-2

	Exhibits B	Does not exhibit B	
Exhibits A	p_{11}	p_{12}	p_{1a}
Does not exhibit A	p_{21}	p_{22}	p_{2a}
	p_{b1}	p_{b2}	

A and B are *positively associated*. They are *negatively associated* when the inequality is reversed.

Corresponding to the sample observations of Table 12-1, suppose there are true population probabilities as recorded in Table 12-2. Thus p_{11} is the true probability of a population member exhibiting both characteristics, and

$$p_{ia} = p_{i1} + p_{i2}$$

$$p_{bj} = p_{1j} + p_{2j}$$

$$1 = \sum_{i,j} p_{ij}$$

Here statistical independence between A and B occurs whenever

$$p_{11} = p_{1a} p_{b1}$$

or, equivalently,

(12.4-7) $p_{11} p_{22} = p_{12} p_{21}$

Since (12.4-5) and (12.4-6) imply

$$n_{11} n_{22} = n_{12} n_{21}$$

unassociation would appear to be the sample expression of the population notion of independence. The following test is based on this idea.

Let the null hypothesis, H_0, as stated in (12.4-7) hold. Then the test statistic

$$z = \frac{n(n_{11} n_{22} - n_{12} n_{21})^2}{n_{1a} n_{2a} n_{b1} n_{b2}}$$

has a distribution that, for large n, approximates χ^2 with one degree of freedom (Hays and Winkler [2, p. 201]). When z falls in the critical region, H_0 is rejected. Generalizations to larger numbers of characteristics may be found elsewhere (see, e.g., Kendall and Stuart [4, Ch. 33]).

References

1. Gerschenkron, A., *Continuity in History and Other Essays* (Cambridge, Mass.: Harvard University Press, 1968).
2. Hays, W. L., and R. L. Winkler, *Statistics: Probability, Inference, and Decision,* vol. II (New York: Holt, Rinehart and Winston, 1970).
3. Holt, R. T., and J. E. Turner, "The Methodology of Comparative Research," in R. T. Holt and J. E. Turner, eds., *The Methodology of Comparative Research* (New York: Free Press, 1970), pp. 1–20.
4. Kendall, M. G., and A. Stuart, *The Advanced Theory of Statistics,* 2nd ed., vol. 2 (London: Griffin, 1967).
5. Krantz, D. H., R. D. Luce, P. Suppes, and A. Tversky, *Foundations of Measurement,* vol. 1 (New York: Academic Press, 1971).
6. Lindgren, B. W., *Statistical Theory* (New York: Macmillan, 1962).
7. Loève, M., *Probability Theory,* 3rd ed. (Princeton, N.J.: van Nostrand, 1963).
8. Mosteller, F., and D. L. Wallace, *Inference and Disputed Authorship: The Federalist* (Reading, Mass.: Addison-Wesley, 1964).
9. Randall, C. H., and D. J. Foulis, "An Approach to Empirical Logic," *American Mathematical Monthly,* 77 (1970):363–74.
10. Walsh, J. E., *Handbook of Nonparametric Statistics,* II (Princeton, N.J.: van Nostrand, 1965).
11. Wilks, S. S., *Mathematical Statistics* (New York: Wiley, 1962).

CHAPTER 13

Empirical relations among variables

The last chapter considered, in part, statistical tests for the existence of relations among variables. These tests are based on how observations of the variables in question fit together. But in many situations (e.g., prediction) merely to know that statistical evidence supports its existence is not enough: Some knowledge of the nature of the relation itself is essential. The only empirical way of approaching such a problem is to ask what sorts of relations best fit the observations at hand. When meaningful numbers are available the usual technique is to assume that the relation has a certain form, say, linearity, and then estimate its parameters. If according to some acceptable criterion the fit turns out to be "good," the assumed form is taken as a reasonable approximation of reality. Parallel procedures in the absence of ratio, interval, and ordinal measures are of interest here.

As remarked earlier, empirical relations are obviously capable of detection even in the absence of measurement. It is only necessary to observe that, under appropriate conditions, certain values of, say, $(x_1, \ldots, x_K)$ arise with certain values of $(\rho_1, \ldots, \rho_M)$. Once such information is obtained, subsequent investigation might include the drawing of structural inferences and the formulation of predictions. This chapter explores these possibilities.

Even without ratio, interval, and ordinal scales, introduction of numbers in the form of dummy variables is often legitimate in order to facilitate analysis. Recall (Section 2.2), any typology or classification scheme permits nominal measurement. That is, given a set X and some decomposition of X into mutually exclusive and exhaustive subsets, S_ν, the objects of X can be assigned real numbers such that within each S_ν, all elements receive the same numerical value. Dummy variates require such a procedure for their definition. But because nominal associations of real numbers to elements of X may be arbitrary, care must be taken to avoid conclusions that depend on the particular scales chosen. (The pitfalls of treating ordinal as if it were interval data in factor and regression analysis already have been illustrated at the end of Section 2.2.) The employment of dummy variables, nevertheless, remains an attractive alternative: Numerical techniques are too convenient and efficient to

ignore. As a result, extensive use of dummy variables appears in the following discussion.

On the other hand, regardless of legitimacy or arbitrariness, it is not
always true that invoking nominal measurement bears additional fruit to
that which would otherwise be reaped. Identical conclusions may sometimes be derived in a simple, straightforward manner without them.
Hence an effort will be made to distinguish precisely those circumstances
in which the calibration of nonquantifiable variables on nominal scales
contributes significantly to empirical analysis.

The chapter begins by considering the inference of theoretical structure from observational information (i.e., the identification problem).
Then dummy variables are introduced and the difficulties involved in
obtaining "true" empirical relations and in prediction are examined. In
the latter regard it is assumed that the structural relations on which prediction is based do not change between the time past observations are
seen and recorded and predictions of future observations are made. A
discussion of models containing both quantifiable and nonquantifiable
variables follows.

13.1   Identification

Theoretical analysis often produces a collection of relations referred to
as *structural*. These summarize all relevant information contained in the
theory about how certain variables and parameters interact. Structures
may be static or dynamic, probabilistic or nonprobabilistic, and so
forth. In so far as theory is concerned, their constituent relations may
contain any number of variables and parameters. There are many possibilities. Due to limitations of space, however, only one fairly general
structure is considered here, namely, that of relation (5.1-1):

$$(13.1-1) \quad x_j = f^j(x_1,\ldots,x_{j-1},x_{j+1},\ldots,x_K,\rho), \qquad j = 1,\ldots,L$$

where ρ is a vector of parameters and the x_j are variables. Both variables
and parameters are assumed to range over clearly defined sets. As
before, (13.1-1) will be abbreviated to

$$x = f(x,\rho)$$

where f is short for $(f^1,\ldots,f^L)$ and x replaces both $(x_1,\ldots,x_L)$ and the
$(x_1,\ldots,x_{j-1},x_{j+1},\ldots,x_K)$.

The main problem with (13.1-1) is that, as it stands, it cannot be
observed directly. The data points (which consist of one value for each
of the components of (x,ρ)) in any collection of observations of it must
satisfy all relations in (13.1-1) simultaneously. Hence there is no general

way to deduce L distinct f^j's from them. But if (13.1-1) were rewritten so as to express x as a function of ρ alone, say with $K = L$ and

(13.1-2) $x = g(\rho)$

where g is a vector of K relations (i.e., $g = (g^1, \ldots, g^K)$), then the data could be used to reveal g. (Alternatively, if g or its properties are known from a theory, an empirical check of the latter is obtained.) Several collections of conditions that are sufficient for resolving (13.1-1) into (13.1-2) have been given in Chapter 5. For example, one approach includes certain invertability restrictions along with the requirement that $K = L$. A way of adding empirical content to (13.1-1), then, is to assume one of these sets of conditions is met. Equation (13.1-2) is called the *reduced form* of (13.1-1).

Knowledge of the reduced form does not make structural information irrelevant, for observation of (13.1-2) only yields associations and correlations. And as useful as they might be for prediction, without appropriate manipulation they cannot provide much understanding of the underlying structural interaction. To know that business cycles are highly correlated with sunspot activity reveals nothing about the causes of cycles or how their peaks and troughs might be smoothed. Furthermore, structural change may result in erroneous prediction unless it is incorporated immediately into the reduced form. Often the occurrence of such a change may be detected independently before it has had time to appear in the latter. The passage of a new law, for example, could induce structural variation. Although the precise impact cannot be known until the reduced form is observed, knowledge of the old structure may permit reasonable modification of predictions. Having no knowledge about the old structure at all, one might not even be aware that modification is necessary. Finally, if (13.1-2) is to be numerically "estimated," structural information can sometimes improve efficiency (Kmenta [6, pp. 573ff]).

Granted, then, that empirical information concerning structure is worth knowing and that it can only be obtained from the reduced form, the next question is how much and under what conditions can it be recovered? This is the so-called problem of *identification*. Although identifiability criteria usually appear as restrictions on the structure alone, it is convenient here to state them primarily in terms of other functions. In a numerical illustration given later, these conditions are implied by restrictions on the original structure. Clearly, the requirements permitting the derivation of (13.1-2) from (13.1-1) must also be included, at least implicitly, as part of the identifiability criteria.

The first thing to notice is that since (13.1-2) is the solution of (13.1-1), a vector (x, ρ) satisfies all relations in the structure if and only if it also satisfies the reduced form. However, there are vectors satisfying at least one less than all structural relations that do not satisfy (13.1-2). These have been lost in the derivation of (13.1-2) as the solution of (13.1-1) (recall the nonquantifiable example of Section 5.1). In reconstructing (13.1-1) from (13.1-2), then, it should not usually be possible to obtain more points (x, ρ) satisfying any one structural relation than there are points satisfying the reduced form. Alternatively, because many structures generate the same reduced form, reconstructions of the original structure beyond what is contained in the reduced form cannot be expected. Thus letting D be the class of all observed data points (x, ρ), if the structure is recoverable at all, then it is recoverable on D. In general, there are many extensions of the structure from D to the rest of the variable–parameter space. Only under special circumstances will the extension turn out to be unique and correspond to the original.

Sufficient conditions, in addition to those required to deduce g from f, are now given that permit recovery of f from g on D. To begin, suppose the parameter vector $\rho = (\rho_1, \ldots, \rho_M)$ has greater dimensionality than that of $x = (x_1, \ldots, x_K)$. Thus $M \geqslant K = L$. Second, assume every g^i has an inverse (Section 4.2) with respect to at least one ρ_j for all values of x and the remaining parameters, and if each g^i has an inverse only with respect to a single ρ_j, then ρ_j is different for each g^i. Alternatively, without loss of generality, it may be supposed that g^i has an inverse at least with respect to ρ_i for all $i = 1, \ldots, K$.

Under these conditions the reduced form, g, may be inverted as follows:

$$(13.1\text{-}3) \quad \rho_1 = \alpha^1(x_1, \rho_2, \ldots, \rho_M)$$
$$\rho_2 = \alpha^2(\rho_1, x_2, \rho_3, \ldots, \rho_M)$$
$$\vdots$$
$$\rho_K = \alpha^K(\rho_1, \ldots, \rho_{K-1}, x_K, \rho_{K+1}, \ldots, \rho_M)$$

where α^i is the inverse of g^i with respect to ρ_i given values for x and the remaining parameters. Now, for any $i = 1, \ldots, K$, substitution of all α^j such that $j \neq i$ into g^i gives structural relation i on D. Thus, for example,

$$x_1 = \beta^1(x_2, \ldots, x_K, \rho)$$

where

$$\beta^1(x_2, \ldots, x_K, \rho) = g^1(\rho_1, \alpha^2(\rho_1, x_2, \rho_3, \ldots, \rho_M), \ldots,$$
$$\alpha^K(\rho_1, \ldots, \rho_{K-1}, x_K, \rho_{K+1}, \ldots, \rho_M), \rho_{K+1}, \ldots, \rho_M)$$

It is clear that $\beta = (\beta^1, \ldots, \beta^K)$, where β^i is defined anaogously to β^1 for each i, must coincide with $f = (f^1, \ldots, f^K)$ on D – otherwise g could not be the reduced form of f. But, as indicated earlier, any extension of β beyond D is not necessarily unique and need not correspond to the original f.

If g^1 also has inverses with respect to ρ_2 and g^2 with respect to ρ_1 so that

$$\rho_2 = \alpha^{*1}(\rho_1, x_1, \rho_3, \ldots, \rho_M)$$

$$\rho_1 = \alpha^{*2}(x_2, \rho_2, \ldots, \rho_M)$$

and if all other α^j's in (13.1-3) remain unchanged, then an alternative reconstruction, $\beta^* = (\beta^{*1}, \ldots, \beta^{*K})$ is obtained such that, say,

$$x_2 = \beta^{*2}(x_1, x_3, \ldots, x_K, \rho)$$

where

$$\beta^{*2}(x_1, x_3, \ldots, x_K, \rho)$$
$$= g^2(\rho_1, \alpha^{*1}(\rho_1, x_1, \rho_3, \ldots, \rho_M), \alpha^3(\rho_1, \rho_2, x_3, \rho_4, \ldots, \rho_K), \ldots,$$
$$\alpha^K(\rho_1, \ldots, \rho_{K-1}, x_K, \rho_{K+1}, \ldots, \rho_M), \rho_{K+1}, \ldots, \rho_M)$$

Evidently β^{*2} is the inverse of β^1 with respect to x_2 given $(x_3, \ldots, x_K, \rho)$, β^{*1} is the inverse of β^2 with respect to x_1 also given $(x_3, \ldots, x_K, \rho)$, and β^* is an equivalent form of β. In general, when more than one g^i has inverses with respect to more than one ρ_j, and hence there is more than one way to rebuild f on D, all derivations yield equivalent results.

There is, however, an important exception arising when exactly $K-1$ of the g^i's happen to vary independently of one or more ρ_j's. Suppose

$$x_1 = g^1(\rho_1, \ldots, \rho_M)$$

and

$$x_i = g^i(\rho_2, \ldots, \rho_M)$$

where $i = 2, \ldots, K$. Then the construction based on (13.1-3) produces a β such that β^1 is independent of ρ_1 and the remaining β^i are independent of both x_1 and ρ_1. On the other hand, inverting g^1 with respect to, say, ρ_M (assuming $M > K$), and leaving all other inversions unchanged, gives a β^* where each β^{*i} depends on all parameters and all variables distinct from x_i. But although β and β^* are not equivalent, they are neither contrary to each other nor inconsistent with f on D: β^* merely describes a different "part" of the structure on D than does β.

Another case in which parameters are excluded from rebuilt structural relations occurs if $K = 2$. Taking the inverted reduced form to consist of α^1 and α^2 from (13.1-3), the reconstructed structure on D is:

$$x_1 = g^1(\rho_1, \alpha^2(\rho_1, x_2, \rho_3, \ldots, \rho_M), \rho_3, \ldots, \rho_M)$$
$$x_2 = g^2(\alpha^1(x_1, \rho_2, \ldots, \rho_M), \rho_2, \ldots, \rho_M)$$

Thus ρ_2 does not appear as an argument of β^1, nor can ρ_1 show up in β^2. Furthermore, if an alternative inversion of g were used, say, inverting g^1 with respect to ρ_2 and g^2 with respect to ρ_1, then ρ_1 would be left out of β^1 and ρ_2 out of β^2. But this is not an exception to the general proposition just derived: As long as g^1 and g^2 have inverses with respect to both ρ_1 and ρ_2, the two reconstructions are equivalent. If either g^1 or g^2 has inverses with respect to exactly one of ρ_1 and ρ_2, then only one reconstruction is possible. The following illustrations will clarify these ideas.

Let $K=2$ and consider initially a nonquantifiable structure defined in tabular form:

f^1: $x_1 = f^1(x_2, \rho_1, \rho_2)$	x_2	ρ_1	ρ_2
b	a	ρ_1^0	$\bar{\rho}_2$
c	b	ρ_1^0	$\bar{\rho}_2$
a	c	ρ_1^0	$\bar{\rho}_2$
b	a	ρ_1'	$\bar{\rho}_2$
c	b	ρ_1'	$\bar{\bar{\rho}}_2$
a	c	ρ_1'	$\bar{\rho}_2$

f^2: $x_2 = f^2(x_1, \rho_1, \rho_2)$	x_1	ρ_1	ρ_2
b	a	ρ_1^0	$\bar{\rho}_2$
a	b	ρ_1^0	$\bar{\rho}_2$
a	a	ρ_1'	$\bar{\rho}_2$
b	c	ρ_1'	$\bar{\bar{\rho}}_2$

As in Section 5.1 the reduced form is

g^1: $x_1 = g^1(\rho_1, \rho_2)$	ρ_1	ρ_2
b	ρ_1^0	$\bar{\rho}_2$
c	ρ_1'	$\bar{\rho}_2$

g^2: $x_2 = g^2(\rho_1, \rho_2)$	ρ_1	ρ_2
a	ρ_1^0	$\bar{\rho}_2$
b	ρ_1'	$\bar{\rho}_2$

Now suppose the set of data points is $D = \{(b, a, \rho_1^0, \bar{\rho}_2), (c, b, \rho_1', \bar{\bar{\rho}}_2)\}$ so that the observed reduced form is as described here. Then both g^1 and g^2 have inverses with respect to ρ_1 and ρ_2. Inverting g^1 with respect to ρ_1 and g^2 with respect to ρ_2 yields, upon substitution back into g,

β^1: $x_1 = \beta^1(x_2, \rho_1)$	x_2	ρ_1
b	a	ρ_1^0
c	b	ρ_1'

β^2: $x_2 = \beta^2(x_1, \rho_2)$	x_1	ρ_2
a	b	$\bar{\rho}_2$
b	c	$\bar{\bar{\rho}}_2$

Clearly, all information contained in β also appears in f. Combining the first (or second) line of the table for β^1 with the first (or, respectively, second) line of the table for β^2 gives the first (or fifth) line of the table for f^1 and the second (or fourth) line of the table for f^2.

On the other hand, inverting g^1 with respect to ρ_2 and g^2 with respect to ρ_1 provides an alternate form, namely, β^*:

$\beta^{*1}:\ x_1=\beta^{*1}(x_2,\rho_2)$	x_2	ρ_2
b	a	ρ_2
c	b	$\bar{\rho}_2$

$\beta^{*2}:\ x_2=\beta^{*2}(x_1,\rho_1)$	x_1	ρ_1
a	b	ρ_1^0
b	c	ρ_1'

Note that β^{*1} and β^{*2} may be obtained from, respectively, β^2 and β^1 by inversion. Furthermore, enough information about (13.1-1) is obtained to permit some structural understanding of reality and, at the same time, allow for the possibility of modifying predictions when structural change is independently observed.

It is also worth examining an example drawn from the quantifiable world. Let

(13.1-4) $x_1 = 2x_2 + \rho_1 + \rho_2, \quad x_2 = x_1 + 2\rho_1 + \rho_2$

define a structure where the x_i and ρ_i are measured on interval scales. The reduced form is

(13.1-5) $x_1 = -5\rho_1 - 3\rho_2, \quad x_2 = -3\rho_1 - 2\rho_2$

and each equation of (13.1-5) has inverses with respect to both parameters. Following either previously described route back to the original structure yields

(13.1-6) $x_1 = \frac{3}{2}x_2 - \frac{1}{2}\rho_1, \quad x_2 = \frac{3}{5}x_1 - \frac{1}{5}\rho_2$

However, in the quantifiable case still further structures that are consistent with the reduced form may be obtained. First adding and then subtracting the equations of (13.1-5) results in

(13.1-7) $x_1 = -x_2 - 8\rho_1 - 5\rho_2, \quad x_2 = x_1 + 2\rho_1 + \rho_2$

and, in fact, applying any linear transformation to (13.1-5) gives a pair of equations from which the reduced form can be derived. Clearly, the points satisfying equations (13.1-4) to (13.1-7) all lie on a two-dimensional plane, Γ, in four-dimensional Euclidean space. This plane is uniquely described by any of these four pairs of equations. But off Γ, equations (13.1-4), (13.1-6), and (13.1-7) are all different.

Now when variables are quantifiable and the structure is linear, the standard approach to identification of linear models can be fitted easily into the general picture. Suppose (13.1-1) is written

(13.1-8) $Ax' = B\rho'$

where A is a K by K matrix of real numbers, B is K by M, and the primes on x and ρ denote their transposes. If the inverse matrix A^{-1} exists, then (13.1-2) is

$$x' = \Pi\rho'$$

where $\Pi = A^{-1}B$. Given a collection of data points D, the entries in Π can be estimated. Thus the determination of structure on D from the reduced form becomes the problem of obtaining values for the entries in A and B from Π.

It is, of course, well known that if a function is linear over some set, and if its coefficients are discovered on any subset – no matter how small – then the same coefficients must apply over the entire set. One enormous advantage of quantifiability and linearity is therefore clear: Once the correct structure is found on D its extension to the remainder of the variable–parameter space is unique and coincides with the original. But as the example of (13.1-4) to (13.1-7) suggests, uniqueness and coincidence cannot be expected without further restrictions. This is where the standard discussions of identifiability of (13.1-8) usually begin (see, e.g., Fisher [2]). The procedure is to look for conditions on A and B that ensure that these matrices can be recovered from Π. Such conditions imply the invertability of (13.1-2) but are not, in turn, implied by it.

To illustrate, consider the structure

$$(13.1\text{-}9) \quad \begin{aligned} x_1 &= a_{12}x_2 + b_{11}\rho_1 + b_{12}\rho_2 \\ x_2 &= a_{21}x_1 + b_{21}\rho_1 + b_{22}\rho_2 \end{aligned}$$

where $a_{12}a_{21} \neq 1$. Equations (13.1-4) are a special case of (13.1-9). The reduced form is

$$(13.1\text{-}10) \quad x_1 = \pi_{11}\rho_1 + \pi_{12}\rho_2, \quad x_2 = \pi_{21}\rho_1 + \pi_{22}\rho_2$$

where

$$\pi_{11} = \frac{a_{12}b_{21} + b_{11}}{1 - a_{12}a_{21}}, \quad \pi_{12} = \frac{a_{12}b_{22} + b_{12}}{1 - a_{12}a_{21}}$$

$$\pi_{21} = \frac{a_{21}b_{11} + b_{21}}{1 - a_{12}a_{21}}, \quad \pi_{22} = \frac{a_{21}b_{12} + b_{22}}{1 - a_{12}a_{21}}$$

There are exactly two sets of conditions on A and B that are sufficient for identification of the complete structure (13.1-9):

    i. $b_{12} = b_{21} = 0$, $b_{11} \neq 0$ and $b_{22} \neq 0$.
    ii. $b_{11} = b_{22} = 0$, $b_{12} \neq 0$ and $b_{21} \neq 0$.

The restrictions of (i) imply $\pi_{11} \neq 0$ and $\pi_{22} \neq 0$; those of (ii) guarantee $\pi_{12} \neq 0$ and $\pi_{21} \neq 0$. In either case each equation of the reduced form (13.1-10) has an inverse with respect to a different parameter. Because the structures obtained under (i) and (ii) are distinct, the quantifiable counterpart to the parameter omission phenomenon in the absence of measurement (described on page 257) is exemplified. It is also clear that structures (13.1-4), (13.1-6), and (13.1-7) are not identified in this sense.

13.2 Dummy variates

Let X be a set of arbitrary objects and let ν be an index running over real numbers. Suppose a typology (Section 2.1) partitions X into nonempty, mutually exclusive and exhaustive subsets S_ν. Such a partition gives rise to any number of 1-1 correspondences between the collection of all subsets, $\{S_\nu\}$, and the reals. Each correspondence defines a nominal scale, f, (Section 2.2) whose use involves nominal measurement. Dummy variables range over sets of the form $f(X)$. Without loss of generality, attention may be confined to the nominal scale:

$$(13.2\text{-}1) \quad f(x) = \nu$$

for all x in S_ν. Then the *dummy variable* with respect to X, $\{S_\nu\}$, and f is a variable $y = f(x)$, which assumes real numbers for values according as x is in appropriate S_ν. Obviously, y depends on the given typology and the choice of scale. Confusion cannot arise by employing the symbol x to represent both the variable ranging over X and the dummy variable y. Context determines the intended usage.

Dummy variables that take on only two values are called *binary*. The typology underlying any binary variable splits X into a subset S and its complement $X - S$. As usually formulated, a binary variable assumes the value 1 when a particular characteristic is present (i.e., say, x is in S) and 0 when it is not present (x is in $X - S$). The associated nominal scale is therefore

$$(13.2\text{-}2) \quad f(x) = \begin{cases} 1, & \text{if } x \text{ is in } S \\ 0, & \text{if } x \text{ is in } X - S \end{cases}$$

Although the use of 0 and 1 is standard, from a definitional point of view all pairs of real numbers are equally suitable.

Any dummy variable may be characterized equivalently in terms of a vector of binary variables. Let $\{S_\nu\}$ be a partition and consider the dummy variate y based on (13.2-1). For each ν suppose y_ν is the binary variable of (13.2-2) with respect to S_ν. Then there is a 1-1 correspondence between values assumed by y and those of the vector of all y_ν's. In particular $y = \nu$ is associated with

$$(\ldots, 0, 1, 0, \ldots)$$

where the 1 appears in the y_ν slot. If the number of sets in $\{S_\nu\}$ is finite, then the vector of binary variables corresponding to y has a finite number of components. From now on all partitions employed here are presumed finite. Hence any model containing dummy variables can be viewed equivalently as a model in which all variable values are vectors of 0's and 1's.

Actually, in the finite case where $\nu = 1, \ldots, n$, only vectors with $n-1$ components are required to represent the original dummy variate. Let $Y^1 = \{(y_1, \ldots, y_n)\}$ be the collection of vectors obtained from the partition $S_1, \ldots, S_n$, where

$$X = \bigcup_{\nu=1}^{n} S_\nu$$

Only one y_ν takes on the value 1 in each $(y_1, \ldots, y_n)$; the remaining $y_\nu = 0$. Consider the $n-1$ dimensional vectors $Y^2 = \{(y_1, \ldots, y_{n-1})\}$ having the same property. Then $y_\nu = 1$ in $(y_1, \ldots, y_{n-1})$ for some $\nu = 1, \ldots, n-1$ is equivalent to $y_\nu = 1$ in $(y_1, \ldots, y_{n-1}, 0)$ since, in either case, x is in S_ν. And because

$$S_n = X - \bigcup_{\nu=1}^{n-1} S_\nu$$

$(0, \ldots, 0, 1)$ in Y^1 says the same thing (namely, x is in S_n) as that of the $n-1$-dimensional vector of zeros. With the addition of the latter, then, the vectors of Y^2 convey identical information to those of Y^1.

It should be noted that whenever X contains only a finite number of elements, any nonquantifiable variable on X has an equivalent representation in terms of a dummy variate based on the discrete typology (i.e., the partitioning of X into single-element sets). Because dummy variables, in turn, have equivalent representations as vectors of binary variables, any simultaneous relations model that is defined for finite sets can be expressed equivalently as a (usually) larger system of simultaneous relations, all of whose variables assume as values only 0 and 1. But, of course, even in a finite world, the discrete typology may not always be an appropriate mechanism for splitting up sets over which variables range. In that case larger partitioning sets and smaller systems of relations (still involving only binary variables) would arise.

Without actually having ordinal, interval, or ratio scales, the use of dummy variables provides numbers that are required for the application of numerical techniques. But transforming nonquantifiable variables into dummy variables may result in a loss of information. Consider a relation

(13.2-3) $x = g(\rho)$

where x is a scalar over X and $\rho = (\rho_1, \ldots, \rho_M)$ is a vector of parameters. Suppose X is partitioned into S and $X - S$ and let x be represented as a binary dummy variable. Then particular objects in X lose their importance – all that matters is the set to which they belong. Hence as long as the sets over which parameters and the variable range have more than two points, (13.2-3) expressed in terms of binary variables necessarily contains less information than the original. The sacrifice of information needed to employ dummy variables is clearly not worthwhile unless conclusions that could not be obtained otherwise are revealed. Even if no sacrifice were involved, it would not help matters much if only an equivalent expression of (13.2-3) is derived. However, in all cases considered subsequently, a little extra does arise by taking x and the ρ_i to be dummy variables. A discussion of exactly what is gained appears after the development of the numerical techniques themselves.

As previously suggested, there are two possible sources of capriciousness in the use of dummy variables. First, the defining typology may be arbitrary. Without any a priori meaningful way to partition X, a typology might still be introduced in order to employ numerical techniques. In this case the discrete typology would probably be most rewarding because no information is lost when all partitioning sets contain exactly one point. A second type of arbitrariness arises in the choice of the nominal scale. Clearly, then, the results of any numerical analysis involving dummy variables have to be interpreted with caution. True numerical relations between the underlying variables cannot be obtained (recall the end of Section 2.2). In succeeding pages several examples of numerical methods are presented. Models in which none of the elements are quantifiable (and hence all variates find numerical expression only in dummy form) are discussed here. Models with both quantifiable and nonquantifiable variables are postponed to the next section.

At the outset the identification issue of Section 13.1 can be reconsidered. Recall, in the general nonquantifiable case the sufficient conditions for identifiability given there permit unique reconstruction of the structure only on the class of all data points D. Any extension off D cannot be unique. For the special case in which all variables are quantifiable on interval scales and the structure is linear as in (13.1-8), stronger sufficient conditions can be given to provide uniqueness of extensions and to ensure the complete recovery of the original system. These stronger conditions, as illustrated in the example of (13.1-9), are expressed as restrictions on the entries of the matrices A and B. They have nothing whatever to do with the variables x and parameters ρ of the model. Hence if the variables of (13.1-1) are thought of as dummy variates, and if the form of (13.1-1) were taken to be linear as (13.1-8), then the numerical requirements on the entries of A and B sufficient for identification would apply regardless of the choice of nominal scale behind any of the dummy variables. (See Fisher [2, Ch. 2] for a general statement of these conditions.) There are, of course, further compatibility constraints that are necessary for passage from structure to reduced form and back again to be meaningful. Thus, for example, when each dummy variable may range over the collection of all integers, the entries of A, B, and $A^{-1}B$ have to be integers as well. But clearly, even in nonquantifiable circumstances, there are situations in which reconstruction of the original structure over a set larger than D might be possible. In fact, if all dummy variables are based on the discrete typology, if it is known that for these dummy variates the structure is linear, and if the foregoing identifiability and compatibility restrictions are met, complete recovery over the entire parameter–variable space is guaranteed. The required assumptions, however, are rather severe.

The remainder of this chapter deals with models that are already in reduced form. Its purpose is to examine numerical methods usually employed to make predictions and determine the reduced form so as to be consistent with a given collection of empirical observations. Because they can often be found elsewhere, general results are not derived. Only highly simplified illustrations are discussed. Actually, attention is confined to the single relation of (13.2-3):

$$x = g(\rho)$$

where x is a scalar and ρ is a vector. As indicated in earlier argument, nothing is lost by supposing that all variables are binary. The symbols x and ρ appear as both binary variables and the underlying nonnumerical variables they represent.

Independently of whatever theoretical or empirical form (13.2-3) might have, prediction of whether x is in S or its complement is possible with discriminant analysis. This involves construction of a numerical function $z = h(\rho)$ and a critical value z^0 such that if knowledge of ρ yields $h(\rho) > z^0$, then $x = g(\rho)$ is predicted to be in, say, S; that is, $x = 1$. If $h(\rho) < z^0$, the prediction is $x = 0$ or x is in $X - S$. Let l be an index referring to S when $l = 1$ and $X - S$ when $l = 2$. Consider those previous observations of (x, ρ) whose x value lies in the set $\{0, 1\}$. Denote the kth one by (x^{kl}, ρ^{kl}). Set

$$z_{kl} = h(\rho^{kl})$$

and write $\bar{z}_l$ for the mean of z_{kl} over k. Frequently the function h is supposed linear,

$$(13.2\text{-}4) \quad h(\rho) = \sum_{i=1}^{M} \lambda_i \rho_i$$

with the λ_i chosen so as to maximize the "separation" of S and $X - S$ by h, relative to the variation within these sets. Measuring the absolute separation by

$$U = (\bar{z}_1 - \bar{z}_2)^2$$

and the within-set variation by

$$V = \sum_{k,l} (z_{kl} - \bar{z}_l)^2$$

the relative separation is expressed as U/V and is maximized with respect to $\lambda_1, \ldots, \lambda_M$. Details are given, for example, by Hoel [4, pp. 179–84]. With the λ_i's determined, z^0 is found by comparing the z's that are computed by using (13.2-4) and past observations of ρ. Similarly, any new observation of ρ provides a value for z, and the prediction depends on whether it is above or below z^0. Although specific numerical values for z and the λ_i depend on the nominal scales of the binary variables, by using 0–1 variates these values turn out to rest only on the manner in which observations fall into sets of the underlying partitions. Hence the arbitrariness of nominal measurement is skirted. The argument is similar to that for regression analysis that follows. The fact that discriminant analysis with binary variables produces something beyond what is obtainable without nominal measurement also is deferred to a later stage.

For the moment, however, note that even expressed in terms of binary variables, g and h are entirely different functions. Because the latter is concocted for predictive purposes only, information about the numerical form of g, given the underlying typologies and nominal scales, has to be obtained by other means. One standard approach when interval scales are available is regression. This possibility is considered now for the case in which all variables are binary.

Suppose (13.2-3) is linear in its (binary) variables and that, due to possible omissions of other significant variables, the equality between left- and right-hand sides is subject to error. To simplify matters further, take ρ to be a scalar (i.e., $M=1$). If observations are distinguished by the superscript t, and if the numerical error for t is ϵ^t, then (13.2-3) becomes

$$(13.2\text{-}5) \quad x^t = \alpha + \pi\rho^t + \epsilon^t$$

where α and π are scalars to be determined by estimation. Clearly, the extra hypotheses (in addition to $M=1$) transforming (13.2-3) into (13.2-5) are difficult to express without numbers. Moreover, the use of binary variables may sacrifice information as suggested earlier. It is usually assumed in regression analysis that ρ^t is nonstochastic and that ϵ^t is a random variable with mean,

$$E\epsilon^t = 0$$

and constant variance

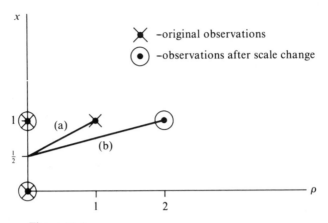

Figure 13-1

$$E(\epsilon')^2 = \sigma^2$$

Since x' is binary, however, the constant variance assumption cannot hold and hence ordinary least-squares estimates are no longer efficient. (There are ways to overcome this deficiency; see Kmenta [6, p. 427].) Still, for present purposes, certain aspects of these estimates are worth considering and, in any case, the general conclusions subsequently derived for them remain valid upon lifting the restriction that x' be binary.

Consider, then, the problem of estimating α and π in (13.2-5). Suppose there are three observations $(x^1, \rho^1) = (0,0)$, $(x^2, \rho^2) = (1,1)$, and $(x^3, \rho^3) = (1,0)$. The ordinary least-squares estimates are $\hat{\alpha} = \hat{\pi} = \frac{1}{2}$. The equation of the regression line is

(13.2-6) $x' = \frac{1}{2} + \frac{1}{2}\rho'$

It is pictured as line (a) in Figure 13-1. Now in Section 2.2 it was shown that both the magnitude and sometimes the sign of regression coefficients estimated with ordinal data depend on the choice of scale. The same is true here. Changing $\rho = 1$ to $\rho = 2$ without imposing any other modifications, the least-squares estimates become $\hat{\alpha} = \frac{1}{2}$ and $\hat{\pi} = \frac{1}{4}$. Such a conclusion is not really suprising in view of the fact that the regression line is "stretched" from (a) to (b) in Figure 13-1 by the alteration in scale. Note, however, that the conditional expectations

$$E[x' | \rho' = 0] = \frac{1}{2}, \quad E[x' | \rho' \neq 0] = 1$$

regardless of whether the range of ρ' is $\{0,1\}$ or $\{0,2\}$. (Goldberger demonstrates that this proposition holds more generally [3, p. 221].) Substituting $\rho = -1$ for $\rho = 1$ in the original data induces reversal of the sign of $\hat{\pi}$.

But there is a sense in which estimated regression coefficients are independent of the nominal scales behind the variables involved. Let x' and ρ' be recorded in binary form and denote the number of observations with $x' = x$ (0 or 1) and $\rho' = \rho$ (0 or 1) by $\theta_{x\rho}$. In the previous example, $\theta_{00} = 1$, $\theta_{11} = 1$, $\theta_{10} = 1$, and $\theta_{01} = 0$. Because binary 0–1 variables are being employed, $\hat{\alpha}$ is the mean of all x''s corresponding to $\rho' = 0$, and $\hat{\pi}$ is the difference between the mean of all x''s corresponding to $\rho' = 1$ and $\hat{\alpha}$ (Kmenta [6, p. 411]). It follows that the general least-squares estimates are

$$\hat{\alpha} = \frac{\theta_{10}}{\theta_{10} + \theta_{00}}$$

$$\hat{\pi} = \frac{\theta_{11}}{\theta_{01} + \theta_{11}} - \frac{\theta_{10}}{\theta_{10} + \theta_{00}}$$

Note the earlier values $\hat{\alpha} = \hat{\pi} = \frac{1}{2}$ may be derived as a special case. Furthermore, $\theta_{x\rho}$ can be defined without reference to the binary variables; all that matters is the sets of the underlying partitions to which the x and ρ belong. Hence estimates of α and π may be obtained independently of nominal scales. Least-squares procedures produce these estimates only when the binary variables assume the numerical values of 0 or 1. All other possibilities may therefore be ignored. An analogous conclusion holds for any number of parameters $\rho_1, \ldots, \rho_M$.

It is worth digressing for a moment to indicate another advantage of taking all dummy variables in binary form. If, for example, the range of ρ' in (13.2–5) were $\{0, 1, 2\}$, then

$$E[x' | \rho' = 0] = \alpha$$
$$E[x' | \rho' = 1] = \alpha + \pi$$
$$E[x' | \rho' = 2] = \alpha + 2\pi$$

Hence

$$E[x' | \rho' = 0] - E[x' | \rho' = 1] = \pi$$
$$E[x' | \rho' = 1] - E[x' | \rho' = 2] = \pi$$

that is, the difference between two pairs of conditional means is identical. Such an implication is not present when x' in (13.2-5) is replaced by two binary variables.[1] Hence the avoidance of binary variables may introduce extra unwarranted relations into the analysis.

---

[1] Replacing ρ' by three binary variables, although logically permissible according to earlier discussion, creates an indeterminacy in estimating the regression coefficients. See Kmenta [6, p. 413].

An alternative way of dealing with (13.2-5) is derived from the fact that the conditional expectation

$$Ex^t \mid \rho^t = \alpha + \pi\rho^t$$

Since x^t can be only 0 or 1,

$$Ex^t \mid \rho^t = 0 \cdot p(0) + 1 \cdot p(1)$$
$$= p(1)$$

where $p(w)$ is the probability that $x^t = w$ ($w = 0$ or $w = 1$). It follows that

(13.2-7) $p(1) = \alpha + \pi\rho^t$

Clearly, $Ex^t \mid \rho^t$ can be interpreted as the expected value of $x^t \mid \rho^t$ or the probability that $x^t = 1$. In accordance with the latter interpretation, the least-squares estimates of α and π in (13.2-5) satisfy the probability property

$$0 \leqslant \hat{\alpha} + \hat{\pi}\rho^t \leqslant 1$$

for $\rho^t = 0$ or $\rho^t = 1$. With respect to the former, there is no guarantee that $Ex^t \mid \rho^t$ is either 0 or 1. But (13.2-7) also suggests that the regression analysis can be based on the substitute model

(13.2-8) $q^t = \alpha' + \pi'\rho^t + \epsilon^t$

where primes denote coefficients that are distinct from α' and π'. Here t refers to groups of individual observations that have the same ρ value (0 or 1) and q^t is the within group frequency of occurrence of $x = 1$. Again, the least-squares estimates $\hat{\alpha}'$ and $\hat{\pi}'$ ensure

(13.2-9) $0 \leqslant \hat{\alpha}' + \hat{\pi}'\rho^t \leqslant 1$

for either $\rho^t = 0$ or $\rho^t = 1$. Note q^t is measured on an interval scale. Equations with both quantifiable and nonquantifiable variables are examined further in the next section.

Two procedures for obtaining predictions about x from ρ have now been discussed. Discriminant analysis gives forecasts of whether x is in S or in its complement $X - S$. Least-squares methods yield statements about the expectation or the probability of finding x in S or $X - S$. The predictions derived in either case are independent of the 0–1 nominal scale. On the other hand, they are still sensitive to the underlying partitions: Modifying the partition behind ρ leaving $S \subseteq X$ unchanged, say, may alter predictions. Thus to eliminate all arbitrariness in the foregoing predictive analysis, the underlying partitions have to be justified. Practical considerations (such as the kind of data) will determine the appropriateness of these two approaches in any particular study. It remains here to discuss the prediction issue in general and to indicate in what way the use of dummy (binary) variables can produce better results than those obtainable without 0–1 nominal measurement.

Consider (13.2-3) in its nonnumerical form. If (13.2-3) is an accurate formulation of reality, then any observation (x, ρ) reveals a part of it; that is, a specific link between an observed x and an observed vector ρ. Because of possible errors in specification and observation, there is no guarantee that the same x will always appear with the same ρ. Instead, any collection of data generally provides a distribution of observed x's corresponding to each ρ. Thus a reasonable prediction for x from any new but previously recorded ρ-value is that x-value with the highest frequency of all those that have already appeared with the given ρ. If only the subset of X in which x might fall is of interest, the reasonable prediction again is the one most likely, as indicated by past experience. It is clear, then, that when prediction is made from new appearances of previously observed values of ρ, little is added by the introduction of nominal scales.

However, it is often necessary to predict x from ρ-values that have never before appeared. These may arise in two distinct ways: (a) a new value for some ρ_i may come up or (b) a new combination of previously observed values of the ρ_i might emerge. In the former case if only the set to which x belongs is important, and if the new ρ_i falls into one of the old partitioning sets of ρ_i-values, then the method previously described can still be applied. But if the new ρ_i creates an extra set, or if partitions of the variable and parameter sets are not specified, an alternative technique is needed. On the other hand, expressing (13.2-3) in binary form it is evident that adding a new ρ_i-value is equivalent to introducing a new variable. And the problem of prediction when new, previously unaccounted for, and unobserved variables arise has not yet been resolved, even when all the variables can be calibrated on interval scales. The only known way of approaching it, in both quantifiable and nonquantifiable contexts, is through judgments and educated guesses. Therefore in this circumstance, too, dummy variables are of little aid in prediction.

It is only with new combinations of old ρ_i's that dummy variables become useful. To illustrate how such situations may arise in the first place, let $M = 2$ and assume two values of the vector $\rho = (\rho_1, \rho_2)$ have been recorded – say, (ρ_1', ρ_2') and (ρ_1'', ρ_2''). Since (ρ_1', ρ_2'') and (ρ_1'', ρ_2') are yet to be observed, the prediction of x from either based on historical frequencies cannot work. But suppose all sets over which parameters and the variable range are partitioned into single-element classes (the discrete typology), equation (13.2-3) is expressed in binary form so that (under the simplifications imposed earlier) x and the ρ_i are all binary variables, and appropriate assumptions are made in order to apply one of the numerical prediction procedures as previously described. Because everything is now numerical, predictions obviously are obtainable from any ρ regardless of its configuration of 0's and 1's – including those configurations that have not yet been observed. The same conclusion applies if nondiscrete typologies are an integral part of the analysis and only predictions of whether x is in S are required. In this way the use of dummy variables makes systematic prediction possible when forecasting without nominal measurement is much more difficult. Certainly, extra – even arbitrary – assumptions (e.g., linearity) may be needed; but these are no different from the standard hypotheses employed for scalable phenomena. Thus numerical methods contribute to prediction here under the same conditions that they facilitate it in usual, quantifiable circumstances: namely, if it becomes necessary to predict x from newly observed combinations of old ρ_i's.

13.3   Models with both quantifiable and nonquantifiable elements

Until now attention has been focused primarily on analytical techniques that are applicable when ordinal, interval, and ratio measures of all variable values are not known. However, in a large class of situations the values of some variables may be capable of calibration. Certainly all propositions (theoretical and empirical) that were derived earlier in the absence of measurement remain relevant in these circumstances. But it may be that the presence of ordinal, interval, or ratio scales for one or more variables permits stronger conclusions. This possibility is explored here in the empirical context of the present chapter.

As before, discussion is confined to the single relation

$$(13.3\text{-}1) \quad x = g(\rho)$$

where x is a scalar and $\rho = (\rho_1, \ldots, \rho_M)$. The parameters and variable are taken to be either calibrated on interval scales or nonquantifiable. In the latter case they are assumed 0–1 binary. Hence appropriate typologies and nominal scales are implicit in the analysis. Frequently the additional hypothesis of linearity also is imposed. In that circumstance (13.3-1) may be written in stochastic form as

$$(13.3\text{-}2) \quad x^t = \alpha + \sum_{i=1}^{M} \pi_i \rho_i^t + \epsilon^t$$

where the ρ_i^t are nonstochastic and ϵ^t has zero mean and constant variance. Sometimes for simplicity and convenience, M is set at unity.

There are two different directions to be taken in studying (13.3-1) and

(13.2-2). These are distinguishable on the basis of whether x is one of the dummy variates. Suppose first that it is not.

Application of regression analysis to (13.3-2) when some ρ_i (but not x) are binary 0-1 is quite standard. Many of the results presented in Section 13.2 carry over. Thus setting $M=1$, $\rho_1=\rho$, and $\pi_1=\pi$, so that (13.3-2) becomes

(13.3-3) $\quad x^t = \alpha + \pi\rho_t + \epsilon^t$

the least-squares estimate $\hat{\alpha}$ is the x^t sample mean associated with $\rho^t=0$, and $\hat{\pi}$ is the difference between the x^t sample mean for $\rho^t=1$ and $\hat{\alpha}$. The expression of $\hat{\alpha}$ and $\hat{\pi}$ in terms of quantifiable observations and the underlying typology is obtained thereby. Of course, estimates are different if the range of the binary variable is not $\{0,1\}$; but as long as ρ^t is binary, $Ex^t|\rho^t$ remains independent of the nominal scale defining ρ^t. The use of nonbinary dummy variables instead of binary ones may, as indicated earlier, introduce extraneous assumptions. Similar assertions hold in general. (Since x is not binary, the constant variance assumption $E(\epsilon^t)^2=\sigma^2$ is not automatically precluded as it was in Section 13.2. If it holds, then least-squares estimates are efficient.)

By slightly modifying the linear format, dummy variables may be intertwined with quantifiable variables in alternative ways. Let $M=2$ and suppose ρ_1 is quantifiable on an interval scale while ρ_2 is 0-1 binary. Then the model

$$x^t = \alpha + \pi_1\rho_1^t + \pi_2\rho_2^t$$

can be thought of as depicting one line in the x-ρ_1 plane when $\rho_2^t=0$ and another line when $\rho_2^t=1$. These lines are parallel and separated by the vertical distance π_2. On the other hand, the lines in the model

$$x^t = \alpha + \pi_1\rho_1^t + \pi_2\rho_1^t\rho_2^t$$

have the same intercept but differ in slope. In either case the presence or absence of a nonquantifiable element causes "shifts" in a quantifiable relation. Both kinds of shifts are combined simultaneously in the model

$$x^t = \alpha + \pi_1\rho_1^t + \pi_2\rho_2^t + \pi_3\rho_1^t\rho_2^t$$

Although not completely linear in all of the ρ_i's, the coefficients in these equations (upon introduction of the usual error term) may, nevertheless, be estimated with regression analysis (Kmenta [6, pp. 419-21]). Thus the interaction of quantifiable and nonquantifiable facets of a model can be stated very succinctly by employing dummy variables. It is clear, however, that such statements can still be made without them.

When x is 0-1 binary and at least one ρ_i is not, several of the corresponding conclusions of Section 13.2 again carry over. Discriminant analysis is exactly as before and much of the discussion concerning regression analysis is also relevant. However, without the binary restriction applied to every ρ_i, the probability property (13.2-9) need no longer hold. That is, with $M=1$ and (13.3-3) replaced by (13.2-8), namely,

$$(13.3\text{-}4) \quad q^t = \alpha' + \pi'\rho^t + \epsilon^t$$

(where q^t is the frequency estimate of the probability that $x=1$ in group t), in general $\hat{\alpha} + \hat{\pi}\rho^t$ can be either larger than one or less than zero for suitably chosen values of ρ^t. Hence regressing q^t on ρ^t to obtain estimates of α' and π' is now inappropriate for predicting the probability that x is in S (or $x=1$).

There are ways to eliminate this difficulty. Least-squares estimates can be obtained with (13.3-4) subject to the constraints (see Judge and Takayama [5])

$$0 \leqslant \alpha' \leqslant 1, \qquad 0 \leqslant \alpha' + \pi' \leqslant 1$$

Alternatively, a simple modification of the model will also do the job. For replacing q^t with the frequency (odds) ratio $q^t/1-q^t$, and assuming log linearity instead of arithmetic linearity, (13.3-4) becomes

$$(13.3\text{-}5) \quad \log \frac{q^t}{1-q^t} = \alpha^* + \pi^* \log \rho_t + \epsilon^t$$

where asterisks denote new coefficients. Use of (13.3-5) is often referred to as logit analysis. Clearly, ρ^t can no longer take on zero as one of its values. But because the choice of zero was arbitrary to begin with, if prediction (not structure) is the only issue, then its replacement by a positive number distinct from unity is of no consequence. Appropriately grouped data can be used to estimate α^* and π^* (Cox [1, Chs. 3–5]). Furthermore, given a newly observed value for ρ^t,

$$E \log \frac{q^t}{1-q^t} \bigg| \rho^t$$

may then be determined and a value for q^t easily found. Thus an estimate of the probability that x will fall in S (or $x=1$) is derived.

Still a third approach dispenses with logit analysis, constrained least-squares, and linearity assumptions. It is based on the hypothesis that ρ is stochastic and distributed conditionally depending on values of x. For the case in which these conditional distributions are normal, Warner [7] obtains an expression for $Ex^t | \rho_t$ and derives the appropriate maximum likelihood estimates required for its use.

Finally, when x^t is binary the conclusions of Section 13.2 about the role of dummy variates in prediction also apply: Dummy variables are of little extra value if it is only required to forecast from a $\rho^t = (\rho_1^t, \ldots, \rho_M^t)$ that has already arisen in the past. When it becomes necessary, however, to predict from a fresh ρ^t whose dummy components have appeared (separately or collectively) in at least one previously observed ρ^t, their contribution can be significant.

References

1. Cox, D. R., *The Analysis of Binary Data* (London: Methuen, 1970).
2. Fisher, F. M., *The Identification Problem in Econometrics* (New York: McGraw-Hill, 1966).
3. Goldberger, A. S., *Econometric Theory* (New York: Wiley, 1964).
4. Hoel, P. G., *Introduction to Mathematical Statistics,* 3rd ed. (New York: Wiley, 1962).
5. Judge, G. G., and T. Takayama, "Inequality Restrictions in Regression Analysis," *Journal of the American Statistical Association,* 61 (1966):166–81.
6. Kmenta, J., *Elements of Econometrics* (New York: Macmillan, 1971).
7. Warner, S. L., "Multivariate Regression of Dummy Variates under Normality Assumptions," *Journal of the American Statistical Association,* 58 (1963): 1054–63.

CHAPTER 14

An empirical application: occupational preferences and the quality of life

WITH J. E. RUSSO

Economists do not yet have a satisfactory understanding of the means by which individuals choose among occupations. Current theory (see, e.g., Friedman [6, pp. 211–25], Scitovsky [13, pp. 97–106], and Stigler [15, pp. 108–10]) is largely based on two assumptions: First, by balancing both monetary and nonmonetary components, individuals arrive at a preference ordering of all possible alternatives. Second, they choose the maximal preference occupation from those not eliminated by relevant nonpreferential constraints. This is fine as far as it goes. However, what are the nonmonetary elements and how are they evaluated? According to Friedman and Kuznets [7, p. 130], they include "such subjective and intangible factors as the prestige value attached to the profession, the opportunity it offers for rendering service and making 'social contacts,' the conditions under which professional work is performed,..." One purpose of this chapter is to obtain a better understanding of these nonpecuniary factors.

The fact that substantial numbers of nonmonetary ingredients may influence the individual's choice of occupation suggests that the theory explaining how choices are made ought to be broadened. If it is to provide more than a superficial understanding of real situations, it has to account for the role these inputs play. Thus the theory should view occupational decisions as choices between distinctive life-styles or "qualities of life," encompassing internal components such as pride and sense of achievement, as well as external factors such as physical working conditions and the type of people to be associated with.

In what follows an attempt is made to develop and test a model along these lines. Very general career–living situations are employed as the elements among which choices emerge. Following Lancaster [12], Iron-

This chapter is reproduced (with minor changes) from *Social Science Research* (1977), pp. 363–78. © Academic Press Inc., New York, 1977. Reprinted by permission of Academic Press. The authors would like to thank the Academic Senate of the University of California, San Diego, for financial support. A more complete version of this study has been published by D. Katzner as *Choice and the Quality of Life* (Beverly Hills, Ca.: Sage, 1979).

monger [9], and Kuenne [11], career–living situations are assumed to be analyzed and evaluated in terms of abstract characteristics. Each arises in one of many possible realizations. Taken together, the collection of characteristic manifestations an individual perceives in a given career–living situation describes, for him, its quality of life. Preferences are taken to be defined over the individual's quality-of-life space, and hence induce an ordering of career–living situations. Upon the introduction of appropriate constraints, selection of preference-maximizing situations proceeds as usual.

The advantages of such an approach are readily apparent. To begin with, it provides a technique for analyzing the structure of individual preferences among career–living situations, and hence, occupations. By uncovering the wide differences in structures thus found, an explanation for the diverse pattern of actual occupational choices is obtained. Furthermore, through revelation of the structures themselves, the possibility of discovering systematic attributes (at least in the minds of individuals) across occupations arises. Therefore general "positive" and "negative" features may become discernible, along with the kinds of modifications that could make less popular occupations more desirable. (If erroneous perceptions concerning any particular occupation are prevalent, they can be detected and steps can be taken to correct them.) Although the empirical side of the present study is too confined to permit such sweeping conclusions, the implications for policy making that aims at improving the quality of life in career–living situations are evident. Future research can hopefully expand the empirical results in this direction.

The specific issues upon which attention focuses here are restricted to (i) development of the model as previously described, (ii) determination, for a few persons, of the structure of their preference in terms of abstract characteristics, and (iii) use of the latter both to test the model and to discover how accurately individuals are able to specify these structures. This chapter also furnishes additional data on the possibility, examined by Easterlin [5], of a positive correlation between income and happiness.

14.1   The model

The starting point is a list of abstract characteristics that are identified by the individual as significant in determining his quality of life. Each characteristic can appear in many different ways. For example, the last paragraph in the "quality of life" section of each of the two career–living situations in Table 14-3 (see Section 14.2) provides two manifestations of the attribute "sense of achievement." The first describes a feeling of accomplishment, especially as a breadwinner, whereas the second, more negative realization alludes to a fear of failure. For any characteristic i, let q_i be defined as that variable that assumes as values alternative realizations of characteristic i. A variable value, then, is a verbal description. The vector consisting of one value q_i for each of the K given characteristics, that is, $Q = (q_1, \ldots, q_K)$, is called a quality of life. The collection of all Q's is the individual's quality-of-life space.

Career–living situations, on the other hand, are characterized in terms of various economic, social, and other parameters that are capable of description by an objective spectator. Let L such parameters be given and denote them by $p_1, \ldots, p_L$. Some p_j are quantifiable (like income); those that are not may be defined analogously to the q_i. Each vector $P = (p_1, \ldots, p_L)$ specifies a career–living situation, and the set of all P's is the career–living space under consideration. Two illustrations of P appear in Table 14-3. The main difference between the p_j's and q_i's is that the former are directly observable, whereas the latter are subjective constructs that need exist only in the mind of the individual in question. Alternatively, although many persons may share the same career–living space, no two of them are likely to have even remotely similar quality-of-life spaces.

The next step is to introduce formal structure in terms of set-theoretic relations among the variables and parameters. Any nontrivial relation necessarily limits the kinds of Q's that are consistent with any P. The idea is to impose enough of these restrictions to be able to associate a unique Q to each P. Thus a function mapping P space into Q space is being sought.

It turns out that a great deal of information about relations among the particular variables and parameters employed in this discussion already exists in the social science and psychology literature. Fromm [8, p. 196], for example, speaks of an "inverse" relation between security and freedom. Coopersmith [2, pp. 28, 242] relates self-esteem to success, occupation, and social status. Blau and Duncan [1, Ch. 4] study the relation between occupation and social prestige, and Katz and Lazarsfeld [10, p. 295] examine the interrelatedness of income and social participation. There are many more. Although few of these relations are given with sufficient precision to be directly employable here, they still suggest the reasonableness of postulating a general structure of the form,

$$(14.1\text{-}1) \quad q_i = f^i(q_1, \ldots, q_{i-1}, q_{i+1}, \ldots, q_K, P), \qquad i = 1, \ldots, K$$

where f^i is a function that identifies a unique value of q_i to each $(q_1, \ldots, q_{i-1}, q_{i+1}, \ldots, q_K, P)$.

Because the studies on which (14.1-1) is based very often deal with relations among the q_i's, they are not concerned with an explicit function that maps P into Q. However, it is very important to be able to derive the latter link, that is, the reduced form, from (14.1-1). Knowing that the reduced form exists guarantees the internal consistency of (14.1-1) and permits determination of the quality of life in terms of parameters. Furthermore, because any collection of actual observations of (14.1-1) must satisfy all equations simultaneously, it is impossible to discover K distinct f^i's empirically. Hence empirical corroboration of (14.1-1) must proceed through the reduced form. Now, in spite of the fact that many of the variables and parameters involved are not, at present, capable of measurement, conditions under which (14.1-1) can be solved to obtain Q as a function of P are known (see Ch. 5; e.g., the existence of appropriate inverses ensures solvability). Adding these restrictions as assumptions of the model yields

(14.1-2) $Q = F(P)$

Relation (14.1-2) was originally proposed by Dalkey, Lewis, and Snyder [3, pp. 94, 95]. In Lancaster's [12] terminology, F represents the quality-of-life "technology."

To obtain a theory of choice among career–living situations, let a preference ordering be defined in Q space. A corresponding ordering is induced on P space by taking all P's associated with the same Q to be indifferent. Introducing whatever constraints are appropriate and invoking the postulate of rationality, choices are obtained in the traditional way.[1] Of course, as interpreted here, choice of a career–living situation implies choice of an occupation.

14.2   Empirical analysis

This section reports on an experiment undertaken to provide empirical support for the model previously outlined.[2] The focal point is the quality-of-life technology F defined in (14.1-2). The experiment had two aims: (i) to provide a simple statistical test of the viability of F and (ii) to determine how accurately F can, in fact, be described.

Empirically, the relation F was obtained in both qualitative and partly quantitative form. In the first instance, it consisted, as originally defined, of an association between verbally described career–living situations and verbally described realizations of characteristics. In the second, verbal manifestations of characteristics were replaced by utility

---

[1] Clearly, the usual assumptions ensuring the existence of maximal preference elements must be made. Recall Section 5.4.

[2] Actually, two experiments were performed. But because the second duplicates the first in many respects, it is not presented here.

numbers that represented evaluations of career–living situations on each characteristic. Here the relation F mapped a verbal variable into a vector of numbers. To keep these cases apart, the subscripts v and n are introduced to indicate, respectively, verbal as opposed to numerical variables. Thus the technological relation (14.1-2) may appear as either

(14.2-1) $Q_v = F(P)$

or

(14.2-2) $Q_n = F(P)$

where $Q_v = (q_{v1}, \ldots, q_{vK})$ and $Q_n = (q_{n1}, \ldots, q_{nK})$. Actually, (14.2-1) and (14.2-2) were equivalent ways of looking at the same thing, since a 1–1 correspondence between the Q_v's and Q_n's was assumed. When (14.2-1) applied, F was called verbal or qualitative, and when (14.2-2) was relevant, F was called quantitative or numerical.

Each of these two forms of F has its own merits. The numerical relation is relatively quick and easy to obtain, but it does not provide a great deal of information. To know only that one career–living situation yields numerically more, say, pride, than another does not reveal the distinction between the verbal realization pride takes when it is "more" from that when it is "less." If policy makers are intent on improving an individual's quality of life, they clearly have to understand the qualitative differences between alternative realizations of characteristics before any meaningful policy can be formulated. Merely asking the individual, say, to rate a set of policy options by personal preference, without insisting that he formally develop in some detail his verbal F, is likely to produce error and be unstable over time. On the other hand, requiring the exhaustive examination suggested here should increase both accuracy and stability. It is also possible that the characteristics as specified in the experiments that follow might appropriately, in the minds of some individuals, be subdivided into two or more components. Security, for example, could involve a person's job, his personal investments, his ability to communicate and interact with others, and so on. If such distinctions existed, the verbal route would detect them, whereas the numerical approach could not. Finally, in determining individual specifications, knowledge of each form of F can clearly help to reveal sources of error in the other.

Both P's and Q_v's were assumed to be evaluated by the assignment of utility (value) to each. Thus functions mapping P and Q_v into utility numbers were presumed. Utility images were written, respectively, as $U(P)$ and $U(Q_v)$. As with F, confusion will not arise by using the same symbol U to denote different mappings. In making comparison, higher utility always meant "more desirable." It was further hypothesized that evaluations of Q_n were made in terms of a linear model; that is, utility was a linear function of the q_{nk}. Information concerning $U(P)$, $U(Q_v)$, and both qualitative and numerical F were obtained from individuals by direct interrogation. Two methods for procuring weights for the linear evaluation of Q_n were considered. They could have been either taken as reported by the individual or determined optimally by regressing $U(P)$ on $(q_{n1}, \ldots, q_{nK})$. Symbolically, these evaluations of Q_n may be written

$$\sum_{k=1}^{K} w_{sk} q_{nk} \quad \text{and} \quad \sum_{k=1}^{K} w_{ok} q_{nk}$$

where w_{sk} and w_{ok} represent, respectively, the stated and optimal weights for characteristic k.

Using arrows to denote mappings and an asterisk to indicate an evaluation procedure, the design of the experiment may be schematically summarized as follows: In qualitative terms, it appeared as

$$P \overset{F}{\to} (q_{v1}, \ldots, q_{vK}) = Q_v$$
$$P \overset{*}{\to} U(P), \quad Q_v \overset{*}{\to} U(Q_v)$$

whereas, quantitatively, it was described by

$$P \overset{F}{\to} (q_{v1}, \ldots, q_{vK}) \overset{H}{\to} (q_{n1}, \ldots, q_{nK}) = Q_n$$
$$P \overset{*}{\to} U(P)$$

$$Q_n = (q_{n1}, \ldots, q_{nK}) \quad \overset{*}{\Big\langle} \quad \begin{array}{l} \displaystyle\sum_{k=1}^{K} w_{sk} q_{nk} = U(Q_n) \\[2mm] \displaystyle\sum_{k=1}^{K} w_{ok} q_{nk} = U(Q_n) \end{array}$$

Note that the numerical formulation of F is actually the composition of F with H (hereafter written as $F \cdot H$).

Because the four evaluations previously described give desirability orderings of the P's, Q_v's, and Q_n's, a basis for testing the model of Section 14.1 is obtained. In particular, the orderings derived from

a. $U(P)$ and $U(Q_v)$,
b. $U(P)$ and $\sum_{k=1}^{K} w_{sk} q_{nk}$,
c. $U(P)$ and $\sum_{k=1}^{K} w_{ok} q_{nk}$,

could be compared using Kendall's τ (see Section 12.4).[3] A high test sta-

---

[3] As it requires only ordinal interpretation of the data, the τ test, rather than the Pearson correlation coefficient, was employed. Because the actual extent of cardinality in the

tistic would mean that the orderings are similar rather than unrelated. This would imply that an F exists and that the evaluation hypotheses are appropriate.

A second statistic obtainable from the τ procedure is the percentage of confirming (identically ordered) pairs. A high percentage could be interpreted to mean that: (i) the cognitive structure expressed as F or $F \cdot H$ was "accurate" and (ii) the valuation procedures (denoted by $*$ above) were satisfactory. Assuming that (ii) was always true, values for this statistic could be taken as measures of the accuracy of F and the composition $F \cdot H$.

In a more informal way, the comparison of (b) has been made by Dalkey et al. [3]. Their experiment covered thirteen persons, each of whom rated eight career–living situations, both as wholes and in terms of twelve characteristics. Correlation coefficients ranging from 0.50 to 0.95 were found. Perhaps because they were implicitly assuming the existence of a numerical F, Dalkey et al. did not test for the significance of their results. Furthermore, they left themselves exposed to the possibility that their subjects did not obtain $U(P)$ and $\sum_{K=1} w_{sk} q_{nk}$ independently. That is, in their experiment, a subject's ratings q_{nk} for all characteristics and all career–living situations remained in front of him while he derived $U(P)$. Hence he had only to remember the weights that he had previously specified[4] in order to reproduce an identical ordering in terms of $U(P)$. But regardless of whether the subjects were successful or even tried to follow this route, the suggestion that they could use the linear model to secure $U(P)$ apparently was implied in the experimental procedure itself. Because the stated weight comparison (b) is necessarily inferior to the optimally weighted (c), the Dalkey et al. approach was repeated here in optimal weight form to correct the preceding deficiencies and to expand its scope. Thus comparison (b) was dropped.

It is clear that the model under examination here varies in specification across individuals. The functions U and F, the weights w_{ok}, the manifestations of characteristics q_{vk} and q_{nk}, and the characteristics themselves can be expected to be different for different people. Furthermore, the particular specification for any given individual depends on his own personal "cognitive structure," that is, on the way he organizes and perceives reality and on the symbols he employs to express his per-

data was difficult to determine, it was safer to use a method that minimized dependence on it. Even under a strictly ordinal interpretation of the data, we prefer the τ test to the Spearman rank correlation coefficient (also described in Section 12.4), due to its simpler interpretation as a descriptive statistic.

[4] For at least seven of the thirteen subjects, the weights were obtained in advance. It is not clear when the remaining six were asked to provide weights. See Dalkey, Lewis, and Snyder [3, p. 110].

Table 14-1. *Characteristics of the quality of life*

Characteristic	Frequency chosen
e: Pride, self-esteem, self-confidence, self-knowledge	3
s: Security, peace of mind	1
a: Sense of achievement, accomplishment, success	2
f: Variety, opportunity, freedom	4
g: Receiving and giving love and affection	2
c: Challenge, intellectual stimulation, growth	3
h: Comfort, congenial surroundings, good health	2
u: Understanding, helping, and accepting others	1
n: Being needed by others, having friends	1
l: Leisure, humor, relaxation	3
r: Respect of others, social acceptance, prestige	0
d: Sense of dominance, leadership, aggression	0
i: Sense of involvement and participation in society	3

ceptions. One of the fundamental difficulties to be overcome in discovering and testing his qualitative F, then, is to enable him to reveal accurately the relevant portion of his cognitive structure. Although vaguely aware of alternative realizations of characteristics such as pride, freedom, and so on, the individual does not mentally carry around an explicit formulation of them. The problem is to induce him to create appropriate precision in his existing cognitive framework. For his qualitative F can only be expressed in its terms and with its symbols. In other words, to list verbally various manifestations of, say, pride, the individual must describe how this aspect of his reality appears to him. And to write down descriptions that are meaningful, he must explain his own perceptions of pride in his own terms.

Five male graduate students in economics served as experimental subjects over a period of roughly nine weeks during the first few months of 1975. They ranged in age between 24 and 32 years.

Each subject was first given thirteen characteristics (adapted from those used by Dalkey et al. [3]) in different random order and asked to choose the five he thought most important in determining his quality of life. (Only five were requested because it is doubtful that human capacity can handle more; see, e.g., Slovic and Lichtenstein [14, pp. 686-7].) The characteristics and their choices are summarized in Table 14-1. Subjects were then presented verbal sketches (summarized in Table 14-2) of thirty career–living situations (P) and asked to write, for each characteristic they had chosen, short realizations or manifestations of that characteristic covering all thirty P's. Combining the five realizations (one for each characteristic) assigned to a career–living situation P produced the Q_v

Table 14-2. *Summary of career–living situations presented to subjects*

	Career situation	Living situation	Yearly income ($)
P_1	Farmer	Live on farm, farm community	15,000
P_2	General store owner–operator, farm community	Live over store, farm community	15,000
P_3	Clothing boutique owner–manager, large city	Inner-city high-rise apartment life, walk to work	30,000
P_4	Programmer, large corporation	Suburban life, 30-min car ride to work	18,000
P_5	Teacher, large crowded inner-city high school	Inner-city dwelling, 45-min bus ride to work	15,000
P_6	Professor, large state university in big city	Pleasant city area, walk to work	22,000
P_7	Construction worker on bridges, roads, etc.	Average city area living	18,000
P_8	Carpenter, small city	Average small-town life	13,000
P_9	Auto salesman, just outside large city	Suburban life, 45-min car ride to work	50,000
P_{10}	Junior officer, large corporation	Suburban life, long train ride to work	40,000
P_{11}	Appliance repairman, medium-sized city	Pleasant area in town	16,000
P_{12}	Accountant, small accounting firm, medium-sized eastern city	Average suburban life, 20-min car ride to work	16,000
P_{13}	Consular official, Tokyo	American-style life	25,000
P_{14}	Associate professor, small New England college	Country life, walk to campus	18,000
P_{15}	Assistant city manager, medium-sized Ohio city	Old, restored area of town	19,000
P_{16}	Lawyer, law firm, large eastern city	Exclusive suburban area, 1-hr drive to work	80,000
P_{17}	Company cab driver, medium-sized western city	Average middle-class, in-town life	14,000
P_{18}	Real estate broker, small midwest city	Better than average area just being developed	22,000
P_{19}	Vice-president, large corporation, Philadelphia	Upper middle-class suburban area, 40-min train ride to work	90,000

Table 14-2 *(cont.)*

Career situation	Living situation	Yearly income ($)
P_{20} Traveling salesman, three southern states	Pleasant middle-class suburban area, outside fairly large city	18,000 plus expenses
P_{21} Department manager, dept. store, suburban shopping center, large metropolitan area	Average suburban area, 10-min drive to work	16,000
P_{22} Country club manager, outside medium-sized city	Live rent-free on club grounds	15,000 plus house
P_{23} Outfielder, major league team, western city	Upper middle-class area in city	37,000
P_{24} Elected member, U.S. House of Representatives, midwestern state	Upper middle-class area in Washington, D.C.	40,000 plus expenses
P_{25} Service-station owner–operator, residential area, small southern city	Average middle-class area, walk to work	15,000
P_{26} Family doctor, medium-sized northwestern city	Upper middle-class suburban area, 5 min to hospital and office	75,000
P_{27} Research assistant, federal agency, large city	Crowded, middle-class area in town, 30-min bus ride to work	14,000
P_{28} Pilot, large airline, based in large eastern city	Upper middle-class area, far from center of city	45,000 plus expenses
P_{29} Partner, business consulting firm, large eastern city	Moderately upper middle-class area, within 30 min of work	37,000 plus expenses
P_{30} Librarian, small public library, medium-sized city	Middle-class area within city, 20-min drive to work	17,000

associated with that P. Two examples appear in Table 14-3. In this way, the qualitative functions F were defined.[5] Quantitative F's (i.e., the $F \cdot H$'s) were obtained by having the subjects rate their characteristic descriptions on numerical scales.

[5] Although it was required that only one Q_v be associated with each P, the possibility that two P's could be mapped into the same Q_v was not ruled out. This is consistent with the

Table 14-3. *The quality of life attributed to selected career–living situations by a representative subject*

Career–living situation P_8

You are a carpenter in a small, but friendly, city. Work is uncertain, but when available, the hours are rigid. There is often overtime. In your spare time, others may hire you for odd jobs or you may make and sell furniture. You manage to get along at a leisurely pace. You live in an average section of town. The big-city congestion, pollution, and crime are relatively absent but so are the cultural mix and the opportunities of city life. Friends are drawn from your living area and around town. You have strong social and cultural ties in your neighborhood. Yearly income: $13,000.

Quality of life

l: Your job and physical environment allow a leisurely pace in each. You have many close friends, through your work and in the community, with whom you can relax and joke daily.

n: You have many friends, both from your job and through your community. You feel a sense of being needed through your work, as you provide a worthwhile, specialized service to those who seek you out.

h: Physical environment is an asset for good health. Your occupation also keeps you healthy. Your home life is very comforting. Nearly all your neighbors enjoy similar activities, thus socializing is easy.

f: The pace of your work provides most of your freedom, with variety and new opportunities arising daily.

a: Your work is goal oriented, the attainment of which gives you a feeling of accomplishment. Overall success is manifested by providing security for you and your family.

Career–living situation P_{26}

You are a reasonably successful family doctor (general practitioner) in a medium-sized northwestern city. Your work is very demanding and you are always under intense pressure. You are regularly off Wednesday and Saturday afternoons and all day Sunday. You have an arrangement with eight other doctors so that approximately every other month you are on call for an entire weekend. You are also on call about one evening every other week, and there may be emergencies requiring your attention at any hour of any night. Your arrangement with the other doctors also permits frequent long-weekend vacations. You live in a large house with a big yard in an upper middle-class suburb just outside of town. You are 5 min away from your office and the main hospital in the area. Pollution, congestion, and crime are minimal. Your friends are scattered about town. There are frequent social functions for doctors in which you participate. You are a member of a nearby country club. Yearly income: $75,000.

Quality of life

l: Leisure time and relaxation are found mainly at home and with close friends who enjoy similar recreational activities. Your demanding work requires that your free time be spent in relaxation.

n: You have many friends, both from your job and through your community. You feel a

---

model of Section 14.1, as long as all P's identified with the same Q_v are indifferent. In practice, however, errors in responses concerning values for the $U(P)$'s arise. Hence when, say, P' and P'' were associated with the same Q and rated differently by the individual, the average of the two ratings was taken as both $U(P')$ and $U(P'')$.

Table 14-3 *(cont.)*

---

sense of being needed through your work, as you provide a worthwhile, specialized service to those who seek you out.

h: You draw nearly all of your comfort from your work, which is stimulating and time-consuming. Your family ties also bring you comfort.

f: Your job allows variety and freedom, both while on the job and while on vacation. The competent organization of your time also brings added freedom.

a: You are under constant pressure to succeed, both on and off the job. Even though you have continually proven yourself by your accomplishments, one failure can be disastrous.

Next, the subjects were asked for the evaluations required for comparisons (a) and (c). That is, they were requested to rate appropriate variables on specific scales. At each stage, they were provided with only the information that was necessary to complete that task. Immediately after obtaining $U(Q_v)$, a check was made to see if the subjects might not have obtained this evaluation from memory, specifically, by first remembering from which career–living situation the Q_v's came and then using $U(P)$'s to generate the $U(Q_v)$'s. Overall, only about 50 percent of the Q_v's were attributed to the correct P's. It appeared that subjects could not have remembered enough information about the latter to be of use in rating the former. (Note that upon obtaining the $U(P)$'s, enough information was available to compute the optimal weights, w_{ok}, as previously described.)

The comparisons of orderings derived from these data appear in Table 14-4 under the heading "Replication 1."[6] Generally, the values of the test statistic z were very significant. Hence the proposed model seemed quite consistent with the subjects' performance. Percentages of confirming pairs were also fairly high, suggesting that both F and $F \cdot H$ were defined with reasonable accuracy.

Of course, it is always possible that a subject's performance could be

---

[6] Strictly speaking, the computation of $\hat{U}(P) = \sum_{k=1}^{K} \hat{w}_{ok} q_{nk}$, where the $\hat{w}_{ok}$ are ordinary regression coefficients, yields smaller variation in the $\hat{U}(P)$ than should be there. This is because the procedure improperly includes part of the random variation in $\hat{U}(P)$ as structural variation "explained" by the regression. A "cross-validation" method was employed to determine the extent of the error introduced from this source. The data were divided into three sets of ten observations each. The predicted $\hat{U}(P)$'s for each set were based on the regression equation estimated from the remaining twenty observations. Thus the regression coefficients were estimated from one set of data and used to predict a different set. However, the resulting values for z and the percentage of confirming pairs were lowered from those of Table 14-4 on the average of, respectively, only 0.06 and 0.4 percent. Also, when ties occurred in any ordering, a conservative estimate of the variance was used in computing the test statistic.

Table 14-4. *Comparison of orderings*

Subject	Replication	Comparison[a]	Test statistic[b] z	Percentage of confirming pairs
1	1	(a)	4.31	77.9
		(c)	5.40	85.0
	2	(a)	5.74	87.1
		(c)	6.47	91.9
2	1	(a)	4.10	76.6
		(c)	4.10	76.6
	2	(a)	5.34	84.6
		(c)	5.98	88.7
3	1	(a)	4.06	76.7
		(c)	4.88	81.6
	2	(a)	3.16	70.5
		(c)	4.33	78.1
4	1	(a)	3.42	72.2
		(c)	4.47	78.9
	2	(a)	5.05	82.6
		(c)	5.84	87.8
5	1	(a)	6.06	89.2
		(c)	5.74	87.1
	2	(a)	5.21	83.7
		(c)	5.57	86.0
Mean	1	(a)	4.39	78.5
		(c)	4.92	81.8
	2	(a)	4.90	81.7
		(c)	5.64	86.5
	Combined	(a)	4.64	80.1
		(c)	5.28	84.2

[a] (a) purely qualitative; (c) optimal weights.
[b] All values of z were statistically significant beyond the .001 level.

bettered through revision. Thus in an effort to improve accuracy, subjects were informed of major disagreements between the orderings obtained from $U(P)$ and $U(Q_v)$ and asked to eliminate whatever inconsistencies in their cognitive structures (written realizations of characteristics), F's, or H's that might have led them into such errors. Comparisons (a) and (c) then were resolicited to measure any improvement. Because he believed the task to be too difficult, one subject (Subject 3) agreed to revise his cognitive structure only with noticeable reluctance. This subject spent considerably less time on the revision than anyone else.

The comparisons of orderings computed from this replication are indicated in Table 14-4. Subjects 1, 2, and 4 improved their performance, whereas that of 3 and 5 deteriorated. The failure of Subject 3 to improve can probably be explained by his attitude. The attitude of Subject 5, on the other hand, was excellent. Indeed, this subject was confident that he had done a better job on Replication 2. Subject 5's decrease in performance was probably related to his high accuracy on Replication 1 (the highest of all subjects over both replications). His drop in performance only placed him in the midst of Subjects 1, 2, and 4.

Excluding Subject 3, the results of Replication 2 were strikingly uniform. In spite of the complexity of the task and the different ways in which these subjects approached it, their performance level on Replication 2 was approximately the same. In terms of the percentages of confirming pairs, comparison (a) produced a spread of from 82.6 to 87.1 percent, whereas the range for (c) was 86.0 to 91.9 percent. It is plausible that rough upper limits for performance can be set at 85 percent in the case of (a) and 89 percent for (c). (Actual figures in the "mean" part of the table are lower, due to the inclusion of Subject 3.)

Another interesting conclusion that emerges from the data of Table 14-4 is that the verbal and numerical approaches [comparisons (a) and (c), respectively] gave very similar results. A plausible explanation for this is that both methods used the same dimensions. Even though the output of each procedure was different, the subjects' possible responses in both cases were constrained by the general nature of the task and the specific dimensional structures they chose. Furthermore, recent work (Dawes and Corrigan [4]) has shown that the weighting of dimensions is usually less important than the selection of the dimensions themselves. And although these studies examined only linear weighting models for combining dimensions, the finding probably generalizes to nonquantifiable situations.

14.3   Income and happiness

It is worth noting that the data gathered here provide some support at the individual level for the recent skepticism of Easterlin [5, p. 90] concerning the existence of a positive correlation between income and happiness.[7] If an individual is happier the higher up he is in his quality-of-

---

[7] Specifically, Easterlin [5, p. 118] found that, within countries, there appears to be some positive association between income and reported happiness. But over time and across countries the association is uncertain.

Table 14-5. *Income and the quality of life*

Subject	Test statistic[a] z	Cumulative probability of z	Percentage of confirming pairs
1	− .79	.215	44.9
2	−1.26	.104	41.8
3	− .21	.417	48.6
4	−1.26	.104	41.8
5	− .20	.421	48.8

[a]Significance at the .05 level required $|z| \geqslant 1.96$ in a two-tailed test.

life preference ordering, then the role of income in determining happiness would, to some extent, be revealed by comparing the ordering of the thirty career–living situations based on $U(P)$ with that based on income. The same test statistic z, was used again. As Table 14-5 shows, the results reveal no significant relationships.[8]

14.4   Conclusion

In summary, this chapter has focused on the theoretical and empirical aspects of occupational choice by examining the structure of individual preferences expressed in terms of abstract characteristics. Both verbal and quantitative models were employed. These were successfully tested, and a rough upper limit on the ability of individuals to specify their quality-of-life technology was determined. Although the study was too restrictive (in the number and variety of individuals surveyed, as well as in the number of career–living situations included) to permit general inferences concerning the quality of life of particular occupations, the latter could presumably be achieved by expanding its scope.

Nevertheless, from the limited empirical findings it may be concluded that the qualitative model captured career–living preferences almost as consistently as did the highly structured quantitative approach. Furthermore, the experiments apparently extracted subjects' cognitive structures for career–living situations in all the richness and generality permitted by verbal expression. Such qualitative information, although more costly to determine, is of considerable potential benefit to policy

---

[8] The validity of these numbers depends, in part, on the representativeness of the thirty career–living situations employed in our experiments. Although designed to cover a wide range of environments, there is no way of determining if they, as a sample, exemplify real-world conditions. To the extent that they do not, conclusions drawn from Table 14-5 should be qualified.

makers or anyone attempting to improve the quality of life for participants in less popular occupations. Various verbal descriptions of attributes like self-esteem (pride) may suggest the specific deficiencies involved. Equivalent knowledge cannot be obtained from numerical representations.

References

1. Blau, P. M., and O. D. Duncan, *The American Occupational Structure* (New York: Wiley, 1967).
2. Coopersmith, S., *The Antecedents of Self-Esteem* (San Francisco: Freeman, 1967).
3. Dalkey, N. C., R. Lewis, and D. Snyder, "Measurement and Analysis of the Quality of Life," in N. C. Dalkey et al., eds., *Studies in the Quality of Life* (Lexington, Mass.: Heath, 1972), pp. 85–137.
4. Dawes, R. M., and B. Corrigan, "Linear Models in Decision Making," *Psychological Bulletin* 81 (1974):95–106.
5. Easterlin, R. A., "Does Economic Growth Improve the Human Lot? Some Empirical Evidence," in P. A. David and M. W. Reder, eds., *Nations and Households in Economic Growth* (New York: Academic Press, 1974), pp. 89–121.
6. Friedman, M., *Price Theory* (Chicago: Aldine, 1962).
7. Friedman, M., and S. Kuznets, *Income from Independent Professional Practice* (New York: National Bureau of Economic Research, 1954).
8. Fromm, E., *The Sane Society* (New York: Rinehart, 1955).
9. Ironmonger, D. S., *New Commodities and Consumer Behavior* (Cambridge: Cambridge University Press, 1972).
10. Katz, E., and P. F. Lazarsfeld, *Personal Influence* (Glencoe, Ill.: Free Press, 1955).
11. Kuenne, R. E., "Quality Space, Interproduct Competition, and General Equilibrium Theory," in R. E. Kuenne, ed., *Monopolistic Competition Theory: Studies in Impact* (New York: Wiley, 1967), pp. 219–50.
12. Lancaster, K., *Consumer Demand: A New Approach* (New York: Columbia University Press, 1971).
13. Scitovsky, T., *Welfare and Competition,* rev. ed. (Homewood, Ill.: Irwin, 1971).
14. Slovic, P., and S. Lichtenstein, "Comparison of Bayesian and Regression Approaches to the Study of Information Processing in Judgment," *Organizational Behavior and Human Performance,* 6 (1971):649–744.
15. Stigler, G. J., *The Theory of Price,* 3rd ed. (New York: Macmillan, 1966).

CHAPTER 15

Getting on without measures

The preceding pages have considered the problem of thinking – in an intellectually sophisticated way – about phenomena that are difficult, if not impossible, to scale. (A detailed summary has been provided in Section 1.2.) In so doing, the objectives set out at the beginning of Chapter 1 have largely been met. At this point, however, it is interesting to observe briefly a few ways in which life structures emerging out of differing cultural and historical circumstances have cohered quite independently of abilities to calibrate. As a practical matter, it turns out that human beings are able to get on surprisingly well without measures or even numbers.

First of all, it is clear that numbers themselves are not needed to count. Certain orthodox Jews, for example, require that at least ten men, a *minyan,* be present to conduct particular religious services. Before they start, a ten-word sentence is recited in which each man is identified with one word. If the sentence is completed, then the minyan has been constituted and the service can begin (Zaslavsky [8, p. 52][1]). As a second illustration, the Kpelle people of Liberia have no independent abstract numbers in their language. Objects are still "counted," however, and the results of any particular count appear in number-words that always must modify a noun or pronoun (Gay and Cole [3, pp. 36–43]).

Whether one uses or avoids numbers, counting is based on certain principles (Gelman and Gallistel [4, pp. 77–82]):

   i. Each object in the set to be counted is identified with a unique tag.

   ii. The tags are arranged in a specific repeatable order.

   iii. The last tag in the order represents a property (the cardinality) of the set as a whole.

---

[1] Taboos against counting certain things are common throughout the world and across the ages. Their source, according to Gaster, is as follows: "To be able to identify a thing precisely is, in ancient and primitive thought, to have potential control over it. It is for this reason ... that knowledge of a person's name is all-important in working magic against him and, conversely, it is for this reason that otherworld beings refrain from disclosing it. To know the exact number of things can produce the same result. Accordingly, all over the world we find a popular resistance to taking a census, counting cattle, crops or fruits, and even to revealing one's age." (Gaster [2, p. 483]).

iv. The sequence in which each object is tagged does not matter.
v. Items (i) to (iv) can be applied to any set of objects.

These principles permit the abstraction of numbers although they need not lead to employment of number-words. To reason with numbers requires still more (Gelman and Gallistel [4, Ch. 10]). Thus it is necessary to recognize the ordering relations of "larger (or more) than" and "equivalence" among underlying sets and to delineate operations (such as that which appears as addition when expressed in terms of numbers) on them. Once again, numbers are not essential to, say, "add," the elements of two sets. The parallel with the "underlying phenomenon" for measurement formally described in Section 2.2 is striking.

Measurement, of course, goes beyond counting. As pointed out in Chapter 2, nominal measurement rests on schemes of classification, ordinal measurement on classification and an independent ordering relation, and so on. But these elements vary across cultures and their occurrence (or lack thereof) and manner of appearance are often reflected in language (see Lee [5] and Whorf [7, pp. 214–19]). It should not be surprising, then, to find certain qualities measured in one culture but not in others. Thus the Nuer of the Sudan have no equivalent expression in their language for "time." They cannot speak of the passage of time, nor can they break it up into sequentially ordered minutes and hours (Evans-Pritchard [1, p. 103]). Similarly, the Western tendency to interpret reality by stringing out events and objects in a linear ordering according to criteria such as chronology, importance, or intensity, does not arise in Trobriand Island culture and language (Lee [5, pp. 110–20]). The ordinal measures that might arise from such orderings could not be relevant to the immediate Trobriand world.

To gain insight into how concrete problems might be solved without measures, consider the two factors, time and distance. With regard to the former, it has already been indicated that the Nuer have no way in their language to express time or its passage. The same is true of the Kpelle (Gay and Cole [3, p. 72]). Still Gay and Cole [3, pp. 72–4] have shown that even in the absence of measures of time, the Kpelle are accurately aware of the "length" of short durations. Both the Nuer and the Kpelle, indeed individuals of many African cultures, observe and use natural and economic divisions of time. The cycle of changing seasons identifies a year, the movement through one cycle of darkness and light defines a day, and market cycles often delineate a concept akin to the Western week (Zaslavsky [8, pp. 62–4], Gay and Cole [3, pp. 71, 72], and Evans-Pritchard [1, pp. 95–102]). Similar statements apply to the farmers, shepherds, and craftsmen of Montaillou, a fourteenth century

French town (LeRoy Ladurie [6, pp. 277–82]). In many cases, time during the day is reckoned either in terms of such natural occurrences as sunrise or the crowing of the cock, or with reference to social and other happenings such as meals and the milking of the cows. Time of day can be judged from the latter because they always occur for everyone after the same sequence of events, each of which covers roughly the same amount of time for each person. Thus by way of illustration, the passage of daytime for the Nuer is marked as a succession of happenings throughout the day (Evans-Pritchard [1, pp. 101, 102]). To schedule a particular activity, say, a meeting, a Nuer might inform the participants to gather after a certain meal. As everyone eats at the same time (i.e., after the same sequence of events), each participant would know exactly when to arrive. Note that these meanings of time often vary as the number of daylight hours increases and decreases with the earth's rotation about the sun.

It is well known that measured distance, d, and measured time, t, are linked by the formula

$$d = vt$$

where v is the (quantified) velocity of an object traveling distance d for t units of time. This relation, however, does not depend on the existence of measures for d, v, and t and is understood (although with less precision) by individuals having little vocabulary for calibration. The people of Montaillou, for example, occasionally thought of time in terms of distance: An interval of the former might be expressed as the (unquantified) time it takes to walk a certain distance (LeRoy Ladurie [6, p. 277]). On the other hand, the Kpelle sometimes speak of distance as time. Thus the distance between two particular points, say, is a day's walk (Gay and Cole [3, p. 71]). Note that from an analytical viewpoint, as long as walking speed can be regarded as constant, the preceding formula ensures that quantified distance can be employed as a measure of quantified time and conversely. But to the Kpelle, two villages whose connecting path crosses mountains would still appear to be farther apart (because the travel time between them would be greater) than if their connecting path had the same length but lay entirely on level ground.

By contrast, the Nuer conception of distance emphasizes accessibility. A village reached by traversing a large stretch of uninhabited brush is nearby compared to one much closer in miles but separated by a river that is difficult to ford (Evans-Pritchard [1, p. 109]). If the river were impossible to cross, then the village would be "infinitely" far away. Of course, such unquantified distances change seasonally as the river dries up and becomes easier to bridge.

The foregoing suggests that successful communication of information and resolution of simple problems in practical life are possible with neither scales nor calibration on them. However, the extent to which rather sophisticated puzzles have also been solved in such a nonquantitative setting is remarkable. Thus Africans and Eskimos seem to have discovered long ago that the house with a circular floor plan is the strongest, simplest, most economical to build and encompasses the greatest area for a given perimeter of all geometric forms in the plane (Zaslavsky [8, pp. 155–6]). Although various parts of the proposition can be established mathematically or scientifically through the use of quantified variables, such lines of reasoning were clearly beyond these peoples' reach. One can only conclude that they arrived at the "round house" through observations and thought processes that did not significantly rely on numerical measurement.

Previous chapters have attempted to make a similar, more detailed statement about the possibility and potential of analysis without measurement applicable, in general, to the conduct of inquiry. It has been argued that the exorcising of numerical quantity upsets neither the philosophical underpinnings nor the mathematical foundation for scientific investigation. Convergence and closeness can still be defined, functions can still be manipulated, systems of simultaneous and periodic relations can still be constructed and examined, and empirical tests and predictions can still be pursued. Notions such as maximization, control, feedback, infinity, probability, and identification also remain relevant to the nonquantifiable world. Analysis in the absence of one or more numerical scales may therefore proceed in much the same way as it does when measures of all variables are available. The main difference is the lack of extraordinary convenience that numbers provide. But convenience is the only loss. Deprivation of it imposes no barrier to the pursuit of intellectual activity.

Earlier pages also have suggested that analyses of nonquantifiable phenomena according to the rules just described can be rewarding. Informal examples taken from the writings of a variety of social scientists including Durkheim, Parsons, and Pareto have been cited in Section 1.1. More formal illustrations of the reworking (and consequent illumination) of already completed studies as well as the development of new theoretical and empirical propositions have been provided, too. Analysis without measurement, then, is more than an hypothetical possibility; it already has borne fruit. Its applicability to the nonphysical sciences and its potential for the enhancement of understanding in them, are established.

Still, the current tendency of researchers to focus on the construction of measures, and on problems that deal only with scalable variables, may not be easy to overcome. But the dangers of avoiding the non-quantifiable are real. At the extreme, one is reminded of Yankelovich's comment cited many words ago (in the epigraph facing page 1) which was inspired by the disastrous penchant of the Johnson administration to analyze and evaluate the status of the Vietnam War solely in terms of the "body count," that is, estimates (and poor ones at that) of the number of enemy soldiers killed. The plain fact is that there are many important issues requiring one to become involved in a fundamental way with entities or phenomena that appear to be impossible to calibrate. To ignore such elements is to increase unnecessarily the risks of error and irrelevance. The muse of science deserves better.

References

1. Evans-Pritchard, E. E., *The Nuer* (London: Oxford University Press, 1940).
2. Gaster, T. H., *Myth, Legend and Custom in the Old Testament* (New York: Harper & Row, 1969).
3. Gay, J., and M. Cole, *The New Mathematics and an Old Culture* (New York: Holt, Rinehart and Winston, 1967).
4. Gelman, R., and C. R. Gallistel, *The Child's Understanding of Number* (Cambridge, Mass.: Harvard University Press, 1978).
5. Lee, D., *Freedom and Culture* (Englewood Cliffs, N.J.: Prentice-Hall, 1959).
6. LeRoy Ladurie, E., *Montaillou: The Promised Land of Error,* B. Bray, trans. (New York: Braziller, 1978).
7. Whorf, B. L., *Language Thought and Reality,* J. B. Carrol, ed. (Cambridge, Mass.: MIT Press, 1956).
8. Zaslavsky, C., *Africa Counts* (Boston: Prindle, Weber and Schmidt, 1973).

Index